How to Manage Spelling Successfully

How to Manage Spelling Successfully is the essential handbook for anyone involved in teaching spelling. Accompanied by its companion workbook, *Activities for Successful Spelling*, it provides a straightforward and coherent programme for developing spelling skills for all, including those who struggle to establish lifelong proficiency.

This book contains a comprehensive exploration of every aspect of spelling theory and associated teaching methods. Day-to-day advice on how to help those with difficulties is underpinned by information on the development of the English language and its spelling rules, with explanations of common language problems. The author provides a wealth of practical advice, including strategies and techniques based on her extensive experience of teaching dyslexic and dyspraxic children. Written in a clear and concise style, the book makes information about complex issues, including the outcome of international research, accessible to the general reader. Included are sections on:

- Spelling processes
- Teaching and learning synthetic and analytic phonics
- The significance of individual cognitive and learning styles
- Assessing and monitoring spelling progress
- Using spelling error analysis when identifying SpLD

Relevant to pupils across the age range, including adult learners, this groundbreaking distillation of best practice effectively demystifies the English spelling system. It organises the myriad spelling rules and conventions into clear categories and reduces them to a manageable size. Primary and secondary school teachers, teaching assistants, specialist teachers, SENCOs, tutors, teacher trainers and lecturers will all find this an indispensable resource.

Philomena Ott is an internationally recognised expert on teaching pupils with specific learning difficulties. She is currently an independent educational consultant, trainer and speaker on dyslexia, conducting seminars and giving lectures around the world.

Related Titles from Routledge:

Activities for Successful Spelling
Philomena Ott
0–415–38574–1

Teaching Children with Dyslexia: A practical guide
Philomena Ott
0–415–32454–8

Day-to-Day Dyslexia in the Classroom – 2nd edition
Joy Pollock, Rody Politt and Elisabeth Waller
0–415–33972–3

Making Progress in English
Eve Bearne
0–415–15996–2

Teaching English Language and Literacy
Dominic Wyse and Russell Jones
0–415–20091–1 / 0–415–20092–X

How to Manage Spelling Successfully

Philomena Ott

Routledge
Taylor & Francis Group

LONDON AND NEW YORK

First published 2007 by Routledge
2 Park Square, Milton Park, Abingdon, Oxon OX14 4RN

Simultaneously published in the USA and Canada
by Routledge
270 Madison Ave, New York, NY 10016

Routledge is an imprint of the Taylor & Francis Group, an informa business

© 2007 Philomena Ott

Typeset in Palatino by Keystroke, 28 High Street, Tettenhall, Wolverhampton
Printed and bound in Great Britain by MPG Books Ltd, Bodmin

British Library Cataloguing in Publication Data
A catalogue record for this book is available from the British Library

Library of Congress Cataloging in Publication Data
A catalogue record has been requested

ISBN10: 0–415–38575–X (hbk)
ISBN10: 0–415–40732–X (pbk)
ISBN10: 0–203–96607–4 (ebk)

ISBN13: 978–0–415–38575–6 (hbk)
ISBN13: 978–0–415–40732–8 (pbk)
ISBN13: 978–0–203–96607–5 (ebk)

To Jonathan, Alexander and Mélanie, Charles and
Claire-Louise in appreciation of their enthusiasm,
faith and fortitude

Contents

Preface

The idea for this book was sparked by seeing at first hand the pain and anguish caused to those who find spelling difficult and challenging and who struggle to write accurately and coherently, whatever the cause. I have included quotations from individuals whose descriptions of their struggles are poignant and often enlightening. They highlight the realities and frustrations of those who struggle with literacy.

It is indisputable that many children have simply not been taught how to spell. They often do not know why words are spelt as they are, nor have they been shown how to memorise what they are asked to learn.

The Rose Review of the Teaching of Early Reading was published in March 2006. It consulted widely and drew upon the results of international studies and recommended the structured teaching of synthetic phonics, which is a focal issue addressed throughout this book. The teaching of phonics has been at the core of specialist dyslexia teaching programmes on both sides of the Atlantic for over forty years. These teaching methods have now been vindicated. It has been officially recognised that that what is good for dyslexic learners is also the way forward for all learners.

Acknowledgements

I could not have written this book without the help and support of those who believed in my burning mission to learn how best to teach dyslexic children. This includes the Trustees of the Churchill Trust, Dr Macdonald Critchley and Tim Devlin who made it possible for me to train at the Scottish Rite Hospital in Dallas where I learned at first hand about Orton–Gillingham teaching methods from masterteacher, Aylett Cox.

My colleagues in the dyslexia world have been generous with their time. I have valued their comments on earlier drafts of chapters of the manuscript and useful advice. I would like to thank in particular: Professor Greg Brooks, Dr Steve Chinn, Ann Cooke, Dr Nata Goulandris, Jean Hutchins, David Jefferson, Bernadette Maclean, Elaine Miles, Professor Maggie Snowling, Dr Bonita Thomson, Dr Michael Thomson and Patience Thomson.

The work has benefited from the permission for the inclusion of examples of the 'realities of dyslexia' from some of my former pupils and their parents. I am grateful to Andrew Balding, Patrick Boggon, Austin Carpenter, Ruth Carpenter, Sue Cuthbert, Christopher Davidson, Paul Lambert, Valerie Lambert, Louise McGregor, Patrick Newell, Elizabeth Reilly, Ross Robinson, Penny Stopps, Emma Townsend, Zoe Townsend, Neil Valentine, Stuart Valentine and Anne Whale for their contributions. I would also like to thank the individuals and parents of children whose work has been included under a pseudonym (these names are in quotation marks).

1 English Spelling's Rich Inheritance

- Spelling defined
- The global influence of the English language as a foundation for a 'world language'
- Timeline of major events, and a who's who in the history of the English language
- The rich legacy inherited by English speakers from many sources and various cultures
- The practical implications and advantages of knowing about the history of spelling
- Spelling reform, including key figures' contributions
- How new technology and text messaging have spawned new spelling conventions
- Dyslexia defined, and why spelling well is not a birthright for all, particularly for those with dyslexia
- Summary and conclusions

Keywords

Alphabet	**Loan words**	**'Odd-bod' spellings**
Dyslexia	**Macron**	**Orthography**
Grapheme	**Mnemonic**	**Phoneme**
High-frequency words	**Morpheme**	

Spelling defined

'English is made up of words from 100 other languages and has over 600,000 words in comparison with 185,000 German words' (Terban 1998). The pronunciation of foreign words has often been adjusted by English speakers but their origins frequently remain visible and are decipherable from their written forms. Rich diversity and cross-cultural influences have had lasting effects on English, especially on its spelling. They help to explain the root cause for many of the spelling irregularities of the language today. The study of the origin and evolution of English is enlightening and particularly effective for spellers because it helps to provide logical explanations for some spelling anomalies and enigmas.

Knowledge is a powerful ally for the speller. This can be demonstrated by studying the origin and definition of the verb 'to spell'. It comes from 'spellen' which was borrowed in part from an Old English word 'spellian' meaning 'to tell, declare, relate, speak' and from 'spel/spell' meaning 'an incantation, charm, to tell a story'. This later became 'spellon', an Old High German word meaning 'to tell', which is related to the word 'gospel'. This in time became the Old French word 'espeller'. By the Middle English period 'spelling' was commonly accepted as meaning 'to write or say the letters of a word one-by-one or to cast a spell by a magical incantation'. The irony of the latter meaning will not be lost on those who find spelling a challenge and who sometimes wish they could work a magic spell to make them manage spelling successfully.

The *Shorter Oxford English Dictionary* (1933) defines spelling as 'the action, practice, or art of naming the letters of words, of reading letter by letter, or of expressing words by letters'. The *National Strategy Literacy Progress Unit: Spelling* (DfEE 2001) states that 'spelling is a letter-by-letter process which involves a set of conscious choices not required in reading'. According to Carney (1994) 'the current meaning of the word spell is knowing the separate letters of a word'. Spelling involves 'the act, process, or system of relating speech sounds to letters and to the written form of the words' (McArthur 1992). For the purpose of this volume spelling is an ability to match the sounds in speech to the letters that represent them as well as an ability to recall the letters that represent these and to use them when reading and writing or when spelling the word orally.

Educationalists, psychologists, neuroscientists and linguists have made extensive scientific studies of the theory, processes and acquisition of literacy during the past twenty-five years and have reached a consensus that 'learning to spell involves the integration of several skills. These include knowledge of phonological representations, grammatical and semantic knowledge, as well as the formulations of analogies with words in visual memory and the knowledge of orthographic rules and conventions' (Lennox and Siegel 1994).

The global influence of the English language as a foundation for a 'world language'

In 1995 English was spoken by more people than other languages with the exception of 1.1 billion who spoke Chinese. Spanish was the third most used. English has the largest and most diverse lexicon of any of the world's many languages. English is the mother tongue of about 400 million people. It is spoken as a 'second language' by over 400 million people in over 70 different countries, and around 2 billion people use and understand a restricted form of English. By 2006 English was the most widely learned and used foreign language. Many of these countries were at one time part of the British Empire. English is used as a 'foreign language' by an estimated 700 million people worldwide. It is the chosen medium of communication between air traffic controllers. Seaspeak is the essential English for International Maritime use. It is used by over two-thirds of scientists for communication. It is universally used in businesses such as the World Bank and at sporting events such as the Olympic Games.

It is the chosen medium for over 80 per cent of electronic communication systems. English dominates the Internet and now is accepted internationally as a world language for use by governments and by individuals who work for multinational organisations such as Nato, the United Nations and the European Union.

To account for its supremacy and diversity it is necessary to examine where our ancestors originated and what languages they spoke.

Timeline of major events and a who's who in the history of the English language	
500 BC	The Celts came from Europe and eventually settled in the British Isles. They spoke a number of different Celtic languages such as Cornish, Welsh, Irish and Scottish Gaelic.
AD 43	The Roman invasion began, followed by a colonisation lasting over 350 years.
449	Angles, Jutes and Saxons invaded and the Anglo-Saxon settlements began.
597	St Augustine and his Christian missionaries arrived in Canterbury.
650	An inscription on an Anglo-Saxon brooch found near Malton, North Yorkshire, is thought to be the earliest surviving example of English writing.
731	The Venerable Bede finished writing the Latin *Ecclesiastical History of the English People*.
787	Viking raiders began sporadic attacks.
871	Alfred King of Wessex translated Latin works into English, and the writing of English prose began.
891–1154	The *Anglo-Saxon Chronicle* was the first extended writing in English. Seven of the manuscripts survive.
1000	The epic Old English poem *Beowulf* was written down though it had been composed earlier.
1066	Defeat of Harold, last of the English kings, by William the Conqueror resulted in the Norman Conquest, which resulted in many Norman words being borrowed. English, French, Latin, Danish, Welsh and Cornish were spoken in different parts of the country.
1362	English was first used in Parliament.
1382–86	Geoffrey Chaucer's *Canterbury Tales* were written.
1384	John Wycliffe translated the Bible from Latin into English.
1399	Henry IV came to the throne and spoke 'His Mother Tongue' as he crowned himself. He was the first king to speak English for state business for three hundred years.
1476	The first printed English book, *The Recuyell of the Historyes of Troye*, was published by Caxton though printed in Bruges.
1478	Chaucer's *Canterbury Tales* were published by Caxton at his printing press which he set up in Westminster in 1476.
1475–1650	The Renaissance: classical influence was established, resulting in thousands of words being added to the English language. Initially there was a backlash – known as the Inkhorn Controversy – against the use of classical words.
1524–25	William Tyndale translated the New Testament into English 'so that the poorest ploughboy could hear God's word' (Bragg 2002).
1582	Richard Mulcaster's *The Elementarie* was published; it took an 'innovative stand on reforming spelling'.

1596	Edmond Coote's *The English Schoole-maister* was published and 'contributed most to the settling of English spelling' (McArthur 1992).
1604	Robert Cawdrey's *A Table Alphabeticall* was the first English dictionary published.
1611	The Authorised or King James version of the Bible was published. It was a major influence on written English.
1623	The First Folio of Shakespeare's plays was published in London.
1702	Publication of the first daily newspaper in English, *The Daily Courant*.
1712	Jonathan Swift wrote a *Proposal for Correcting, Improving and Ascertaining English*, arguing that English should be spelled and pronounced consistently.
1755	Samuel Johnson's *Dictionary of the English Language* was published.
1828	Noah Webster's *American Dictionary of the English Language* was published.
1852	*Roget's Thesaurus* was published.
1928	*The Oxford English Dictionary* (OED) was published. James Murray had been editing it from 1879.
1998	CD-ROM of *The Oxford English Dictionary* made available.
2000	*The Oxford English Dictionary* went on-line.

Adapted from McArthur (1992), Crystal (2002) and Bragg (2003)

The rich legacy inherited by English speakers from many sources and various cultures

Britain, though an island, was invaded by many tribes, each of which brought its language and culture. English evolved and changed with each of these invasions. By studying these early inhabitants and particularly the 'seven primary chronological groups' (McArthur 1992) of place names associated with pre-Celtic, Celtic, Latin, Old English, Norse, Norman French and Modern English we can see how the invading tribes influenced the language of the indigenous population.

Pre-Celtic

Pre-Celtic invaders spoke languages of which little is now known. River names survive from this period such as Avon, Itchen, Soar, Tamar, Thames and Wey and are evidence of the existence of these languages.

Celts

They were among the earliest invaders, and examples of the language spoken during a thousand years of this era survive in only about two dozen words, mainly found in English place names such as:

Aviemore from 'mor' meaning big

Penrith from 'pen' meaning top of a hill

Personal names such as 'Gareth' and 'Eoin' survived as well as 'O'Neil' and 'McCarthy', and words such as 'glen' and 'loch' are evidence of Celtic influences.

Romans

The Romans invaded Britain in AD 43 and stayed for over 350 years. There are about two hundred surviving words such as 'fork' 'kettle', 'street', 'wine'.

They left us a rich legacy including a network of roads and landmarks which still are evident in the countryside. Hadrian's Wall and Fishbourne Palace are lasting reminders of their presence, as is the evidence from place names, including:

Catterick from 'cataracta' meaning waterfall

Doncaster from 'caster' meaning army camp

Latin was spoken and used in religion, scholarship and politics for over fifteen hundred years in Britain from the time of the Roman invasion.

Anglo-Saxons

Saxons, Angles, Jutes, northern Germanic and Danish tribes came from northern Europe in about AD 450, as well as Frisians, whose language according to Bragg (2003) 'was a strong parent of English'. The Angles, who gave their name to the English language, came from Angeln now in Schleswig in Germany. These invaders were called Anglo-Saxons, a term used to describe their language and culture which had a pervasive influence and is the nucleus of the English we speak. Crystal (1995) points out that 'the earliest English alphabet was devised by missionaries in Britain who used the Irish forms of the Latin alphabet to present the sounds of Anglo-Saxon as phonetically as possible'. There are over a thousand Anglo-Saxon 'now more properly referred to as Old English' (Barnhart 1988) words in current use; most are one-syllable words

HANDY HINT

ANGLO-SAXON HIGH-FREQUENCY WORDS

Nist (1966) summed these up wittily in the person of the man who:

loves his mother, father, brother, sister, wife, son and daughter; lifts his hand to his head, his cup to his mouth, his eye to heaven and his heart to God; hates his foes, likes his friends, kisses his kin and buries his dead, draws his breath, eats his bread, drinks his water, stands his watch, wipes his sweat, feels his sorrow, weeps his tears and sheds his blood; and all these things he thinks about and calls both good and bad.

The spelling and pronunciation of Anglo-Saxon words are sometimes problematic. Originally they were written in the runic alphabet called the 'Futhork'. They include many 'high-frequency' words such as 'house', 'woman', 'eye' and the question words 'what', 'when', 'where', 'why', 'which'. Thousands of new place names evolved during this period and have survived, including:

Berkhamsted from 'stede', meaning site or settlement

Birmingham from 'ham', meaning home/hamlet

Christian missionaries

The monasteries and Church used Latin, which was also used in the scriptures such as in the surviving *Lindisfarne Gospels* and *Book of Kells*. The Roman alphabet was the chosen script. According to Crystal (2002) 'the missionary influence resulted in around 450 new words coming into the language' which were associated with the church such as:

gospel   heaven   hell   mass   monk   priest

Vikings

They were invaders who came from Scandinavia and began their incursions in about AD 787. About a hundred and fifty words, such as 'beck' and 'ransack', survive from this period. Evidence of their settlements are found in over fifteen hundred place names which indicate Old Norse influence including:

Bowness from 'ness', meaning headland

Whitby from 'by', meaning village

We owe to Scandinavian languages such as Old Norse words including:

awkward   birth   dirt   guess   knife   window

Crystal (2002) draws our attention to the fact that 'the verb to be, the most widely used English verb' is Scandinavian. Poor spellers struggle to spell the various tenses, particularly 'are', 'being', 'were', as well as words such as 'they', 'their'.

Normans

In 1066 Harold, the 'Last of the English Kings', was defeated on Senlac Hill near Hastings by William Duke of Normandy. The Norman French conquerors gained control of the church, judiciary and government. The affairs of state and church were recorded in Latin and Norman French which their rulers spoke. Bragg (2003) asserts that as 'the English laboured, the French feasted'. Place names which survive from this period include:

Beaulieu, meaning beautiful place

Belvoir, meaning beautiful view

Bovey Tracy and Melton Mowbray are examples of names surviving from manorial family names (McArthur 1992). Surviving words include:

beauty   biscuit   castle   money   please   sword

From the time of the Conquest, a study of the surviving literature and the many surviving Old French words provides a rich source of information about the origins of our language. They repay the spelling scholar with invaluable insights about why many of our spellings are as they are, as well as yielding information about the origins of some notorious irregular spellings. English spelling borrowed 'qu' for /cw/ sound as in 'queen'. To avoid visual confusion between 'u' and 'v' the letter 'o' was substituted. This accounts for the spelling of words such as 'come', 'love', 'done'. French, English and Latin were spoken by different members of society. The common people continued to use English as their spoken tongue and it was mostly unwritten. French was used in the courts of law until 1362 and for writing legal documents until the 1450s. The church continued to use Latin for its liturgy and the scriptures.

In 1362 English was used for the first time at the opening of Parliament. Spelling was a mixture of two systems, Old English and French. The way words were spelt depended on how they were pronounced in the many regional accents, which resulted in different spellings of the same word. When William Caxton introduced his printing press in 1476 he made the decision to use the prevailing pronunciation then used in London as a basis for spelling. Venezky (1976) pointed out that English spelling was unreliable at this period and cites evidence from the work of Caxton, who spelt Bruges, where he had lived for thirty years, in the following six different ways:

brugges   bruges   Brudgys   Brugis   Bruggis   brudgis

Bragg (2003) points out that 'there were over five hundred ways of spelling the word 'through' and over sixty forms of the common pronoun 'she'.

Modern English

Modern English place names date from around 1500 (McArthur 1992). Later, Tunbridge Wells was named after springs discovered there. Maida Vale commemorates a battle won in southern Italy.

The practical implications and advantages of knowing about the history of spelling

People learn about spelling in many different ways and they also remember how to spell words using a variety of methods and strategies. Palmer (2000) opined that 'every word has a story, and [that] the stories are often enshrined in the spelling'. Mnemonic devices, which are memory aids, can be used to learn a spelling. An acronym or a sentence which includes the letters may help to recall the letters in the word, and can be made more memorable with an illustration. This may be a valuable 'adhesive' for those with good visual skills but poor auditory memory.

The links provided by knowledge of the history of a word such as its Latin or Greek origins may help others to cement those words in long-term memory. For instance 'cent' is a Latin word for a hundred and knowing this helps the speller to remember how to spell 'century' (hundred years), centurion (soldier in charge of a hundred men), 'centilitre' (one-hundredth part of a litre). Word study helps to develop awareness, recognition of spelling patterns and meanings, which helps to develop an automatic recall of the word when reading or writing.

However, according to Crystal (1995), pupils 'are not generally told why spellings are as they are, or about how these spellings relate to the way words are pronounced. Without such a perspective, spelling becomes a vast, boring and time-consuming task.'

How can this oversight be dealt with? A study of the history and development of our language pays handsome dividends for spellers, including poor spellers, because it gives them a roadmap with signposts to help them choose correct options – knowing is understanding.

Guidelines and categories for French loan words

Over ten thousand French loan words were assimilated into English in the Middle Ages. Many of these words are still in use today and are associated with:

- food and drink, such as 'appetite', 'sausage'
- law, such as 'evidence', 'verdict'
- religion, such as 'cathedral', 'miracle'
- government, such as 'chancellor of the exchequer', 'parliament',
- clothes, such as 'brooch', 'collar'
- furnishing, such as 'curtain', 'cushion'

Many of these words have silent letters or poor letter-to-sound match and may cause poor spellers great difficulty. The white knight who took up the challenge to improve spelling was no other than Richard Mulcaster, an eminent schoolmaster who was subsequently the first headmaster of Merchant Taylors' School and later High Master of St Paul's School in London. He published in 1582 the first part of *The Elementarie*, which was a textbook about education. It is significant that he recommended a list of words for spelling based on 'government by sound, custom and reason'.

He led the way for the reform of English spelling, and influenced Edmond Coote, who wrote *The English Schoole-Maister* (1596), which was the first bestseller written on spelling and by 1737 was in its fifty-fourth edition (Scragg 1974).

The Renaissance saw the re-emergence of interest in classical civilisation. Latin and Greek became more important and many new words were introduced to the lexicon at that period. Today 'Latin roots can still be identified in 52 to 56 per cent of the words in any English dictionary' (Cox and Hutcheson 1988). Many explorations and scientific discoveries were made at this period and resulted in loan words from Spanish, Italian, French and Portuguese being used by English speakers. 'Words from up to fifty other languages came into English' (Crystal 2002).

During the reign of Queen Elizabeth I there was a great expansion in naval trade, and the soldiers and explorers introduced about twelve thousand new words to the language. The Elizabethan age produced many great poets and dramatists, many of whom revelled in the expansion of vocabulary. William Shakespeare is admired and revered for his contribution to English literature. His language continues to enlighten the minds and enrich the souls of succeeding generations. To do so he used twenty thousand different words in his writings and added up to two thousand words to English. His works have been translated into over fifty languages, and quotations from him occupy seventy pages of the fourth edition of *The Oxford Dictionary of Quotations*.

Bragg (2002) claims that Shakespeare 'laid the foundations for a world language'. The First Folio edition of Shakespeare's work published in1623 included examples of spelling such as 'doe' for do; 'goe' for go; 'heere' for here. Spelling was clearly not universally consistent. This could be explained by the different spelling conventions followed by individual printing typesetters. Shakespeare had definite views on spelling and uses one of his characters, Holofernes in *Love's Labour's Lost*, Act V Scene i, to mock the use of French spelling in English because 'I abhor such fanatical phantasms, such insociable and point-device companions; such rackers of orthography, as to speak dout; det when he should pronounce debt, – d, e, b, t, not d, e, t'.

The results of the many borrowings from French, Latin and Greek meant that spelling became very challenging. There was little standardisation of spelling in Tudor England and as yet there were no national standards or yardsticks. There was however a perceived need for guidance about spelling as well as for an understanding of 'hard' words so that people could understand them when they heard them. In 1604 the first dictionary of 'hard words', *A Table Alphabeticall*, was published by William Cawdrey. It consisted of 2,445 words. He did not succeed, however, in ironing out spelling inconsistencies in published works because even on the title page of his dictionary 'worde' and 'word' are used on the same page.

Spelling reform, including key figures' contributions

The desire for reform in English spelling has a long history dating from 1569 when John Hart pleaded for words to be spelled by their sound. In 1712 Jonathan Swift proposed an English Academy to 'fix' the language so that words could be spelled and pronounced consistently. In 1740 the French Academy changed the spelling of 36 per cent of French words. Pleas were made from time to time by successive generations of writers in both England and America. There were many influential individuals who wanted to see spelling reformed as well as simplified.

Noah Webster had the singular distinction of succeeding in changing the spelling of many words in the English language primarily through his *Dictionary*, which continues to this day to be the authority for American spelling.

It is now well established that British and American English have differences in spelling. There are also a number of grammatical and pronunciation differences as well as meaning and syntactic differences. The advent of globalisation, which has been influenced by film, television, the Internet and the news media, has seen the acceptance of some of these differences in British English and many are now in common use in everyday communication.

There were vast waves of immigration to America. Slavery introduced many black Africans to the country. Throughout the nineteenth century millions of Europeans fled to the New World. These emigrants brought 'loan words' as well as borrowing words from the native Indians. These included some of the following:

Spanish
ranch   rodeo   stampede   tacos

Dutch
boss   coleslaw   cookie   snoop

French
chowder gateau poker saloon

Italian
espresso pasta pizza spaghetti

German
delicatessen frankfurter kindergarten pretzel

Yiddish
bagels kosher mazuma nosh

Black English
groovy hip nitty-gritty rap

American Indian
moccasin skunk totem wigwam

(Crystal 2002)

British spelling reformers

John Hart in 1551 complained that English writing is 'learned hard and evil to read' (Crystal 1995) and in 1569 he advocated that words should be spelt strictly by their sound.

In Britain during the nineteenth century Isaac Pitman was at the vanguard of spelling reform because there was a poor match between sound and symbol: For example the /sh/ sound can be spelt in many ways, as the following words show.

addition	division	ocean
anxious	Egyptian	mission
Asian	fashion	ship
chauffeur	fuchsia	sugar
conscience	luncheon	

Pitman founded a 'Fonetik Soseiti' and created a shorthand system called Stenographic Sound-Hand in 1837. In 1840 he published 'an augmented Roman alphabet called Phonography' which was a landmark in reform. In 1876 the National Union of Elementary Teachers called for a Royal Commission to consider spelling reform. The British Spelling Reform Association was founded in 1879, and among its distinguished members it included Alfred Lord Tennyson and Charles Darwin.

It evolved into the Simplified Spelling Society in 1908. Its leading luminaries included Daniel Jones of University College London. He campaigned for the promotion and acceptance of the International Phonetic Alphabet. Supporters included George Bernard Shaw, who advocated the advantages of a phonemic spelling system as a labour- and money-saving device.

When he died in 1950 Shaw bequeathed a proportion of the royalties from his estate for a period of twenty years to simplify English spelling. As a result the Shaw alphabet was devised. It consisted of forty letters to match the phonic sounds. It was not accepted by the public. Mont Follick MP introduced a private member's bill to Parliament to reform spelling in 1949. He proposed that the Simplified Spelling Society's publication *New Spelling* should be used in primary schools. The Bill reached the Committee Stage in 1953 but it never reached the statute books owing to lack of public interest.

Sir James Pitman, grandson of Isaac Pitman, devised and introduced the initial teaching alphabet (i.t.a.) in 1959 to help children when learning to read. It consisted of 44 shapes to represent each of the 44 sounds in English. It used 24 letters of the alphabet but left out 'q' and 'x'. It was supported by the Ministry of Education. It enjoyed initial popularity and was used in a number of countries, but it was consigned to the top shelf in libraries and was forgotten about and left to gather dust in cupboards in classrooms as the teaching profession became increasingly disenchanted with it.

The Simplified Spelling Society (SSS) is still working for the 'reform of English spelling for the benefit of learners and users everywhere' (2003). It argues that the alphabetic principle represents speech sounds but 'English has not systematically modernised its spelling over the past 1,000 years and today haphazardly observes the alphabetic principle'. Upward (2003) of the SSS argues that 'for phonics to work effectively, we need simpler spelling that corresponds to the sounds of words, and the variants are therefore to be preferred for pedagogical reasons'. Various initiatives have been tried to reform spelling on the 'basic principle that anyone who knows the pronunciation of a word should be able to spell it' (Carney 1994).

More recently there were howls of derisive laughter as well as anger when the British government's examination watchdog, the Qualifications and Curriculum Authority (QCA), told schools to adopt 'internationally standardised' spelling for scientific terms such as 'fetus' for foetus, 'sulfate' for sulphate. Professor Bernard Lamb, a geneticist and London branch Chairman of the Queen's English Society, stated that the QCA had no business imposing US spellings. He said, 'I can see arguments in favour of standardisation but why not use British spellings as the standard?' (*The Times* 2000b). The then schools standards minister Estelle Morris contacted the QCA and decreed that 'English pupils should use English spellings' (*The Daily Telegraph* 2000). On the other side of the fence an editorial in *The Times* (2000a) argued that 'standardisation of the spelling of scientific terms would be good science and good English'. However it drew the line on wholesale spelling reform and thundered that a 'phonetic revolution of spelling would be barbarism'. Each attempt to modify or change has ended in failure. The British public does not like, nor do the majority of people want, change in spelling.

Another major chink in the armour of the 'spelling watchdogs' and the self-appointed custodians of English spelling has been caused as a result of the use by the advertising industry of playful invented spellings such as Heinz Meanz Beanz, Kwiksave, Toys 'R' Us. Creative spelling has become a feature of tabloid newspaper headings and is used extensively in advertising. There has been a proliferation of trade names with eye-catching unconventional spellings. Is this the thin edge of the wedge? Only time will tell whether new spelling conventions will prevail.

How new technology and text messaging have spawned new spelling conventions

Has the technological communications revolution resulting in e-mailing and text messaging broken down the last bastion of standardised spelling usage and opened up a way to spelling simplification?

The underlying principles of texting could have been designed as the answer to the prayers of people with dyslexia who struggle to use conventional spelling. Some poor spellers have been using phonetic spelling simply because they were unable to remember standardised spelling. Texting has unwittingly provided some additional advantages for those who find spelling an impediment to traditional written communication. It reduces the knowledge they require to communicate and, by masking errors, takes away the stigma attached to poor spelling as 'creative' spelling becomes acceptable.

An extract from an essay by a 13-year-old schoolgirl illustrates these principles and the strategies involved in texting:

My smmr hols wr CWOT. B4 we usd 2go2 NY2C my bro, his GF & thr 3: kds FTF. ILNY, it's a gr8 plc

My summer holidays were a complete waste of time. Before, we used to go to New York to see my brother, his girlfriend and their three screaming children face-to-face. I love New York. It's a great place.

Daily Mail 2003

The following are examples of mobile phone text message abbreviations that have made their way into the new edition of the *Concise Oxford Dictionary*:

ATB	All the best	BBLR	Be back later
B	Be	BFN	Bye for now

Dyslexia defined, and why spelling well is not a birthright for all, particularly for those with dyslexia

The word dyslexia is derived from the Greek 'dys' (meaning poor or inadequate) and 'lexis' (words or language).

Dyslexia is a learning disability characterised by problems in expressive or receptive, oral or written language. Problems may emerge in reading, spelling, writing, speaking, or listening. Dyslexia is not a disease; it has no cure. Dyslexia describes a different kind of mind, often gifted and productive, that learns differently. Dyslexia is not the result of low intelligence. Intelligence is not the problem. An unexpected gap exists between learning aptitude and achievement in school. The problem is not behavioral, psychological, motivational, or social. It is not a problem of vision; people with dyslexia do not 'see backwards.' Dyslexia results from differences in the structure and function of the brain. People with dyslexia are unique, each having individual strengths and weaknesses. Many dyslexics are creative and have unusual talent in areas such as art, athletics, architecture, graphics, electronics, mechanics, drama, music, or engineering. Dyslexics often show special talent in areas that require visual, spatial, and motor integration. Their problems in language processing distinguish them as a group. This means that the dyslexic has problems translating language into thought (as in listening or reading) or thought into language (as in writing or speaking).

International Dyslexia Association (1998)

CASE STUDY: 'ANDREW' (47 YEARS)

This response to a questionnaire uses original spelling, grammar and punctuation.

How old were you when you discovered you were dyslexic?

I was told at 5 [that] you are very clevar [with an] IQ 142 But work and school will be very difficult.

Are other members of your family dyslexic?

My father [who is] 70 [and my three] brothers and my sister is slightly and all my 3 childran. [My father and his twin brother used to have rubber bands tied on their fingers to help them tell left and right, when they were at school. My eldest brother has a son and daughter who are both mildly dyslexic. My younger brother has one severely dyslexic son and the other two are mildly so. My sister has a dyslexic son and her daughter is not. She is the only one in the third generation of the family who is not dyslexic.]

Did you ever have an embarrassing or upsetting incident at school?

Techars could not understand me writing ought words and then getting them wrong agane.

Can you recall an amusing or funny incident associated with your dyslexia?

At unavrasity a gerl at the end of the lectur taped me on the sholdar and asked it I was Polish. She said that she had forotan her specticals and had been try ing to read [my notes] ovar my sholdar.

Do you have any recurring difficulties?

I spel foneticly and I cant sea spelling mastakes.

What examinations have you passed?

I have an MA from [a Scottish University] and a banking exam Dip AIB.

Did you receive any 'special considerations' when you sat examinations?

At unavrsaty I dictated to a tape machen, in the Banking exam I dictated to somone who wrote in long hand.

Do you find using the spell-checker on the computer useful?

If often dose not recognise what I am tiping in.

SUMMARY AND CONCLUSIONS

1   Explanations for some of the causes of the difficulties traditionally associated with the complexities of English spelling are hidden among the roots of the language and are often veiled by changes over centuries.

2   English place names can be used to provide a thumbnail sketch of the lives of the various settlers who came to our shores and gave us words from their mother tongues.

3   English spelling has a rich linguistic and broad cultural heritage. The language has imbibed and borrowed words from a multitude of nations and cultures as well as retaining linguistic fossils from our forebears, such as 'papa' which was first spoken fifty thousand years ago at the beginning of the Ice Age. The most influential sources were Scandinavian languages, French, Latin and Greek. Britain's armies and colonies as well as its trading added to our rich linguistic heritage. New words were coined as a result of cultural changes and scientific development, and with territorial exploration. This Babelisation of English is a significant factor in some of the complexities in our spelling and pronunciation.

4   The dominance of English as a first language is a phenomenon, and World English is a reality. The British Council teaches more than half a million people English each year. English as a second language has become increasingly more common. There are now more non-native speakers worldwide than native speakers. Seventy per cent of the text used on the Internet is in English. Some demographic studies predict that Arabic, Hindi and Urdu will in fifty years' time be spoken by statistically more people. However English will surely still be the universal currency.

5   The study of etymology and knowing about the history of the language help to enlighten learners and clarifies meanings of words that would sometimes otherwise be obscure or challenging to spell.

6   For hundreds of years various individuals have sought to standardise and simplify English spelling.

7   Noah Webster succeeded in his war of independence from British English spelling domination. Many spelling conventions were conceded when British English became American English. English speakers in Australia, New Zealand and South Africa have developed their individual vocabulary, grammar and pronunciation. In more recent times English has become an official second language in a number of countries and differences are found such as in the English spoken in India, Africa, Malaysia, Singapore and Jamaican Creole which include loan words from their indigenous languages, as well as new words.

8   Many individuals and organisations such as the Simplified Spelling Society have sought to change, amend and simplify English spelling, but in vain. The public does not have a stomach for change – the status quo continues.

Regional variations in pronunciation persist, as in the north of England where people have a bath before 'breekfust' while people in the south of England have a 'barth' before brekfust'. But even if they talk like that, standard English and its spelling prevail but issues surrounding standard English pronunciation are controversial. According to Quirk et al. (1985) 'the traditional spelling system generally ignores both the stages in pronunciation over time and the variations in pronunciation through space; despite its notorious vagaries, it is a unifying force in world English'.

9   From the beginning of the new millennium a chink has appeared in the spelling reformers' armour. Standard spelling, which many regard as a 'world heritage site', has been under attack as text messaging and e-mail play an increasingly prominent role in mass communication. Abbreviations, acronyms and 'creative' spelling are used and punctuation is often ignored. A rearguard action is being fought including that of examiners who ordered pupils to 'Delete text message style' (*TES* 2002).

10   The BBC has raised the profile of spelling by organising a national spelling contest. The television quiz show *Hard Spell* involved a hundred thousand children in a thousand schools in a competition to find 'Britain's best young speller aged eleven to fourteen. The most consistently misspelt words were 'caterwaul', 'pleasurable', 'rankle' and 'totem'. The winner was Indian-born Gayathri Panikker, who clinched the title by spelling 'chihuahua', a breed of dog named after its Mexican place of origin. The deciding word was 'dachshund', another breed of dog named after the German *dachs* (badger) and *hund* (dog). The producers claimed that 'spelling is compelling'. It may well have been for millions of viewers and certainly was for the competitors but what of those who simply cannot spell?

11   Some children are instinctively good spellers. The majority of children need to be taught how to manage spelling successfully including ways to remember spellings. Others such as children and adults with dyslexia often find spelling a minefield. The International Dyslexia Association's most recent definition highlights this (Reid Lyon et al. 2003) and states that 'dyslexia is a specific learning disability that is neurobiological in origin. It is characterised by difficulties with accurate and/or fluent word recognition and by poor spelling and decoding abilities.' The objective must be to make it less so with the use of better methods and strategies, greater understanding of how best to teach and learn spelling, and with the assistance of the best possible use of technology and electronic communication.

2 Spelling Processes

- Are there differences in how individuals learn and remember spellings?
- Practical suggestions for an informal survey of the strategies and techniques that individuals use when spelling
- Brain function and its significance for cognitive and learning styles
- Are there implications for practitioners and individuals about the research outcome for those with acquired dyslexia versus developmental dyslexia?
- Brain function examined during post-mortem and neuro-imaging studies
- What processes are involved in spelling?
- Stage models for the development of spelling skills
- Why learning to read and learning to spell are like conjoined twins
- Summary and conclusions

Keywords

Acquired dyslexia	Magnetic resonance	Skywriting
Amalgamation theory	imaging (MRI)	Specific developmental
Analogy	Metacognition	dyslexia
Auditory skills	Mnemonic	Specific learning
Automaticity	Morphemes	difficulty
Cerebral dominance	Multi-sensory learning	Spelling stage
Cognitive style	Neurolinguists	Spelling strategy
Dysplasias	'Odd-bod' spellings	Strephosymbolio
Ectopias	Phonological	Visual memory
Kinaesthetic skills	awareness	Working memory
Learning style	Rapid automised	
Long-term memory	theory (RAN)	
'Look-and-say' method	Short-term memory	
of reading	Sight words	

Are there differences in how individuals learn and remember spellings?

The variations in how individuals approach learning spelling can be measured. They can be established by informal observation in a one-to-one situation or in a classroom of a group of children while doing a spelling test. The test could consist of a dictated list of individual spellings or a short prose passage. Dictated sentences provide an even better diagnostic test measure than individual dictated words because many other essential subskills such as sequencing, grammatical knowledge, punctuation and working memory are simultaneously involved. This testing should be done over an extended period, preferably over three consecutive weeks for example when the weekly spelling test is given. The teacher or teaching assistant can make a note of individual responses. The results may then be used to provide indications of the most consistent methods and dominant strategies used by individuals when they spell.

Observation of a mixed ability group of pupils in a mainstream classroom will usually provide evidence of the various strategies individuals use. These could include some of the following, depending on individual preferred learning style.

PRACTICAL SUGGESTIONS FOR AN INFORMAL SURVEY OF THE STRATEGIES AND TECHNIQUES THAT INDIVIDUALS USE WHEN SPELLING

Use a dictated passage which includes 'odd-bod' spellings (Ott 1997) and observe and record the following:

- The pupil who repeats the word 'cat' and sub-vocalises it (or moves the lips) as he or she sounds out and segments the phonemes of the word and matches these to the graphemes /c/ /a/ /t/ shows that he or she has good auditory skills and can apply sound-to-symbol matches.
- He or she may tap out the syllables using the fingers to help to remember the constituent four parts in the word /in/ter/est/ing/ and then he or she spells each chunk. This shows that he or she has good phonological and motor memory.
- The individual who closes his or her eyes as if he is turning on a personal mental video recorder to help to recall the pattern of letters and a visual representation of the word shows that he or she has strong visual skills. He may 'see' the arches in the word 'McDonald's'. Other visualisers according to neuro-linguistic programmers (O'Connor and Seymour 1990) turn their eyes upwards and 'look' at the letters in their mind's eye.
- Another pupil may use analogy and rhyme to help him or her to recall the spelling of the /k/ sound at the end of a word when he or she wants to spell 'back'. They could for example recite the nursery rhyme

    > Jack be nimble
    > Jack be quick
    > Jack jump over the candlestick

    to help recall words with similar endings which have 'ck'. This shows that he or she has good oral skills.
- Strong visualisers remember letter patterns, especially those which occur frequently or which they have studied, such as 'ight' or 'ing'. When they want to spell 'string' they may say 'bring' because it rhymes and they can see the pattern.

- Someone else may scribble the word quickly on a piece of rough paper and try a few versions of the letters before choosing the final version. They are relying on visual memory of the word usually from exposure to print when reading.
- Someone who has good motor memory may trace the letters of the word on the desk or use skywriting or write the word to help remember the spelling pattern. This shows that they have good kinaesthetic skills, and the motor memory helps them to remember the letter sequence.
- Others can apply a spelling rule or convention such as 'no English words end in "v"' as in 'live', showing that they have good verbal skills.
- Some pupils may use a mnemonic device as a memory aid to help remember an irregular word such as 'because' and he or she may say the sentence 'big elephants can't always use small entrances'. They then know that the first letter of each word represents the letters in the target spelling, showing good verbal and visual skills.
- Some pupils will just write the word quickly and easily because they have internalised and learned it. The spelling is stored in their long-term memory, and it is ready for instant recall. They can spell automatically and with the minimum of effort.

Orton (1931) drew attention to another behaviour sometimes observed in a pupil who is unsure of the sound-to-symbol match. For example when the target word is 'Dido' he may spell it as 'Diedough'. Orton describes this approach as 'sight implants' and argues that the errors manifested are because 'such a boy did not know the sound of the letter' but had been taught by a sight method (look-and-say) to recognise whole words. This speller tried to circumvent the problem by using a visual strategy, including an attempt to recall the letter pattern 'ough' for 'o'. But because like many dyslexic individuals he has poor visual memory he continues to misspell words, particularly when taught by a mainly visual approach.

Dyslexic spellers are sometimes caught in a Catch-22 situation for spelling. When they are unable to remember whole word spellings or spelling patterns, they spell phonetically and rely on tuning their ears to the sounds they want to spell. Many of them fail when using this method because of their fundamental phonological problems. They produce unconventional letter combinations which at times appear to be bizarre when they match the sounds to incorrect letters because of poor phonological skills because they cannot segment the sounds. This accounts for the chronic nature of their spelling difficulties and is a core deficit in the condition.

On the other hand good spellers are able to use a variety of strategies to spell, depending on their preferred learning styles and on whether the target word is a regular or an 'odd-bod' spelling. They may use a combination of multi-sensory methods particularly when trained to do so. An over-reliance on a particular strategy such as phonetic spelling may be an indication of a specific learning difficulty. These observations in a 'real' learning environment prompt us to seek explanations about the different ways individuals perform the spelling task. It prompts the question 'Do individuals' brains function differently and do individuals learn in different ways, and if so, what are the implications for teachers?'

Brain function and its significance for cognitive and learning styles

Much of our knowledge about language and brain function has come from the study of neurolinguistics and from the work of neuroscientists. The father of the dyslexia movement, Samuel Orton, was a neurologist as well as a psychiatrist and psychologist who worked primarily with individuals with learning difficulties.

The British pioneer, a Scot named James Hinshelwood, was an ophthalmologist. He was a clinician as well as a diagnostician, and he took a keen interest in teaching reading and writing to his patients. He made some very farsighted observations including recommending using as many 'cerebral centres as possible' (Hinshelwood 1917).

Orton (1937) hypothesised that 'the process of reading is a much more complex activity requiring the physiological integrity and interplay of many brain areas'. His theory was that letters and words were transposed in a mirror image in individuals with dyslexia because they did not have well-established lateralisation of the hemispheres of the brain. He called this 'strephosymbolio'. He postulated that this was why the letters 'b', 'd', 'p' and 'q' and whole words such as 'dog' for god, 'left' for felt were reversed. This was frequently cited up until the 1970s as a primary symptom of the condition. This theory has now been superseded by neuropsychologists using neuro-imaging technology.

Dyslexia is associated with a host of difficulties which involve reading, writing, spelling and language as well as problems with symbolic information, memory and sequencing speed of processing, such as when undertaking arithmetic or music. The quest for explanations and solutions to these problems resulted in studies being undertaken in a number of centres worldwide to try to establish how individuals learn, as well as studying the causes of dysfunction. Researchers examined brain dysfunction as well as studying the similarities and differences between acquired dyslexias and specific developmental dyslexia. Ellis (1993) reviewed the literature from the 1970s of neuropsychologists, particularly about patients who had had strokes, and concluded that 'whatever dyslexia may turn out to be, it is not a reading disorder'.

Are there implications for practitioners and individuals about the research outcome for those with acquired dyslexia versus developmental dyslexia?

Many authorities, including academic researchers and theoreticians, as well as experienced practitioners now agree that a defining characteristic of dyslexia is a lack of cohesion in its manifestations, as well as a disparity between unexpected strengths and weaknesses regardless of ability. However when there is early recognition of specific developmental dyslexia, and when appropriate teaching is given, it can be compensated for and many difficulties can be overcome. The prognosis is not usually as optimistic for those with acquired dyslexia. In some cases it depends on the location of the brain damage and on the individual's earlier education history.

The symptoms of the dyslexia may overlap but the outcome is the major difference between the two conditions. This is why dyslexia is one of the key disorders in the systematic investigation of the architecture of the mind and its basis in the brain (Frith 1997). These studies of neural architecture and function do have practical implications for the outcome and for how we teach dyslexic people and on how individuals learn.

CASE STUDY: 'JACKIE' (24 YEARS) AS TOLD BY HIS MOTHER

Jackie has mild, but widespread cerebral palsy that slightly affects everything he does. This definitely clouded his primary school days. Any problems he had were presumed to be caused by his physical difficulties. Although we had been told by the Local Authority educational psychologist that he had a very high IQ, some of his teachers gave the impression that they considered that he was just a bit slow mentally.

From the age of 5 he started absconding from school and by the age of 10 was doing this on a daily basis. At home during the holidays he was quite different and full of fun but was a very unhappy child during term time. We could not understand why he was quicker than his older brother when he was doing mental arithmetic but he could not work out sums on paper. One day when he was looking up the meanings of 'fear' and 'instantly' in the dictionary he became very frustrated because he knew they didn't fit into the context. He asked me to help him and I pointed out that the words on the list in front of him were actually 'fever' and 'insanity'.

He was sent to a school for physically disabled people when he was 11 years old. He wasn't accepted by his peers and was taunted by a pupil who said, 'What are you doing here, you're not handicapped?'

When he was 13 I watched a television programme about dyslexia and 'couldn't believe' the insights it gave me. It took another two and a half years, culminating in a formal appeal to the Secretary of State for Scotland, to prove that he was indeed dyslexic. He was formally assessed for dyslexia. At the time we as parents presumed that he had 'acquired' dyslexia. Later it was discovered that he had 'specific developmental dyslexia'. Subsequently it was established that there are many other members of our family who are also dyslexic.

At the age of 15 he had a reading age of 8 years 9 months and a spelling age of 8 years 3 months. He was sent to a specialist school and went on to gain GCSEs, A levels and a BSc (Hons) in Biotechnology and a MSc in Molecular and Cellular Biology. When he was sitting his BSc examination he was given extra time and had a scribe and extra time when doing his Master's degree. The diagnosis of 'specific developmental dyslexia' and appropriate teaching changed his life.

Brain function examined during post-mortem and neuro-imaging studies

The pioneering work of Dejerine (1892) described the different functions of the left and right brain hemispheres. It has been since been confirmed that dyslexia has a neuro-biological basis. Research has found evidence in the left posterior brain region. Geschwind and Levitsky (1968) established that the majority of all individuals have asymmetric brains.

The Wm Underwood Company gave a bequest to the Orton Dyslexia Society in 1980 to establish the Orton Dyslexia Neuroanatomy Laboratory at Harvard University Medical School's Department of Neurology which was based at the Beth Israel Hospital in Boston. The director of the dyslexia research laboratory was Albert Galaburda (1993), who had been a student of Geschwind. He and his medical team carried out autopsies on individuals who had had dyslexia (Rosen et al. 1993). They found as a result of eight autopsies on six male and two female dyslexic individuals that there were structural differences in their brains and that their brain function was different. They had ectopias (brain warts) and dysplasias (scars) on the planum temporale, which is the language area of the left hemisphere of their brain, but no brain damage. The two halves of their brains were symmetrical whereas in 'the control brains [normal readers] 85 per cent show asymmetry, the larger side usually being the left'. Larsen et al. (1990) when using MRI scans were able to show in a study of a adolescents that all dyslexics who had severe phonological problems had symmetrical brains. Neuro-imaging studies have used magnetic resonance imaging (MRI) technology to map brain activities on a computer screen. Shaywitz and Shaywitz (1998) carried out an experiment which included 29 adults with dyslexia and 32 adults without. Their results indicated differences between the brain function of both sets of subjects. There was under-activation in the posterior brain region of the individuals with dyslexia. This occurred while they were rhyming letters and words, reading words and letters, and while putting words into categories. These abnormalities are on the language area of the left hemisphere of the brain. This may account for the language impairments often experienced by those with dyslexia.

The right side of the brain is the dominant side for many dyslexic people. According to Geschwind (1982) this 'may explain the superior right hemisphere capacities exhibited by dyslexic children'. The implication for practitioners is that dyslexia is a developmental disorder with a biological basis which when understood can prevent misunderstanding.

HANDY HINT

Cox (1978) when paying tribute to Samuel Orton proclaimed that we should 'heed the beat of Dr Orton's different drum' which she explained meant that 'the educational system must begin to meet the individual child's learning needs rather than to continue to require the child to meet the system's needs'.

This has since frequently been paraphrased by others such as Chasty (1990) when he suggested that 'if this child doesn't learn the way we teach, can we teach him the way he learns, and then develop and widen his competencies in learning?'

What processes are involved in spelling?

The word 'spelling' implies different processes and a variety of approaches.

- It can involve writing down a word using the correct letters to match the sounds of the word when it is pronounced. To do this the individual needs to be familiar with the letters (graphemes) and must be capable of matching these to the sounds (phonemes) that represent them.
- Spelling can also depend on visual memory, a personal lexicon – a word bank. The word is held in a mental lexicon because it has been memorised. Words can then be recognised as correct, for example when proofreading, or when doing a multiple-

choice activity. Some argue that 'spelling is mainly a visual skill' (Hilton and Hyder 1997). Peters and Smith (1993) stated that 'the most important factor in learning to spell is the VISUAL element . . . spelling depends on looking with interest, intent and intention to reproduce a word'. Critics such as Thomson (2003) argue that many would dispute this, 'arguing that it is primarily phonological encoding with all the processes of phoneme awareness, segmentation, onset/rime'.

- Spelling also implies knowledge of spelling rules and conventions, including generalisations. This knowledge can be acquired naturally from repeated exposure to words in print, or derived from explicit teaching or from an arbitrary source such as a dictionary or a spell-checker.
- Spelling can also be generated by knowledge and experience of affixes including prefixes, suffixes and roots including morphemes (the smallest meaningful unit in a word) such as 'ing' or 'ed'.
- Spelling is helped by the use of semantics, which involves studying the meaning of words. For instance, 'tele' comes from Greek and means 'coming over a long distance'. Etymology explains the history of words and their derivations. It is also useful to remember spellings such as 'telephone', 'telepathic', 'telescope', 'television'.
- The more experienced speller also uses analogy to generate spellings or to remember spelling patterns. The knowledge that the sound ī is spelt with 'ight' as in 'night' helps to spell 'flight' and 'light'. However some spellers with poor visual memory fail when using this method just as some readers fail when taught to read by using the 'look-and-say' method.
- Memory devices such as mnemonics help those with good language skills to remember the letters. However Hutchins (2003) points out that 'there is a limit as to the number of mnemonics dyslexic spellers can recall'.
- Some learn to spell by using motor memory to recall the spelling patterns. This is often done by copying out lists of words, or by using the computer keyboard, or by jotting down the letters. Some spellers do this with their eyes closed. This is evidence for why multimedia software (including talking word processors) when combined with graphics helps improve spelling, as do packages which include games for overlearning and reinforcing spelling. Multi-sensory learning is effective.
- Using a spell-checker, particularly one with a speech option on the computer or a handheld version, helps the speller to learn, check and reinforce spellings. The use of colour to highlight silent letters or tricky parts helps to raise awareness of spelling conventions and processes which good spellers use effectively. Speech recognition software often helps improve spelling, not least because the spellings are provided and all the words that appear on the screen are correctly spelt.

Stage models for the development of spelling skills

A number of academics have defined certain phases in the development of children's spelling skills. These have been refined, enhanced and developed into a theory of stages in spelling development. They have ranged from influential figures such as Frith (1980), who describe the 'three stages in the spelling process' by linking it to spelling error analysis, to critics such as Treiman (1993) and Snowling (1994) who argue that not all children move automatically from one stage to the next. This is often evident in older pupils with dyslexia. They may still be struggling to remember basic spelling patterns, or sounding out the word to match the letters, while other examples of their spelling may show that they are using strategies such as semantics to spell. This highlights the uneven pattern of skills and weaknesses evident in their spelling. Learning to spell is normally part of a continuous developmental process during which the apprentice spellers' skills are honed by practice, fine tuned by experience of print when reading and burnished by personal use when writing.

Repeated practice and experience lead to mastery of spelling conventions and the understanding of the principles for most spellers. However some, including people with dyslexia, have persisting difficulties because spelling with automaticity does not become a reality for them. They have to think about how to spell even high-frequency words such as 'once', 'forty', 'were'.

Why learning to read and learning to spell are like conjoined twins

Orton (1931) argued that children with a marked reading disability are almost always bad spellers 'and that 'an ability to spell is treated as of more or less minor importance'. Bradley and Huxford (1994) offered convincing arguments for why learning to read and spell are inextricably linked. Like conjoined twins they are 'built on the same foundation, [but] they do not develop simultaneously' according to Bosman and Van Orden (1997). They should however be taught in tandem because 'grapheme–phoneme relations are used for reading, phoneme–grapheme relations are used for spelling' (Ehri 1997). To decode words when reading, the pupil needs to know the 44 sounds which are represented by 26 alphabet letters which have lowercase and uppercase shapes. Some behave regularly: sounds such as /b/ are represented by the letter 'b' in 98 per cent of words. Other sounds such as long /ē/ sound can be spelt in over sixteen different ways. To encode words when spelling the pupil needs to know about the seventy or more possible letter combinations which represent the sounds. The National Literacy Strategy (DfEE 1999a) lists 'some of the 140 (approx.) letter combinations illustrated within words'.

The reader, when taught to recognise syllables in words such as /per/form/ance/, can then blend and read the word. The speller when he pronounces the word can break it into syllables such as /con/duct/ing/ and spell it once they have learned about the conventions of language. According to the NLS Literacy Progress Unit (DfEE 2001) 'Spelling is a letter-by-letter process which involves a set of conscious choices not required in reading . . . Spelling is regular enough to repay systematic teaching.'

Adams (1997), when evaluating her review of the scientific research on reading and its acquisition, reported that the 'most surprising of all, research has taught us that what enables this remarkable swift and efficient capacity to recognise words is the skilful reader's detailed and automatised knowledge of their spellings and spelling–speech correspondences'.

A succinct explanation of the inseparable bond between reading and spelling processes which she called the amalgamation theory was given by Ehri (1980). She argued that spellers need to know and use a combination of 'phonological, morphological, orthographic, semantic and syntactic skills' (Ehri 1997). Reading and spelling are interconnected 'like circuits on a switchboard' (Moats 1995).

SUMMARY AND CONCLUSIONS

1   Spelling is a complex process which involves the interplay of a variety of approaches and is often dependent on cognitive style which is matched to a chosen learning style. Stanback (1980) reviewed the literature on teaching spelling and concluded that there is no one best method. Techniques and strategies should vary according to the words to be learned as well as the individual's preferred learning style.

2   Brain studies provide evidence of the significance of cerebral dominance, and show how this may affect cognitive style and the learning strategies used in spelling acquisition and retention.

3   Many spellers use a variety of processes and strategies when learning spelling. Some spellers are unable to do so, often because of constitutional difficulties, including dyslexia.

4   Spelling skills develop over time, mainly through practice and experience.

5   Reading and spelling development go hand-in-hand: each has a role to play and they are mutually beneficial. Beginner readers use logographic strategies and recognise whole words whereas beginner spellers use phonological skills. Ehri's (1980) experiments showed that, according to the 'amalgamation theory, not one but several subskills are involved and need to be acquired'. Children need to recognise letters and word patterns when they decode words. They then need to match the sounds they hear to the letters that represent these when they want to encode a spelling. Shaywitz (2003) proclaimed that 'Spelling is intimately related to reading, not only because sounds are kept linked to letters but because words are being encoded – literally put into code instead of merely being deciphered or decoded'.

6   Teaching and learning spelling are progressive processes which need to be structured to the level of development of pupils. Pupils learn best when spelling is taught systematically and in a structured manner over time. Spelling needs explicit instruction for the majority of pupils, particularly for those who otherwise will fail to 'catch it' because of inherent difficulties. Scheerens (1992) analysed research from across the world when considering the essence of good teaching. This influenced the authors and played an important role in formulating the NLS Framework for Teaching (Beard 1998). It recommended that successful management of the teaching of spelling should include structured teaching which involves:

   - Making clear what has to be learnt
   - Dividing material into manageable units
   - Teaching in a well-considered sequence
   - The use of materials in which pupils make use of hunches and prompts
   - Regular testing for progress
   - Immediate feedback.

3 Alphabetic Knowledge: The Keystone of Language

- Evidence of the alphabet's central role in literacy acquisition
- Difficulties associated with acquiring alphabetic knowledge
- How modern technology 'levels the playing fields' for those with sequencing, short-term and working memory difficulties with alphabet skills
- Practical suggestions and guidelines when choosing and evaluating dictionaries
- Does the choice of dictionary matter to spellers?
- Why experience and exposure to letters and the alphabet pay dividends for apprentice learners
- Practical suggestions to develop letter knowledge and for raising awareness of the alphabetic system
- Guidelines using tried and tested means to help novice learners establish alphabetic mastery
- The significance of alphabetic adroitness
- Summary and conclusions

Keywords

Alphabet	Inflected words	Pictograms
Dictionary	Logograms	Quartile
Headword	Pangram	QWERTY keyboard
Holoalphabetic	Pedagogy	Syllabograms
Ideograms	Phonograms	Transparent languages

Evidence of the alphabet's central role in literacy acquisition

Humans are programmed biologically to speak, and children are pre-programmed to use receptive and expressive language as part of normal development. Written language is a human invention and an acquired skill. 'Speech and writing are two separate systems of signs, the sole purpose of the second is to represent the first' (Saussure 1916).

The Sumerians of ancient Mesopotamia, in what today is Iraq, are credited with inventing writing about five thousand years ago (McArthur 1992). Some of the oldest surviving evidence includes examples of writing in cuneiform (wedge-shaped symbols) of 6 and 7-year-old schoolboys' work.

There are two kinds of writing. One is a picture-based system which uses:

- pictograms which are pictures to represent objects
- ideograms which are marks such as numbers to represent concepts
- logograms which are icons to represent words. These were used in Sumer, Egypt and China.

The other kind of writing is a sound-based system which uses:

- syllabograms which are syllabic symbols used to represent small units of pronunciation as in Japanese *kana*.
- phonograms which are letters to represent individual sounds. These letters representing sounds are known collectively as alphabets. They match phonemes to graphemes.

The invention of the alphabet is said to be one of the greatest human inventions and, according to Havelock (1986), the world would never be the same again. The alphabetic principle was invented in West Asia in about 1700 BC and was known as the North Semitic alphabet: it was used in Canaan and Phoenicia. All later alphabets including the Phoenician, Greek, Etruscan and Roman alphabets are descendants. The Roman alphabet was the most influential, primarily because of Rome's mighty power, including its conquering armies. To govern its far-flung empire it needed administrators to enforce its laws and edicts. These were written down using the Roman alphabet. The Roman alphabet continues to dominate Western European languages, just as the Cyrillic alphabet dominates the languages of Eastern Europe.

The Anglo-Saxons had no written true representation of their language. They used an alphabet composed of runes which were 24 angular letters, as a result Old English was originally written in the runic alphabet called the Futhork. The Roman invaders used the Roman alphabet. This was adapted for use in English because certain sounds in Anglo-Saxon (Old English) were not used in Latin. The modern English alphabet was derived from the Roman alphabet and has 26 letters. The number of letters in alphabets varies. The smallest alphabet consists of 11 letters in the Rotokas language of the Solomon Islands and the largest of 74 letters in the Khmer language spoken in Cambodia. There are now about a hundred alphabets in the world and about three thousand languages are spoken.

In alphabetical languages the letters of the alphabet represent the speech sounds and a letter can represent several sounds: this is the alphabetic principle used to read and write. Alphabetical skills, including visual familiarity with the symbols and their relationship to the sounds in language, are the building blocks of literacy. Badian (1995) conducted an experiment on a group of pre-school children and followed their progress to the sixth grade (11–12 years). Her main finding was that 'letter naming and visual symbol matching were the only pre-school measures that had consistently significant correlation with reading and spelling at all or most grade levels when verbal IQ and age were controlled'. This highlights the importance of visual as well as oral knowledge of the alphabet because 'there is not a one-to-one correspondence between sign and sound' (Man 2000).

Many children can recite the alphabet before they come to school. Mason (1980) conducted a study and found that two-thirds of the 4-year-olds tested could recite the alphabet. A screening programme was carried out for four successive years on a cohort of 7–8-year-olds in a primary school. There were two classes of 34 children who were of average or above average ability who had already had two and a half years of formal teaching. The results showed that up to six children each year could not recite the alphabet, and in many instances, could not write it in sequence in lower case letters. These children had had formal teaching of the alphabet at the age of 4 in the kindergarten and each classroom had an alphabet frieze on the wall. Of those who failed to perform the alphabet task many were later assessed as being dyslexic. Waites (1980) conducted a study of writing the alphabet in normal and 198 dyslexic children and his results showed that 'at age ten, almost 40 per cent of our dyslexic children were still making errors compared with only 15 per cent of the normal population at that age'.

Difficulties associated with acquiring alphabetic knowledge

Difficulties with alphabetic knowledge are not manifested only in small children. Among a group of twenty-six teenagers at a specialist school for dyslexic boys all had difficulties with the alphabet. There is anecdotal evidence from dyslexic adults that suggests they 'get lost' when saying the alphabet. 'I know it but I have to keep going back to the beginning when I want to look something up in the Yellow Pages' (Whale 2001). Sir Jackie Stewart, one of the most celebrated Scots of the twentieth century, three times Formula One World Champion, confessed 'to this day I cannot recite the alphabet' (Caithness 1997).

This highlights some of the sequencing difficulties associated with dyslexia as well as the associated difficulties with short-term and working memory. Some individuals have difficulties remembering the visual representation of a letter.

Comments such as 'I never can remember the difference between a "j" and a "g"' are frequently heard. A 10-year-old pupil when asked to practise writing the alphabet went home and said to his mother 'I don't know why I have to do all this babyish stuff again'. He subsequently discovered that he could say the alphabet aloud, but became hopelessly lost when he was asked to write it in sequence, because of the mental effort of remembering the visual representation of the letter shape at the same time. He could not perform this task with automaticity. It is therefore not surprising that pupils like him have difficulties when they want to spell a word. Later some of these individuals have difficulties when they learn to use a keyboard. They cannot remember the layout of the keyboard because they have poor visual memory and consequently they type exceedingly slowly. Others find learning and using the so-called QWERTY sequence on the keyboard (which describes the letters on the top line) very challenging when learning to touch-type.

Comments like 'use a dictionary and check your spelling' often appear at the bottom of a pupil's work. This is a reasonable request for the majority of pupils. For some dyslexic pupils it is an unreasonable request which is just like asking someone with a twisted ankle to run in a marathon.

How modern technology 'levels the playing field' for those with sequencing, short-term and working memory difficulties with alphabet skills

Some individuals, as we have already seen, find using a dictionary or a reference book difficult. When and if they do succeed in finding the word they want to spell, it takes them an inordinately long time to do so. They have to keep going back to the beginning of the alphabet and saying it to find out what the next letter is. They have difficulties with short-term and working memory when they have to hold a piece of information in their head long enough to add on another piece of information. When they can cope with finding words by the initial letter they become very confused when searching a list of words all beginning with the same initial two or three letters. The problem is compounded when the word they are searching for has a different fourth letter and so on because they have difficulties with working memory. Fortunately many of these challenges have been eliminated by modern technology for those with poor sequencing skills. At the touch of a key the computer will find the word, give the meaning and the correct spelling. What a relief it is when a long list such as a bibliography can be alphabetised by a click of the mouse. But in many classrooms these methods are not used because the dictionary is venerated as the saviour of poor spellers. In reality it is often a thorn in their sides.

PRACTICAL SUGGESTIONS AND GUIDELINES WHEN CHOOSING AND EVALUATING DICTIONARIES

Use a dictionary with bold print particularly for the headwords. The font size and line spacing are key considerations. The use of colour is helpful for pupils with visual discrimination difficulties. Dictionaries that are tabulated on the side for each letter make for quicker access.

It is helpful if guidance is given for the pronunciation of words using diacritical marks as well as the stress-pattern. The easiest method is that used by Burchfield (1981). In his guide for the BBC on recommendations for pronunciation he gives a word that rhymes with the target word: 'ate' as in late. Other dictionaries use the International Phonetic Alphabet (IPA) to provide guidelines using symbols for the sounds of any language. It uses symbols based on the roman alphabet as well as inverting roman alphabet letters and Greek alphabet letters. For those who have difficulties with visual perception and visual discrimination these symbols are very difficult to remember and to use. Such help systems provide a very useful guideline for readers and spellers and should be more widely adopted, especially by those who struggle to decode and encode.

It is easier if the whole words are given rather than just a list of possible endings. Poor spellers may know the root word 'like' but often they use the dictionary to check on the spelling of 'likely', 'liking', 'likeable'. This is also significant when dealing with doubling letters such as 'commit' and 'committing'.

Choose the size and number of entries to match the literacy levels of the individual. The *Oxford Young Reader's Dictionary* (www.oup.com) has the alphabet on every page, gives the plural of nouns and the different forms of verbs, a guide to pronunciation and an example sentence using enlarged text which is also approved by the Royal National Institute for the Blind (RNIB).

Younger pupils find dictionaries with colour and illustrations attractive and easier to use. Pictorial cues also help to speed up the process.

Clear definitions are important and should be followed with an example of usage. A dictionary that says where the word has come from, for example 'juggernaut' from India, or 'dram' from Scotland, or 'coleslaw' from Holland, helps to provide clues and may later help to trigger the spelling of these loan words.

Some pupils find using a spelling dictionary, which gives the phonemic approximation of the spelling and the words, useful such as the *Dictionary of Perfect Spelling* (Maxwell, 2005) (www.barringtonstoke.co.uk) which gives the misspelling in red and the correct spelling in black as well as a 'key to suffixes, compounds and spelling rules' at the bottom of each page. For instance, if the individual wants to spell 'cucumber' they might look under the 'qu' entries. This is the sound they perceive at the beginning of the word. Critics point out that seeing the incorrect spelling in print can reinforce the error in the speller's visual memory. The author of the *ACE Spelling Dictionary* (www.LDAlearning.com) (Moseley 1993 and 1995) described three case studies which found that using a phonetic dictionary was 'an adjunct to the process of writing' and 'many pupils said that they became more confident as writers' after using the dictionary. A very interesting study would be to examine the spelling and writing output in timed conditions of a group of matched ability, and a control group of dyslexic people using different dictionary tools.

It is essential to have an up-to-date dictionary that has been revised within the preceding five years. This ensures that new words or phrases such as those associated with technology, including the Internet (which has generated its own language), are included. Many words have been compounded to create new meanings such as 'mouseclick'. Others have had prefixes added such as 'cyberspace' or 'hypertext'. Many people find hypenation a challenge, which is not surprising when we spell-check a document. Another innovative feature is the frequent use of abbreviations and acronyms such as 'Com' meaning Computer, Communications, Compatibility or 'ISP' meaning Internet Service Provider.

Text messaging using a mobile phone has generated a whole new language mainly using abbreviations derived from letter sounds as well as symbols such as '2day' (today), 'B4' (before), 'Cul8r' (see you later).

Homophones are a recurring source of confusion for poor spellers. The voice-activated spell-checker is a great help particularly when the target word is given in a sentence which helps with meaning. Speech recognition software (SRS) is also a boon.

A dyslexic 12-year-old said that he rarely used the dictionary. He preferred to use a thesaurus – 'then I know that I have chosen the correct word even if I have spelled it incorrectly such as "are" or "our"'.

Spell-checkers with a compatible dictionary such as the *Franklin* (www.franklin.com/uk) and the *Junior Oxford Dictionary* are very useful as a resource, because when the spell-checker gives the correct spelling it also gives the page number for the dictionary entry. This facility circumvents sequencing difficulties and gives the required information.

Many dyslexic spellers are frustrated when confronted with American spelling on a spell-checker so it is important to choose one with British English spelling.

Others argue that seeing the correct spelling on the screen acts as a reinforcement and that eventually this can lead to an improvement in spelling. The *Oxford Pop-up Dictionary* is a CD-ROM which is a useful multimedia resource: it includes the *Oxford Thesaurus, Dictionary of Quotations* and *World Encyclopaedia* (www.oup.com).

Handheld spell-checkers particularly those with a speech option (such as Speaking Homework Wizard, www.dyslexic.com) are a lifeline to poor speller when they write, and allow the individuals to function on a par with the majority of their peers.

CASE STUDY: 'RICHARD' (19 YEARS)

I am a 19 year-old undergraduate at Oxford University reading politics, philosophy and economics (PPE). My spell-checker on my computer opened up a whole new world to me. I was able to think about what I wanted to say rather than thinking how I might spell what I had in my head.

I can honestly say it has changed my life. I can now compete on a 'level playing field' (Ott 1997) with my fellow students. I'm still haunted by flashbacks of the pain and frustrations of my schooldays. I shall never forget my sense of shame and humiliation when I was in Year 6 and my teacher ripped out my essay in front of the whole class and said, 'this is just downright laziness and carelessness, I know you have a spelling problem but even a 6-year-old can spell their own address'. She then told me to write out my essay (which was in longhand) again and added, 'Be sure to check your spelling in your dictionary.' I could not do this because I did not know which words were wrong nor could I 'find' words like 'question' when I looked under 'kw'.

Does the choice of dictionary matter to spellers?

There are different types of dictionaries available. Each one has distinctive features which can be an additional resource and support for the specific spelling needs of individuals.

- *Pocket dictionaries*. Their chief feature is their portability.
- *Spelling dictionaries* give definitions and include the spelling changes when endings are added. The *ACE Spelling Dictionary* is an aurally coded sound-based dictionary.
- *Concise dictionaries* contain more words and phrases and more explanations than pocket versions.
- *Writing dictionaries* are designed to make writing and spelling easier.
- *Phonetic dictionaries* include the *Dictionary of Perfect Spelling* (Maxwell, 2005). It was designed for those with 'spelling difficulties'. The words are arranged alphabetically with the incorrect (mainly phonetic) spelling given in red and the correct spelling along side it, such as 'fysicks' for physics, 'kemistry' for chemistry. It is simple and straightforward to use as is the *Primary Spelling Dictionary* its companion volume (2006).
- *Specialist dictionaries* include foreign language and subject dictionaries.
- *School dictionaries* come in many forms to meet the age and educational level requirements of pupils.
- *Unabridged dictionaries* such as *Chambers Twenty-first Century Dictionary* include word and phrase definitions, word usage, history and guidance on pronunciation. The *Oxford English Dictionary* (OED) (1989) has been hailed as 'one of the wonders of the world of learning' and it 'defines over half a million words in twenty volumes'.
- *CD-Roms and electronic dictionaries* including pocket spell-checkers are available for many dictionaries including the Oxford University Press dictionaries. Seiko Instruments Inc. have produced three handheld devices that include a dictionary, thesaurus and spell-checker which are linked to the Oxford dictionaries. James and

Draffan (2004) conducted a review of the accuracy and effectiveness of electronic spell-checkers when dealing with 264 spelling errors including regular and irregular words made by dyslexic children and adults. The number of words corrected depended on the 'severity' of error, which they described as simple, moderate or severe errors, as well as on the strategy the speller used. More phonetic errors than visual errors were corrected. The *Franklin Literacy Word Bank* (known as LWB 216) (www.dyslexic.com) includes the contents of *The Oxford Primary Dictionary*, which was found to be the best handheld spellchecker.

Why experience and exposure to letters and alphabet pay dividends for apprentice learners

'Solid familiarity with the visual shapes of the individual letters is an absolute prerequisite for learning to read' was Marilyn Jager Adams', (1990) battle cry in *Beginning to Read: Thinking and Learning about Print*, her 'landmark synthesis of research' (Adams et al. 1997). It has been described as the most important and influential book about the teaching of literacy skills written during the whole of the twentieth century. In other words readers ultimately need the simultaneous recognition of the individual letters visually, orally, aurally and kinaesthetically for automatic use. Eventually this will include recognition of the letters in lower case and upper case and in printed and handwritten forms.

HANDY HINT

Read et al.'s (1986) studies showed that 'the crucial factor seems to be explicit instruction rather than specific encounters with the letters of the alphabet'.

PRACTICAL SUGGESTIONS TO DEVELOP LETTERS KNOWLEDGE AND FOR RAISING AWARENESS OF THE ALPHABETIC SYSTEM

Treiman (1993) argued that 'exposure to print rather than explicit teaching, is the important factor in the learning of orthographic patterns'. This also applies to the individual letters.

The following hints and strategies are useful to develop skills:

- Encourage the child to look at labels and signs such as 'exit', 'station', 'Toys "R" Us', 'Tesco' or 'Harry Potter' on the side of a bus, carrier bag, shop window, book cover.
- Read the labels on the products in the shopping aisles of the supermarket. Discuss them while packing them away in the cupboards at home. Did we buy Heinz tomato ketchup or Asda own label? Which brand of toothpaste did we choose, Colgate or Macleans?
- Talk about and compare different well-known logos and fonts in trade names such as Coca-Cola or Kelloggs. This can be enhanced by comparison with the advertisements on television such as those for B&Q and of course will be even more memorable if the jingle 'you can do it if you B and Q it' is discussed at the same time.
- Mealtimes can be enlivened by looking at the packets and seeing how much information can be obtained from the name. Are we having Häagen-Dazs chocolate ice

cream or Baskin Robbins vanilla ice cream? It is important to know whether the can of Campbell's soup is mushroom or oxtail before you open it.

- Reading place names and road signs on the way to school or on a car journey is another opportunity for raising awareness of the world of print that bombards us in paper, in print or even in edible alphabet spaghetti hoops.
- Parents reading to their children can point to the words as they read them. This helps to highlight the fact that words go from left to right on the page. There are punctuation marks that make us ask questions, and full stops that slow us down to help us to understand and remember what is being read.

When the spark has been ignited, the world of print can be illuminated by the familiarity with the alphabet. This will lead in time to a realisation that those who know the code can then make sense of words. Later they will be able to write words to make sense of what they want to say, just as when doing a jigsaw puzzle they will need to look at the shapes and configurations as well as the orientations of the individual letters. By turning the letters around they can say something different. 'b' turned the other way can be 'd' as in 'big'/'dig' and 'm' upside down can be 'w' as in 'mill'/'will'.

Guidelines using tried and tested suggestions to help novice learners establish alphabetic mastery

Alphabetic knowledge consists of many different competencies, as well as complementary skills that need to be developed in tandem for easy, quick access. A person must be able to say the letters, write them in upper and lower-case, recognise them in print and in cursive form, as well as being able to sequence them orally and visually, quickly, with automaticity. Here are some suggestions to help establish the required skills.

- Recite the alphabet orally. This can be reinforced by singing it to a tune such as 'Twinkle, Twinkle Little Star.' However it is important that the individual does not say the letters too quickly so that the individual letters elide.
- Ask the pupil to lay out a set of wooden alphabet letters in a semicircle and then count them to establish that there are 26 letters in the English alphabet.
- Write the alphabet sequentially, first with a wooden or plastic model of the letters, then without a model saying the letter names simultaneously.
- Say the alphabet in alternating pairs with a partner. (The teacher says 'A, B', the pupil says 'C, D' and so on.) It is helpful to remind the pupil to keep saying the alphabet subvocally to help keep his or her place.
- Say the alphabet in alternating triplets with a partner.
- Ask the pupil to say what letter comes *after* a specific letter in random order.
- Ask the pupil to say what letter comes *before* a specific letter in random order.
- Ask the pupil to say what letter comes *between* letters in random order.
- Ask the pupil to write the alphabet in upper case and lower case, with each letter on a new line (A, a; B, b etc.), while saying the letter names aloud.
- Ask the pupil to close their eyes and move some of the letters around. Then ask them to guess what letters have been switched, then ask them to put these in the correct order.
- Make up riddles such as "I am thinking of the letter that comes just before o. What is it?'

- Divide the alphabet into quartiles and use the mnemonic <u>E</u>lephants <u>M</u>ake <u>S</u>quirts to help him remember where each quartile ends. This will also be useful for learning dictionary skills later. It cuts down on the time required to locate letters and words.
- Place five letters in sequence, but insert an extra letter. The objective is to identify the 'odd one out'.
- Choose a letter in the first half of the alphabet, such as C. Then ask the pupil to continue to name the next five letters. Do the same for a letter in the second half.
- Ask the pupil to find for example the first consonant in the alphabet or the third vowel.
- Put three wooden letters in a bag. Ask the pupil to put a hand in the bag and to identify them by feel.
- Give the pupil an individual wooden letter to name, and ask them to say what letter precedes and what letter follows it.
- Ask for example for the fourth letter name, tenth letter name or the last letter in the alphabet.
- Use magnetic alphabet letters on a board or the fridge door for reference and to help develop visual familiarisation. Games can be played such as asking the pupil to find the letter for the first word on their dog's can of pet food.
- Play games with laminated letters on cards including bingo, snap, dominoes.
- Make A3 laminated letters and cut these out. Place them on the floor. Ask the pupils to throw beanbags and to name the letter the bag lands on. This can be done to music with a radio or tape recorder. When the music stops the pupil must run and stand on a letter which they must name. If they are unable to name it they forgo their turn. Take away a letter each time the music stops so that there is always one letter less than the number of players. The winner is the pupil who succeeds in naming all the letters and is the only remaining player. A reward for the winner makes the game more fun and more memorable.
- Use alphabet wall charts and friezes in classrooms or bedrooms, and encourage the pupils to refer to these.
- Use a variety of worksheets with missing letters in sequence, and ask the pupils to fill these in when they are able to write the letters.
- Use puzzles and jigsaws which reinforce the alphabet, including computer packages which have a multimedia input such as the CD-ROM *abc*, and the talking animated alphabet *Sherston* (2003) (www.sherston.com) which teaches initial sounds, letter shapes and sound–symbol relationships. *Alpha sound Xavier* (1998) (www.xavier.bangor.ac.uk) teaches basic letter sound and name correspondences. *AtoZap* (www.r-e-m.co.uk) has a number of useful software packages to help pupils explore the alphabet in an amusing and interactive way.
- Use carpet tiles or sandpaper and ask the pupil to trace the letter to develop kinaesthetic awareness, and to help develop a visual pattern of individual letters.
- When the pupil is able to say and write the individual letters, ask them to copy out a pangram (holoalphabetic) sentence such as 'The quick brown fox jumps over the lazy dog'.

The significance of alphabetic adroitness

Chall (1967) in her classic text *Learning to Read: The Great Debate* found that the best predictor of beginning reading achievement is the child's knowledge of the names of the letters of the alphabet. Many subsequent studies have confirmed these findings. Adams (1990: 61–4) reviewed these and explained the significance of 'knowing letters' for learners.

- Speed and accuracy in recognising the letter names indicates that the individual will find it easier to learn the sounds associated with the letters.
- Ease and fluency, arising from automatic recognition, when naming the letters is also highly predictive and important when learning to read and spell because the individual will be able to recognise words and word patterns later.
- Letter names and sounds often are strongly correlated, so the individual will be able to master the sounds and understand the alphabetic principles.
- The ability to name objects, digits and colours at speed was shown by Denckla and Rudel (1976) in their Rapid Automized Naming Theory (RAN) to be a good predictor of future reading ability.

Adapted from Adams (1990, pp. 61–4)

Shankweiler and Liberman (1972) found that 'in reading an alphabetic language like English the child must be able to segment the words he knows into the phonemic elements that the alphabet shapes represent'.

Furthermore it has now been shown by many research studies that the second most important predictor of later success in learning to read and write is a knowledge of phonemes. Even more important is an awareness that the word *cup* can be represented by the sounds /c/ /u/ p/ and that the word *puppet* can be divided into syllables pup/pet and that the word *crisp* can be chunked into letter clusters – the onset 'cr' and the rime 'isp'.

SUMMARY AND CONCLUSIONS

1   Many preschool children can say the alphabet. Dyslexic people even as adults have persisting difficulties with alphabetic skills. Learning the alphabet for them is not 'as easy as ABC'.

2   Ehri (1997) insisted that 'acquiring knowledge of the alphabetic system is central to development and should fall within the province of spelling instructions'. However this can be a cause of ongoing difficulties for some readers and spellers.

3   Technology is the ultimate solution for those who have sequencing difficulties associated with alphabetic skills.

4   Dictionaries and thesauruses should be chosen with care because the size of font, use of colour, spelling layout and the use of whole words which have the inflected forms written in full are prime considerations.

5   The choice of dictionary should match the age, development and current literacy skills of the user.

6   Alphabetic knowledge is built up over time but requires explicit teaching for many learners. The Rose Review (Rose 2006) cited Rowe's (2005) findings on behalf on the Australian government's report on teaching reading that 'the incontrovertible finding from the extensive body of local and international evidence-based literacy research is that for children during the early years of schooling (and subsequently if needed), to be able to link their knowledge of spoken language to their knowledge of written language, they must first master the alphabetic code'.

7   The alphabet is the keystone of language acquisition knowledge and is the amalgam that cements the letters in words. Without this the whole of the language edifice is endangered because words, sentences and text each require familiarity and automaticity with the letters and letter patterns when reading and writing.

4 Phonics: Resolving the Big Issues

- Phonics' historic centre-stage role in the acquisition of literacy
- Transatlantic concerns about declining reading standards raised by whistleblowers, resulting in the outbreak of a 'phonics war'
- Responses to concerns about declining reading standards in US and UK schools
- The way forward – A National Literacy Strategy including phonics
- Training standards for those charged with delivering literacy skills
- The NLS objectives for teaching phonics
- The whys and wherefores of the 'long tail of underachievement' in reaching expected standards in National Curriculum tests
- Plugging the gaps in basic skills with the NLS's Additional Literacy Support
- Specific difficulties associated with delivering Additional Literacy Support for those with dyslexia
- Practical suggestions for teaching and learning the bare essentials of phonics
- Checklist for phonics
- Summary and conclusions

Keywords

Analytic phonics
'Code emphasis' reading method
Grapheme
Keywords
'Meaning emphasis' reading method
Multi-sensory learning
NLS Additional Literacy Support (ALS)
Phoneme

Phonics
Phonological awareness
Phonology
'Progressive education' movement
Segmentation skills
Synthetic phonics
Systematic phonics
'Whole language' movement
'Whole word' reading method

Phonics' historic centre stage role in the acquisition of literacy

The Phoenicians devised a system of mapping the sounds of speech to symbols which were called letters. The set of letters became the alphabet. Each letter in the Greek alphabet was represented by a single sound and children learning to read were taught phonics (Chall and Popp 1996). Balmuth (1992) argued that the phonic teaching method, which teaches reading and spelling by sounding out the individual letter sounds, then blending and synthesising the sounds to produce a word, was first devised in the fifteenth century by a German teacher called Valentin Ickelsamer.

There are two forms of the phonic method – the analytic method and the synthetic method. The analytic phonics method teaches the child to look at the whole word and to break it into chunks: the 'onset', which is the initial consonant or consonants, and the 'rime', which is the vowel and the final consonant(s), when reading and spelling. The synthetic phonics method teaches the child to look at the word and then to break it into the individual sounds which he or she blends when reading and segments when spelling.

It is easy to sound out words in a 'transparent' language such as Spanish which has a strong sound-to-symbol match. In English it can be difficult, particularly with the Old English words which used Latin letters to represent the Germanic sounds. The problem was exacerbated by the subsequent inroad of words from other languages.

One of the first phonic readers to be published in Britain, *Reading Without Tears* was a landmark text (Bevan 1857). Other titles followed, and the most influential were Nellie Dale's (1900) *Dale Readers*. According to Morris (1986) 'from the turn of the century until the Education Act of 1921 phonics continued to be very much in vogue in the UK'.

After the First World War many changes took place in society as well as in education. From the 1920s onwards the 'progressive education' movement developed, which resulted in greater importance being given to the 'meaning emphasis' method of reading instruction. Easily decoded texts with unknown words being deciphered by using contextual cues were used when reading was being taught. Later the the so-called 'whole word' sight method became increasingly popular. 'Basal readers' known as 'reading primers' in the US and 'reading schemes' in the UK were produced, such as the Beacon Readers (Fassett 1922), which still included phonics. 'Look-and-say' reading methods which taught pupils to recognise whole words primarily through visual memory and by memorising 'sight words' gradually became the preferred teaching method.

It is of significance that there were however opposing views about reading methods from mid-Victorian days onwards, especially for those who were struggling to learn to read. Evidence of this can be found in the work of the founding father of dyslexia, the Scotsman James Hinshelwood. In his seminal text (1917) he discusses the importance of using what he calls 'the old fashioned method' – the ABC method which involved spelling the word aloud while saying the names of the letters of the alphabet. It emphasised learning the alphabet and later the phonemic link to the letter, rather than the 'modern method' – the 'look-and-say' method – to ensure success in learning to read. Orton (1931) also had strong views on the preferred reading method for children, and pointed out that 'the method of instruction in reading seems to play an important part and many of the children with isolated spelling disabilities are found to have been taught to read by the whole word or "sight" method which has failed to establish the sound association with individual letters necessary for the reproduction of word spelling'.

Individual teachers and schools exercised their autonomy (which nowadays would be described as professional judgement) about how much direct and systematic phonics to teach. The two major approaches to teaching reading were the 'meaning emphasis' method, which teaches the use of contextual cues, and the 'code emphasis' method, which teaches explicit decoding skills. Both had their followers and co-existed peacefully.

In the postwar UK there was increasing disquiet about poor standards of literacy. Some critics blamed this on the use of 'progressive' teaching methods which placed greater emphasis on the individual child's needs, rather than on traditional forms of teaching including phonics and explicit decoding skills. Daniels and Diack (1954) were the leaders of the 'phonic revolt' and spearheaded a rearguard action with the publication of the Royal Road Readers (Daniels and Diack 1960). This was in response to their research, which they claimed showed that integral and systematic phonics is important for initial teaching of literacy. They initially enjoyed some popularity but their books and others like them gradually went out of fashion. The 'whole language' movement became the vogue. Leading advocates such as Goodman (1986) argued that explicit teaching of reading is like oral language and is unnecessary. Reading skills developed naturally by exposure to good literature and it was not necessary to teach sound–symbol relationships. He asserted that teachers made learning to read difficult 'by breaking whole (natural) language into bite-size, abstract little pieces'. Meanwhile there were a number of government enquiries and reports including the Plowden Report and the contentious Black Papers (Cox and Dyson 1969) which highlighted disquiet about reading standards and reading methods, as well as concerns about national reading standards in the UK. However problems with literacy at this period were not confined to this side of the Atlantic.

Transatlantic concerns about declining reading standards raised by whistleblowers, resulting in the outbreak of a 'phonics war'

The debate about falling literacy standards and reading methods was propelled into the public domain in the US with the publication of Rudolf Flesch's book *Why Johnny Can't Read: And What You Can Do About It* (1955). It caught the eye of the media and was serialised in national newspapers. It was top of the *New York Times* bestseller list for thirty weeks. It was the touchpaper which ignited an education atom bomb. Even today the fallout can still be felt in educational circles.

The backlash and public outcry about falling reading standards, which Flesch attributed to the teaching methods used, was fanned by his 'abrasive style and persuasive arguments'. He pleaded that English is a phonetic language and that teaching it should be done by using phonic methods. He claimed that many professionals regarded these methods as old-fashioned, dull, boring and repetitive. There was a lot of mud slinging and according to Adams (1990) 'he called out the profit motive and impugned the intellect and honesty of experts, schools and publishers'.

In the short term his campaign was effective in raising public debate about reading standards, and it resulted in the US Office of Education Cooperative Research Program in First-Grade Reading Instruction (Bond and Dykstra 1967). Jeanne Chall (1967) was one of its most influential members. She published the results of her research in the classic text *Learning to Read: The Great Debate*. 'The overall findings were that a code emphasis, no matter what it was called – whether a spelling method, a phonic method – a direct, an explicit or a systematic phonics method – produced better results than a meaning emphasis. The results were better than a whole-word, sight and story method for children in general, and especially for children at risk' (Chall 1997).

In spite of the careful investigations Chall carried out at home and abroad, as well as the evidence she gleaned from worldwide research, hers was a voice crying in the wilderness. She reviewed the work of many researchers, for example Joyce Morris (1959), who had studied five-year-old pupils in English schools and found that the use of initial phonics significantly improved reading attainments. Her conclusions, findings and message also largely fell on stony ground. There was however a small but devoted band of 'synthetic phonics' followers, many of whom were disciples of Orton and Gillingham and users of their teaching methods. They continued to fight on in the 'phonics war' in the US.

None the less the followers of the 'whole language' movement won the biggest battles. By the 1970s it had become popular for teaching literacy and during the 1980s it was the chosen method of teaching reading in many schools both in the US and in the UK. Its most influential advocates were Frank Smith (1978) and Kenneth Goodman (1986), who argued that children learned to read and spell just as they acquired spoken language. Critics such as Liberman and Liberman (1990) pointed out that 'the basic assumptions of Whole Language are wrong' but their words and those of Orton–Gillingham fell on stony ground. In schools users of synthetic phonics were given 'suitable reading materials of their choice'. Children were sent to the 'reading corner' to choose a book from the class library and encouraged to read it themselves. Supporters claimed that children's reading would develop naturally. This approach was dubbed the 'psycholinguistic guessing game' because of the emphasis placed on the use of contextual cues to aid meaning and understanding when reading. During this time many British schools began to abandon reading schemes, many of which had been used by generations of children when learning to read. The teaching profession was divided in its evaluation of reading schemes such as the *Janet and John* series (O'Donnell and Munro 1949). Critics said that they were often unimaginative because of their sequential story lines and that too often they depicted cosy, middle-class life. Other commentators decried the repetitive use of 'controlled' vocabulary and the stilted contrived phraseology used in many reading schemes.

Meanwhile millions of dollars were spent on research. A number of studies such as Stedman and Kaestle's (1987) showed that between 20 and 25 per cent of the US school population had problems with reading. There was a general consensus that illiteracy was a major problem. According to the Orton Dyslexia Society (1986), 'illiterate adults account for 75 per cent of the unemployed, one-third of the mothers receiving Aid to Families with Dependent Children, 85 per cent of the juveniles who appear in court, 60 per cent of prison inmates and nearly 40 per cent of minority youth; of people in the work place 15 per cent are functionally illiterate, including 11 per cent of professional and managerial workers and 30 per cent of semiskilled and unskilled workers'.

Responses to concerns about declining reading standards in US and UK schools

The US Department of Education commissioned Marilyn Jager Adams (1990) and Mary Marcy Stein (1993) to examine and report on teaching reading. Adams's findings were published in *Beginning to Read: Thinking and Learning about Print*. She proclaims in her *tour de force* text that 'most surprising of all, research has taught us that what enables this remarkably swift and efficient capacity to recognise words is the skilful reader's detailed and automaticised knowledge of their spellings and spelling-speech correspondences'. Her report confirmed that educationalists had ignored Chall's findings of thirty years earlier.

HANDY HINT

Adams (1997), when she reviewed the scientific research worldwide, found that:

First, the capacity for reading English with fluency and reflective comprehension depends integrally on deep and ready knowledge of spellings and spelling–sound correspondences. Second, for many if not most children acquisition of this knowledge depends on insights, observations and behaviours that are not forthcoming without special instruction.

Adams (1997) argues that 'explicit phonics instruction is more effective than implicit phonics instruction'.

There was a rude awakening about the consequences for individual pupils when the National Assessment of Education Progress (NAEP) showed that more than 40 per cent 'of tested fourth graders [9–10-year-olds] were basically unable to read grade-appropriate texts' (Adams 1997). There was a national outcry when 70 per cent of Californian pupils 'failed or were waived from the test' because of their reading difficulties. The National Reading Panel (Institute of Child Health Development 2000) phonics subgroup showed that 'systematic phonics instruction helped children learn to read better than all forms of control group instruction'.

In the UK there were mounting concerns about education standards in schools and among school leavers. The government set up an inquiry into the teaching of English language resulted in the Kingman Report (1988). This influenced the content of the National Curriculum (NC) (1988) when it was introduced. When the NC was revised the English Orders in the National Curriculum (DfEE 1995) brought the teaching of phonics to the forefront.

The issues surrounding international comparisons of literacy standards are complex and elicit mixed results depending on the tests used as well as sample sizes. However 'a distinctive feature of British performance is the existence of a long "tail" of under-achievement which is relatively greater than that of other countries' according to Brooks et al. (1996). A report commissioned from Ernst and Young (1993) estimated 'the costs to the country of illiteracy, in lost business, remedial education, crime and benefit payments to be over £10 billion per annum'. The International Adult Literacy Study (IALS) carried out by the Organisation for Economic Co-operation and Development (OECD) (1997) showed that 23 per cent of the population of England and Wales were functionally illiterate. The programme for International Student Assessment (PISA) OECD (2000) examined literacy levels which showed that the UK ranked seventh of the fifteen countries taking part. Royal Mail (2003) carried out research among a thousand consumers about business communications. The survey claimed that 'spelling and grammar mistakes cost UK business over £700 million a year' and 'communication gaffes as a whole cost UK business nearly £4.6 billion a year'.

The way forward – A National Literacy Strategy including phonics

In response to public and political pressures the National Literacy Project was established in Britain in 1996. Education standards became an important issue in the public domain. In response the Labour Party (1997) pledged in its election manifesto to 'encourage the use of the most effective teaching methods, including phonics for reading'.

The National Literacy Strategy (NLS) was published. In 1997 the incoming Prime Minister Tony Blair issued his since often quoted mantra 'Education, education, education' and promised that education standards would be near the top of the political agenda of his new government. The Secretary of State for Education and Employment David Blunkett in his foreword to *The Literacy Strategy Framework for Teaching* (DfEE 1998) set a 'target of 80 per cent of 11 year-olds achieving the standards of literacy expected for their age by 2002' and he 'put his money where his mouth was' and offered to resign from office if this target was not met.

Teachers were initially daunted by the demands of the NLS, which included a Literacy Hour. Some criticisms were made about the prescriptive processes in the objectives for the three levels of teaching for each term of the seven primary school years. Some felt that it was 'too regimented' and far 'too standard'. Questions were raised about the content and rationale. Some of this disquiet and concerns could have been prevented by the inclusion of a bibliography in the *Framework for Teaching*. An acknowledgement of the sources for a number of the recommendations and initiatives would have been helpful. Many teachers were in the dark about these, and many were unaware of the findings of the most respected international research which was the basis for many of the ideas and recommendations used for teaching in the NLS. The *Review of Research and Other Related Evidence* (Beard 1998) was not widely publicised. This included a condensed explanation of the rationale about the whys and wherefores of the NLS strategy and should have been compulsory reading for all students, teachers and teaching assistants charged with implementing the NLS in our schools. It should have been studied in tandem with the NLS *Framework for Teaching*. It clarified the main issues, provided explanations as well as the research evidence for implementing the key targets, and 'follows the recommendations of such reviews of research evidence as that in *Beginning to Read* by Marilyn Jager Adams which was commissioned by the US Congress'. The NLS has drawn its teaching approaches from successful initiatives in the US including Slavin's (1997) *Success for All*. Its chief features were 'direct, interactive teaching' and 'systematic phonics in the context of interesting text'.

'The policy and strategic justifications for the NLS can thus be seen to be underpinned by several international sources, including scholarly generalisations from published research and current initiatives in the USA and Australia, especially those designed to boost the performance of disadvantaged students' (Beard 1998). The Framework for Teaching (1998) emphasised that 'During Key Stage 1 the teaching of phonics, spelling and handwriting complements this [writing] process and should be used systematically' and 'there must be a systematic, regular and frequent teaching of phonological awareness, phonics and spelling throughout Key Stage 1'. A curious omission from the glossary was a definition of phonics. While advocating systematic phonics it is curiously silent about whether children should initially be taught reading by the analytic or the synthetic phonic method. Not surprisingly this lack of specific guidance from the DfEE at the time perhaps reflects the polarisation of views among educational professionals. This was the key issue in the phonics debate and was the underlying cause of continuing uncertainties among the teachers about the teaching of phonics. It continued to cause bitter disputes and disagreements among those who believe that beginning readers should first learn analytic phonics (reading whole words by breaking them into chunks) or those who believe that they should first learn synthetic phonics (reading by sounding out words broken into individual phonemes). The NLS advocated using the 'Searchlight' model for reading which included a mixed approach of whole words, phonics, contextual cues and memorisation of the 'high-frequency' word lists.

The Office for Standards in Education (Ofsted) is charged with reporting on the major issues including and involving the teaching of literacy from inspection evidence. The unresolved issues about how and what phonics method to use showed according to a report of Ofsted (1998) that 'in a significant number of schools, teaching of phonic skills was haphazard and superficial'. Ofsted (1999) reported that 'schools need to ground their work in a systematic approach to phonics but ensure that pupils' individual development is fully supported by a wide range of strategies'. The NLS (DfEE 2001a) states that 'phonics consists of skills of segmentation and blending, knowledge of the alphabetic code and understanding of the principles which underpin how the code is used in reading and spelling'. A review of the *Times Educational Supplement* (*TES*) website on 2 January 2002 showed that the word 'phonics' had generated 69 articles as well as numerous letters, which was an indication of interest nationally. One of the most bitter and vitriolic arguments was whether the NLS resources could be interpreted as recommending the teaching of analytic or synthetic phonics first.

Training standards for those charged with delivering literacy skills

Another outstanding issue was about teachers' knowledge and understanding about how, what, when and why to teach phonics.

A number of studies were carried out to establish the level of understanding individual teachers had about the teaching of reading, reading methods and their knowledge of the structure of language. In the US, Moats (1994) conducted an informal survey of linguistic knowledge among fifty-two educational professionals who were 'very experienced in classroom teaching' and who had been teaching for between five and twenty years.

They were asked 'to define terms, locate or give examples of phonic, syllabic and morphemic units and analyse words into speech sound, syllables and morphemes'. The results showed that they had poor phonic knowledge and that they struggled with the terminology. Fromkin and Rodman (1993) showed that 'at least six weeks of study and practice must be devoted to these' by those undertaking initial teacher training.

The US government continued to grapple with key issues associated with literacy. The National Institute of Child Health and Human Development (2000) showed that reading scores had been in decline throughout the 1990s in many of its schools. The National Reading Panel recommended more research on the knowledge teachers needed to teach reading effectively, particularly their 'knowledge of phonology'. A study was carried out by McCutchen et al. (2002) into teachers' knowledge of literature and phonology. Tests were conducted to examine the phonological knowledge of teachers. The Informal Survey of Linguistics Knowledge devised by Moats (1994) was administered. The average score for the primary school teachers was about 30 per cent and the conclusion was that 'the overall low scores of the teachers on the phonological survey are noteworthy, and troublesome'.

In the UK the Code of Practice (1994) and the Educational Reform Act (1996) have resulted in teachers being required to acquire additional skills and knowledge about teaching those with special education needs because as many as 20 per cent of pupils have special needs at some period of their education, including problems with literacy and numeracy. An Ofsted (1999) report about the teaching of phonics stated that 'many teachers still lack the confidence to teach reading and spelling through a systematic phonics approach'. The revised Special Educational Needs Code of Practice (2001) stated that 'schools must have regard to' and 'must not ignore' the Code and it emphasised 'preventative work to ensure that children's special needs are identified as quickly as possible and that action is taken to meet those needs' (Morris 2001).

This implies knowledge and understanding of the needs and how to deal with them for all teachers. Stannard (1999), when director of the NLS, argued that 'What matters is that children are systematically taught the phonic code'.

The Special Educational Needs and Disability Act (2001) provided legislation to ensure that those with disabilities are not treated unfavourably in schools, colleges and universities. This applies to classroom organisation, the curriculum, teaching, learning and examination arrangements. Governing bodies are responsible for the implementation and for due consideration for the needs of those with disabilities. Local Education Authorities (LEAs) are responsible for providing learning support teachers and teaching assistants. Know-how and understanding as well as staff training are all part and parcel of good practice in 'dyslexia-friendly' institutions at each level of education at primary, secondary and tertiary level.

The disquiet about the teaching of phonics continued to send shocks through the educational establishment, not least because of the findings in *Watching and Learning 3* (2003), known as the Fullan Report, an evaluation by the Ontario Institute for Studies in Education of the NLS which indicated that many teachers were still not confident about teaching phonics. The former director of the NLS, John Stannard (2003), stated that he agreed with the findings of the Fullan Report that 'some teachers are not sufficiently skilled' and 'more professional development is needed'. The government's Standards and Effectiveness Unit of the DfES convened a Phonics Summit in March 2003 (Ofsted 2003) to discuss the teaching of phonics in the National Literacy Strategy because of continuing concerns which centred on a significant omission in the systematic teaching of an effective programme of phonic knowledge and skills (DfES 2003). Evidence given to the Education and Skills Committee about teaching children to read (House of Commons 2004) raised questions about 'the quality of the training and the content of the training' teachers receive, particularly about the teaching of phonics and the lack of awareness of the research evidence for this. The report concluded that 'there is still a significant proportion of schools in which the importance of phonics in improving pupils' reading and spelling has not been recognised'. The Rose Review (Rose 2006) looked at evidence from international research including the Clackmannanshire Study (Johnston and Watson 2005). This showed that children who were taught synthetic phonics were eight or nine months ahead in spelling and seven months ahead in reading, and they concluded that the synthetic phonics approach 'is more effective than the analytic phonics approach'. The Rose Review recommendations included systematic phonics to be 'taught discreetly' in a 'broad and rich language curriculum' which 'should start by the age of five' using 'multi-sensory methods'. Guidelines were to be given in a new Primary National Strategy Framework.

The NLS objectives for teaching phonics

The DfEE (2001a) sets out the objectives for teaching phonics which include teaching children to:

- identify sounds in spoken words (phonological awareness);
- recognise the common spellings for each phoneme (phoneme-grapheme correspondence);
- blend phonemes into words for reading;
- segment words into phonemes for spelling.

The *NLS Framework for Teaching* (DfEE 1998) included suggestions and recommendations for when each of these should be taught.

As well as the NLS resources, including *Phonics: Progression in Phonics* (DfEE 2001a) and the *NLS Literacy Progress Unit* (DfEE 2001b) there are many commercial resources to teach phonics.

The whys and wherefores of the 'long tail of underachievement' in reaching expected standards in National Curriculum tests

There have however been concerns from teachers that many pupils are still failing to attain the standards necessary to read and write to access the curriculum as well as failing to reach the standard expected in National Curriculum tests.

These include many pupils who have special educational needs, including those who have specific learning difficulties. There are varying estimates for the numbers of individuals with specific learning difficulties. The British Dyslexia Association states in its literature that 4 per cent of the population are severely dyslexic and up to 10 per cent have some degree of the manifestations of the condition. They based this on the American Psychiatric Association (1994) figures that 4 per cent of the population are affected to a significant extent.

There is no evidence of agreement on a standard definition of what the condition constitutes or of the age of the participants or the diagnostic measures used to identify these individuals. Until a large-scale survey is carried out in individual countries, worldwide estimates of the prevalence of the condition remain 'guestimates'. Furthermore the issues surrounding different languages and the implications for dyslexic individuals have only begun to be addressed by the scientific community. Frith (1997) draws attention to what she describes as 'dyslexia-friendly languages', implying that some languages such as Spanish, Italian and Finnish have a closer sound-to-symbol match and that their orthographies are more transparent, meaning that there is a clearer match between sounds and letters. Finnish is among the most transparent languages in the world, which may play a significant part in explaining why Finland's schoolchildren are usually top of international literacy comparative studies. Frith (2002) points out the impact of different writing systems in European countries and concludes that 'learning to read and write in different European countries is a very different experience for young children starting school'. Wimmer and Mayringer (2002) found that although 'the typical German dyslexic child can read correctly more or less any German word' they do so slowly and laboriously because of 'impaired reading speed'.

There are many associated difficulties other than reading and spelling which must also be considered when establishing whether that individual is dyslexic or not.

There has been a growing awareness that there are major differences in the achievement of boys' and girls' basic skills. Analysis of the 1998 Key Stage 2 Standard Achievement Tests (SATs) showed that boys' writing was particularly weak.

'In 2000 83 per cent of pupils gained level 4 in reading as opposed to only 55 per cent in writing' (DfEE 2001). In 2006 (TES 2006) at Key Stage 3, 66 per cent gained Level 5 in reading: 74 per cent for girls and 59 per cent for boys. This shows that the gender gap persists across the ages. Is there a link between the sex differences in SATs scores and the gender differences associated with dyslexia, which indicate that there are 3.3 male to 1 female dyslexic people (De Fries 1991)?

Figures have not been published to establish the numbers of pupils with specific learning difficulties in maintained schools in the UK. The British Birth Cohort Study of 12,905 10-year-old children was a longitudinal study. Miles et al. (2003) concluded that 'the results also confirm the widely held view that dyslexia can occur with varying degrees of severity'. They argue that severe literacy difficulties can no longer be regarded as significant in the diagnosis: 'it appears that the necessary *and sufficient* condition for dyslexia is the overall pattern of difficulties'.

Some evidence can be found from the numbers of pupils with statements of special educational needs which are provided by the LEAs. The numbers of pupils with special educational needs varies across the country and 'continues to be something of a postcode lottery, or at least depends upon the region of England or local education authority in which the child lives' (*TES* 2001a). The Audit Commission's report (2002) described SEN support as 'inequitable' and said that children in some areas are five times less likely to receive a guarantee of additional help than others. Anne Pinney, author of the report, said that it costs £2,000 to assess and produce a statement and that this money could be better spent in addressing the children's needs in school rather than in assessing them. Furthermore a statemented pupil can have a wide range of learning difficulties ranging from physical, emotional, cognitive, behavioural psychological to specific learning difficulties. However a higher percentage of statemented pupils do have specific learning difficulties than other disabilities. 'Of the £3.6 billion special needs budget, 70 per cent is spent on preparing and implementing statements for the most needy 3 per cent. Local authorities spent £100 million a year writing statements.' The Audit Commission (*TES* 2002) says that 'most children with special needs such as dyslexia, autism and behavioural problems are denied help thanks to the weight of bureaucracy'. The DfEE estimates that up to 20 per cent of pupils will be on their school's special needs register at some time during their primary school years.

Plugging the gaps in basic skills with the NLS's Additional Literacy Support

The government responded to criticisms and political pressure by introducing the NLS Additional Literacy Support (ALS) (1999) 'to help pupils in Key Stage 2 who have already fallen behind in literacy' (Barber 1999). The DfEE allocated a £22.15 million budget for this in 1999–2000: a large part of this sum was to be spent on additional classroom assistants who were to have a 'key role in delivering ALS'.

Training was provided as well as support materials, including scripted lessons and a timetable for each of the four modules of study. There is a phonics element in each of the four modules, which are to be delivered over a period of thirty-two weeks. The programme is to be delivered in twenty-minute slots four days a week.

It appeared that lessons had been learned from the implementation of the Literacy Hour and from the *Framework for Teaching*. There were recommendations that individual pupils needed longer and more overlearning to grasp and remember basic skills. There was an acknowledgement that the pace of delivery needed to be slower. However some experienced specialist teachers still have reservations about the efficiency and effectiveness for mastery of spelling and writing skills of the ALS. Their major concern is about the breakneck speed as well as the breadth and complexity of some of the lesson materials, as an example shows. Lesson 12 Phonics Module 4 aims to do the following in twenty minutes with a small group of pupils:

1   Spelling words with word endings 'er' and 'y'
    Time 5 minutes

2   Reading 4 and 5 syllable words
    Time 5 minutes

3   Revision of consonant and vowel digraphs
    Time 5 minutes

4   Learning to read and spell tricky words
    Time 5 minutes

> The National Literacy Strategy: Additional Literacy Support
> Module 4 (DfEE 1999)

Specific difficulties associated with delivering Additional Literacy Support for those with dyslexia

The following illustration highlights the difficulties associated with teaching Lesson 12 Module 4 to a pupil with dyslexia.

Pupils with dyslexia may frequently have word naming difficulties (Denckla and Rudel 1976) as well as difficulties with processing language at speed (Wolf 1991). It will be necessary first to review concepts and terminology such as vowels and consonants and to teach the spelling of words ending in 'y' such as 'baby', 'fly', 'donkey'. It will also involve revising the concept and rules for pluralisation such as 'babies', 'flies', 'donkeys'. It also involves rules for adding suffixes to words ending in 'y' which involves three different spelling conventions:

*   rely   relied   reliable
*   copy   copying   copyist
*   employed   employer   employing

> (Ott 1997)

Teaching and learning how to spell words ending in 'er' will need an explanation about the grammar of adjectives, including comparison of adjectives.

This can be challenging and confusing for some, particularly when names and definitions have to be produced at speed within the group. (Anecdotal evidence can be found for this from 11-year-old Tom who, when asked what a verb was, replied, 'Oh, that's an easy one: a – e – i – o – u'. He confused the word 'vowel' with 'verb'.

There are oral language issues associated with learning syllables, as well as reading difficulties. The pupil may need to rehearse and revise key concepts such as a definition of a syllable, and that every syllable must have a vowel. The word 'vowel' may have to be revised including knowledge of long and short vowels, which are required to identify the different types of syllables such as open and closed. The following applies to Activity 1 of Lesson 12, Phonics Module 4.

1   If the objective is to teach adding 'er' as a suffix it will be necessary to revise as well as having prior knowledge of the terms – root, suffix, vowel, consonant. Then the pupil needs to learn that there are different ways to add the suffix 'er' to a root word which are as follows.

- Words with one syllable and one short vowel and ending in one consonant double the consonant before adding the ending 'er' such as big – bigger; hot – hotter.
- Words with a root word ending in two consonants just add 'er' such as sing – singer; bang – banger.
- If there is a vowel digraph before the /er/ sound just add 'er' such as paint – painter; feed – feeder.
- If the word ends in 'y' change 'y' to 'i' before adding the ending such as lucky – luckier; happy – happier
- If the word ends in a magic 'e' drop 'e' before adding the ending such as bake – baker; hike – hiker

2   It is also necessary to know and understand the function of the syllable division line and syllable division formula to break words into '4 and 5 syllable words' using a worksheet as recommended. Again it will compound difficulties and will have little value to attempt to cover so much ground at such a pace. The time allowance of five minutes suggested for this activity is unrealistic.

3   Revision of the concepts of consonant vowel digraphs is a tall order for any pupil. Those with good auditory memory will be able to remember them orally. Visual learners will need rehearsal with the use of concrete resources such as flashcards or plastic letters. However to use this knowledge when writing it would be preferable to include a written activity to practise and revise the digraphs. Those who work with pupils with specific learning difficulties have long been aware of the importance of a structured and systematic approach to teaching and learning skills, and the significance of not overloading the mental capacities of these pupils who have difficulties with short-term and working memory, as well as with processing language particularly at speed. They do not internalise or automaticise language including phonological knowledge quickly or easily.

The prudent approach would be to revise in this specific lesson the various ways for spelling long /ā/ sound which the pupils will have previously learned including:

'a'	April	'e'	they
'a-e'	hate	'ei'	reign
'ai'	chair		
'ay'	day		

There is little chance that five minutes will be long enough to gallop over this ground orally, not to mention having enough time to reinforce the spellings in a multi-sensory way through reading examples in meaningful contexts or by using them in writing either through dictated sentences or as a writing activity. Adams (1990) argued that 'like arithmetic without application, phonics without connected reading amounts to useless mechanics'.

4   This part of the lesson could be undertaken within the recommended time as the number of 'tricky' words to be learned is manageable. It will also depend on the prior knowledge and skill of the individual pupils, and on familiarity with the mnemonic 'o u lucky duck' to remind them of the 'ould' spelling pattern in words such as 'could', 'would' and 'should'. There is a recommendation that the lesson should end with work on the notoriously difficult homophones 'their'/'there'.

To teach and learn spelling requires time, practice and experience, as well as repeated repetition and reinforcement, for the skills and information to become internalised for automaticity for all pupils. Pupils with dyslexia demonstrate that they often require a significantly longer time to internalise skills because of the deficits now known to exist with skills involving the cerebellum (see Nicolson 2001).

Practitioners and individuals with dyslexia will testify that learning to spell and write requires greater effort for them than for the majority of their peers. It takes much longer than the recommendations in the Key Stage 3 support materials. 'Five minutes of fast paced teaching time' will result in further failure and frustration for many including pupils with dyslexia. They need more intense teaching throughout the Primary School years at an appropriate pace depending on individual needs. Teaching assistants are well placed to provide this help.

HANDY HINTS

Good readers need four experiences of sight words to read by sight

(Ehri 1997)

Spellers need 50 experiences of a word for mastery.

(Fernald 1943)

According to Ofsted 'evidence continues to indicate that the quality of phonics teaching in primary schools is variable and if pupils do not know about phonics they need to be taught' (DfEE 2001a). Adams (1990) asserted that 'teaching phonics is a task that requires disciplined, sequenced coverage of individual elements and their interrelations as well as continuous evaluation of students' levels of mastery'. In other words teaching individual isolated aspects does not work. In the past pupils with perceived spelling difficulties were often taught isolated spellings which arose in their writing. Filling in letters or word patterns on worksheets does not work in the long term because they often fail to memorise what they have copied as a rote activity. What is necessary is an intrinsic knowledge of the basic principles of spelling. Furthermore, Brooks and Weeks's (1998) research confirmed that 'children approximately doubled their normal rates of learning spellings once they had discovered their own successful method of learning'.

Bos and Reitsma (2003) carried out a study which showed that 'memorising of the spelling of words is not considered to be effective, learning to memorise stories [using mnemonics] and specific rules is thought to be quite effective at the same time'.

PRACTICAL SUGGESTIONS FOR TEACHING AND LEARNING THE BARE ESSENTIALS OF PHONICS

The pupil needs to learn the following.

Letters, vowels and consonants

Letters have four properties which are necessary to read and write words. They are:

1	Names	A	B	C	'aye' 'bee' 'see'	
2	Sounds	/ah/	/buh/	/k/		
3	Shapes	A	a	*a*		
4	Feel (this is motor memory of the letter pattern when it is written)					

The letters represent the speech sounds in words. Adams (1990) states that 'to establish the link between a letter and a sound, the learner must first establish a clear image of each'. There are 44 sounds used in speech in English.

Readers need to learn to write and recognise the individual letters in lower case and upper case and eventually the cursive shapes. This involves memorising 78 symbols for the letters in the alphabet.

Key terminology needs to be taught and used, such as vowels and consonants. Reinforce this with games and computer packages.

The concept that every word must have a vowel must be well established. Colour is useful for this. A mnemonic device to establish this is that a word is like a sandwich. Sandwiches have a filling which can be seen. The colour of the filling tells what kind of sandwich it is.

The 'vowel filling' tells you the sound of the word. It is important to be aware that many dyslexic individuals confuse the vowel sounds, particularly the short vowels.

The definition that the 'consonants are all the other letters in the alphabet' is more easily remembered by someone with word naming and word retrieval difficulties. Sets of wooden alphabet letters can be used to classify consonants and vowels, as can games, puzzles and using the computer and worksheets. 'Death by workbook' is a cry that is sometimes heard because of inappropriate use which includes using worksheets purely as a copying activity with no oral or aural input. However worksheets do play a role in skilful remediation programmes when the pupil uses the materials in a variety of ways, including rehearsing and reinforcing the skill orally, auditorally, visually and kinaesthetically.

The concept of sounds at the beginning (initial), middle (median) and end (final) needs to be taught and practised using multi-sensory methods. Henderson (1985) drew attention to the fact that 'linguists say that letter-sound relationships are governed by their environment or position in a word'. Ball and Blachman (1991) found that training in 'phonemic analysis was the most beneficial' and 'that phonemic analysis appears to play a greater role in reading acquisition than any other linguistic analysis' (Blachman 1997). Morais et al.'s (1979) work with adult illiterate Portuguese who never went to school showed that they could score only 19 per cent on tests of phoneme deletion and substitution tasks. Those adults who were taught to read in adulthood using phonemic analysis scored 70 per cent in the same tasks. This provides evidence that segmentation of phonemes does not come naturally. Playing games such as I Spy and using oral activities help to establish what sound a word such as 'rat' begins with or ends with. Ask pupils to tell you what 'cat' says if the /c/ is left out. As skills with phonemic segmentation develop they can then be asked what the word says if they add /fl/ to 'at'.

Keywords

The keyword is a term that needs to be established early in whatever programme or sequence of phonics being used. A mnemonic device that can be used is to talk about a key and what a key is used for – usually to open a door or unlock something. A keyword is a target word made by using a picture on the back of the card which is used consistently to 'unlock' the sound of the letter on the front of the card. The keyword then can be used as a key to 'unlock' the sounds. Put these on index cards which can be laminated. Make separate sets for:

- short vowels
- long vowels
- digraphs
- blends
- assimilations.

Write the letter on the front of the card in:

A (upper case)
a (lower case)
a (cursive).

Put the keyword illustration on the back of the card. (The word should not be written on the card.) Use as large a font as possible and different colours for the three forms of the letters. Store these in a card index box and use for daily reinforcement in the classroom and for home work to help develop instant recognition of the four properties of the letters. This approach was developed by Gillingham and Stillman (1956) and has since been used in many hybrid programmes such as Hickey (1992), Hornsby and Shear (1993), Bramley (1995) and Ott (2007).

Teach the short vowels with a keyword such as:

/ă/ ăpple   /ĕ/ ĕlephant   /ĭ/ ĭgloo   /ŏ/ ŏrange   /ŭ/ ŭmbrella

Reinforce these with finger puppets which depict the short vowels. Use them by asking the pupil to raise a finger when they hear /ĭ/ sound in a word. Play games and activities and use worksheets to identify missing short vowels in words. Pick out the 'odd one out' when given words with different short vowel sounds. The research evidence of Lundberg, Frost and Petersen (1988) showed that 'the effect on ability to perform phonemic tasks was quite dramatic when later learning to read and spell for the children who had used games and oral activities'. Later they can learn to read and spell words with short vowels.

Long and short vowels, digraphs and blends

The concept of long vowels can then be introduced, initially as an oral activity by learning that long vowels say their names. Then the pupil can learn the vowels that are long.

1   Vowels are long at the end of an open syllable such as 'he', 'go'.
2   Vowels are long when there is a magic 'e'. Magic 'e' is at the end of a word. A mnemonic device to teach this is: 'Magic Mrs "e" casts a spell and makes the vowels say their name but she keeps quiet.'

hăt	hāte	pĕt	Pēte	pĭp	pīpe
nŏt	nōte	tŭb	tūbe		

3   Vowels are also long when there is a vowel digraph such as in 'train' or 'seed' (terminology used to explain the long vowels will need to be developed further).

   •   A syllable is a beat. Every syllable must have one vowel sound. Syllables can be divided with a syllable division line. Pupils need plenty of practice in this initially orally and later when reading and writing (Chapter 12 includes a detailed account of these processes).
   •   The concept of closed and open syllables can be introduced. Closed syllables end in a consonant and they have a short vowel. Open syllables end in a vowel and the vowel is long (Ott 1997).
   •   Digraphs are two letters making one sound such as /sh/ in 'shop' or 'dish' as well as /ch/, /ck/, /th/, /wh/, /ph/, /gh/. There are consonant digraphs, and vowel digraphs which will be learned later as a spelling concept.

There needs to be additional practice using oral activities such as saying nursery rhymes like 'Old Mother Hubbard went to the cupboard to get her poor dog a bone' or the tongue twister 'Peter Piper picked a peck of pickled peppers'. The NLS puts major emphasis on the importance of rhyme and alliteration as well as on blending and synthesising sounds to help develop phonemic and phonological awareness in response to international research findings on language acquisition.

   •   The blends are letters that are found next to each other which sound separately but quickly such as the consonant blends.
   •   The assimilations are 'nt', 'nd', 'nk', 'nch', 'ng', 'mp'.
   •   The terminology and explanation of the 'onset' which is the initial consonant or consonant cluster needs to be developed orally, using plastic letter blocks, and in written forms using the most commonly used forms. The 'rime' is the vowel and the consonant(s) in the word.

Checklist for phonics

The 44 sounds of the English language are as follows.

Consonants (18)

/b/	bus	/h/	hat	/l/	log	/r/	rat	/w/	wig
/d/	dog	/j/	jam, gym	/m/	man	/s/	sun, city	/y/	yak
/f/	fan, photo	/k/	cat, kid,	/n/	nut	/t/	tin	/z/	zip
/g/	gun		choir	/p/	pot	/v/	van		

Vowels

Short vowels (5)
(say their sounds)

Long vowels (5)
(say their names) in open syllables, in the middle, at the end of words and in magic 'e' words

ă	ăpple		ā	ācorn	brāin	plāy	cāke	
ĕ	ĕlephant		ē	ēmu	trēē	trēat	Pēte	
ĭ	ĭnk		ī	īron	fīght	tīē	crȳ	wīne
ŏ	ŏrange		ō	ōpen	gōāt	snōw	nōte	
ŭ	ŭmbrella		ū	ūniform	glūē	stēw	tūne	

Consonant digraphs (6)

(two letters making one sound)

/sh/	ship		/ph/	phone
/ch/	chin		/wh/	whip
/th/	thumb (unvoiced)	⎫	/gh/	laugh
/th/	that (voiced)	⎭		

Vowel/consonant digraphs (4), all with 'r'

/ar/ car
/er/ herb
/or/ corn
/ur/ nurse first

Vowel digraphs (3)

/ai/ train /ea/ seat /oa/ boat

Vowel diphthongs (3)

/oo/	saying	/ŏo/	cook	⎫
/oo/	saying	/ou/	pool	⎭
/ow/	saying	/ow/	cow	
/oy/	saying	/oi/	boy, coin	

SUMMARY AND CONCLUSIONS

1   The teaching of phonics has been in and out of fashion throughout the past century because education like many other fields of human endeavour is subject to constant reforms, fashion and trends. It has also been subject to change as a result of the input from research and from practitioners including 'master' teachers' experiences.

2   The polarisation of the views of educationalists about how to teach reading, including phonics, has extended beyond the walls of academia. There are continuing disputes about when and whether to teach analytic or synthetic phonics. Practitioners who have long experience of teaching dyslexic children (Cox 1980) know that synthetic phonics needs to be taught when the child is learning to read and spell, but before doing this children should learn about analytic phonics purely as an oral activity. The NLS puts great emphasis on the initial teaching of rhyme and rhythm as an oral activity, and with the use of games activities. However, reports that 'Ofsted backs synthetic rather than analytic phonics' caused a storm of renewed protests (*TES* 2001b) among practitioners in the UK.

3   Moats and Foorman (2003) carried out further research on teachers' knowledge of language and reading, and demonstrated that 'teachers' knowledge of and ability to apply concepts of phonology and orthography accounts for significant variance in young children's reading and spelling achievement'.

   This was confirmed by a study by Cunningham et al. (2004), who found that teachers' knowledge of children's literature, phonological awareness and phonics was critical for teachers of reading. Teachers 'cannot teach what they do not know' asserted Nolan, McCutchen and Berninger (1990).

4   Both the British and the US governments have made education reform and an improvement in literacy a key policy issue and as result the education budget has been targeted for additional funding.

5   The National Literacy Strategy and the revised National Curriculum have had a major impact on what and how children are taught in schools. The *Final Report of the External Evaluation of England's National Literacy and Numeracy Strategies* (The Fullan Report) (OISEUT 2003) concluded 'that much has been accomplished but much more is needed to be done to address the reform agenda more comprehensively'. Brooks (2003), House of Commons (2004) and the Rose Review (Rose, 2006) turned the tables and established that the problem was not how teachers taught reading using the NLS mixed method of strategies Searchlight model (DfEE 1998) but that they were instructed to use this approach. The teaching profession should not be pilloried but the authors of the NLS should be held accountable for their fundamentally flawed teaching recommendations which were 'daunting and confusing' (Rose 2006).

6   Children are still falling through the net and there are ongoing concerns about a national 'tail of underachievement' especially among boys, particularly with

continued

their writing skills. There is increasing concern about the lack of basic literacy and numeracy among some college students. Classes have been introduced to teach these in some establishments. Low literacy levels are a significant factor in the high number of students who drop out and fail to complete their courses.

7   Some pupils, such as those with specific learning difficulties, often still struggle with literacy at Key Stage 3. Some teachers feel that the needs of these pupils are not being fully addressed. 'I get very frustrated with the Literacy sometimes because I know it's going over the heads of quite a lot of the children in the group – what I've got to teach them' (Year 3 teacher, OISEUT 2003). Is this an indication that the content and pace of support materials for those with learning difficulties is insensitive to their needs and fails to deliver?

8   'Learning the alphabet is a visible task, in that the letters are in front of the child and can be seen. Yet phonemes, or sounds in words are fused together in the speech stream, which is glued together within words. To become aware of phonemes is difficult, unless someone points them out' Nicolson (1997). Goswami (2002) argued that an 'awareness of phonemes, the abstract units in the speech stream represented by letters, seems to develop as a consequence of learning to read and write (or as a consequence of direct phonemic training)'. Ofsted (2004) inspectors reported in *Reading for Purpose and Pleasure* that the teaching of phonics was 'uneven'. Phonics needs to be taught systematically, cumulatively and with an understanding of what to teach, when to teach it and why to teach it. The issue is not whether phonics should be taught, but arguments still rumbled on about whether the synthetic or analytic method should be used. Rose (2006) has silenced the critics and recommends that 'synthetic phonic work should start by the age of five'. The Primary Literacy Strategy has been rewritten to include the recommendations that phonics should be taught 'explicitly, systematically, early and well'.

5 Phonological Skills: Theory, Research, Practice

- Pioneering influential language acquisition studies
- Landmark research (including results from longitudinal studies)
- The 'phonological deficit hypothesis' theory
- Research evidence of specific oral language problems
- The 'double-deficit' theory including phonological and naming-speed deficiencies
- Anecdotal evidence of phonological and specific language difficulties associated with and accruing from dyslexia
- Guidelines for choosing tests for the assessment and diagnosis of phonological difficulties
- Practical suggestions to develop phonological and listening skills
- Summary and conclusions

Keywords

Auditory perception	Phonology
Behavioural psychology	Phonological awareness
Linguistics	Phonological decoding
Longitudinal study	Pre-readers
Magnocellular pathway deficits	Structural linguistics
Ocular-motor factors	

Pioneering influential language acquisition studies

Midway through the twentieth century there was a growing awareness of the importance of language and its impact on learning. Commentators pointed out that a breakdown or a failure in the development of skills can occur in receptive and expressive language, and that this can be a primary or a secondary cause of learning difficulties as well as being a significant factor for those with specific learning difficulties including dyslexia. Vellutino

(1979) argued that dyslexia is a 'verbal deficit'. It may implode and impact on developing speaking, listening, reading and writing skills.

Linguistic studies helped to develop new theories about how humans develop and use language. Linguists such as Noam Chomsky (1986) believed that humans have a 'genetic disposition to language'. From this premise they asserted that language should not be taught in a mechanistic way. It should be 'concerned with competence' and meaning, and from this hypothesis the 'whole language' movement developed. Followers believed that learning to read is a natural, effortless, process just as developing spoken language is for the majority of humankind. This thinking was poles apart from the behaviourists' views expressed by Leonard Bloomfield (1933), whom many regard as the father of structural linguistics. He believed in a structured and systematic approach to learning and teaching language. He proposed that it should be learned by habit and from repeated exposure to structured teaching materials such as that provided in certain reading primers. This was the main objective of phonic readers such as *Let's Read* (Bloomfield et al.1964). Critics of these materials argue that meaning is sometimes subsumed by the need for controlled vocabulary and for a structured approach resulting in the use of strangulated syntax and contrived sentences such as:

Can an elk sit in an elm? Not a big elk,

An elk must not risk it. An elk must sit in a glen.

Other researchers, while acknowledging the importance of phonology, studied visual factors such as ocular-motor factors and most recently magnocellular pathway deficits in a quest to find the answers to why some individuals struggle to acquire literacy skills. Biological factors including biological differences in individuals were examined. Neurological factors, including brain architecture, were also being investigated by a number of researchers. Norman Geschwind (1965), the founder of behavioral neurology, as a result of his work with adults with aphasia and their resultant frequent loss of language skills such as colour naming, hypothesised that those with developmental reading difficulties may also have difficulties with certain language functions.

Elkonin (1963) carried out groundbreaking studies in Russia on the importance of phoneme analysis. Bruce (1964) was the first to describe difficulties with phonological awareness when he devised a test for children who had to repeat a word after a specific sound was removed. At the forefront of studies in the US on the influence of language, particularly the sounds in their own language of very young children, were Isabelle Liberman and her co-workers at the Haskins Laboratories in Connecticut. They conducted an experiment to establish whether beginning readers could tap out phonemes and the number of syllables in spoken words (Liberman et al. 1974). This line of enquiry had proved to be productive for Elkonin (1973), who asked children to move a counter for every phoneme they heard in a word. Many subsequent studies have shown that 'neither experience with speech nor cognitive maturation is sufficient to acquaint a person with the principle that underlies all Alphabets' (Liberman and Liberman 1990).

This evidence showed that language deficits can be evident in pre-school children and that discrete language skills are often not acquired naturally but have to have explicit teaching (Scarborough 1990; Snowling et al. 2003).

The hunt continued to find out more about the significance of these findings and the impact it could have on learning as well as teaching outcomes for teaching individual children. These studies resulted in what became known as the 'phonological deficit hypothesis' theory, 'one of the great success stories in science' (Stanovich 1992).

Landmark research (including results from longitudinal training studies)

British research (including results from longitudinal training studies)

Authors	Sample size (each with matched controls)	Age of subjects (mean age)	Key findings
Bradley and Bryant (1983)	368	3–5 year-olds	Children at age 3 had to carry out sound categorisation tasks from spoken words. Children who were given sound categorisation training with alphabet letters were the most successful.
Maclean, Bryant and Bradley (1987) and Bradley and Bryant (1991)	65	3–6 year-olds	Children's knowledge of nursery rhymes at age 3 still accounted for variance in spelling scores when tested three years later. Rhyme must play a special part in the connection between nursery rhymes and spelling.
Bradley (1987, 1988) and Bradley and Bryant (1991)	65	6–7 years	Children were given phonological training skills for forty ten-minute sessions over two years. 'When phonological training was given it had a remarkable effect on children's spelling' progress (Bradley and Huxford 1994). 'The foundations for spelling are laid down before the children come into contact with print at all, in their early language play and especially in their games' (Bradley 1988).
Hatcher, Hulme and Ellis (1994)	128	6–7 years	They used four groups and four different teaching approaches. Each had two thirty-minute sessions for twenty weeks. The children who received 'phonological awareness training with systematic reading instruction did best' and were 'the only intervention group to show an improvement in spelling'.
Johnston and Watson (2005)	300	6–7 years	Three groups were studied. The first learned by the synthetic phonics method, the second by the analytic phonics method, the third by analytic phonics including phoneme awareness method. The synthetic phonics group were seven months ahead of chronological age in reading, and nine months in spelling after training.

continued

Scandinavian research

Authors	Sample size (each with matched controls)	Age of subjects (mean age)	Key findings
Lundberg, Frost and Petersen (1988)	235	6 years	As a result of training Danish children each day for eight months in games and oral language exercises they found that 'segmentation ability does not seem to develop spontaneously' and 'the crucial factor seems to be explicit instruction'. 'The effect on rhyming and on word and syllable awareness were comparatively modest, whereas the effect on the ability to perform phonemic tasks was quite dramatic.'
Lie (1991)	208	6–7 years	As a result of training Norwegian children in phoneme, segmentation and blending, at the end of Grade 1 they scored 'significantly higher in spelling' which showed that 'phonological awareness is much more involved in early spelling than in early reading'.
Borstrøm and Elbro (1997)	36	6 years	They studied a group of Danish children considered 'at risk' of manifesting difficulties with literacy acquisition because each child had at least one parent with dyslexia. They were trained to recognise single speech sounds and letter sounds which were reinforced with games and pictures for thirty minutes each school day for seventeen weeks. 'The "at risk" children were in fact able to acquire phoneme awareness at a fairly normal rate – but this required an intense and phonemically based programme.'

United States research

Authors	Sample size	Age of subjects	Key findings
Liberman, Shankweiler, Fischer and Carter (1974)	46 49 40	5 years 6 years 7 years	They conducted a syllable tapping and phoneme counting game. In each age group segmentation of words into syllables was the easiest task. 46 % of pre-school children and 90 % of first-grade children could do it. By contrast none of the pre-schoolers could segment by phonemes but by first grade 70 % could.
Ball and Blachman (1988, 1991)	90	5–6 years	They showed that 'after intervention, the phoneme segmentation group outperformed both control groups on phoneme segmentation and

United States research (continued)

Authors	Sample size (each with matched controls)	Age of subjects (mean age)	Key findings
			reading measures' when trained to move disks to represent sounds in words. 'Children can be taught to segment words and this skill has an impact on early reading.'
Torgesen, Wagner and Rashotte (1994)	60	5–6 years	Subjects were given phonological training in groups of three or four children for twenty minutes, four times a week for twelve weeks. The group who had training outperformed other 'at risk' children on a segmentation task. It also provided evidence that phoneme awareness training in small groups is more effective than classroom teaching.
Torgesen (2001)	60	8–10 years	Each session was fifty minutes long. Subjects had sixty-seven and a half hours of one-to-one training for five days a week for eight weeks. The children who were trained in phonological awareness and synthetic phonics showed the most progress despite their severe specific learning difficulties when spelling words.
Molfese et al. (2002)	400	Birth and 8 years	They used electroencphalography (EEG) to examine 'brain activity and responses to speech sounds at birth', and later on language and reading tasks at age 8. Tests showed that seventeen children were poor readers. The EEG studies carried out at birth on newborn infants had correctly classified 81.25 % of the sample of children who had difficulties with perception of speech sounds. Children who develop normal language skills were better able to discriminate between speech sounds at birth than children who develop poorer language skills. They identified fourteen of the seventeen children with dyslexia and six of the seven poorer readers and concluded that 'responses to speech sounds correlate highly with later language performance measures'.

The 'phonological deficit hypothesis' theory

International studies were carried out in Britain, Canada, Scandinavia and the US. Troia (1999) reviewed the literature and found evidence of sixty-eight published studies about the impact of phonological deficits and phonological training experiments for individuals, including those with a genetic risk of dyslexia.

HANDY HINT

The key points of the research reported above are as follows.

- **Phonological awareness, including an ability to manipulate and segment sound segments in words, is the best predictor of later reading achievement. Phonemic awareness is the most powerful predictor of early reading acquisition and includes a knowledge of synthetic phonics to segment and blend the sounds (later confirmed by Rose (2006).**
- **Poor phonological skills are indicative of learning difficulties.**
- **Phonological awareness skills can be taught, and children who have had the training in these skills make greater progress when they learn to read.**

The pathfinding study was conducted by Liberman et al. (1974). They established that no pre-school children could segment words into phonemes and only 17 per cent of kindergarten children could. In a nutshell it has now been established by international research studies that phonological skills, including knowledge of phoneme, syllables and rhyme, facilitate learning to read and that those who struggle or fail to acquire and develop phonological skills often later have reading and writing difficulties. Stanovich (1992) described this as 'one of the great success stories in science'.

Frith (1997) attributed the causes of dyslexia to biological, cognitive and behavioural factors. The biological evidence of Paulesu et al. (1996) showed abnormal brain activities in individuals with dyslexia.

The cognitive evidence of Goulandris and Snowling (1991) showed that poor visual memory results in an inability to remember a sequence of letters when spelling. The behavioural evidence includes poor reading, word naming, working memory, phonological awareness and non-word repetition difficulties (Snowling 1981). But by common consensus (Lundberg 2002) 'the common core problem, the hallmark of dyslexia is assumed to be a dysfunctional phonological module'.

Training in phonemic and phonological awareness is possible, and when successfully taught can minimise difficulties some individuals have when learning to read. The theory, research and implementation of phonological training for beginning readers have great significance for all involved and who are responsible for basic literacy.

The role played by spoken language and the difficulties associated with it have continued to play a pivotal role in research, diagnosis and support for those with learning difficulties, particularly dyslexia. Spoken language is the scaffolding that underpins written language both when encoding letters in words and when spelling and decoding letters in words when reading.

Research evidence of specific oral language problems

Research has now shown that, in addition to the core deficit of poor phonological aware-ness, there are additional deficits associated with difficulties in processing and producing language. Denckla and Rudel (1976) identified difficulties with rapid automised word naming, known as the RAN theory. They showed that colour-naming speed rather than colour naming accuracy distinguishes children with dyslexia from normal readers. Catts (1989) found evidence of a tendency to mispronounce words. Brady (1986) carried out a number of experiments to examine short-term memory deficits and found that poor readers 'were significantly less accurate on the more difficult multi-syllabic and pseudo-word stimuli' as well as having 'reduced sensitivity to rhyme'. Katz's (1996) studies showed that 'phonological deficiencies account for the naming deficit of poor readers'.

Poor readers had no significant difficulties with hearing, including perception of environmental sounds, animal noises or mechanical sounds. They had a 'generally defi-cient auditory perceptual ability, but it related specifically to the processing requirements of speech'. Wolf (1997) demonstrated that, in 'comparisons with average readers, the naming speed deficits in dyslexic readers appear persistent and severe, extending from prereading stages through early adolescence'.

An ability to read nonsense words (Rack et al. 1992) was found to be highly predictive of reading difficulties as well as indicating weaknesses in phonological processing and phonic skills. Snowling (1981) showed that dyslexics are poor at non-word repetition tasks. Four-year-old children who found non-word repetition tasks difficult were found when tested at 8 years to manifest difficulties in acquiring written language skills (Gathercole et al. 1994).

The 'double deficit hypothesis' including phonological and naming speed deficiencies

A number of studies by academics such as Bowers and Wolf (1993) showed that 'serial naming speed' and slow processing of language play a significant role in the underlying skills that are necessary for reading. They dubbed this the double-deficit hypothesis. They have demonstrated that 'the process underlying naming speed represents a second core deficit in dyslexia, largely independent of phonological processes' (Wolf et al. 2000). Poor naming speed and word retrieval difficulties affect spelling. Someone who says 'rember' has little chance of spelling the word 'remember' with three syllables.

Anecdotal evidence of phonological and specific language difficulties associated with and accruing from dyslexia

These examples are from the spontaneous speech of pupils who have been assessed as dyslexic with Full Scale IQ WISC–IIIUK scores ranging from 95 to 135 in children aged eight to thirteen years.

- When 11-year-old Kevin was asked by the headmaster what his teacher Mr Tollit's name was, he replied 'Mr Toilet'. He was firmly reprimanded because it was assumed that he was being impertinent. When he was later asked what his tutor's name was he replied 'Mr Tutor'. When pressed to give his tutor's name not his position, he again replied 'My tutor is Mr Tutor'. It transpired that the man's name was Mr Chuter. Owing to his poor auditory perception skills he could not discriminate between the /oi/ and /o/ or the /ch/ sound saying /sh/ which he confused with /t/.

- A class of 12–13-year-olds were discussing videos they had watched during the holidays and who their favourite actor was. Twelve-year-old James said his favourite actor was Arnold 'Sports Neggo'. Further questions elicited more information and one of his friends shouted out, 'Oh! You mean Arnold Schwarzenegger!'
- Another dyslexic boy in the same class said that he loved Harry Potter, and his favourite part was when Harry was sent to Hogwarts 'school of misidry'. His teacher prompted him and said, 'Oh! You mean school of wizardry.'
- When 13 year-old Henry was asked by his mother what he had been learning about in his Religious Education lesson yesterday he replied, 'We were doing something about parables, but it was very different from what we did in our English lesson this morning. After we listened to a story the teacher said, "For your homework write five parables [paragraphs]".'
- The geography teacher had been discussing the possible causes of the foot-and-mouth outbreak in Britain which had started in Northumberland. He said that it had then been spread from there to an abattoir in Essex. Thirteen-year-old Andrew put his hand up and said, 'I thought an abattoir is a place where you keep water and I can just imagine all the sheep swimming around in it.' He had confused the word with 'reservoir'. Eight-year-old Thomas told his teacher that 'I had a great time at Auntie Sue's wedding on Saturday when I was a stage and wore a quilt'. He was a page and wore a Scottish kilt.
- Nine-year-old Sophie when talking about Diana, Princess of Wales's funeral said, 'I felt so sad when her coffin was put into a purse [hearse] and was driven off'. When eight-year-old Ali's teacher pointed to a drawing he had just done she asked him what the burglar had in his hand, he replied, 'a trifle'. The burglar had a rifle.
- Ten-year-old Adam ran through the doorway and shouted out that he had a great day at school. He said, 'We had a book expedition [exhibition] at lunchtime and this afternoon we had a rugby match and I kicked a conservatory [conversion].'
- Ten-year-old Penny told her friend that her dad was going into hospital because he 'has a Cadillac'. Her father was having an operation for a cataract in his left eye.
- Thirteen-year-old Raj went to school one Monday morning with his arm in a sling and his teacher asked him what was the matter with it. He said that he had hurt it when playing football and the doctor had told him that he had a 'green twig fracture'. He actually had a greenstick fracture.
- Twelve-year-old Pamela went home and told her mother that her maths teacher was not in school this week because of something to do with a 'railway carriage'. Her teacher had in fact had a miscarriage.
- Ten-year-old Georgina was asked, 'What were you learning about in your English lesson today?' She replied 'We were doing "colossals", you know like when you say, it's raining cats and dogs'. 'We also did something about pouring and rasin.' She had been learning about colloquialisms and metaphors.
- Twelve-year-old Ross when talking about Sir Barnes Wallis the inventor of the bouncing bomb, said to his history teacher in the next lesson, 'Can we do more about Warwick Willis?' 'Who?' said the teacher. 'Oh! That chap who wanted to make an earthquake bomb [bouncing bomb].'

These examples of deficits in receptive and expressive oral language provide some concrete anecdotal evidence that substantiates the research findings that there is a deficit in core language skills. Further examples of these difficulties will be found in reading and spelling errors.

CASE STUDY: 'LIAM' (9 YEARS)

'Liam' had a younger sister and an older brother. He had reached most of the development milestones, but there were delays in his speech and language development. He was almost three years old before he could talk and be understood, and received speech therapy once a week between the ages of four and six years. He struggled when he learned to read but gradually his reading skills improved and at the age of 9 years he was reading on a par with his chronological age level on a standardised word recognition test. He still however had profound difficulties with spelling and certain aspects of expressive and receptive language.

Throughout his childhood he had had intermittent bouts of hearing loss resulting in grommets being inserted on two occasions because of otitis media (glue ear).

His mother reported that he was constantly being reprimanded in class for not paying attention and his school reports said, 'he must listen to instructions more carefully and not switch off' and should not 'daydream'. When he was in Year 3 (7–8 years) the school SENCO asked his mother to arrange to have his hearing tested as she thought that he 'might be slightly deaf'.

He was seen yet again by an ear, nose and throat consultant who tested him. He was prescribed two hearing aids after his visit to the hospital clinic. He hated these and cried a lot and complained of the 'terrible noise' in his ears.

His mother having already observed his behaviour when he had been suffering from otitis media was not now convinced that he had a hearing loss. She sought other possible explanations for his difficulties. One day when reading an article on dyslexia in a magazine as she sat in the hairdresser's, she said, 'I recognised that 'Liam' had many of the symptoms they described'. She decided to have him assessed. Her suspicions were confirmed. He was dyslexic, and it was later discovered that his elder brother and sister were as well, as were his father and paternal grandfather.

After the assessment he was given one-to-one tuition by a specialist teacher, and pleaded to be allowed to remove his two hearing aids saying 'I can hear all right'. During the lessons it was apparent that he had profound phonological and phonemic difficulties, which were compounded by poor auditory perception as well as marked difficulties with word naming and word retrieval but had normal hearing and did not require hearing aids. In time he responded well to the help he was given and gradually began to learn ways and means to compensate for and overcome his specific learning difficulties.

Guidelines for choosing tests for the assessment and diagnosis of phonological difficulties

Educational publishers both in the UK and US have responded to the need for teachers, psychologists and other professionals to have suitable standardised testing materials, including informal tests. There are four different categories of tests: for phonemic knowledge, phonemic knowledge, diagnostic screening batteries and computerised screening test batteries.

Phonemic awareness

Title	Author and publisher	Content	Age range	Administration time
Phonological awareness in Young Children: A Classroom Curriculum	M.J. Adams, B.R. Foorman, I. Lundberg and T. Beeler (1998) (Paul H. Brookes Publishing Co. Baltimore, MD)	Detecting Rhymes Counting Syllables Matching Initial Sounds Counting Phonemes Comparing Word Lengths Representing Phonemes with Letters	5–7 years	30 minutes
Sound Linkage: An Integrated Programme for Overcoming Difficulties	P.J. Hatcher (1994) (Whurr Publishers Ltd, London)	Syllable Blending Phoneme Blending Rhyme Phoneme Segmentation Phoneme Deletion Phoneme Transposition	4 years 8 months to 6 years 8 months	5 minutes

Phonological Knowledge

Title	Author and publisher	Content	Age range	Administration time
Phonological Assessment Battery (PhAB)	N. Frederickson, U. Frith and R. Reason (1997) (NFER – Nelson, London)	Alliteration Naming Speed Rhyme Spoonerisms Fluency Non-Word Reading	6 years to 14 years 11 months	30–40 minutes
Comprehensive Test of Phonological Processing (CTOPP)	R. Wagner J. Torgesen C. Rashotte (1999) (Harcourt Assessment, Oxford)	Blending Non-word Repetition Colour and Digit Naming Phoneme Reversal Segmenting words and Non-words	5–24	30 minutes

Phonological Knowledge (continued)

Phonological Abilities Test (PAT)	V. Muter, C. Hulme and M. Snowling (1997) (Harcourt Assessment, Oxford)	Rhyme Detection Rhyme Production Word Completion Phoneme Deletion Letter Knowledge Speech Rate (sub-test) Letter Knowledge (sub-test)	5–7 years	30 minutes

Diagnostic Screening Test Batteries

These include tests of phonological knowledge

Title	*Author and publisher*	*Content*	*Age range*	*Administration time*
Dyslexia Early Screening Test (DEST)	A. Fawcett, R. Nicolson and R. Lee (2001) (Harcourt Assessment, Oxford)	Rapid Naming Bead Threading Paper Cutting Digits and Letters Repetition Shape Copying Spatial Memory	3 years 6 months to 4 years 5 months	10–15 minutes
Dyslexia Screening Test (DST)	A. Fawcett and R. Nicolson (1996) (Harcourt Assessment, Oxford)	Rapid Naming Phonological Discrimination Postural Stability Rhyme/Alliteration Forwards Digit Span Digit Naming Letter Naming Sound Order Shape Copying Vocabulary	4 years 6 months to 6 years 5 months	30 minutes
Dyslexia Screening Test (DST)	A. Fawcett and R. Nicolson (1996) (Harcourt Assessment, Oxford)	Rapid Naming Bead Threading One Minute Reading Test Postural Stability Two Minute Spelling Test Nonsense Passage Reading One Minute Writing Verbal Fluency Semantic Fluency	6 years 6 months to 16 years 5 months	30 minutes

continued

Diagnostic Screening Test Batteries (continued)

Dyslexia Adult Screening Test (DAST)	A. Fawcett and R. Nicolson (1996) (Harcourt Assessment, Oxford)	Rapid Naming Phonemic Segmentation Nonsense Passage Reading Verbal Fluency One Minute Spelling Non-verbal Reasoning Semantic Fluency Postural Stability Backwards Digit Span One Minute Writing	16 years to adult	30 minutes

Computerised Screening Test Batteries

These include tests of phonological knowledge.

Title	Author and publisher	Content	Age range	Administration time
Lucid Cognitive Profiling System (Lucid CoPS)	C. Singleton, K. Thomas and R. Leedale (1996) (Lucid Research Ltd, Beverley, East Yorkshire)	Phonological awareness Auditory discrimination Auditory short-term memory Visual short-term memory Visual and verbal sequencing	CoPS 1 4 years to 8 years	30 minutes
Lucid Assessment System for Schools (LASS)	(as above)	Visual memory Auditory-verbal memory Phonic reading skills Phonological processing ability Single word reading Spelling/reasoning	8 years to 15 years	45 minutes

Linguistic skills, including phoneme and phonological skills, develop over time, mostly as part of normal development, but may be slower or late for those with specific learning difficulties. This has been confirmed by the research of Bowey and Francis (1991), who found that phonological skills develop gradually from early rhyming abilities to an explicit understanding of phonemes. There is a wealth of evidence which shows that these skills can be taught as an oral language activity, thus ensuring that the prerequisite building blocks of language are in place when reading and writing are taught. They include the following skills.

PRACTICAL SUGGESTIONS TO DEVELOP PHONOLOGICAL AND LISTENING SKILLS

Listening should be proactive. Some children find listening difficult, particularly if they are bombarded by sound. Noise can degrade what the listener hears, for example when someone is talking against the background sound of a television programme, or a reporter who is using a mobile phone against a background of motorway traffic.

Children can learn to listen and learn about sound using some of the following approaches.

Record familiar household sounds such as the audible microwave signal at the end of the cooking sequence, a flushing lavatory, the sizzling of frying in a chip pan. Sounds such as the crumpling of a piece of paper, the rattling of coins, striking a match, tearing paper, ticking of a clock can be listened to when the child is blindfolded and can be asked to identify these. Sounds in the classroom can be recorded such as the scraping of a chair as it is moved away, the banging of a desk or a teacher writing on the board with chalk. These help to develop auditory discrimination. The test can include sounds made by animals or the music used to introduce a television programme such as *Neighbours*.

Auditory memory can be developed by playing games. In one game the objective is for a player to give a name in response to 'I went to a party and I met . . . [a friend's name]', then the next player repeats the name the first player gave and then adds another name and so on. The player who can repeat and give the most names is the winner. This can also include games about buying food in a supermarket, birthday presents or choosing holiday destinations.

Dancing to the 'Hokey Cokey' helps with learning about directionality as well as following oral instructions simultaneously. The game Simple Simon Says is useful for developing sequencing, listening and memory skills: 'Simple Simon says, "Put your right leg in, your right leg out, in-out and shake it all about, that's what it's all about".'

Action songs such as 'Heads, Shoulders, Knees and Toes' or 'I'm a Little Teapot' help to develop rhythm, and rhyme and movement linked to oral language skills.

Put on one person a blindfold such as the eye masks given to airline passengers on long-haul flights. Then the other person makes a sound such as a knocking sound. The objective is for the blindfolded person to say where in the room the sound is coming from, for example the window, the door, the teacher's desk.

Tell a familiar nursery rhyme but change the words around. Then ask the child what was wrong and ask him or her to give the correct version such as:

Jack be nimble, Jack be quick,
Jack jumped over the candlestick.

Jack be nimble, quick as a fox,
Jack jump this little box.
(Cherry 1971)

Play Chinese Whispers. A player has to listen to what the person on the right says. They then have to repeat it to the next person seated on their left in the group, who are seated in a circle, and so on. This helps to develop listening as well as expressive language skills.

Play Musical Chairs. Give the instruction before switching on the music.

'Skip to the chair, when the music stops. Children must move all around the room. Then turn off the music and follow the instruction. This helps develop short-term and working memory.

Ask the child to pretend to be a television presenter and to give instructions about 'How to boil an egg' just like the cookery writer Delia Smith – or Jamie Oliver, who is dyslexic. This develops sequential language, word naming and word retrieval skills.

Play a game using a mobile phone to give directions to home, school or the library.

Older children can be asked to listen to a recording of a radio broadcast. Then they can be asked questions about the contents such as 'What new building did the Queen officially open today?' 'In what country have there been huge bush fires?' 'Where are the next Olympic Games being held?' 'Who is the England football captain?'

Play How Good a Detective are You? Choose a well-known fairy-tale such as *Little Red Riding Hood*. Give each child a pencil and paper. Explain that they have to find the 'mistakes' in the story when you read it and then put a tick on the sheet of paper. Give a mark for each correct tick and a bonus if the child can substitute the correct response. Read the story as follows. 'Little Red Riding Hood went to the supermarket. She went on her bicycle and she met Robin Hood on the way. A tiger was watching her and followed her. He knocked on the door of her auntie's cottage', etc.

A digital camera can be used to make recordings of, for instance, the fire service, delivering milk, the postman or postwoman on their rounds or an ambulance at the scene of an incident. Then the children can watch this and talk about the activities.

A useful resource for 'understanding spoken language and using spoken language' as well as the underlying phonemic and phonological skills is C. Delamain and J. Spring, *Speaking, Listening and Understanding: Games for Young Children* (Speechmark Publishing Ltd, Bicester, 2003).

Rhyme, rhythm and song

Clinical experience and evidence from parents and adult dyslexic people provides evidence of ongoing difficulties with rhyme production and remembering the words of songs: 'I still can't remember the words of the Lord's Prayer or the National Anthem' (Sir Jackie Stewart OBE). Practical suggestions for developing rhyming skills include:

- Saying rhymes
- Word play on the rhymes such as 'Little Bo Peep has lost her – cat – dog' and then completing the rhyme
- Acting out rhymes such as 'Old Macdonald Had a Farm'. The production of the various farm animal sounds is invariably a source of fun and merriment
- Dancing to music and acting out the rhythms which develop motor skills and memory for the rhyming word. Action songs such as 'London Bridge Is Falling Down' can be used. Generations of children have learned co-ordination and listening skills when singing 'Here We Go Round the Mulberry Bush' while carrying out actions simultaneously

Skipping and hopping to music while singing tunes such as 'The Farmer's in His Den' help to develop rhythm and rhyme awareness in a multi-sensory way. The children form a ring and hold hands, and dance round singing while one is chosen to be the farmer and stands in the middle of the ring.

> The farmer wants a wife,
> The farmer wants a wife.
> Hey ho diddly oh,
> The farmer wants a wife.
> (*The child in the middle then chooses another child to be the wife.*)

The wife wants a child,
The wife wants a child,
Hey ho diddly oh,
The wife wants a child.

Marching to the words of tunes such as 'The Grand Old Duke of York' helps to develop awareness of sound, and an ability to co-ordinate this to movement enhances awareness and discrimination in addition to an appreciation of life's futilities.

Beating time to rhymes helps to develop auditory perception:

Polly put the kettle on,
Polly put the kettle on,
Polly put the kettle on,
We'll all have tea.

Rhymes involving numbers help to develop numeracy and sequencing skills:

Ten green bottles standing on the wall,
(Hold up both hands with all fingers extended)
Ten green bottles standing on the wall,
But if one green bottle should accidentally fall,
(Bend one finger down over the palm)
There'll be nine green bottles standing on the wall.

Nursery rhymes can be used as models for different kinds of linguistic features including alliteration. These are commonly known as tongue twisters.

If Peter Piper picked a peck of pickled pepper,
Where is the pickled pepper Peter Piper picked?

She sells seashells on the sea shore
The shells that she sells are not sea shells I am sure.

Children can be helped to generate their own rhymes. This is more challenging, particularly for those with word naming difficulties. Model this by singing:

Here we go round the mulberry bush, the mulberry bush, the mulberry bush.

Then continue a chosen activity to the same tune using the refrain:

This is the way we brush the dog, brush the dog,
This is the way we comb our hair, comb our hair etc.

Using percussion instruments such as drum or tambourine can be useful to reinforce rhythmic skills. The child has to remember the rhyme pattern and simultaneously use a hand while playing the instrument and keeping time.

Attention can be drawn to the different types of rhyme patterns such as internal rhymes or at the end of the line as in:

Three blind mice, three blind mice,
See how they run, see how they run.

Children can be helped to produce their own vocabulary-building skills, rhyming words by word play. Tell them a story about the children who were practising for their Christmas concert and they were singing the carol 'Nowell, Nowell the angel did say' when suddenly the Angel Gabriel appeared in the classroom and he said to Zoe 'How many letters are there in the alphabet?' Zoe said, 'There are 25', 'Oh, no!' said Angel Gabriel, 'there are 26 letters.' 'But we've just been singing "no L"' said a rather surprised Zoe.

Children can listen to stories and they can be encouraged to follow the words by pointing at them with their fingers as they listen. This helps to develop an awareness of print and the direction of the letters on the page as well as pattern of the words.

Reading poetry to children awakens their appreciation of language as well as the structure of language. Some contemporary children's authors such as Michael Rosen (1991) have compiled anthologies of their favourite poems and include examples from popular poets. Benjamin Zephaniah is dyslexic and is the author of a number of poetry collections. He has produced humorous verses for *Chambers Primary Rhyming Dictionary* (2004).

Many children spend a considerable amount of time watching television. Many know and learn advertising slogans and jingles easily and quickly. A collection of these could be tape-recorded. Then play them. Have a competition to see who can complete the jingle and say what programme or product it advertises.

Children's interest in poetry can be awakened by the oral recitation of the poem. They can become aware of language, rhythm and rhyme. Themes can be chosen, for example animals, with poems such as G.K. Chesterton's 'The Donkey' or William Blake's 'The Tyger' or Spike Milligan's 'Look At All Those Monkeys'.

SUMMARY AND CONCLUSIONS

1   The human infant is programmed to speak because humans have 'a genetic disposition to language'. Some commentators believed that learning to read was a concomitant of learning to speak and from this theory emerged the 'Whole Language' movement. This was counter to the theories of the 'behaviourists', who argued that reading and spelling should be taught in a structured and controlled manner. Lundberg et al.'s (1988) study showed that pre-school children can be taught phonemic awareness without formal reading instruction by playing listening games, rhymes and ditties and by playing with sentences and with initial sounds and ultimately segmenting words into phonemes. A follow-up study by Lundberg (1994) provided evidence showing the long-term benefits for those pre-school children who received this training.

2   Scientists began to provide evidence that 'phonological awareness normally develops over a number of years, progressing from early rhyming abilities to explicit awareness of the individual phonemes' (Moats 1994).

3   International research and longitudinal training studies showed that phonemic and phonological skills need explicit teaching which can make the difference between success and failure for some children, particularly those who have difficulties with matching the sounds they hear to choosing the letters to repre-

sent them. Bus and Van IJzendoorn (1999) reviewed the literature on 37 studies and concluded that 'the training studies settle the issue of the casual role of phonological awareness in learning to read: Phonological training reliably enhances phonological and reading skills'. Bowey and Francis (1991) showed that children develop the following skills orally and in the following order.

- Syllables   rab/bit   sun/set
- Onset and rimes   /m/ /ash/   /t/ /ank/
- Individual phonemes   /p/ /e/ /n/   /f/ /i/ /sh/

4 Training studies which used explicit phonological training 'had a remarkable effect on the children's progress' over a period of five years and offer convincing evidence in support of a cause–effect relationship between phonological sensitivity and learning to spell' (Bradley 1987, 1989, cited in Bradley and Huxford 1994).

5 Phonological deficits are now recognised as a core deficit for people with dyslexia. There is also a parallel deficit which is evident when speech and language is processed and produced particularly at speed. These automised word naming (RAN) difficulties and word retrieval difficulties have been dubbed the 'double deficit' hypothesis. It has been shown that 'early naming speed is most predictive of later word recognition [for reading]' (Wolf 1997).

6 Scarborough (1990) showed that 'very early language deficits in dyslexic children' are predictable in children who have a family history of dyslexia. Snowling et al. (2003) confirmed that the 'family risk of dyslexia is continuous' and that language delays are 'early precursors' of difficulties. Difficulties with word naming and a tendency to use malapropisms and spoonerisms as well as difficulties with remembering or following directions or instructions persists. It is not as a result of poor hearing or inattention. For some it remains a lifelong characteristic of the condition for which there is now compelling research evidence about the nature and manifestations. Frith (1997) argues that 'dyslexia is a lifelong developmental disorder with a biological origin'.

7 There is a plethora of text materials to help the diagnostician identify problems. Most are user-friendly and easy to administer and to interpret. One of the most exciting and innovative uses of these materials is their potential to identify children 'at risk' at a very early age. The benefits are twofold. Early identification can act as a signal to indicate help with phonemic and phonological skills. This has been shown to be effective and efficient, and some children who respond to the early support do well and then proceed to learn to read as easily as the majority of their peers. For those with significant difficulties, including those with a genetic disposition to dyslexia, early confirmation of suspicions of the existence of the condition can then be used to set in motion the apparatus for a full assessment to confirm the findings. This can eliminate frustration and failure particularly when the characteristics of the condition are clearly earmarked.

continued

These can then be used as a clarion call to parents and teachers that this child does have special educational needs and requires immediate and appropriate teaching intervention.

8   Traditional rhymes and games using music, movement and play are very important in the development of lifelong learning. Bradley showed that 'the foundations for spelling are laid down before the children come into contact with print at all, in their early language play and especially in the rhyming games (Bradley and Huxford 1994). Oral language is the foundation stone for literacy. The authors of the National Literacy Strategy (DfEE 1998) have clearly been influenced by the international research findings and place a significant emphasis on teaching and language skills which can be seen in the training materials the DfES has produced. Pre-reading and phonic skills are acquired mainly through spoken language activities and not by sitting passively in front of a television or at a computer screen. Children need to practise and develop their language skills with human interactions. The more often they do so, the better the outcome.

6 Matching Instruction to Developmental Skills

- Is a theory for spelling instruction necessary, and, if so, why?
- Does it matter for individuals when, what, why and how spelling is taught?
- Theory, research and evidence of progressive stages in spelling development
- What are the main characteristics of spelling at the different stages of spelling development? Evidence from spelling error analysis and categorisation
- Errors associated with the different stages of development
- Practical implications for teachers and learners of stages in spelling development
- Summary and conclusions

Keywords

Behavioural psychology	Learning styles	Simultaneous oral
Developmental	Maturation lag	spelling (S-O-S)
psychology	Piaget's cognitive	Strategy
Developmental	developmental	Theory
stages	theory	Vygotsky's zone of
Direct instruction	Scaffolding activities	proximal
Explicit teaching	Spelling error	development theory
Individual education	categorisation	(ZPD)
plans (IEP)		

Is a theory for spelling instruction necessary, and, if so, why?

Gross (1996) asserted that 'a good theory should be internally consistent and economical, making as few assumptions as possible and it should also offer practical guidance in solving everyday problems'.

Theoretical knowledge of how individuals learn, and how best to teach them, has been ongoing. It has assumed greater significance for teachers and learners and has resulted in developments in learning theory and in the teaching of thinking skills, as well as a greater understanding of learning styles. However, the tools (tests) used to label learners as visual, auditory or kinaesthetic have been criticised by some as 'unreliable' or of 'dubious value' (Coffield 2004). Developmental psychologists formulated a theory that children develop intellectually at different stages. The child needs to be guided through a process of discovery at each stage of development to enable him or her to develop and proceed to the next stage.

The theory, implementation and understanding of how children develop is frequently based on the work of Jean Piaget (1970), who is regarded as the father of developmental psychology. He concluded, after lifelong studies, that development is a continuous process. He hypothesised about how the errors made by children in various situations, including play, could be used to provide evidence of the stage of development they had reached. This resulted in a theory that children should be taught discrete skills and that each step in acquiring that particular skill should be taught specifically and in a structured sequence.

HANDY HINT

To acquire an academic skill requires direct instruction which:

- **is academically focused, teaching academic skills directly**
- **is directed and controlled by the teacher**
- **uses carefully sequenced and structured materials**
- **gives students mastery of basic skills**
- **sets goals that are clear to students**
- **allocates sufficient time for instruction**
- **uses continuous monitoring of student performance**
- **provides immediate feedback to students**
- **teaches a skill until mastery of the skill is achieved.**

Rosenshine and Stevens (1986)

Does it matter for individuals when, what, why and how spelling is taught?

Piaget's cognitive developmental theory hypothesised about 'when and how children think and how their thinking changes as they mature'. He claimed that children go through four stages in intellectual development:

- The sensorimotor stage (0–2 years) when the child reacts with the environment and learns through sensory or motor experience.
- The pre-operational stage (2–7 years) when the child tends to think about how things seem rather than by logical principles. They can use symbols and language to interact and learn about the environment.
- The concrete operational stage (7–11 years) when the child performs operations with the use of concrete objects.
- The formal operational stage (11–15 years) when the child can reason using statements and can think about hypothetical situations and deal with abstract ideas to solve problems.

This theory implies that there is a predetermined growth rate for physical and cognitive functions which explains why some children have a delay in a particular ability or skill such as speech or motor skills. However, this is not universal, and it is evident that some children have a maturation lag which can be ascribed to a delay in the development of cognitive and physical skills. The word 'mature' is derived from a Latin word (*maturare*) meaning to ripen. 'Lag' implies growing or developing more slowly, and as a consequence gradually falling behind.

For some, this is may be a temporary delay which can initially lead to a diagnosis of a specific learning difficulty and/or of special educational needs (SEN). These difficulties may later be overcome. Others may fail to reach certain milestones for their age and ability and may have permanent disabilities. For example children who experience a delay in the development of speech may require speech therapy. Those with visual difficulties may require glasses or need to use coloured lenses or coloured paper. Others may be dyspraxic and have a delay in the development of motor skills, and may require occupational therapy.

Children who have poor neuromuscular development and poor physical co-ordination due to cerebral palsy, or those with dyslexia and dyspraxia, may have long-lasting and persisting difficulties with skills including fine and gross motor skills. Others have oral and written language skills deficits. This can include slow or poor processing of expressive and receptive language, as well as inaccurate reading and poor spelling because of poor phonemic or poor phonological skills. Many of these individuals respond well to appropriate teaching methods which often includes multi-sensory teaching which helps to compensate for and overcome many of their earlier difficulties.

The theory about stages in development was applied to other areas of intellectual activity. This included knowing about what to teach an individual dyslexic learner when he or she begins to receive specialist teaching. Followers of the Orton–Gillingham teaching methods are trained to use diagnostic assessment measures to identify the specific stage of development in literacy skills the individual has reached. Test results and observations made by the teacher should also highlight the strengths and weaknesses of the individual. Experienced practitioners do not assume previous knowledge in the learner. They first establish literacy skills using standardised tests. This then allows them to identify the point at which skills have broken down or where skills have yet to be acquired or established. Teaching can then be tailored to the existing knowledge and to the specific educational needs of the individual child or adult learner.

There is increasing recognition that individuals have different learning styles, and that teaching should be matched to meet the needs of individual learners. One-size learning does not fit the needs of all pupils, and all pupils do not respond to the same teaching methods. 'The teaching method needs to match an individual's learning style' and, according to Brooks and Weeks (1998), research 'shows that children's rates of acquiring spellings can be much enhanced by simply applied individual learning strategies used with their usual English and spelling programmes'. This applies to all spellers but has additional significance for those with specific learning difficulties.

Vygotsky (1962, 1978) showed that tasks can be divided into different levels of difficulty. He explained how very difficult tasks will be beyond the individual's capacity and how very simple tasks will be too easy for the individual. The middle way is when a task is neither too easy nor too difficult. Learning is best done when it is in the 'zone of proximal development' (ZPD), meaning the level nearest to and appropriate for the current skills and present developmental stage of the individual.

Pupils who are asked to undertake tasks that are too difficult or beyond their current skills often fail to learn. This is a common observation made about individuals with dyslexia. It is heartbreaking and soul-destroying for a teenager or a mature student who has the courage to 'try again' to be presented with textbooks and reading resources that are too difficult because of gaps in, for example, his or her knowledge of phonemes and phonological skills. Furthermore, if presented with the same teaching strategies and the same teaching methods that they have already used and failed with, they may continue on the same downward spiral of failure, and once again not succeed in achieving the literacy levels they aspire to. Some abandon their attempts to keep pace with their peers because of repeated failure, and comments like 'Your spelling is downright careless' can trigger depression and despair.

> **'Alex' (9 years) said, 'I'm not going to bother doing any more revision for my history exam. We had a test on Monday and even though all my answers were correct I only got 9 out of twenty marks. Every time I made a spelling mistake a mark was taken off – it's just not fair!'**

CASE STUDY: 'STEVEN' (22 YEARS)

I was in Year 8 [12–13 years] and was having a rough time at school because of the speed I worked at in the classroom. I was always falling behind and had constantly to stay in at breaktimes to catch up with my work. One day, which will always stick in my mind, was when a teacher kept the whole class back until I learned to spell the word 'merriment' correctly. This was the period before breaktime so most of my close friends and enemies could not wait to get out of the classroom and were as eager as I was to leave the room.

It took me the whole of breaktime (fifteen minutes) to learn to spell the word 'merriment' aloud. This was extremely hard for me as everyone in the classroom was watching me as if I was some performing monkey in the corner of the room. To make it even worse I had been made to stand up.

This happened during my first month in a new school. This fifteen-minute episode made me feel so small and knocked out of me the little confidence I had in any situation, for some considerable time. This episode certainly haunted me for the duration of my secondary school days.

Theory, research and evidence of progressive stages in spelling development

Scientists, educational professionals and parents have long been conscious that individual children meet developmental milestones at approximately the same time and also that a number of children experience delays. Observers study the discrete changes that occur at different stages of development in acquiring skills, including spelling.

Charles Read (1970, 1971) carried out pioneering studies in this as part of his doctoral dissertation at Harvard, and broke new ground when he claimed that 'children's perception of speech sounds might differ from adults' (cited by Henderson 1985). He found that children who had not yet had formal spelling lessons could nevertheless spell words. He observed that they did so by using letters to denote a sound. In other words they 'invented spellings' by using phonemic strategies.

He identified the defining characteristics of the stages in the development of spelling, and pinpointed how children's spelling changed as they developed. He demonstrated this by examining children's spelling errors, and showed that the pattern of errors made by children changed as the child grew older and gained experience.

HANDY HINT

Spelling errors are a window on the underlying processes used by spellers, and can be used to shed more light on the current levels of skills and knowledge as well as identifying difficulties.

These groundbreaking research findings on spelling led the way to a greater understanding of what to teach, when to teach and how to teach spelling. These insights about the progression of skills should have paved the way to making the teaching of spelling as a rote memorisation task increasingly less used in classrooms. It has however taken many years for these insights to be disseminated and accepted in mainstream education in the US and the UK.

Edmund Henderson (1985) and his colleagues at the University of Virginia mapped out the sources of information used by spellers, evaluated the sequence of stages children go through, and processed children's experience when learning to spell. From these results a theory of the different 'stages', 'levels', 'steps', 'categories' or 'phases' in the development of spelling evolved.

What are the main characteristics of spelling at the different stages of spelling development? Evidence from spelling error analysis and categorisation

Many commentators, including Gentry (1982), Henderson (1985), Treiman (1993), Brown and Ellis (1994), Moats (1995) and Ehri (1997) have contributed to our knowledge and understanding of the main issues and theories, about stages of spelling development skills, by analysis of children's spelling errors.

There are five distinct stages in spelling development according to Moats 1995. We shall look at these in detail below.

1   Precommunicative
2   Semiphonetic
3   Phonetic
4   Transitional
5   Morphophonemic (Derivational)

An analysis of spelling is carried out by examining the errors made in the target words of spelling tests, and in the errors made in a sample of extended writing.

The errors in the sample of extended writing are often significant for diagnostic purposes, because writing sentences, which involves processing information and considering the vocabulary and contents as well as remembering grammatical conventions, including punctuation, imposes greater demands on the subskill requirements for the speller. It consequently makes greater demands on his or her ability to spell than do dictated tests of single-word spelling. It may provide important evidence of where and why skills have broken down. Spelling error analysis can be used to scrutinise and categorise the errors. The following is an overview based on a review of possible sources of error, which include:

- poor phonemic skills, including segmentation difficulties
- poor phonological skills, including sound segments in words
- visualisation weaknesses, including poor orthographic knowledge of letters and letter patterns
- lack of morphemic knowledge, including affixes
- indications of poor sight vocabulary, including high-frequency words
- lack of understanding and inability to use derivations and syllabification.

Errors associated with the different stages of development

Precommunicative stage

Some commentators describe this as the preliterate writing stage.

- Marks are made on paper with a variety of implements, such as crayons, pencils, felt pens.
- Often writing is a continuous line of scribbles which may sometimes be interspersed with random letters such as the initial letter of a word. Sometimes numbers such as '2' are used for to/two. Drawings can be substituted for words.
- Some children can write their own names even though they have no letter/sound knowledge.
- Writing may go from left to right on the page.

Semiphonetic stage

- A letter name may be used to spell a word and there is a beginning of a realisation that letters represent sounds in speech: 'pt' for pet, 'ur' for your.
- There is a tendency to omit letters: 'stap' for stamp, 'tod' for told, 'uv' for other.
- There is a tendency to use consonants more than vowels such as 'bg' for big, 'hd' for holiday. Ehri (1991) says this is 'because consonants begin and end most words and because many vowel sounds are not found in letter names'.
- Some words are spelt correctly as sight words, such as the high frequency words 'the', 'play'

Phonetic stage

- Sometimes spellers may be able to map all the sounds in a word even if their choice of letters is not correct. In other words they can identify individual sounds even if they cannot match them to the correct letter. Often they are poor visualisers who have not internalised conventional spelling patterns: they use 'nexed' for next; 'saise' for says.
- They use the vowel name to spell long vowel sounds in words such as 'tran' for train; 'tri' for try.
- If the final consonant does not match the sound, they may use the letters that represent the sounds they hear: 'bocks' for box; 'glace' for glass.
- Magic 'e' (sometimes referred to as silent 'e' or lengthening 'e') makes the vowel long, and makes it say its name. This is a consistent source of confusion for some spellers. Some add 'e' to almost every word even though they are clearly short vowel sounds such as 'pine' for pin; 'hate' for hat.
- When they encounter the past tense of the verb which adds 'ed' but says /t/ /d/ /id/, many spellers use their knowledge of sound-to-symbol match rather than their knowledge of grammar, such as 'lookt' for looked; 'talkd' for talked and 'mendid' for mended.
- Some develop a sight vocabulary for spellings and for individual spelling patterns. These are words that they can spell instantly; in other words they have a mental picture of how the word is spelt which can be retrieved automatically.

Transitional stage

- Some begin to use visual cues. The use of 'eta' for eat, 'silm' for slim, indicates that a speller knows and has seen the word, even though they are unable to recall the correct sequence of the letters in the word. This error is frequently seen in the spellings of individuals with dyslexia.
- They begin to use vowels in each syllable: 'eightee' for eighty; 'reackermen' for recommend.
- They become more aware of spelling patterns: 'wrighting' for writing.
- They use vowel digraphs more frequently, often as a result of frequent exposure to them in print: 'lickwied' for liquid.
- Knowledge of where syllable boundaries occur develops over time for normal spellers. This helps when deciding whether 'tennis' has one 'n' or two. It has two because there are two closed syllables. It helps to explain why 'tiger' has one 'g' not two because there is an open syllable which ends in a long vowel followed by a closed syllable.

Morphonemic (Derivational) stage

This is called the conventional stage by Beard (1998).

- Spellers at this stage misspell words with indistinct schwa sounds when the vowel is not accentuated, such as 'buten' for button; 'blloon' for balloon. Henderson (1985) claimed that 'the misspelling of schwa accounts for a higher and higher proportion of errors as children advance through the grades'.

- Adding suffixes to words is often problematic, and includes difficulties such as knowing when to double consonants or when to drop 'e' in words such as 'loved', 'lovely', 'hoped', 'hoping', 'hopeless'. Spelling a suffix such as 'ed' is a continuing source of difficulty for some: 'ineojde' for enjoyed.
- Knowledge of root words is an essential crutch for spelling. Knowing that 'television' is a derivation of 'vision' and that 'tele' means 'operating over a distance' helps. A poor speller may use 'tellevishun' for television.
- Prefixes can be problematic for those with insufficient knowledge of Latin or Greek derivations, and may for example result in 'ilegal' for illegal; 'sircumfrence' for circumference.

Practical implications for teachers and learners of stages in spelling development

These findings have widespread pedagogic implications for teachers and learners, particularly for those with dyslexia.

HANDY HINT

In a nutshell, when the individual's stage of development has been established by testing and an analysis of their spelling errors, teaching should then be matched to the individual's needs as well as the individual's preferred learning style. Schlagal (2001) asserted that 'teaching students beyond their developmental level invites rote memorisation of words, an inefficient and often impermanent form of learning'.

There has been a growing awareness of the following points.

- For some individuals spelling remains an 'insuperable obstacle' (Rawson 1986) and they have great difficulties in learning to spell.
- Some people, including many individuals with dyslexia, remain chronically poor spellers throughout their lives.
- Some individuals do not progress beyond Stage 3, and use phonetic spelling as their main spelling tactics, as shown by Patrick in the case study in Chapter 1. According to the studies of Lennox and Siegel (1994), 'poor spellers at all grade levels had more difficulty than grade-matched good spellers in producing accurate phonological matches to the target word'.
- Some poor spellers have very poor visual memory, so consequently they have very small sight vocabularies. They continue to misspell high-frequency irregular words such as 'one', 'two', 'forty', no matter how often they see or use the words.
- Extraneous factors such as stress when sitting examinations or fatigue can affect an individual's spellings.
- Some poor spellers can spell words in isolation, particularly words they have studied for a test, but then misspell these same words when using them in their writing. This is why dictated sentences are a better diagnostic measure of spelling skills than word lists.
- Spelling ability cannot be established by the results of just one standardised dictated word spelling test such as a 'one-minute' test.

- Geschwind (1982) recalled that Orton had pointed out 'that there were children in whom difficulties in learning to read had never been present, yet who spelled extremely badly'. This may account for failure and academic underachievement in otherwise academically gifted pupils who are let down by their poor writing skills.

Anecdotal evidence for these findings has come from schools which came near the top of examination league tables with high-achieving pupils. Establishments in the independent sector of education such as Eton College, Harrow, St Paul's and Winchester have departments and members of staff who are specialist teachers who provide 'learning support' for their dyslexic pupils. Schools such as St Edward's in Oxford, Millfield and Shrewsbury have had dyslexic scholars according to anecdotal evidence, as have other preparatory and public schools. In the maintained sector of education many exciting initiatives have occurred, such as a policy to create 'dyslexia-friendly' schools pioneered by Swansea LEA and now promoted by many LEAs. There is a statutory obligation for all schools to provide for the needs of pupils with SEN as specified in the Code of Practice. The Special Educational Needs and Disability Act 2001 (SENDA) covers all aspects of education and is mandatory in all schools. It is unlawful discrimination if a pupil is treated 'less favourably' and if 'reasonable adjustments' are not made for those with disabilities. This could mean providing differentiated spelling lists. A pupil might alternatively be allowed to use a computer program to learn spelling rather than the pencil and paper approach. In practice this may mean that the pupil may be allowed to use a laptop in lessons and in examinations and that allowance may be made for poor spelling and presentation. Provision, support and recognition of the needs of dyslexic pupils have taken gigantic leaps forward, particularly for those with the greatest needs. Those with less severe manifestations of dyslexia still slip through the net and are often not identified until late in their education (Ott 2006).

There has been a surge in the past decade in the numbers of students attending universities and colleges of higher education. A report by the National Working Party on Dyslexia in Higher Education (1999) 'revealed that the incidence of dyslexia in higher education may be estimated at about 1.2%–1.5% of students', that is about '20,400–25,500 students' of the total 1.7 million students. Of these students 57 per cent had already declared themselves to have dyslexia on entry to higher education, the remaining 43 per cent being identified or diagnosed as dyslexic after admission.

It is common knowledge that tutors are alerted to students who are later assessed as dyslexic mainly because of their poor spelling, poor presentation skills and difficulties with essay-writing skills. These individuals may have struggled for years with implications of undiagnosed dyslexia, and have suffered stress and anxiety which can hinder performance (Bartlett and Moody 2000).

Morris et al. (1986) conducted a study and found that, when pupils were scoring 40 per cent or less in tests, there was marked deterioration in the quality of their errors. They often had more than just one incorrect letter, and their spellings were often far removed from the correct spelling of the target word. Furthermore their spelling attempts were sometimes bizarre. This showed that these pupils were out of their depth. They called this a 'frustration level' and concluded that when this happens learning does not occur, nor are the words studied retained in long-term memory. The examples in Fig. 1 of spelling tests taken by John (9 years) show that he is being asked to learn words beyond his current stage of spelling development.

CASE STUDY: 'LOUISA' (27 YEARS)

Louisa has a twin brother who was diagnosed as severely dyslexic when he was 7 years old. Her problems were therefore regarded as 'somewhat insignificant'. She always had 'great difficulties writing essays with sentences that made sense'. She managed to get 'C' grades in her exams, but her teachers always felt she was potentially an 'A' grade pupil 'if only she could write down what she knows'. She was awarded a Sixth Form Art scholarship. She later attended a school of art and was awarded a BA 2.1 degree in Textiles and Design. She was then accepted by Goldsmiths' College of Art to read for a MA. She was devastated when she was failed at the end of her course 'because of the quality of her written work' in her dissertation. In discussion her tutor suggested to her that she 'might be dyslexic'. The College arranged for a psychological assessment to be carried out. It established at age 27 that she was dyslexic. She appealed to the University and was finally awarded a Master's Degree.

HANDY HINT

Pupils who were taught at their appropriate instructional level were found at the end of the academic year to have retained 85 per cent of the words they had been taught. Those who were 'out of their depth' only retained 45 per cent of the words learned by the end of the academic year, even though some of these pupils did well in weekly spelling tests. Those in this group of poor spellers had forgotten the spellings they had learned in 'six weeks time'.

Morris et al. 1995a

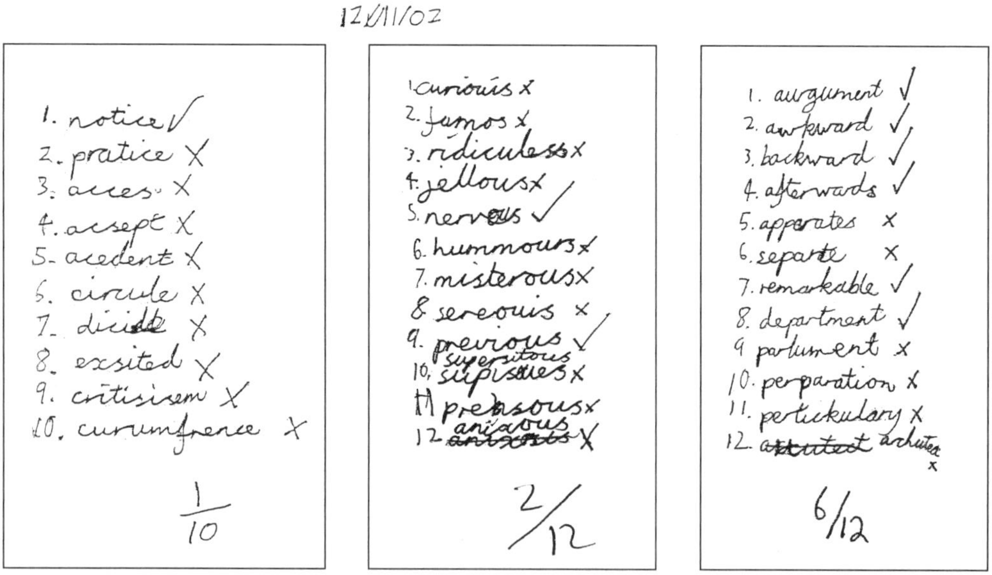

Figure 1

A follow-up study conducted by Morris et al. (1995b) showed that, if pupils are given lists of spellings to learn which are compatible with their skills and stage of development, 'significant gains can be made by poor spellers. However they sometimes misspell many of these same words when they are using them in writing which also involves composition and sequencing.'

Good spellers go on learning about spelling almost indefinitely, often as a result of reading experience. They flex their skills with practice and experience, and use many cognitive skills simultaneously when they need to think about the spelling of a word which they cannot visualise or recall automatically, if they do not have access to a dictionary or an electronic spelling device such as a spell-checker.

SUMMARY AND CONCLUSIONS

1   Learning to speak comes naturally to humans. Writing is a human invention. Spelling does not come naturally to most people. It requires direct instruction from an external source. This can include personal interaction, such as by reading and word study of the visual features, which helps develop awareness and know-how about the mechanics of written language. Direct explicit instruction about spelling is necessary for normal spellers. Spelling is an acquired skill, but there are wide variations in how quickly and easily it is acquired by the majority of the population. Some languages such as English are more difficult to spell (Caravolas et al. 2003); others are less difficult because it is easier to 'sound out' the speech sounds and they have fewer spelling irregularities (as in Italian). However cross-linguistic comparisons by Lingren et al. (1985), Wimmer (1996) and Landerl et al. (1997) showed that dyslexic children have 'impaired spelling ability'. 'English poor spellers were more impaired than their French counterparts' according to Caravolas et al. (2003).

2   Spelling skills develop and are acquired as a gradual process over time. Some individuals acquire these easily and with little apparent effort often because they are strong visualisers. Others struggle to latch on to the spelling code. Learning to spell can be a nightmare for some, and poor spelling may be as persistent for them as a running sore. Comments like 'Why can't I be just like everyone else and be able to remember my spellings that I spent a half an hour learning last night?' are often a repeated heartfelt cry from poor spellers.

3   What are the possible causes of chronically poor spelling? Levine (1994) considers that delays in acquiring skills may be the result of a learning disability, or that they may be an indication of 'neurodevelopmental dysfunctions which are gaps, delays or variations in the way a particular child's brain is developing'.

4   The National Institute of Child Health and Human Development (NICHD) (Lyon 1995) studies confirmed that children who have difficulties in learning to read (and write) often had maturation delays and, when given pre-school explicit instruction in, for example, phonological awareness, often overcame the effects

continued

of the delays and achieved on a par with peers of similar age and ability. Individuals develop skills at different times and at different rates. Reid (1998) contends that 'although children with specific learning difficulties have some common core difficulties they do not represent an identical discrete entity with individual profiles'.

5   It has been established that learning to spell is usually part of a developmental pentagon process for normal spellers, and that skills develop in a quantifiable order. The current stage in a speller's developmental levels of skills can be pinpointed by analysing the individual spelling errors. It is important to remember that one stage can overlap with the next stage, particularly in older spellers. There are no precise demarcation lines. However when using reliable diagnostic tools, and with experience gained from using spelling error analysis and categorisation, teachers can make reliable estimations about the stage of development reached by an individual speller. This information can be included in individual education plans (IEPs).

6   Misspelling analysis is useful and may provide a snapshot of underlying weaknesses and the causes of these, as well as providing clues about the spelling strategies best used, whether phonological or visual. Spelling error analysis plays a significant role in the diagnosis of dyslexia.

7   Information and evidence gathered can then be used when deciding upon the appropriate level of intervention. Moats (1995) concurs with this approach and pointed out that 'instruction can, and should, be matched to the level of knowledge the child is ready to assimilate'.

8   The Disability Discrimination Act 1995, which has been amended to the Special Educational Needs and Disability Act 2001 (SENDA), has had a profound influence on effective provision for those with disabilities such as dyslexia. Establishments have to make 'reasonable adjustments' to accommodate specific needs when designing curriculums and in their delivery such as making allowance for spelling errors. 'Pupils do not need to use completely correct spellings to gain marking credit' except in the spelling test. Spellcheckers are allowed in English (except in the spelling test) 'for those with SEN' and those 'who use them as part of normal classroom practice' QCA (2005).

7 The Evolution of Spelling Instruction

- • The significance of teaching methods
- • Orton's key findings and their relevance for current practice
- • An overview of popular resources for teaching spelling in mainstream classrooms
- • Explanations for why traditional weekly spelling tests often result in poor progress for those with dyslexia
- • The practical implications of spelling research for classroom practitioners
- • Summary and conclusions

Keywords

ABC reading and spelling method
Cerebellum deficit theory
'Chinese' spelling style
'Compensated' dyslexia

'Phoenician' spelling style
Rote memory
Special educational needs (SEN)
Spelling stages
Spelling styles

Visual memory
Visual sequential memory
Whole language reading method
Whole-word 'look-and-say' reading method

The significance of teaching methods

One of the earliest recorded examples of teaching reading using the phonological method, according to Olson (2002), was described in *The Shortest Way to Reading* (1527) by Valentin Ickelsamer, who recommended taking the name 'Hans' and sounding out the four letters /H/ /a/ /n/ /s/.

There is evidence from as long ago as 1660 that some children 'could scarce tell six of letters at twelve months' end, who if they had been taught in a way more agreeable to their meane apprehensions, we might have wrought more readily upon their senses, and affected their minds with what they did' (cited in Hoole 1969). Is this one of the earliest recorded references to learning difficulties, and does it give an indication of a variation in individual learning styles?

Spelling was historically regarded as a mainly visual activity. Spelling books such as *The English Schoole-Maister* (Coote 1596) were used to teach reading and writing. Spelling primers such as Webster's *The American Blueback Spelling Book* (1790) were widely used in America. Webster (1783) considered that 'spelling is the foundation of reading and the greatest ornament of writing'.

Learning to read and learning to spell were interdependent, according to Diack (1965), 'until well into the 19th century in both England and America; the teaching of reading was inseparably associated with the alphabet and spelling'. 'To learn to read the ABC method was used which was the discovery of [how] a word was made, as sentences were spelled by letter-name and spoken word-by-word in guided recitation' (Henderson 1985). Spelling the word aloud while saying the names of the letters of the alphabet was the main method used to learn spellings.

Towards the middle of the nineteenth century the phonics method, which involved sounding out the individual letter sounds and then blending them, was used to learn to read and began to be adopted by many American and later British educators. But spelling continued to be taught to children by giving them lists of words to memorise, often by repeating the letter names /k/ /aa/ /tee/ for 'cat'. According to Henderson (1985) 'by the 1870s a synthetic phonics method of teaching reading was at last established', however 'spelling was thought to require brute memory'. The whole-word reading method, which had its beginnings in the nineteenth century, became popular in the US from the beginning of the twentieth century and was known colloquially as 'look-and-say'. Children were given books with good illustrations, and were encouraged to memorise and recognise whole words rather than systematically sound out the letters. Edmund Burke Huey (1908) was its principal advocate in the US. In the last quarter of the twentieth century the 'whole language' method advocated that children should be allowed to read books of their choice and they learned to recognise whole words, often by using contextual cues.

Advocates of this method said that reading is linked to oral language (Goodman 1967), and would therefore develop naturally without direct instruction. As each of these methods was promoted, imposed, rejected or accepted by teachers and schools, an individual reader's chances of learning to crack the code often depended on whether the reading method they were using matched the way they learned. Increasingly a polarisation of views developed about teaching methods as evidence and concerns continued to appear about standards of literacy and about the cohorts of pupils leaving school with low literacy levels.

Open warfare erupted from time to time about the best way to teach reading and spelling. There are still many unresolved issues about reading and spelling instruction for teachers and learners, particularly for those with special educational needs.

There is a growing body of knowledge about variations in learning styles, as well as a growing volume of scientific literature about those who learn differently, often because of a specific learning difficulty such as dyslexia.

The significance of appropriate teaching methods and their influence on learning styles has become even more important. The quest for answers has resulted in a reappraisal of the doctrines of great educators of the twentieth century such as Maria Montessori (1912), who worked with young children who were 'at risk' academically, as well as

Samuel Orton (1937), who worked with individuals whom he had identified as having severe reading and spelling disabilities. He asserted that 'occasionally a poor reader will learn to spell fairly readily by rote auditory memory and when examined upon recently acquired lists of words will show a fair degree of skill' (Orton 1931). He argued however that 'children with a marked reading disability are almost always bad spellers'. He hypothesised that this could be due to a defect of visual memory.

With the benefits of hindsight we now know that Orton was correct in his assumption that many poor spellers have poor visual memory. When auditory skills (now referred to as phonological and phonemic skills) were poor, they could not be used to compensate for poor visual skills, which in turn compounded the difficulties of individuals with reading and spelling problems. Orton continued to make a study of his dyslexic patients' needs, including what they needed to learn to manage spelling successfully.

Orton's key findings and their relevance for current practice

- Many people with dyslexia learn to read, albeit slowly or inaccurately.
- Some individuals have a 'special disability in spelling [which] may stand out as an isolated defect'.
- 'Compensated' dyslexic students and adults who have responded to teaching and overcome many of their earlier difficulties often have persisting difficulties with spelling.
- The method of instruction in reading seems to play an important part in the development of literacy. Many of the children with isolated spelling disabilities are found to have been taught by the whole word or 'sight' method which has failed to establish the sound association with individual letters necessary for the reproduction of the word in spelling.
- 'The vowels are a particularly fertile source of errors', and errors occur more frequently with vowels than with consonant sounds. Short vowel difficulties are a hallmark of the spelling feature of children with dyslexia.
- Some of the recurring features of the poor speller's difficulties include 'additions' and 'confusions of similar sounds', which shows how useful spelling error analysis can be.
- 'No one procedure can be advised for bad spellers.'
- Orton advocated using 'nonsense syllables' to help with the 'enunciation of the sounds of the short vowels' and he opined that they were useful because 'they exclude the practice effect in known words'. This idea was later adopted by researchers who established that using non-word reading and spelling tests are diagnostically useful for identifying difficulties with phonological and phonemic awareness. This is because contextual cues cannot be used as an aid to spelling or as a decoding strategy.
- He insisted that children should be taught the name and the sounds of the letters simultaneously, and that 'learning the sounds of the letters was of little use in itself and that synthesizing them into a spoken word was of cardinal importance and must be carefully taught'.

Orton assigned the task of organising the teaching procedures to Anna Gillingham at the Language Research Project of the New York Neurological Institute (1932–36), according to June Orton (1966). She and her associate Bessie Stillman implemented Orton's principles and techniques for teaching which they had developed and refined and called 'the alphabet method'. They published their teaching manual privately in 1946. This collaboration resulted in the landmark text *Remedial Training for Children with Specific Language Disability in Reading, Spelling and Penmanship* (Gillingham and Stillman 1956). June Orton (1966) proclaimed that the manual 'was a storehouse of treasures for teachers, schools and parents, especially during the long period when the teaching of phonics was banned in most places and such materials were not published elsewhere'. This text is now acknowledged as the progenitor of many multi-sensory phonics and spelling programmes. It advocated the simultaneous use of visual, auditory, kinaesthetic and tactile (V-A-K-T) methods. Orton wanted pupils to use the letter sounds when spelling the word aloud, because they represented the phonemes in the words. Gillingham wanted pupils to use the letter names when spelling aloud because she argued that the sounds could not be used to spell irregular words. According to Sheffield (1991), followers of what became known as the Orton–Gillingham method now use Orton's synthetic phonics approach initially. The classic dyslexia teaching programmes use Gillingham and Stillman's idea of a keyword for each sound which is written on an index card. These cards are used for frequent practice and overlearning. The pupil looks at the card with the letter and says the letter name. Then the card is turned over, and the keyword picture helps to trigger the sound automatically.

This helps to develop phonemic skills, which the research of Lundberg et al. (1988) showed can be improved with explicit teaching. These can be reinforced with multi-sensory methods using the eyes, the ears, the lips and the hands to learn.

The Orton–Gillingham theory, principles and methods have stood the test of time. They have resulted in a number of programmes based on their principles with the addition of individual authors' distinctive background experience, and continue to be hugely influential worldwide in teaching individuals with specific learning difficulties. Likewise many of its principles and techniques have begun to be incorporated into mainstream education curriculums and research projects.

Practitioners who work with people with dyslexia tend to use a variety of materials and resources. Reid (1998) and Schneider (1999) reviewed the literature on teaching programmes. Ott (2006) and Patoss (2006) include information about resources for teaching. Smith et al. (1998) includes information about spelling and learning resources.

An overview of popular resources for teaching spelling in mainstream classrooms

Until fairly recently many of those working in mainstream education continued to teach spelling as a rote memory task. This included using spelling lists of 'useful words' such as subject-based lists. Essential spelling lists such as Schonell's (1932) included graded lists for children aged 7–12 years and were, he said, 'grouped according to common difficulty'. Schonell's (1932) spelling book is still one of the main teaching resources for weekly spelling lists in mainstream schools throughout the UK. The example from Schonell's book (Fig. 2) shows that often a variety of spelling rules and conventions, including suffixes and irregular spellings, were included with no explanation. The only instruction was to 'learn these for the test next week'.

In the US, word frequency lists such as the Dolch (1936) list, which included sight words with irregular spellings, were used. Lists such as Hanna's (1971) were influential

Figure 2

in introducing lists with more structure and an emphasis on the regularity of English spelling patterns. Another memorisation strategy suggested by Clymer (1963) among others was to teach spelling rules or generalisations. The contents of many of the published spelling books used on both sides of the Atlantic were influenced by these authors.

Many of these resources depended on visual memory skills as well as on reasoning skills. Weekly spelling tests were the norm in schools throughout the country and children were given lists often with little structure in the words to learn. Sometimes these lists consisted of useful words which had evolved from school work. Learning spelling was primarily taught by the use of visual channels. When children made spelling mistakes they were frequently asked to correct their errors and told to copy each correction six times. It was presumed that repetition would help them to memorise the spelling pattern.

Cripps (1984) used word families and words of similar appearance for his spelling lists, and emphasised the importance of the 'eye' for spelling. His more recent materials such as *A Hand for Spelling* (1995) emphasise teaching through learning letter patterns, and using cursive handwriting, which enhances motor memory for letter patterns.

Spelling Made Easy: Multi-sensory Structured Spelling (Brand 1989) used word patterns which were taught as the title suggests, and included dictation passages which used the words in meaningful contexts, so that the teaching of patterns was not just a visual memory activity.

Peters and Smith (1993) argued that 'the most important factor in learning to spell is the visual element' and that 'vision is our preferred sense'. They advocated that spellers should be encouraged 'to see if it looks right' 'just by looking at it'. They concluded that 'spelling depends on looking with interest, intent and intention to reproduce a word, and this reproduction obviously occurs in writing'. This, they said, was 'encapsulated in the familiar 'look-cover-write-check routine', an idea borrowed from Horn (1919).

Many of these approaches do not take account of the specific difficulties which some spellers, including those with dyslexia, have with visual memory, nor do they include the oral and aural sub-skills which can be a useful element to enhance learning when spellers 'say' the word aloud.

Another method was suggested by Mudd (1997). She exemplified her strategies by describing a spelling lesson when teaching 7–8-year-olds who were writing about 'Our Pets'. 'Two children kept fish and introduced the word aquarium into our discussion: This was an ideal opportunity to consider the Latin word aqua and its related words. Suggestions from the children included aquatic, aquamarine, aqua-lung, Aquarius. The children soon spotted the aqua pattern in the words; looking carefully at patterns within words is a vital part of spelling instruction.'

The National Literacy Strategy (DfEE 1998) awakened fresh interest in how to teach spelling and what spellings to teach. Teaching analytic phonics using onset and rimes was seen as very useful. A number of publications were developed to teach analytic phonics and spellings such as *Phonological Awareness Training: A New Approach to Phonics* (Wilson 1993), usually known as *PAT*, which, according to Reid (1998), 'is a specific programme on a particular aspect of literacy development phonological awareness. Its essential component is the use of analogues to help children read and spell.' Brooks et al. (1998) summed it up as a 'daily 10-minute programme [which] provides intensive work on three skills within the same activities: identifying sounds, blending phonemes together and segmenting or isolating sounds in words'. When it was evaluated, 'the experimental [children] made scarcely any more progress than would have been expected from normal schooling and development'. Others use the worksheets for additional reinforcement and revision. Many schools put great emphasis and spend much time on pupils learning to read and spell the 'high-frequency' lists of words in the NLS (DfEE 1998). Many of these words are 'odd-bod' spellings, so consequently are often challenging for poor spellers as well as having few examplars such as 'once', 'forty'. It might be more productive for poor spellers to concentrate on learning regular spelling patterns using systematic synthetic phonics, particularly those generating large word families Brooks recommended in his report on the DfEE's (2003) Phonics Seminar that 'within the 100 most frequent words, only those that are irregular should be taught as sight words'. This also applies to their spelling. Poor spellers need to learn regular spellings first, then irregular spellings.

Explanations for why traditional weekly spelling tests often result in poor progress for those with dyslexia

- There are often too many words to learn.
- The words are often too difficult for individual children's current skills (Fig. 3).
- The words do not match the current developmental stage of the speller.
- Words have little relevance, or the meanings are unfamiliar.
- Not enough time or opportunity is given to revise and rehearse words.
- Spellers are not given enough opportunities to use the spellings in their own writing.
- Opportunities are not provided to re-test spelling in a week or month's time to ensure that the words can be retrieved from long-term memory with automaticity.
- Word lists often have little structure, such as the use of a spelling pattern rule, or generalisation. Sometimes when attempts are made to include a spelling pattern the target words also include additional spelling rules, such as adding a suffix to the root word.
- There is often little instruction about learning strategies such as the use of mnemonics for 'odd-bod' spellings.
- Help is sometimes not provided to identify preferred learning styles, such as spelling by analogy for good visualisers, or using the S-O-S method for those with good oral/aural skills, or the use of technology for those with good kinaesthetic skills.

In response to the recommendations made in the NLS (DfEE 1999) and DfEE (2001) a number of useful and user-friendly materials have been produced to help teachers and classroom assistants implement the Strategy. For example *Key Stage 3 Literacy Progress Unit – Spelling* draws on the results of international research about the teaching of literacy.

A number of commercial spelling programmes have been developed and linked to the spelling objectives of the NLS. They include:

- *Searchlights for Spelling* (Buckton and Corbett 2002), which is a systematic scheme for teaching spelling patterns using multi-sensory activities (www.cambridge.org).
- *Focus on Spelling* (Sweeney and Doncaster 2002), which builds up phonic knowledge and teaches spelling rules as well as a variety of spelling strategies (www.Collins Education.com).
- *Big Book Spelling* (Palmer and Morgan 2003), which uses 'look-say-cover-write-check' methods and includes prose, poems and picture stories to teach spelling patterns in meaningful contexts (www.ginn.co.uk).

These new and more enlightened approaches will surely lead to an improvement in spelling skills in the country's classrooms for the majority of pupils. However, children still continue to struggle, and there is still a 'tail of underachievement' in spelling for a sizeable number of pupils. This has been an ongoing concern. Academics and practitioners continued to seek explanations why many individuals fail to 'crack the code'. This has included investigating and studying the errors children make when they spell.

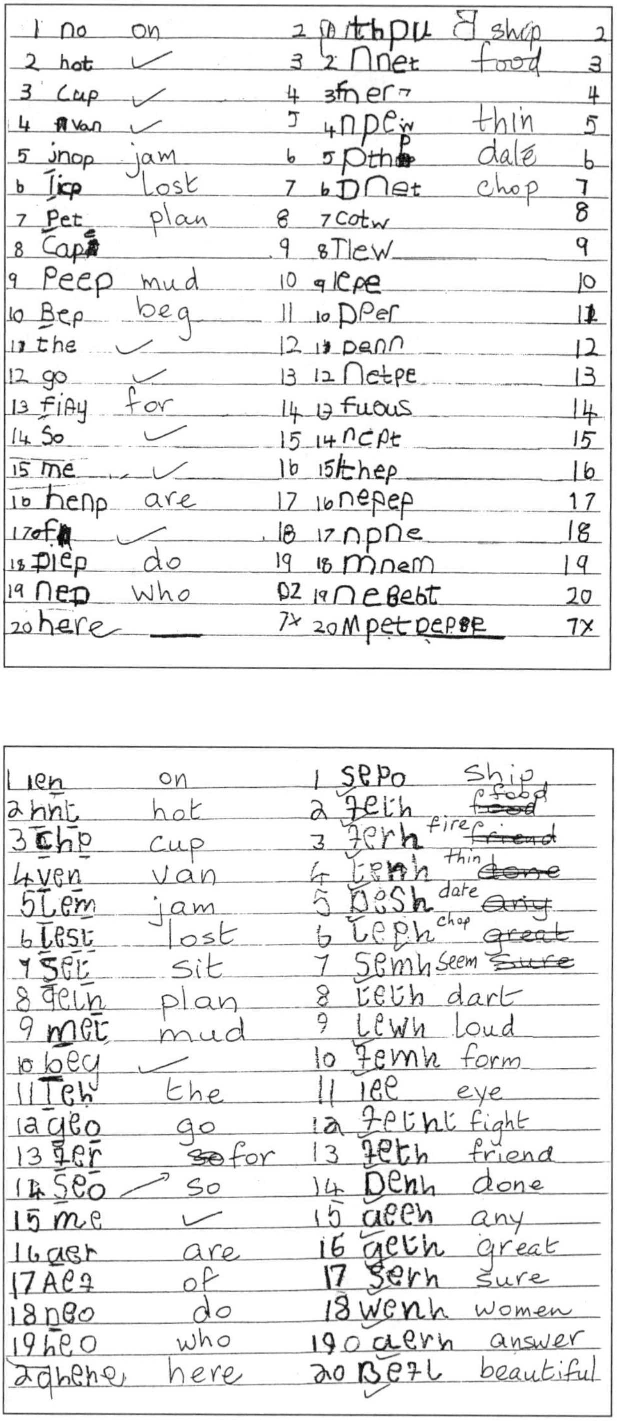

Figure 3

The practical implications of spelling research for classroom practitioners

Spache (1940) analysed children's spelling errors, and divided them into various categories which included the omission, addition, reversal and substitution of letters. These were attributed to a failure to memorise letter strings or spelling patterns within words. Researchers such as Jensen (1962) worked on experiments on memory, and on the recall of a series of letters, patterns and digits on the assumption that visual memory could be trained. The inference was that this could be transferred to learning spelling. In the classroom this resulted in individuals being asked to correct their spelling mistakes and then to copy out the corrections six times. This worked for those with good visual memory skills who could memorise the spelling pattern. For those with poor visual memory it was a waste of time. Some of these individuals even failed to copy their own corrected spellings accurately. Part of the training sometimes included recommendations to 'use the dictionary to correct your spelling mistakes'. For a dyslexic speller who has difficulty saying the alphabet and remembering the sequence of letters this was a futile, frustrating chore. Those with poor visual sequential memory often miscopied the word. This approach to spelling continues to result in repeated failure for many children. Anecdotal evidence shows that this approach is still widespread in many schools.

In the 1960s researchers began to study linguistics and how children acquired spoken language. They established that learning to spell involves a plethora of simultaneous subskills, but this message often did not reach individual classrooms – old habits die hard. Teachers in some schools still adhere to the belief that 'teaching spelling is about repetition, repetition'.

Academics sought to find answers about how children learn to spell, and how best to teach all children to spell, including those who find spelling problematic. The main areas of research included the following.

- Lundberg et al. (1980) studied phoneme skills to establish how they affect reading and spelling. Cataldo and Ellis (1988) drew attention to the predictive use of a test of phonemic awareness.
- Bradley and Huxford (1994) confirmed that training in phonological skills had 'a remarkable effect on [the] children's spelling progress'.
- Longitudinal studies on the impact of training studies in phonological skills, and later in learning to read, and on early spelling, such as Lundberg et al. (1988) showed that phonological awareness is much more involved in early spelling than in early reading. Liberman et al. (1985) showed that phonological skills account for variations in spelling proficiency.
- Another line of research was ongoing into the staged developmental processes involved in spelling. Unlike theoretical research, this often involved studying children's learning behaviour. Read (1971), as already shown, led the way in the study of how novice spellers use different strategies at different stages of development. Frith (1976) found that some 12-year-old children, who read well but who had appalling spelling, used the same strategies that 6½-year-old beginner spellers used. She argued that children initially use visual cues for reading, and phonological cues for spelling. She concluded that over time a combination of strategies and techniques are used to decode and encode words by good readers and spellers.

Spelling ability develops with age and experience for normal spellers. Spelling ability for those with dyslexia develops more slowly and often incompletely. Bruck (1987) conducted a study of adults who had been diagnosed as children and found that 'major deficits were most apparent for single word decoding and spelling skills'.

Researchers such as Nicolson and Fawcett (1990, 1994) showed that dyslexic people do not develop skills easily, quickly or with automaticity, resulting in 'severe deficits for spelling'. They require longer and more explicit teaching to do so because of what Fawcett and Nicolson (2001) described as the cerebellum deficit hypothesis. Furthermore these researchers claimed that 'cerebellum impairment would therefore be predicted to cause the 'phonological core deficit'. They concluded from their studies of cases of 'pure' dyslexia that 'spelling' may be the most persistent to remediation, and in another experiment, involving 126 children with dyslexia matched with a control group, 'spelling had the most extreme effect' on the results.

Teachers and learners need to be aware of these underlying constitutional difficulties and variations in how spellers learn, and on the implications for how individuals are taught and learn. Fig. 4 opposite shows a letter written by a dyslexic man to his MP. He was reduced to tears when the MP returned the letter to him with corrections.

Baron and Strawson (1976) coined the terms 'Phoenician' and 'Chinese' to describe the individual learning and spelling styles of certain individuals. Baron et al. (1980) defined 'Phoenician' spellers as 'those who rely heavily on the rules' and 'Chinese' spellers as those who 'rely heavily on word-specific associations between each word and its associated pronunciation'. Stanovich (1992) pointed out that 'Chinese' types have difficulties with phonemic skills but have good skills with the memorisation of orthographic patterns and whole-word recognition when reading. Ellis (1993) pointed out that 'Chinese' readers use a whole word recognition as their main reading tactic and that 'Phoenician' readers use a mainly sounding out approach as their main tactic. The hypothesis is that some spellers may use the same approaches, depending on whether they are stronger visually or auditorially. Ellis (1993) concluded that 'it would make the life of researchers easier if dyslexics fell neatly and tidily into a small number of different sub-types, but they do not, and any attempt to force them into mutually exclusive categories distorts the nature of dyslexic reality'.

Mr Stephen Halsall.

Sunday, March 11, 2001.

Neil Turner.
Labour Member of Parliament for Wigan.
Gerrard Winstanley House,
Crawford St.
Wigan.

Dear Sir.

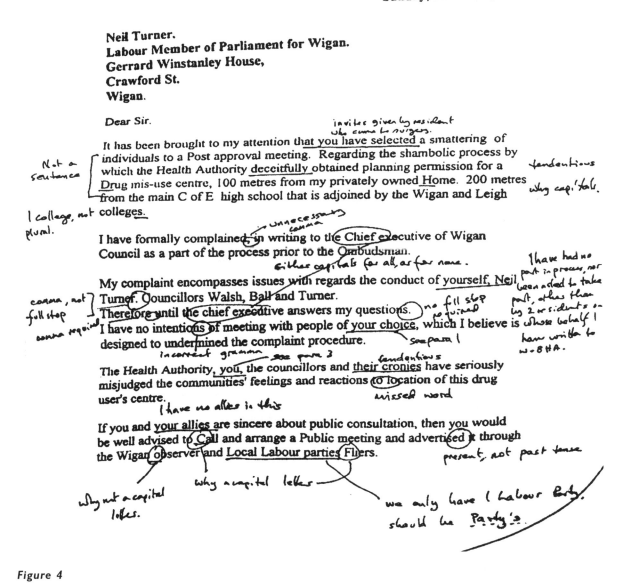

invites given by resident who came to surgery.

It has been brought to my attention that you have selected a smattering of
individuals to a Post approval meeting. Regarding the shambolic process by
which the Health Authority deceitfully obtained planning permission for a
Drug mis-use centre, 100 metres from my privately owned Home. 200 metres
from the main C of E high school that is adjoined by the Wigan and Leigh
colleges.

Not a sentence

tendentious

why capitals.

1 college, not plural.

I have formally complained, in writing to the Chief executive of Wigan
Council as a part of the process prior to the Ombudsman.

unnecessary comma

either capitals for all, or for none.

My complaint encompasses issues with regards the conduct of yourself, Neil
Turner. Councillors Walsh, Ball and Turner.
Therefore until the chief executive answers my questions.
I have no intentions of meeting with people of your choice, which I believe is
designed to undermined the complaint procedure.

comma, not full stop

comma required

no full stop required

see para 1

I have had no part in process, nor been asked to take part, other than by 2 residents on whose behalf I have written to W-BHA.

The Health Authority, you, the councillors and their cronies have seriously
misjudged the communities' feelings and reactions to location of this drug
user's centre.

Incorrect grammar *see para 3* *tendentious*

missed word

I have no allies in this

If you and your allies are sincere about public consultation, then you would
be well advised to Call and arrange a Public meeting and advertised it through
the Wigan observer and Local Labour parties Fliers.

present, not past tense

why a capital letter

why not a capital letter.

we only have 1 Labour Party. should be Party's.

Figure 4

SUMMARY AND CONCLUSIONS

1   Some critics lay the blame for poor spelling on an over-reliance on visual strategies for the way individuals are taught to spell.

2   Many poor spellers are born with a genetic disposition to weaknesses in processing language. However, others missed schooling or were not taught spelling during the time when spelling was deemed less important than creative writing. Some have been brought up in a different linguistic environment and others learn English as a second language, which may affect their spelling skills.

3   The methods of instruction and the resources used to teach spelling do matter and affect the success or failure of the outcome. Chew (2001) collected data from a longitudinal study of a whole year group in a large sixth form college 'showing that 16-year-olds are better spellers if they were started on phonics in infant school than if they were started off on [the] sight word[s] [reading method]'.

4   Orton–Gillingham materials and programmes derived from them have stood the test of time. Theory, research and practice emanating from their work has now been successfully adapted for use in mainstream classrooms world-wide.

5   Traditional teaching methods including the use of weekly classroom spelling tests teach some poor spellers little except pain, anger and frustration. Henderson (1985) pleaded that children should not be asked to write their misspelled words ten times because repetitions 'do not reinforce recall'. They 'fatigue the hand, numb attention, promote error, and actually block the very memory mechanisms which it was hoped they might support'.

6   The NLS (DfEE 1998) has resulted in a more enlightened approach to teaching all children spelling. There is now clear guidance about learning to spell using a variety of methods. The message has gone out to schools nationwide and has become part of the resources for delivering the National Curriculum.

7   There is a greater acceptance and understanding of poor spellers including dyslexics' needs because of the impact of the SEN Code of Practice. Examination boards allow 'access arrangements' for candidates with SEN, including those with poor writing skills or indecipherable spelling. The Special Educational Needs and Disability Act 2001 (SENDA) has made it unlawful to discriminate against someone because of a disability such as poor spelling resulting from, for example, dyslexia.

8   However there are still pockets of resistance and people who blame nurture not nature as the underlying cause of spelling errors, and who say that individuals like Stephen Halsall (Fig. 4) are responsible for their 'careless' errors and poor punctuation and spelling.

8 Matching Teaching Methods to Learning Styles

- Evidence of public concern about spelling standards
- Current practice, processes and underlying principles for the development of strategies and skills
- Informal test to establish preferred spelling method
- Hemisphere function studies and their relevance for cognitive and learning style
- Practical implications of learning styles
- Neurobiological research evidence
- Gardner's theory of multiple intelligences and their characteristics
- Practical implications of the theory of multiple intelligences for teachers and learners
- The significance of learning styles and the implications for all spellers, especially dyslexic people
- Guidelines and suggestions for using learning strategies to meet the needs of poor spellers
- Using preferred cognitive style to match preferred learning style
- Checklists to establish individuals' preferred spelling style
- Summary and conclusions

Keywords

Cognitive style	Learning strategy	Paired spelling method
Electro-encephalography (EEG)	Learning style	Positron emission tomography (PET) scans
	Learning style inventories	
Fernald's method	Metacognition	Simultaneous oral spelling (S-O-S) method
Horn's 'look-say-cover-write-check' method	Multiple intelligences theory	
High-frequency words	Neuro-linguistic programming	
Learning skill		

Evidence of public concern about spelling standards

There have been a number of reports in the media in recent years about spelling standards, notably among school leavers. Employers' organisations such as the Institute of Management (quoted in Lepkowska 1997) claimed that '[education] standards have dropped over the past 10 years, while GCSE and A-level results have improved dramatically'. A headline in a national newspaper proclaimed that 'Alarming evidence of a decline in educational standards emerged in a nationwide survey of spelling skills yesterday' (Clark 2001), showing that 'Spelling is in Crisis'. In a short test 'only two out of 1,000 people aged between 15 and 50 could pick out all 14 glaring errors in a short passage of text. Professor Loreto Todd of Ulster University, who carried out the research, said that, if her findings were representative, 4–15 per cent of today's school leavers are functionally illiterate. The government has continued its vigorous crusade to drive up national standards in literacy. There have been many initiatives to help those with low literacy and poor literacy skills.

The DfEE's (2000) *Supporting Pupils with Special Educational Needs in the Literacy Hour* was a 'tool kit' for teachers, which exemplified a wide range of teaching methods and strategies. It included suggestions for what pupils should be taught, including 'spelling strategies such as using a spelling log [a list of personal spellings], building up spellings by syllabic parts using known prefixes, suffixes and common letter strings' and learning spelling conventions and rules.

Key Stage 3 National Strategy. Framework for Teaching English: Years 7, 8 and 9 (DfEE 2001) included: specific spelling objectives for each year level. It recommended 'learning rules, and developing strategies' such as the 'look-say-cover-write-check' method. It also included a General Spelling List of seven hundred words which included 'common homophones and confusions' and Subject Spelling Lists. Yet, according to Driscoll (2002) in a government review of national test results at Key Stage 2, 'accuracy in spelling has declined'. More than half of 11-year-olds struggled with words such as 'future', 'perfectly', 'change', 'known'. The word 'technique' defeated most of the six hundred thousand pupils who sat the test, appearing as 'techneck' or 'tecacneak'. 'Spelling mistakes that more than half of seven-year-olds made in their Key Stage 1 tests [included]: turnd/ternd; climd/climb; pavment/pavemnt; now (instead of know)' (*TES* 2004).

This is evidence that, in spite of the gigantic expenditure by the government and the Herculean efforts made by teachers and pupils to improve literacy standards, spelling did still not improve in many schools across the nation. *The Times* (2003) reported that 'many teachers are given virtually no training in teaching [children] how to read [and spell] and, as David Bell, chief inspector of schools for Ofsted, puts it, 'the Government's programme of literacy teaching at primary level is confused'. A number of studies including surveys have been conducted in the US about the role of teachers' knowledge about word structure and its relationship to teaching spelling (Spear-Swerling and Brucker 2003). 'Findings such as ours suggest that teachers may not learn the essential insights if they must rely only on teaching experience, use of structured reading programmes, use of screening tests, or willingness to implement higher academic standards. Because teachers improved with coursework, our data suggest that teachers' formal knowledge is acquired through explicit instruction and ample practice with each of the concepts at issue' according to Moats and Foorman (2003). This is why it behoves us to consider that 'the recollection of the past is the promise of the future' (Rawson 1987) when evaluating spelling methods.

Current practice, processes and underlying principles for the development of strategies and skills

What are the options when considering spelling methods and principles? They include judicious use of some basic principles and general strategies as well as the following procedures which have been adapted to meet individual needs, strengths, weaknesses and preferred learning style.

Horn's 'Look-say-cover-write-check' method (1969)

This involves the following processes:

1 Look at the word and take a snapshot of it.
2 Pronounce the word while looking at it and listen to the sounds it makes.
3 Say the letter names while looking at them and spelling them aloud.
4 Cover the word and look at it in the mind's eye with eyes closed.
5 Write the word using cursive writing.
6 Check the spelling by comparing it with the original version.

This method is a multi-sensory approach. It has elements to match individual learning styles. Visualisers will remember the letter patterns when they use their eyes to look at the letter shapes and take a snapshot of these. Auditory learners will remember the sound-to-symbol matches when they use their ears and lips to remember the phonemes and syllables. Kinaesthetic learners will remember where their fingers go when they use their hands, involving motor memory when they write the word. This method can be used to learn regular and irregular spelling. It also lends itself for use on a computer as the eyes can be averted from the screen for the 'cover' part. This method was devised and first used by Ernest Horn in 1919. This approach was brought to the attention of many teachers and children while using the NLS (DfEE 1998) *Framework for Teaching*.

Peters' (1985) adaptation recommended 'look-cover-write-check'. The missing component was 'say'. It is a vital part because it helps to match the sounds to the letters in the words, which helps those with good phonological skills but poor visual skills. Children who have been taught phonics find it useful. Hatcher, Hulme and Ellis (1994) showed how important the 'phonological linkage' is. It includes explicit teaching of phonics, including sounds and the letters that represent them.

Fernald's method (1943)

According to Cotterell (1970), this involves the following processes:

1 The word is written by the teacher using cursive writing on a piece of A4 paper.
2 The teacher pronounces the word slowly and clearly. Then the pupil repeats it.
3 The pupil looks at the word carefully and notes any particular tricky letters, prefixes or suffixes (which can be highlighted).
4 The pupil then traces over the letters using the index finger of the hand he or she writes with, while simultaneously saying the letter names aloud as he or she traces over them.

5   Then the pupil folds over the paper.
6   The pupil writes the word from memory using cursive writing.
7   The pupil then turns the paper back and checks his or her spelling with the target word on the page. The pupil repeats the process if necessary until able to write the word correctly from memory.
8   Then the pupil uses the word in a meaningful context either in a sentence or in a piece of spontaneous writing.

Using the eyes to look at the letters and using colour to highlight morphemes, including plurals and affixes and silent letters, matches the learning style of those with good visual memory. Kinaesthetic learners benefit from using their tactile sense when they trace over the letters as well as their motor memory when they write the letters in a cursive script to enhance motor memory skills. It works well for spellers who have reached the conventional spelling stage when they know and use word patterns and derivations. It uses whole words rather than focusing on individual sounds because it emphasises whole words. Experienced practitioners recommend the use of the Fernald method for irregular spellings such as those found in the NLS high-frequency Lists.

Simultaneous oral spelling (S-O-S) method

This was devised by Gillingham and Stillman (1956) and still forms the backbone of regular spelling strategies for many specialist teaching programmes. It involves the following processes (based on Childs (1956) and Orton (1966)):

1   The teacher says the word.
2   The child repeats the word.
3   The child spells the word orally, i.e. names the letters representing the sounds.
4   Finally the child writes the word naming each letter aloud.
5   The child reads back what he or she has written.

Sheffield (1991) pointed out that Orton insisted that the child should 'sound the phonograms while writing them' when using phonetically regular words. Gillingham and Stillman's (1956) pupils were asked to say the letter names because they argued that these could also be used for nonphonetic (irregular) words. Initially children are now taught to say the individual letter sounds using synthetic phonics when spelling. Later they use the letter names when phonemic and graphemic skills have been firmly established. This method has elements to match the learning styles of good listeners with its emphasis on listening to the teacher as he or she pronounces the word, and then it uses visual memory to match the sounds to the letters that represent these. Kinaesthetic memory is used to write the word, and visual memory to read the word after it is written.

This multi-sensory method works well, particularly for someone with dyslexia who has developed phonemic skills, and has learned to use phonological skills. Some poor spellers find the S-O-S spelling method very effective. Many of them continue to use this strategy to underpin and compensate for their poor visual memory. This was confirmed by a training study by Thomson (1991) which showed that 'simultaneous oral spelling produced better learning than visual inspection' for dyslexics but 'would not bolster relevant skills for irregular words, whereas it would aid the skills required for regular word spelling'.

Goulandris (1994) described a training case study in which a 'treatment-resistant' severely dyslexic boy was given alternative types of spelling intervention to evaluate their effectiveness and to find ways and means to improve his spelling. Before the experiment, at 11 years 7 months, Full Scale IQ 124 and after three years of weekly specialist one-to-one teaching he still had a spelling age of 7 years 10 months and a reading age of 9 years 11 months, which is regarded as 'treatment-resistant'. The first part of the experiment used a multi-sensory approach in which he said the target word, formed the word with plastic letters, divided it into syllables or onset and rimes, finger traced the letters on a variety of surfaces then 'checked to see that the spelling was accurate'. The second part of the experiment used a visual approach. He was told to read the word, spell it with plastic letters, then to 'close his eyes and create a mental image of it' and to project the word on to 'three different surfaces in the room and to change the colours of the writing'. Then he wrote the word, checked it and corrected it if necessary.

The results showed that his spelling retention immediately after the intervention and when tested six weeks later was 100 per cent accuracy on the words taught using the multi-sensory techniques. He had 100 per cent accuracy immediately after intervention and 80 per cent accuracy six weeks later on the words taught using the visual learning technique. At the end of fourteen weeks' intervention his spelling on a standardised test showed his 'spelling age improving by approximately one and a half years and reading accuracy and reading comprehension improving approximately by two years'.

The S-O-S method was originally devised for use in the one-to-one situation with a teacher or a parent to support the learner and can be very effective when used by teaching assistants. Daily reinforcement is a key ingredient in most specialist teaching programmes (Cox 1980). Hatcher and Rack (2002) showed that 'those children who made good literacy gains had followed steady routines, while those who did not do so well had followed interrupted schedules'. Those who made most progress had spent twenty minutes per day, five days a week spread over twenty-nine weeks on various literacy tasks which were part of the forty-eight hour SPELLIT Home Support Programme.

Brooks and Weeks (1998) carried out an experiment to 'examine the individual learning strategies and cognitive development of both children experiencing difficulty and children experiencing no difficulty, and [to] compare the effectiveness of different teaching methods'. The incidence of dyslexia was not recorded. Sixty children aged 6 to 8 years in three different schools were involved. Their best learning method was established from the following methods:

1 Neuro-linguistic (NLP)
2 Look-cover-write-check (LCWC)
3 Analogies with onset-and-rime
4 Phonics
5 Simultaneous oral spelling (S-O-S)
6 Tracing
7 Own voice
8 Mnemonics
9 Picture links
10 Word-in-words

'After 5 months, the rate of increase in spelling age of the group using the individual methods [preferred learning style] doubled, while the others increased at a usual "chronological rate".' The 'S-O-S [method] resulted in the largest gain across all schools.'

Neuro-linguistic programming (NLP) method

1   Write the word on a card.
2   Ask the pupil to turn on his or her personal video in the mind's eye and to take a snapshot of the word.
3   Ask the pupil to note the letters that have ascenders or descenders or other visually memorable features including letter patterns.
4   Turn the card face downwards and ask the pupil to keep looking at the letters in the mind's eye.
5   Ask the pupil to name the letters seen. If he or she turns the eyes upwards, he or she is visualising the letters.
6   Then turn the card face upwards and the pupil checks the spelling.

This method is a strongly visual approach and suits those who have good visual perception and visual memory. This was popular in mainstream classrooms. However, it is important to remember that some individuals with dyslexia have very poor visual memories while others have outstanding visual skills.

Visual-auditory-kinaesthetic-tactile (VAKT) method

This is in fact another name for the S-O-S method. It is a multi-sensory method which, according to Gillingham and Stillman (1964),

is based upon the constant use of association of:

• How a letter or word looks
• How it sounds
• How the speech organs or the hand in writing feels when producing it.

Cox (1980) explains this very succinctly and says that the pupil:

1   Listens
2   Echoes
3   Spells
4   Writes
5   Reads.

The SEN Code of Practice (COP 1994) resulted in special needs teaching being undertaken in mainstream classrooms, often now with the help of the SENCO and Learning Support Assistants. The SEN (COP 2001) and SEN Toolkit (DfES 2001) offer guidance and practical advice about day-to-day matters for SENCOs and learning support assistants including teaching assistants.

Topping (2002) devised 'paired reading' as a strategy which uses peers, parents and volunteers. It 'is a kind of supported or assisted reading' and 'should be [given] three times per week for a minimum of 20 minute for at least the first four to six weeks'.

Topping (1992) devised a 'paired spelling process' based on S-O-S principles, which is as follows:

- Read the word aloud (together and alone).
- Choose a visual or a verbal cue for the word.
- Say the cue together.
- The speller says the cue while the helper writes the word.
- The helper then says the word while the speller writes the word.
- The speller says the cue and writes the word.
- The speller writes the word fast.
- The speller reads the word.
- All the spellings are written fast at the end of the session; if the speller makes a mistake he or she must repeat each step of the process.
- The helper praises the speller.

Schlagal and Schlagal (1992) drew attention to the importance of remembering that 'there is no one method for teaching spelling. The approach used should vary according to the structure of the word as well as the individual learner's capabilities' cited by (Moats 1995). Rack and Hatcher's (2002) research showed that 'It is not the case that one programme is always best; one programme is better for pupils with one set of characteristics and another programme is better for children with a different set of characteristics'. A distillation of the major contributors to the research studies about dyslexia, as well as the contributions of experienced and successful practitioners, all point to one key ingredient for teaching – multi-sensory learning. Multi-sensory learning uses the eyes to look, the ears to listen, the lips to say and feel the movements of speech, and the hands to use the sense of touch while writing to feel movement. The crucial ingredient is that all these senses should be activated simultaneously.

Informal test to establish preferred spelling method

This test can be undertaken with the help of a teacher, parent or teaching assistant.

- Choose twenty words that have irregular spelling patterns. (See Appendix 5: 100 words most often misspelt by children in Ott (1997).)
- Test the individual by dictating the first twenty words on the list. Then choose the first ten words that have been misspelt. For older pupils words can be chosen from NLS lists such as the Key Stage 2 (DfEE 1999) Spelling Bank (Appendix 1 and 2) or Key Stage 3 Year 7 Spelling Bank (DfEE 2001) (Appendix 3).
- The list of ten words is practised each day at the same time for about five to ten minutes Monday to Friday for one week using the 'look-say-cover-write-check' method. Keep a record of the number of spellings known at the end of each session. Re-test on Friday and note the results.
- Another list of ten words is chosen, using the same approach to identify unknown or difficult spellings using the pre-test for choosing the target words. Practise these each

day at the same time of day for five to ten minutes using the Fernald's method. Keep a record of the number of spellings known at the end of the session. Re-test on Friday and note the results.

- Another list of ten words is chosen, and ten new target words are learned by using the simultaneous oral spelling method. Re-test on Friday and note the results.
- Another list of ten words is chosen and these ten target words are learned by using the computer and S-O-S method, or the 'type-think-and-spell' method, or the neuro-linguistic programme method.

At the end of the four week experiment:

- Identify which method was most effective judging by how quickly the ten target spellings were learned each day.
- Establish by checking the results for each method at the end of the weekly trial.
- Establish from anecdotal evidence from the pupil which method they felt was most effective.
- Re-test on the forty target spellings four weeks later, then in three months' time.

These results can help to establish the speller's preferred spelling method.

Hemisphere function studies and their relevance for cognitive and learning style

Rawson (1987), when looking retrospectively at major mileposts in the study of dyslexia, reflected on 'how we got to be what and where we are', asserting that brain studies were of major significance. She affirmed that 'the neurological revolution of the late '50s which is still in full cry' began a new epoch. She revealed that 'my awareness of this new era' began with the publication of 'Speech and Brain Mechanisms' (Penfold and Roberts 1959) to which she attributes 'the whole opening up of the right cerebral hemisphere'.

During the nineteenth century it was established that the brain comprises two hemi-spheres, left and right, which are connected by the corpus callosum. The whole brain processes information but each hemisphere deals with different functions which Dejerine (1892) first reported. 'Each cerebral hemisphere contains a frontal lobe, a temporal lobe, an occipital lobe, a parietal lobe, and a motor area. The motor area of each hemisphere controls the muscular activities of the opposite side of the body' (Lerner 2000).

It has been established that each hemisphere has different specialisms and functions which may account for preferences in thinking skills and learning style skills. The left hemisphere is responsible for speech and language in most individuals. Wernicke's area is involved with the understanding of language and Broca's area with the production of language. The right hemisphere is traditionally associated with visual or spatial skills, artistic ability and creativity. Both sides of the brain are active in many tasks, for example in mathematical tasks; the right side appears to be more implicated in pattern recognition and orientation, the left side appears to be more implicated in numbers, calculations, symbols and formulas. Springer and Deutsch (1984) showed that the right hemisphere is responsible for musical performance while Miles and Miles (1999) pointed out that the left hemisphere is responsible for reading musical notation. Both areas of the brain are simultaneously involved in many activities. The terms left and right are used to describe the following (based on Given and Reid 1999):

Left brain functions	*Right brain functions*
Logical thinking	Creativity
Orderly common sense	Holistic thinking
Systematic sequential tasks including time	Pattern recognition
Detailed processing	Spontaneous ideas
Deals with details such as names	Sees in whole pictures
Controls language	Artistic abilities, colour
Deals with numbers including calculation	Musical performance skills
Processes symbols, formulas, including notation	Orientation
Reading	Mechanical skills
Writing	Recognises faces
Spelling	Visio-spatial skills
Lyrics of songs	

There has been increasing interest in studying the cerebellar function of the brain. The cerebellum is the 'hind brain' and accounts for 40 per cent of the brain surface. It has two hemispheres which are responsible for different functions. Traditionally it is associated primarily with motor skills and automatic movements.

Fawcett and Nicolson (2001) showed that people with dyslexia lack automatisation of skills and have difficulties with balance, coordination and motor skills, and they argue that 'there is now overwhelming evidence of the importance of the cerebellum in language'.

Paulesu et al. (1996) used a PET scan to conduct an experiment with well-compensated adult dyslexics. It involved phonological tasks, including rhyming tasks and remembering letters. The results showed that they did not activate the insula part of the brain which is responsible for an ability to repeat speech (Frith 1997) thus showing brain dysfunction in this area. Frith (1997) hypothesised that 'this study suggests that dyslexia might be due to a disconnection between language systems'.

It is possible therefore to hypothesise that, when someone writes, the left hemisphere is sequencing ideas, processing the vocabulary and dealing with spelling, while the right hemisphere is involved with motor skills, including handwriting, and with the creative and imaginative aspects.

Knowing about the right brain and left brain functions empowers learners. Knowing that one is predominantly left or right lateralised helps to identify preferred learning style and to match this to cognitive style to optimise learning and remembering. However, it is important to remember that some tasks involve both hemispheres of the brain simultaneously.

When neuro-imaging techniques such as those used in experiments carried out by Helenius and Salmelin (2002) become more widely available, they will help to locate and show the different parts of the brain being activated when tasks such as reading or spelling are being undertaken. This may help when establishing preferred learning style and learning strategies for individuals.

Practical implications of learning styles

Spellers with a dominant left brain may find it useful when learning spelling to:

- learn word patterns by matching them to sound patterns with onset and rime such as 'ight' sequence in 'bright', 'fight', 'light', 'might' (utilising rhyming and sequencing skills)
- use mnemonics such as '<u>our</u> dear mother uses great rig<u>our</u> and vig<u>our</u> for every endeav<u>our</u> (utilising analysis, logic and language skills when saying the sentence)
- count syllables in words to heighten awareness of the letters and sounds: /mag/ni/fi/cent/ won/der/ful/ly (utilising sequential skills)
- use word derivations to help remember that 'signature' has been derived from sign or that 'automatic' has been derived from 'auto' meaning self (utilising logic).

Spellers with a dominant right brain may find it useful when learning spelling to:

- use clapping to count syllables in words such as 'difficulty' to help establish phonological awareness. Words such as 'Mississippi' or 'difficulty' can be chanted 'Mrs d – Mrs i – Mrs ffi – Mrs c – Mrs u – Mrs lty' (utilising rhythm and rhyming skills) for strong verbalisers
- use colour when they 'take a snapshot' of a word they want to learn (strong visualisers can recall words in colour)
- use the computer keyboard: this helps some to learn the letters because they can utilise motor memory to remember where their fingers go as well as visual memory to memorise patterns
- use a computer package with graphics to help remember pictures and associate letter patterns with the pictures (utilising ability to remember word patterns and pictures)
- use a mnemonic such as 'he can do *business* on the *bus*' with an illustration of someone working on a laptop (using visualisation skills).

It is important to be aware that for most cognitive activities both hemispheres are involved, which explains why multi-sensory strategies are so effective as a learning strategy for dyslexic people. Rawson (1987) reminded us that 'whether or not our theory is right, I do not know, but I do know that the methods of retraining which we have derived from that view point have worked'.

'The left hemisphere of the brain is the dominant side for 90 per cent of people and is responsible for speech and language processing irrespective of whether the individuals are left or right handed. Language is located in the left side of the brain for 98 per cent of right handed people and for 71 per cent of left handed people' according to Hiscock and Kinsbourne (1987).

Neurobiological research evidence

Scientific knowledge of brain structure and functioning has moved forward in gigantic leaps since Geschwind and Levitsky (1968) showed that most people have asymmetrical brains. Galaburda and Kempner (1979) in a *post mortem* study of a dyslexic man showed that his brain was symmetrical. Another significant step forward along the road to discovery about brain function and brain architecture was taken with the use of brain imaging using positron emission tomography (PET) and magnetic resonance imaging (MRI) scans. Posner et al. (1988) showed that different regions of the brain were activated by words presented visually and by words presented auditorally. Larsen et al. (1990) when using MRI scans found that 'all dyslexics with severe phonological problems had symmetry of the plana temporale'.

Lyon's (1995) study of children with dyslexia showed that the frontal regions of their brains were symmetrical.

Geschwind (cited in Galaburda 1993) 'suggested the possibility that, together with deficits related to the affected area, certain brain lesions could result in "superior functions" in the unaffected hemisphere' and that 'such a mechanism may explain the superior right hemisphere capacities exhibited by dyslexic children' (Barraquer-Bordas, 1993). However, findings from neuro-imaging (Shaywitz et al. 1998) showed that 'no fewer than seventeen regions of the brain were activated when dyslexic subjects were reading.

Electro-encephalography (EEG) was used by Molfese et al. (2002) in a sample of four hundred newborn infants to establish those who had difficulties discriminating between speech sounds. When these same children were tested when 8 years old, '14 of 17 dyslexic children 82.4 per cent' had been correctly identified at birth as having poor language skills. Neuro-imaging confirms that there is a biological basis for dyslexia.

Gardner's theory of multiple intelligences and their characteristics

Geschwind (1982) noted that 'dyslexics themselves are frequently endowed with high talents in many areas'. This characteristic was later explored by Howard Gardner.

Gardner (1987) worked as a neuropsychologist, 'studying the acquired alexias'. He was concurrently associated with the Graduate School of Education at Harvard University and involved in a research project with normal and gifted children about 'the nature and realisation of human potential'. He put forward what he himself acknowledges as 'contentious' opinions about the nature of intelligence. This was at a time when intelligence and intelligence testing had been 'placed on a very high pedestal in American society and in Western societies [including Britain] as well'. Gardner disagreed with Terman (1921) about the 'unitary view of intellect'. He challenged the views of Binet, the founding father of IQ testing (Binet and Simon 1916) who asserted that 'intelligence is a fundamental faculty . . . to judge well, to comprehend well, to reason well', argued that 'an intelligence is an ability to solve a problem or to fashion a product which is valued in one or more cultural settings'.

Gardner in his book *Frames of Mind* (1983) hypothesised that there are seven different intelligences:

1 *linguistic skills* which are involved in reading, writing, listening and talking
2 *logical and mathematical skills* which are involved in numerical computation, legal argument, solving logical puzzles and most scientific thinking
3 *spatial skills* which are used in design and technology, computer programming, marine navigation, piloting a plane, driving a car and working out how to get from A to B, figuring out one's orientation in space. They are also used in the visual arts by artists and architects, or when playing chess or when recognising faces. Certain topics in mathematics such as geometry use them.

4 *musical skills* which are involved in singing, playing an instrument, conducting an orchestra, composing and, to some extent, musical appreciation
5 *bodily and kinaesthetic skills* which are involved in the use of one's whole body or parts of it, to solve problems, construct products and displays. They are used by dancers, athletes, actors, acrobats and surgeons
6 *interpersonal skills* which are involved in understanding and acting upon one's understanding of others – noticing differences between people, reading their moods, temperaments, intentions. It is especially important in politics, sales and psychotherapy and teaching
7 *intrapersonal skills* which are involved in self-management, self-understanding symbolised in the world of dreams.

To these have been added *naturalist skills*. These are involved in landscape design and horticulture and may be possessed by gardeners, ecologists and conservationists. Gardner (1987) concluded that 'I don't think any intelligence is inherently more or less important than others'. This re-evaluation of intelligence was influential particularly for those who are dyslexic and for those who worked with dyslexic people. West (1997) argues that dyslexia is a 'gift' and that it predisposes people to skills and talents associated with the right-brain functions.

Practical implications of the theory of multiple intelligences for teachers and learners

Those who work and live with people with dyslexia – including Gardner, who observed dyslexia first-hand in his son – have 'long known that individuals learn in different ways and that education is most effective when these individual differences are taken into account or even placed at the fore' (Gardner 1987). We must teach them in ways that meet their special needs and match their particular learning styles. All pupils benefit when teaching matches their personal learning styles. For pupils with special educational needs, teaching via their personal cognitive style may include using visual, auditory, tactile or kinaesthetic learning strategies, and the choice between these can have a significant impact on the outcome.

It can mean the difference between educational success or a continuous spiral of frustration and failure. It is imperative to teach dyslexic pupils how best they learn. This is why teaching study skills (including thinking about how to think and learning about how to learn) enhances learning and has now become the linchpin for a successful outcome for those who compensate and overcome their inherent weaknesses. Knowing what to learn and how to learn makes the learning process more effective and more efficient for those who have specific learning difficulties.

The significance of learning styles and the implications for all spellers, especially dyslexic people

There has been a growing realisation among individual learners that it is important to know and understand one's own learning style, and then to develop learning strategies to maximise skills, knowledge and performance. This 'thinking about thinking' was described by Yussen (1985) and is known as metacognition. *Meta* is a Greek prefix which means 'alongside, among, co-existing'. *Gnostikos* means 'knowing, able to discern'. Metacognitive skills are an ability to study and understand how we think and the processes involved in thinking. Being aware of one's personal mental processes is considered highly significant when acquiring and implementing learning strategies.

From the mid-1940s onwards, cognitive psychologists began to study how individuals learn and why some individuals fail to learn. There are two aspects to learning. The first is: how do people learn? The second is: what methods do they use to remember what they have observed? Kolb (1976) asserted that there are four types of learner, those who:

- need to be personally involved in the learning activity
- need to follow a step-by-step sequential thinking and learning approach
- need to process and be actively involved in problem solving
- need to be involved in risk-taking and in making changes.

Learning styles theories had been developed for example by Kolb (1976), and there was a growing awareness that learning styles were linked to strengths and weaknesses and that it is possible to describe these characteristics. From this, questionnaires were developed which were used to identify learning style characteristics.

Dunn et al. (1975) were among the first to devise a diagnostic instrument to help establish preferred learning styles using self-reported methods. This later led to Dunn and Griggs (1989) advocating that teaching methods should match individuals' learning styles. This led to theories about how learning strategies should match individuals' learning styles. Cotfield et al. (2004) conducted a review of learning style theory as well as evaluating thirteen different learning style instruments. They were highly critical of the 'bedlam' of contradictory terminology, the 'status of the research, the simplistic assumptions made' and the 'overblown claims' made by some of the test authors.

There are over a hundred instruments especially designed to identify individual learning styles, according to Grinder (1991). The easiest and the quickest to use are informal questionnaires. They make statements such as 'I prefer to work on my own while I am studying' which are designed to elicit a 'yes' or 'no' response. Others include Levine's (1993) PEEX (6–9-year-olds) and PEERAMID (9–16-year-olds) and Given and Reid's (1999) *Informal Teacher and Parent Learning Style Inventory*.

Guidelines and suggestions for using learning strategies to meet the needs of poor spellers

Individuals can be shown how to recognise and be aware that they learn better when they use a particular sense such as their eyes, ears, lips or hands which equates with their cognitive style. These strategies can be tailor-made to meet the needs of the poor speller as follows:

- The spelling programme can be individualised to meet the needs and existing skills of the individual according to the developmental spelling stage. This can be established from analysing individual spelling mistakes, and from information gleaned from diagnostic standardised spelling tests.
- Teaching basic skills in a systematic way, including onset and rime, syllables and pluralisation, can be reinforced when the pupil is proofreading and editing his or her own work.

- Pupils need to be given time to practise and learn spellings. They need more intensive practice and more frequent rehearsal because skills take longer to become internalised and automaticised for them.
- A variety of spelling methods and strategies should be used which should be matched to individual learning styles, such as the Fernald method for irregular spelling. The S-O-S method for regular spellings and a computer package to reinforce and enhance visual, auditory and kinaesthetic memory should be employed.
- Using a handheld spell-checker with a list of personal 'spelling demons' is a splendid way to enhance spelling and proofreading skills.
- Using a tape recorder is a powerful tool for those with good auditory skills. Pupils look at the word, say the word and spell it aloud on tape. Then they rewind the tape and listen to themselves saying the letter names. They then write the word. Then they replay the tape while correcting the spelling.
- Bos and Reitsma (2003) conducted a survey among experienced teachers to evaluate the effectiveness of nine different spelling methods for poor spellers. Their results showed that 'offering no information' at all was considered to be least effective. For most sets of words, combining the rule strategy with spelling information about the whole word was considered the most effective exercise. They argued that, for those with good language and working memory skills rules act as a scaffold when applied.

Using preferred cognitive style to match preferred learning style

Such skills are linked to hemispheric specialisation and to brain functions carried out in the left or right hemispheres. Gardner's theory of multiple intelligence has great significance, particularly for dyslexic individuals, on how individuals should learn and be taught. Riding et al. (1997) carried out a research study using EEG and found 'a clear link between both of the style dimensions and brain cortical activity' and argued that 'the finding of significant style effects on EEG is important as providing physiological evidence for the existence of style'.

The preferred learning style can be established by using an informal learning styles inventory which will identify how individuals prefer to learn and what learning strategies to use.

Visual learners

It can identify visual learners who:

- learn from pictures and diagrams
- like to use mind maps and colour such as when planning essays or note taking
- draw, doodle, use cartoons to memorise key facts and mnemonics
- take a 'snapshot' in their mind's eye of a page from a book or a scenic view of a place they have visited
- can recall in their mind's eye faces and patterns as well as the layout of diagrams or maps
- find spelling using analogy and word patterns helpful because they are poor synthesisers and have poor phonological skills
- find that videos, film and overhead transparencies are effective means of learning.

MATCHING TEACHING METHODS TO LEARNING STYLES 111

Auditory learners

It can identify auditory learners who:

- listen and remember
- can follow lectures and discussion and remember the content
- have good oral memory skills and can remember the words of songs, ditties or poems and use them to learn and remember
- use music and rhythm and rhyme to enhance memory, recall and understanding
- shine in oral tests
- find tape recorders and personal stereos useful when learning.

Tactile/kinaesthetic learners

It can identify tactile or kinaesthetic learners who:

- like to make notes while listening
- remember by making a model such as by baking a cake
- find that visiting a museum, exhibition or a factory shop floor enhances their learning and recall
- find that the computer and CD-ROMs are a great enabler for them

Knowing and understanding individuals' learning style can be used to enhance skills including spelling.

Checklists to establish an individual's preferred spelling style

Visual skills

		Never	Sometimes	Often
1	I have to think hard to remember how some letters are made.			
2	I compare words with others with similar spelling patterns, such as 'bring' with 'swing'.			
3	I find it hard to copy spellings accurately from the board.			
4	I find it hard to proofread. I don't pick up on my own mistakes.			
5	Sometimes when I am asked to copy out and correct my own spelling mistakes I make mistakes when copying the corrections.			
6	I find it hard to learn spellings if the font is very small.			
7	I sometimes miscopy spellings from the board when given lists for a test.			
8	I spell the same word in different ways on a page of text.			
9	Sometimes my teachers say my spelling errors are due just to carelessness because I make mistakes with spelling homophones such as 'two'/'to'/'too'.			

	Never	*Sometimes*	*Often*
10 Some days my spelling is fine, other days, especially when I am tired, I make mistakes in words like 'because', 'were'.			
11 I sometimes make the same mistake over and over again in words like 'their'.			
12 I sometimes put letters in the wrong order in the words. I know that I have seen the word before but I simply cannot remember the correct order for the letters.			
13 I sometimes rehearse the word and try spelling it in different ways and then check to see which version 'looks' right.			

Auditory skills

	Never	*Sometimes*	*Often*
1 I find it hard to remember the wording of spelling rules.			
2 I find it hard to remember the sentences with mnemonics such as 'I will eat a piece of pie'.			
3 I sometimes omit letters and syllables from words such as 'rember' for 'remember'.			
4 I sometimes confuse words that sound alike such as 'are' and 'our' 'witch' and 'which'.			
5 I sometimes confuse the spelling of words including certain sounds such as /chip/ for ship, /fan/ for van.			
6 I find it difficult to learn spellings by rote memorisation.			
7 I find it hard to sound out words. Sometimes I leave out bits of the word.			
8 I sometimes say when I rehearse a word that I want to spell, 'that doesn't sound right'.			
9 It helps me to spell words if I clap out the syllables.			
10 I find it helpful if I use the spelling pronunciation when I break words into syllables such as /Wed/ /nes/ /day/.			
11 I use a tape recorder and spell the words out. Then I press play and listen to the letters. Then I repeat this until I can spell the word.			
12 I find it helpful to spell the word aloud.			
13 I sometimes whisper the word to myself under my breath.			
14 I find that using headphones when using the computer helps when I type and listen to the spelling.			

	Never	Sometimes	Often
15 I find it helpful to use the spelling rules such as 'q and u go together'.			

Tactile/kinaesthetic skills

	Never	Sometimes	Often
1 I have to write spellings down to remember the letters.			
2 I find that my spelling improves when I use the computer. My fingers help me to remember the letter pattern.			
3 It helps me to remember my spellings if I copy them out when I learn for a test.			
4 It helps if I use word patterns and get these to rhyme with similar words and tap these out with my fingers.			
5 I find it useful to use strategies such as 'chin slapping' or clapping when I am counting syllables.			
6 I find it useful to jot down spellings and my fingers seem to remember the syllable patterns of letters.			
7 I find that using a dictionary to find a spelling and then copying it out helps me to remember the spelling.			
8 I sometimes trace words on the table with my finger before I write them.			
9 I find that using a spell-checker helps me learn the spellings.			
10 I sometimes 'skywrite' spellings with my finger.			
11 When I want to spell a word I just think about where my fingers go on the keyboard and this helps me to remember the letters.			

SUMMARY AND CONCLUSIONS

1 Employers often express concerns about literacy standards of employees who are poor at spelling.

2 The government has continued to try to improve the teaching of spelling in the nation's schools.

3 There are lessons to learn from the classic teaching methods and strategies for spelling derived from some of the great educators and master teachers of the twentieth century.

continued

4   'Dyslexia is one of the key disorders in the systematic investigation of the architecture of the mind' (Frith 1997). Biological evidence produced by the neuroscientists who study brain function and brain structure has increased understanding about the condition and is now beginning to have a major impact on diagnosis and remediation for practitioners and for people with dyslexia. Roger Sperry was awarded a Nobel Prize for Medicine in 1981 for 'his research on left-brain and right-brain hemisphere brain functions'. This has significance for theorists and practitioners. The understanding of the brain's architecture is beginning to yield explanations for dyslexic people's exciting talents. The use of MRI scanners produces crystal-clear images of the body, including the brain, and can be used to determine the parts of the brain that respond to various thoughts and processes when using *in vivo* brain imaging equipment. Sir Peter Mansfield was awarded a Nobel Prize for Medicine in 2003 for his work in changing the face of medical research and diagnosis. The search for further explanations and how best to use this information has just begun.

5   There is a shifting of emphasis away from the discrepancies and difficulties manifested by dyslexia, to a groundswell of interest in the positive attributes of the condition spearheaded by Gardner's theory of multiple intelligences. He asserted that intelligence is a collection of separate, independent but interacting functions (cited in Gross 1999). This has been linked to anecdotal evidence of successful and talented dyslexic people who often have good right-brained skills. A study conducted on three hundred millionaires 'found that 40 per cent of the businessmen and women they studied were diagnosed with learning difficulties and they hypothesised that "dyslexia" can turn out to be a route to riches' (Gill 2003).

6   There is consensus of opinion that individuals learn in different ways. Different individuals have ingrained preferences for how they learn best. Teaching thinking skills, and the learning strategies to complement these such as mind-mapping, have become a buzzword in education circles and have now begun to be adapted for use in mainstream classrooms.

7   The challenge for educators is to identify these individual cognitive styles. Coffield (2005) evaluated '13 different learning styles instruments but only one met the minimal criteria for a proper psychological test'. Meanwhile teachers will have to use informal measures to show individuals how to maximise their learning and minimise their weaknesses by using an appropriate learning strategy to match their learning style for the task being undertaken.

8   There are a number of outstanding issues to be resolved about learning styles. For instance, not all children find mind mapping effective or useful, as is sometimes claimed. It works especially well for those who are strong visual learners. Should, for example, teachers attempt to modify their mode of presentation and the resources they use to meet the specific needs of individual pupils? How can individual differences be catered for in mainstream classrooms? The good news is that technology including multi-media resources, can help to make it possible to match individual cognitive and learning styles in dyslexia-friendly classrooms.

9 Assessment, Identification of Difficulties, Spelling Error Analysis

- Popular prevailing trends for monitoring spelling standards and progress in schools
- An overview of some of the difficulties experienced by poor spellers
- Guidelines for test selection to ensure appropriate tools for the job
- Suggestions and options for popular spelling tests
- Can spelling errors be classified?
- Practical implications for practitioners from spelling error analysis
- Using miscue analysis as a window on an individual's spelling difficulties
- Hallmark features and patterns of errors made by poor spellers, particularly those with dyslexia
- Are there differences between the spelling of individuals with dyslexia and normal spellers?
- 'My Spelling'
- Sixty-nine ways to spell 'dyslexia'
- Summary and conclusions

Keywords

Analytical errors
'Chinese' spelling style
Cloze
Criterion reference tests
Discrepancy criteria
Individual Education Plan (IEP)
Invented spellings
Liquid sounds
Miscue analysis

Morphophonological errors
Norm-referenced tests
Percentiles
Phonetic errors
'Phoenician' spelling style
Phonological errors
Raw scores
Schwa vowels
SEN Tribunals

Spelling age
Spelling quotients
Standard age score (SAS)
Standard deviation scores
Standardised scores
Standardised spelling tests
Stanines
Statement

Popular prevailing trends for monitoring spelling standards and progress in schools

Generations of schoolchildren have traditionally been subjected to a weekly spelling test. The aim and objectives of the weekly spelling test vary from school to school and from classroom to classroom. Preparation for and administration of the test also vary. Teaching and testing include some of the following processes, and words chosen to study for the test could have been included for the following reasons.

- Lists of words were taken from spelling books. Some of the spelling word lists were graded according to word frequency, difficulty and the age of the pupils, such as Schonell's *Essential Spelling List* (1932) of 3,200 words which he compiled from Thorndike and Lorge's (1944) Word List and Horn's (1926) *Basic Writing Vocabulary* as well as from his own studies of London elementary schoolchildren.
- Weekly tests have included lists of words of a particular letter pattern, the so-called 'word family' lists such as Brand's (1984).
- Lists of 'the most common and appropriate words' such as those that were included in the National Literacy Strategy's Spelling Bank (DfEE 1999) have been used.
- Lists of high-frequency words such as those given in the *National Literacy Strategy Framework for Teaching* (DfEE 1998) have been used. The NLS also recommended 'copying out personal misspellings six times, then being re-tested on these at a later date.'
- Lists from a specialist teaching programme such as Alpha to Omega (Hornsby and Shear 1994) have been used.
- The Key Stage 3 National Strategy (DfEE 2001a) included lists for subject spelling and a general list. *The Key Stage 3 National Strategy* (DfEE 2001b) Spelling Bank includes guidance for spelling objectives with lists of examples and a spelling list of 'commonly misspelled' words to learn.
- Lists of awkward or irregular spellings including spelling demons, the 'odd-bods' (Ott 1997) or '100 words most often misspelled by children' (Johnson 1950) have been used.
- Individual teachers generated lists from words misspelt by pupils or from subject vocabulary across the curriculum and then wrote the words on the board. Pupils copied the words into their spelling notebook. This is known as the 'test-study' method, which the report of the Scottish Council for Research (1961) said had 'one vital omission; there is no indication to the child of the way in which he should set about learning the spellings of the word'. The DfEE (2001c) quotes Crystal (1995) who pleaded that 'a major factor [in poor spelling] is that children are rarely taught how to spell'. The instruction usually was to learn these spellings for the test which would take place one week later. The lists were often sent home to be learnt, usually with the help and support of parents or carers. Some children learned the set spelling by saying the names of the individual letters aloud. Other children copied out the spellings and were tested for mastery by their parents. The number of practices depended on the complexity of the spelling list and on the skills of the learner as well as the different criteria used by teachers for the construction of lists.
- The weekly spelling test was part and parcel of most school curricula for well over a hundred years. Spellings were tested, and the results individual children achieved

were frequently read out in public, and those who attained a perfect score were given a merit award which could be displayed on the classroom wall. The fate of the poor performers often depended on the teacher's perception of the child, who was judged by whether he or she was 'lazy', 'stupid', 'idle', or had some sort of 'learning difficulty' or retardation'.

- Some teachers gave 'mammoth tests' of up to a hundred words, often at the end of the term or the end of year. These words could be a summary of the term's or year's work.
- Teachers and individuals have long known that some pupils are naturally good spellers. These individuals know how to spell the majority of words in their day-to-day writing. They can memorise more difficult words, and remember them when they have studied them, and they get full marks in the weekly spelling test. They can later recall how to spell these words in their personal writing.
- Teachers, individuals and parents have also been aware that some pupils, despite inordinate efforts to learn spellings, have great difficulty remembering individual words or word patterns and gain consistently low scores in weekly tests.
- Other individuals can memorise spellings and remember them for the test. However, they may misspell the same words in a week's time or when they use them when multi-tasking in their own writing.

An overview of some of the difficulties experienced by poor spellers

Poor spellers include those who:

- struggle with letter sound–symbol matches because of poor phonemic skills. They often confuse the vowel spellings and have great difficulties with the unstressed 'schwa' vowel sounds.
- can spell phonetically regular words but find non-phonetic spellings very challenging
- develop spelling skills, and can visualise words and remember them when writing the spellings in isolation for a test, but forget these same words when using them during various writing processes
- spell erratically: skills appear to break down in situations involving speed and stress, particularly during examinations or tests.
- have poor phonological skills and cannot grasp the code. These include individuals with dyslexia, including adults who have overcome their earlier reading difficulties.

Spell-checkers provide limited help for some profoundly poor spellers, often because their reading skills are so limited that they cannot make the correct choice of spelling, leading them to use bizarre corrections such as 'gypsy tummy' for 'gyppy tummy'. Spell-checkers with a speech option can help to eliminate this type of error.

There are many good diagnostic tests of spelling on the market which may be used to establish performance in spelling. Informal testing provides some information about competence or weaknesses, but standardised scores are essential for purposes of comparison, accuracy and reliability. They are also important when setting attainment targets, and when monitoring progress when children have special educational needs and have been given an individual education plan (IEP). They also form an important part of the battery of tests used in the assessment of specific learning difficulties. Frith (2002) argued that 'spelling, being a more demanding task, is a more sensitive test and is likely to reveal dyslexia more readily than reading'.

Guidelines for test selection to ensure appropriate tools for the job

Standardised spelling tests have been developed as a result of testing a large representative sample of pupils. A scale of average scores is worked out from these results which can then be used to compare performance nationally, and attainment levels with other pupils of a similar age. Standardised tests are designed to produce the same results whenever and wherever they are administered because they have been trialled on large cross-sections of pupils over a wide locality. Standardised tests should normally not be repeated within a period of six months.

Before making a decision about which tests to buy, the following factors should be considered.

Cost is a major factor. Some tests are very expensive, such as the *Wide Range Achievement Test* (WRAT) (Wilkinson 1993). Test booklets such as the British Spelling Test Series booklets are an additional expense that has to be budgeted for. Photocopying of test booklets is often not permitted.

Age-range bands can be narrow, such as in the Parallel Spelling Tests, which may mean having to buy a series of the same tests. The wider the age span the better, particularly when the pupil is functioning well below or well above the chronological age, as often happens in the case of individuals with dyslexia.

The time it takes to administer the test is an important consideration. This has become increasingly significant because of the number of pupils involved in screening programmes and assessments that Special Education Needs Co-ordinators (SENCOs) are required to undertake. Some tests can now be corrected and marked using a computer package. It is important that the test meets the educational objective. Cost-cutting or saving time should be a secondary consideration.

There is often a necessity for a broad range of information when writing individual education plans (IEPs). These require difficulties to be enumerated as well as advice on processes, strategies and short-term goals which are 'different from or in addition to those' used by the majority. These should be S-M-A-R-T targets, which according to Lloyd and Berthelot (1992) are:

- Specific
- Measurable
- Achievable
- Relevant
- Time related

Tests such as the British Spelling Test Series are useful because they test different spelling subskills which can be targeted for improvement, such as visual discrimination when proofreading written work or auditory discrimination when doing dictation.

Parallel forms when available are useful for monitoring progress and for annual reviews. They are also useful when measuring and comparing targets with those recommended by the National Curriculum, and by the *National Literacy Strategy, Framework for Teaching* (DfEE 1998). Parallel forms of tests such as Young's (1998) lessen the chance of overexposure from frequent repetition through the school years, and the temptation to 'teach' the test words specifically or even inadvertently.

Are the results valid and does the test measure or assess what it claims to? Thomson (2001) surmised that 'a psychological or educational test is simply a means of measurement and, as we shall see, the names given to tests are sometimes quite arbitrary and do not necessarily reflect accurately the underlying cognitive or behavioural traits that they purport to measure'.

The vogue is for shorter tests, often because of time constraints. Turner (1997) maintained that the *Wide Range Achievement Test* (WRAT) (Wilkinson 1993) 'with only 40 items is efficient'. On the other hand Moats (1995) postulated that 'test scores that are based on two or three items are unreliable' and argued that it may be necessary to add supplementary words of 'appropriately selected list of words at the person's instructional level'. Some of the older tests, such as Schonell (1932), had more target words which provided more examples for a miscue analysis of spelling errors which are diagnostically significant as well as useful for practitioners when planning teaching intervention. However, this test is no longer recommended because its norms are outdated and it does not provide a 'standardised score'.

Is a test suitable for the task and is it appropriate for the current skills of the pupil? It is inappropriate to test a pupil with English as a second language if it has been designed for pupils with English as their mother tongue. There are problems associated with translations, such as the word-for-word difficulties, but even more important are the issues involving the test 'concepts'.

It is important to be aware that the contents and reliability of some tests are controversial. Once popular tests may be outdated and do not take into account the findings of up-to-date research about, for example, dyslexia. Turner (1997) commented that 'the Vincent and Claydon Diagnostic Spelling Test (Vincent and Claydon 1982) is based on the work of Margaret Peters and the hypothesis which has lost ground in the 1980s and 1990s, that spelling is a visual skill'.

Are the norms reliable? Will the same results be obtained when used across an age range of pupils and on different occasions, such as for a progress reviews? Will the results be the same when the tests are administered by different testers?

Does a test include a standardised score? A standardised score of 100 is average. It can be used to compare the child's performance with pupils nationally and of the same age. The percentile rank shows where the pupil ranks nationally with pupils of the same age. If a pupil is on the tenth percentile, it means that 90 per cent of pupils did better than he or she did. Examination boards such as the Qualifications and Curriculum Authority and the Joint Council for General Qualifications) specify that attainments must be recorded as 'standard scores' when submissions are made for access arrangements. Standardised scores are also required when pupils are being assessed according to the Code of Practice Guidelines, and play a significant part in for example the decision whether to statement a pupil when using the discrepancy criteria.

Do the tests provide sufficient information? Some of the newer tests are very short. Some spelling tests do not provide sufficient information for analysis and for the diagnostic evidence required when identifying special educational needs which call for 'special educational provision' because a pupil is having a significantly greater difficulty in learning than the majority of children of the same age'. In Frith's (1997) opinion 'tests always tap many different underlying abilities and are subject to many influences' and 'a score, regardless of whether it is within the normal range or not is only a good pointer'. It is therefore important to be aware that test results represent a sample of the individual's performance on a specific task and that many underlying factors can affect the results. They provide a snapshot about skills, which is why tests of extended pieces of writing also play an important role in the diagnosis of special learning difficulties (SpLD) which affect certain cognitive skills as opposed to a general learning difficulty which affects most aspects of learning (Ott 1997). This is particularly important when assessing adults.

Is a test up to date? Tests with norms pre-dating 1980 are regarded by critics as unreliable because of developments and changes to vocabulary, culture, research findings and the curriculum. The research findings of Brooks, Gordon and Kendall (1993) showed that a 'decline in spelling standards over many years has invalidated the results of some tests'. Turner and Chew (2003) compared performance on the WRAT, Vernon and Schonell tests and concluded that 'Schonell tends to produce a consistently lower "spelling age", especially with older pupils' because of 'a consistent decline in standards of spelling for this age group [sixth form college students] over fifty years, at least among pupils of average ability or below'. All three tests showed 'a high intercorrelation' 'but only the WRAT-3 offers norms that reflect contemporary standards in spelling ability'.

Is the test user-friendly? Training is required in the use of some tests. Many tests require practice, particularly when errors and the pupil's responses have to be recorded, such as when administering a reading test, for later analysis. Is the manual useful and helpful? What restrictions, if any, are placed on the use of the test? Some, such as the Wechsler Objective Reading Dimensions (WORD) (Wechsler 1993), which also has a spelling test, are 'closed' tests and their use is restricted to clinical and educational psychologists or to specialist teachers using them 'under the supervision of a psychologist'. This test also provides an 'expected' standardised score which relates to the IQ for comparison with the 'observed (actual) standardised score which indicates the discrepancy, if any, which can have statistical significance'.

Are there different spelling options available, such as dictated word lists, including regular and irregular words, proofreading or written cloze procedures (which involve fitting in missing letters, missing words or missing parts of sentences (Ott 1997))? Each of these tests different aspects of spelling skills, such as in the British Spelling Test Series (Vincent and Crumpler 1997). However it is important to be mindful that 'it is also useless to give a test of proof-reading ability or one that has multiple choice answers and hope to make inferences about written spelling generated by the student' according to Moats (1995).

The Richmond Test of Basic Skills (Hieronymus et al. 1988) includes a spelling test which consists of 114 questions for all six levels of attainment. Spelling is assessed by using lists of four given words. The objective of the test is to 'look for mistakes in spelling' or to be able to decide that there are 'no spelling mistakes'.

Measuring spelling skills by this method can be compared to those who consider a single-word recognition test as a reliable measure of reading skills. The British Psychological Society's Working Party's report *Dyslexia, Literacy and Psychological Assessment* (1999) stated that 'dyslexia is evident when accurate and fluent word reading and/or spelling develops very incompletely or with great difficulty'. Eminent practising psychologists such as Thomson (2001) found this 'ironic' and Burden (2002) found it 'naïve and unhelpful' as a definition of dyslexia. Reading and spelling skills encompass many more underlying skills which cannot be measured accurately or reliably using single word recognition tests or single word dictated spellings.

Tests such as the Richmond test do not provide enough information about spelling skills, nor do they provide sufficient material to carry out a miscue analysis of the errors which is a crucial part of the diagnostic procedures used to identify specific learning difficulties. Moats (1995) concluded that 'thorough assessment should also include direct tests of related processing skills such as phonological analysis of words, handwriting speed and accuracy, recognition of orthographic patterns and knowledge of specific sound/symbol relationships'.

Suggestions and options for popular spelling tests

Popular spelling tests used in the UK

Unless stated otherwise single word spelling tests take 3–5 minutes depending on age and ability.

Title	Author, date and publisher	Age range	Administration time	Content
Graded Word Spelling Test	P.E. Vernon (1983) 2nd edition (1998) (Hodder and Stoughton, London)	6–16 years		Single word dictated test Recommended by JCGQ (2002).
Single Word Spelling Test	L. Sacre and J. Masterson (2002) (NFER-Nelson, London)	6–14 years	30 minutes	Nine tests graded to match Key Stages 1, 2, 3. Includes NLS: high-frequency lists, and NLS Spelling Bank words.
WORD: Wechsler Objective Reading Dimension (includes a spelling test)	D. Wechsler (1993) (Harcourt Assessment, Oxford)	6–16 years 11 months		The scores on these tests and the scores on the WISC IQ test can be used to establish a predicted standard. 'This discrepancy analysis is, in my opinion a crucial first stage in the identification of specific learning difficulties because it points to specific underachievement' (Thomson 2001).
The Wide Range Achievement Test – 3 (WRAT – 3)	G.S. Wilkinson (1993) (Harcourt Assessment, Oxford)	5–75 years		Short test consisting of forty target words in total. It includes a test of letter name(s) and letter writing as well as individual dictated words. Contains no American English spelling. It includes a standardised score. It has two forms.
The British Spelling Test Series	D. Vincent and M. Crumpler (1997) (NFER – Nelson, London)	5–24+ years	30–40 minutes	Five different levels and parallel forms of each. battery of tests including: single word dictated spellings; cloze questions; dictated passage, proofreading and correction of spelling errors. The British Spelling Test Series 3

continued

Popular spelling tests used in the UK (continued)

Title	Author, date and publisher	Age range	Administration time	Content
				has an age range of 9 years 11 months to 15 years 1 month. Someone with a severe specific learning difficulty with a chronological age of 10 years may be able to spell only a few words correctly on the test. BSTS 2 may be more appropriate choice and provide more relevant information for a miscue analysis.
Parallel Spelling Tests	D. Young (1998) (Hodder and Stoughton Educational, London)	6–15 years	20 minutes	6 tests for each year group: 'tests offer an effective and useful way of measuring attainment in spelling in relation to the requirements of the National Curriculum and the National Literacy Strategy Framework for Teaching' (Young 1998).

Popular spelling tests used in the US

Some of these are now widely available and used in the UK.
These single word spelling tests take 3–5 minutes depending on age and ability

Title	Author, date and Publisher	Age range	Content
Peabody Individual Achievement Test – Revised (PIAT – Revised)	American Guidance Service, Circle Pines, Minnesota	5–17 years	Part of diagnostic battery of tests including a spelling test.
Test of Written Spelling – 2 (TWS – 2)	S.C. Larsen and D.D, Hammill (1986) (Pro-Ed, Austin, Texas)	6–17 years	This includes regular and irregular word lists.
Woodcock-Johnson Tests of Achievement (Revised)	R.W. Woodcock and M.B. Johnson (1989) (Action Dyslexia, Egham)		Part of a diagnostic battery of tests including word spelling and proofreading.
Kaufman Test of Educational Achievement (K – TEA)	A.S. Kaufman and N.L. Kaufman (1983) (Harcourt Assessment, Oxford)	6–17 years	Includes words with prefixes and suffixes. Useful to establish the nature of individual difficulties. Can be used to establish the appropriate level of instruction.

Can spelling errors be classified?

Treiman (1993) undertook a study of the spellings of 43 6- and 7-year-old children for a period of two school years. Her findings were published in a text which is a tour de force of 350 pages of facts, figures and opinions and also includes a review of the literature on spelling. She classified the 5,617 spelling errors she collected.

HANDY HINT

Treiman divided errors into two categories. One she called legal errors, which 'are thought to indicate the use of the phonological spelling route' such as 'kat' for cat. Illegal errors 'point to use of rote memorisation or unsuccessful use of the phonological route' such as 'braod' for broad (the 'Phoenician' approach). Today these errors would be ascribed to someone as using a visuo-spatial 'Chinese' approach. She proclaimed that an 'appreciation of the knowledge that lies behind the children's errors can help teachers respond to the errors appropriately'.

Practical implications for practitioners from spelling error analysis

Treiman's (1993) main findings were that

- Children omit unstressed (schwa) vowels more frequently: 'vegetable' 'machine'.
- The more phonemes in a word, the more likely it is that the vowel is omitted.
- Vowels are omitted more often in the middle of words than at the beginning or end of words. This why learners often find it hard to spell words with magic 'e' when he wants to spell the word 'ate'. The letters 'a' and 't' are in much closer approximation to what spellers hear. They say 'aye', 'tee' because the letter names are a good match for what their ears hear.
- Vowel-consonant 'r' spellings are challenging. Children have a tendency to omit the vowel before the 'r' ('nachr' for nature).
- They have a tendency to omit 'l' and 'r' ('mik' for milk; 'gaden' for garden).
- They sometimes omit the second consonant when using consonant-blend spellings. This type of error accounted for 27 per cent of the total errors made ('crips' for crisps).
- They often omit the nasal letters 'n' and 'm' at the end of syllables or words particularly when there is a voiceless consonant such as in the assimilations 'ng' 'nt' 'nk' 'nd' 'mp' ('wet' for went).
- They are more likely to omit a consonant in a rime than in the onset of a word. Treiman concluded 'that children's spelling is to a large extent, an attempt to represent the phonological forms of words. It is not just an attempt to reproduce memorised sequences of letters.' This has important implications for how all children should be taught spelling, particularly those with specific learning difficulties, and shows the importance of teaching systematic, synthetic phonics to beginners.

Louisa Moats's (1995) work has also been very influential in the study of spelling errors, and for an understanding of how individuals learn to spell. It highlights specific difficulties as well as establishing what the speller knows about spelling, and helps identify strategies used to spell.

She began, when known as Louisa Cook (1981), by studying the spelling errors of children. Later, as Moats, (1983) she compared the errors of older dyslexic children with younger normal spellers and then studied adolescent spellers' errors and classified them. She (Moats 1995) reported that 'through grade six and beyond, a large proportion of common spelling errors occurs on words having suffixes that change the spelling of a base word, especially those that involve the doubling rule and the silent e rule'. Children also had difficulties with spelling the past tense of verbs when 'ed' is added. The various ways of spelling, for example, /k/ sound was problematic, as was the spelling of schwa vowel sounds particularly in words with Latin origins.

Using miscue analysis as a window on an individual's spelling difficulties

Good spellers use a variety of strategies including phonological, morphological, semantic and orthographic knowledge which develop with age and experience. Poor spellers need to be taught these skills systematically over time to compensate for their weaknesses or failure to acquire these skills. Evidence of the non-emergence of skills to match normal development, or persistent difficulties in automising these skills, can be found by an analysis of their errors using miscue analysis.

This can be carried out by examining spelling errors which have been recorded during testing with standardised tests, as well as by examining the spelling errors made in an extended sample of the pupil's writing. The errors are scrutinised after testing, and are analysed and categorised. They can provide a snapshot of the underlying weaknesses in spelling such as poor phonological skills and/or poor visual sequential memory, as well as evidence about the strategies used by the speller.

This information can later be used when writing individual education plans (IEPs). Spelling error analysis plays a significant role in the diagnosis and later remediation of dyslexia. It frequently highlights and indicates a pattern of errors:

- Poor phonemic knowledge: 'kat' for cat
- Poor phonological awareness: 'finkin' for thinking
- Poor orthographic knowledge of individual letters or word patterns: 'brite' for bright
- Poor morphemic knowledge: 'mendid' for mended
- Poor sight vocabulary with high-frequency irregular spellings: 'thay' for they.

The information may include analogical errors which are made when an individual attempts to match a word from visual memory to a particular word pattern, such as spelling 'nite' for night 'because it rhymes with bite'. Good spellers make comments about spellings and say, 'That does not look right.' Others say, 'Oh! I can spell "bought" so sought must have the same letters.'

The errors may include phonetic errors which are made when there is a mismatch between phonemes (sounds) in words and the graphemes (letters) that represent the sounds such as 'cet' for get, 'pot' for pod or 'pit' for pet. These errors arise as the result of poor phoneme awareness due to an inability to match the sound segments in words to the letters that represent these sounds. In other words spellers are unable to tune in their ears to sounds in words and then match these to the letters that represent them.

They may include orthographic errors which are made by those who cannot visualise letter shapes and letter patterns. They may reverse or invert letters as well as transposing the order of letters in whole words: 'left' for felt. This is also an indication of poor visual sequential memory.

Spellers may look at the letters on the page, but when they attempt to copy them they cannot retain letter the pattern. They produce spellings such as 'dune', 'deon', 'dun', 'done' because of their working memory difficulties, so the spelling may have the letters miscopied in incorrect order, for instance when doing spelling corrections for homework.

Mistakes may involve phonological errors which are made when there is a mismatch between knowledge of word parts such as syllables, endings, blends, vowel digraphs: for example 'rember' for remember; 'crips' for crisps; 'tran' for train. These errors arise as a result of poor phonological awareness due to an inability to identify, manipulate, segment and blend individual consonants and vowels. Another explanation for these is that the individual has poor auditory sequential memory: because of working memory difficulties he or she cannot remember the sound segments for long enough to transcribe them into the letters to represent the parts of a word.

When analysed and categorised, spelling errors can be used to plan appropriate and effective intervention. This information is also useful when included in IEPs when short-term targets which are 'different from or additional to those' of a pupil's peers are specified. Miscue analysis might indicate that the pupil is having persistent difficulties with segmenting words, which would indicate the need for work on syllable skills, or it might pinpoint the need to teach the pupil to use different strategies such as the 'look-say-cover-write-check' method to match his or her learning style.

Hallmark features and patterns of errors made by poor spellers, particularly those with dyslexia

These can be categorised as follows.

Phonemic or orthographic errors

- These arise because the individual is unsure of how to match individual letters to sounds in the initial medial or final position, as in 'diraf' for giraffe; 'peg' for pig; 'waks' for wax.
- The child is unable to segment words into the individual phonemes and match these to the correct letters, as in 'dg' for dog.
- Children confuse homophones, as in 'tow' or 'otw' for two. Some would call these visual sequential memory errors.
- Children reverse and invert whole words or letters, as in 'bol' for doll; 'left' for felt; 'conld' for could.
- The speller may transpose the order of letters in words, as in 'aingn' for again which Goulandris and Snowling (1991) attributed to poor visual memory.
- Incorrect letters are doubled, as in 'eeg' for egg; 'speeling' for spelling. This also indicates that a visual approach is the main spelling strategy.

Phonological errors

These arise because the individual is unable to discriminate between individual sounds, synthesise the sounds or process all the parts of words, especially multisyllabic words.

Muter et al. (1998a) found that segmentation ability in children of 4 to 6 years was a predictor of reading ability and that grammar and phonology contributed significantly to the development of spelling ability in the same children at 9 years (Muter et al. 1998b). Kibel and Miles's (1994) studies showed that 'dyslexics often failed to spell consonants in clusters', as in 'bot' for blot.

- Letters are omitted particularly in blends, as in 'dum' for drum.
- There is a confusion between the consonants used at the end of words, as in 'pot' for pod; 'lid' for lit.
- Short vowels are confused, as in 'pet' for pit.
- The nasals are sometimes omitted, as in 'lad' for land; 'youg' for young.
- /m/ and /n/ are confused in 'phome' for phone.
- Long vowel spellings are confused, as in 'roill' for royal; 'lowd' for loud.
- Consonant digraphs are confused, particularly at the end of words, as in 'cach' for cash.
- Incorrect boundaries are used, as in 'al ways' for always; 'onsuponton' for once upon a time'.
- Some omit vowels from syllables, as in 'amnt' for amount; 'rman' for remain.
- Letters are added to words, as in 'ftyer' for fire.
- Syllables are omitted as in 'intring' for interesting.

Morphophonological errors

- The past tense of the verb is problematic. The concept of adding 'ed' does not become automised and poor spellers' difficulties are compounded by their phonological difficulties and their tendency to spell phonologically. In practice this means that /t/ /d/ /id/ are used at the end of verbs because this is the perceived sound-to-symbol match: 'walkt' for walked; 'filld' for filled; 'rentid' for rented. Good spellers use their semantic skills and grammatical knowledge to deal with these words.
- Omission or addition of letters for plurals is also found: *'wishis'* for wishes; *'babyes'* for babies.
- Pupils are unsure of the spelling conventions when adding suffixes, such as the rules for doubling when adding suffixes, or the rules for adding suffixes to words ending in 'e': *'hoped'* for hopped; *'lovley'* for lovely.
- Pupils confuse prefixes, as in *'inposible'* for impossible.

Types of errors commonly made

Sawyer et al. (1999) conducted a study to examine the phonological coding errors of a hundred pupils aged 7 to 15 years who had been assessed as having dyslexic difficulties, to examine among other things the 'types of errors commonly made'. The results were presented as percentages of the total number of errors made from 2,025 given words:

1	Nasals (adds/deletes/substitutes m or n)	5.14%
2	Substitutes nasal for liquid sounds	0.04%
3	Liquids (adds/deletes/substitutes l or r)	4.34%
4	Omitted consonant (excludes m, n, l, r)	3.11%

5	Substitutes consonants	16.49%
6	Adds consonants	3.06%
7	Adds final e	10.96%
8	Substitutes vowel	39.75%
9	Omits vowel	2.22%
10	Omits final e	3.16%
11	Incorrect sequence	2.02%
12	Substitutes word	1.73%
13	Reversal	7.41%

Are there differences between the spelling of individuals with dyslexia and normal spellers?

There is a consensus that 'as compared to normal children of the same age, dyslexics perform poorly on any type of spelling test' (Treiman 1997). There is an ongoing debate surrounding these issues. 'Poor spellers do use qualitatively different spelling strategies i.e. their spelling is "deviant" rather than simply "delayed"' (Brown and Ellis 1994). Caravolas et al. (2003), when comparing English and French-speaking poor spellers, showed that English poor spellers were 'significantly more handicapped, by the writing system than the counterparts learning a more consistent orthography (i.e. French). 'The more important finding is that poor spellers of both English and French produce fewer phonologically acceptable attempts than their skilled peers.' On the other hand Treiman (1997) reiterated that 'dyslexics' spelling errors are qualitatively similar to those of younger normal children. Far from being bizarre or unmotivated, dyslexics' misspellings usually have a linguistic basis.'

When doing a miscue analysis it is important to be aware that there can be a variety of explanations for individual spelling errors, such as a pupil who spells 'holiday' as 'nld'. The use of 'n' for 'h' in 'holiday' can be explained as a lack of orthographic knowledge because the pupil did not know what 'h' looked like. It can also be explained as due to poor visual perception, because the pupil cannot remember the shape of the letter and thus omits the ascender in 'h'. This could also be attributed to poor motor memory skills because the pupil cannot automatically remember how to write 'h'. The use of the initial and final letters shows that the pupil has poor phonological skills and can perceive only the first and last sound, probably because they have poor auditory working memory. The omission of two of the syllables can be explained as due to poor phonological awareness. The omission of 'day' can be explained as due to poor morphemic knowledge.

HANDY HINT

It is important to be aware that error types do not always fit neatly into defined categories when a miscue analysis of spelling is undertaken.

However, a pattern of errors often becomes apparent in an individual child's written work over an extended period, such as when there is evidence of phonological errors repeated in several assignments. Learning style and learning strategies will also be evident and can provide useful information about gaps in underlying skills. Evidence may also be provided about the teaching method used, as with the dyslexic pupil who has had an intensive phonics programme of spelling instruction and who uses that as their only spelling strategy.

HANDY HINT

When doing a diagnostic assessment for dyslexia, the results of ten to fifteen minutes of 'free writing' are useful for corroborative evidence of a spelling error pattern. This may or may not be evident from the results of the standardised tests, particularly if spelling attainments have been measured by a dictated list of single words. Word lists that have regular spellings are easier than those that include irregular spellings. This is also significant when assessing older pupils, particularly those who may have had additional learning support including specialist teaching. A sentence completion test such as Hedderly (1995) is also useful, not least because it provides a measure of writing speed which has become increasingly significant for examination candidates when access arrangements such as additional time allowance are required.

Other factors to consider when analysing spelling errors are to establish which of the five stages of spelling development the individual has reached. Some severely dyslexic pupils never progress beyond the third developmental stage, and rely on spelling matching the sounds to symbols as their main spelling strategy.

HANDY HINT

Phonetic spelling is often seen as a hallmark feature of dyslexia, and for some is a lifelong characteristic of the condition, as was shown by the case study of an adult in Chapter 1 (p. 13).

A pattern of errors

These errors were made by 'Patricia' (10 years 9 months) in her 'free writing'.

9 September 1999

manely	(mainly)
agaist	(against)
moster	(moisture)
to	(too)
reserch	(research)
explan	(explain)
desighn	(design)
difficultyies	(difficulties)
aplied	(applied)
ether	(either)
rapped	(wrapped)
couler	(colour)
imedietly	(immediately)
saten	(satin)

aply	(apply)
prosess	(process)
serfise	(surface)
untill	(until)

11 September 1999

wile	(while)
haserd	(hazard)
biogradable	(bio-degradable)
sofened	(softened)
permantly	(permanently)
pacaging	(packaging)
modling	(modelling)
coms	(combs)
camra	(camera)
safty	(safety)
botles	(bottles)
electical	(electrical)
compents	(components)

12 September 1999

containes	(contains)
hasards	(hazards)
incuded	(included)
envirments	(environments)
desserts	(deserts)
consernse	(concerns)
our	(how)
enviremint	(environment)
naturel	(natural)
sentense	(sentence)

15 September 1999

trafic	(traffic)
aligator	(alligator

29 September 1999

hight	(height)
layor	(layer)
vally	(valley)

20 October 1999

difficute	(difficult)
foundions	(foundations)

8 November 1999

paterns	(patterns)
settlment	(settlement)

22 November 1999

tereced	(terraced)
moterway	(motorway)

8 January 2000

desidid	(decided)
buisness	(business)
moterway	(motorway)
suport	(support)
sinserley	(sincerely)

9 January 2000

enviremental polution	(environmental pollution)
exaught	(exhaust)
heavey	(heavy)
gragh	(graph)

10 January 2000

convinient	(convenient)
dos'nt	(doesn't)

12 January 2000

constuction	(construction)
increace	(increase)
privit	(private)
viacle	(vehicle)
extent	(extend)
travle	(travel)

The following is an example from 'Patricia's' extended writing. The misspelt and wrongly capitalised words are in bold.

Adverizments

Threats and jingles are both **Advertizment, People** say if you wear this men will like you or you'll be popular. There is one **Advert** on T.V. **were** this man puts on **deodrant** and all these **buetfell** women follow him. Also **Jingles** are **use, litte** catchy **song** that makes you think of the product. Of course only T.V. and **Radio** can have jingles but posters can **wright threats**. Adverts are **ment** to **purswayed** people to buy **there** products and really you know it is all **rubish** but your insides want to be like that. So I think **Advertisments** do work

CASE STUDY: 'BILLY' (11 YEARS)

Billy had a Full Scale IQ WISC 100. The instructions he wrote for 'How to Mend a Bicycle Puncture' give a clear insight into how dyslexia affected his spelling. He was unable to draft or revise his work simultaneously while word-processing because of his working memory difficulties. He could not process information and think about the secretarial aspects at the same time. He later used the spell-checker, but often needed assistance with reading the spelling options when doing the corrections.

How to mend a puncher

1 Get out puncher kite
2 Get out talles
3 Get bike and turn over
4 Take off the while
5 get tier tall and then take out the inner Chubb
6 pull out the inner Chubb
7 Pump up the inner Chubb
8 Fill up a bole with water
9 Put the inner Chubb in the water
10 look for the bubbles

11 Place thinger on the while
12 dry tiear and keep hand on whiole
13 let the inearchob down
14 Mark where the whoile is
15 Rub with sand paper
16 Cover whole with glow
17 get poch out and place on glow arer
18 whate for parch to drie
19 pot inchob back in the tiear
20 put tiear on bike
21 blow up tiear
22 my bike is now redy to be used

How to mend a puncture

1 Get out puncture repair kit.
2 Get out the tools and pump.
3 Get bike and turn over [upside-down].
4 Take off the wheel.
5 Get tyre tool and then take out the inner tube.
6 Pull out the inner tube.
7 Pump up the inner tube.
8 Fill up a bowl with water.
9 Put the inner tube in the water.
10 Look to see where the bubbles come from.

11 Place finger on the wheel.
12 Dry tyre and keep hand on hole.
13 Let the inner tube down.
14 Mark where the hole is.
15 Rub with sandpaper.
16 Cover hole with glue.
17 Get patch out and place on glued area.
18 Wait for patch to dry.
19 Put inner tube back in the tyre.
20 Put tyre on bike.
21 Blow up the tyre.
22 My bike is now ready to be used.

'My Spelling'

From clinical experience and evidence from practitioners as well as from compensated dyslexics, it is clear that spelling is an ongoing cause of difficulty. Stuart (11 years) captivated an audience at the Royal Albert Hall in London when he recited the following.

My Spelling

You can call my writing illegible
And the grammar quite obscene,
But when my pen hits paper
I know what I mean.

My punctuation may be random
And my meaning hard to see
But my spelling is unique
And has originality.

It's often called dyslexia
But I don't think that's true
I just have good imagination
And a different brain from you.

Sixty-nine ways to spell 'dyslexia'

Evidence of the dilemmas faced by a speller who is dyslexic is vividly and unforgettably portrayed by sixty-nine ways to spell 'dyslexia'. These were generated in the spontaneous writing of 12 to 16 year-old pupils at Mark College, a specialist school for pupils with dyslexia. They could also be used to provide further evidence using miscue analysis of the different types of spelling errors.

bicslexy	desixere	disllyer	dyislexer
bslecr	dexiler	disixier	dylxcear
byxlayer	dicelecser	dislyixa	dysecixya
dcecker	didslexr	diyslexi	dysixia
decky	diestecer	dixlexer	dyslecser
decxlexer	dilexsite	dixlexyer	dyslecsiae
delexser	diseixer	dixia	dysleksia
drsaler	dislecsia	dixseepcer	dyslexai
desexeyer	dislecy	dixsleer	dyslexcia
desixer	disleicer	dizlexy	dyslexea
desixyer	dislexa	dsislexsyur	dyslexia
deslegia	dislexea	dslexic	dyslexic
deslexcv	dislexear	dsixerser	dyslexyer
dslexek	dislexer	dsixseyer	dysxlier
deslexey	dislexeyr	duislecur	dyxier
deslexia	dislexia	dyasxe	
deslixe	dislexier	dycilcer	
desixer	disleyer	dyslexer	

SUMMARY AND CONCLUSIONS

1 Old habits die hard. The weekly spelling test is part of most schoolchildren's routine. Goulandris (personal communication) pointed out that many of the once popular methods of teaching spelling are now known to be ineffective for many pupils. Spelling has long been the Cinderella of the teaching of the three 'r's, 'reading', 'riting' and rithmetic'. It has once again become a significant feature in children's lives. This has happened because of the emphasis the NLS gives to teaching literacy. In the past spelling instruction and using the lists of the spellings taught was often the personal choice of individual teachers. Teaching spelling is no longer a hit-or-miss activity in classrooms and is now part of the National Curriculum. The outcome and success of spelling policy is measured in national tests, including SATs.

2 Some children have persistent difficulties with spellings, which may be a lifelong condition. Frith (1997) asserts that 'no one who has experience of dyslexia would doubt that dyslexic children become dyslexic adults, regardless of the improvements they show in reading'. There is much anecdotal evidence, from dyslexic adults as well as from practitioners, of lifelong struggles to spell even the most basic words; others spell phonetically because they do not master spelling conventions or remember visual patterns.

3 There is a wide selection of spelling tests available. 'Tests offer an effective and useful way of measuring attainment in spelling in relation to the requirements of the National Curriculum and the National Literacy Strategy Framework for Teaching' (Young 1998). Some are more appropriate for use when identifying dyslexia. They are also important when setting targets for IEP plans and when reviewing progress.

4 Misspelling analysis, though time-consuming, is often reliant on judgement and is not an exact science – different explanations can be given for different types of errors but it is a diagnostic tool. Treiman (1997) pointed out that 'children who make many non-phonetic errors are believed to lack appreciation of the alphabetic principle'.

5 Miscue analysis plays an important role in the identification of specific strengths and weaknesses. It plays a significant role when establishing the spelling strategies used by spellers and can be a useful indicator of learning style as well as providing information for future teaching and learning. Frith (1994) considered that 'spelling has always afforded a privileged window into the mind, and spelling errors are a magnificent glass in that window'.

6 Misspelling is a significant feature in the dyslexia syndrome. It can be bewildering, distressful and irritating for individuals. There are, however, now many educational tools which can be used, including early identification, appropriate specialist teaching, and learning support from teaching assistants as well as the compensatory marvels provided by the use of modern technological support such as spell-checkers.

10 Are Spelling Rules Necessary and Helpful?

- Debate and polarisation of opinions about the terminology
- Influential upholders and supporters of the concept of rules
- Why did spelling rules evolve?
- Practical suggestions for the basic skills apprentices need before learning rules
- Different categories of rules
- Classification of rules and generalisations
- Guidelines for teaching rules and conventions as recommended in the National Literacy Strategy
- Checklists for the best options for spelling consonant sounds
- Checklists for the best options for spelling short and long vowel sounds
- Summary and conclusions

Keywords

Alveolar sounds	Lexicographers	Spelling conventions
Borrowed words	Loanwords	Spelling
Clymer's list of phonic	Major spelling rules	generalisations
generalisations	Minor spelling rules	Spelling rules
Core spelling rules	National Literacy	Stanford spelling study
Derivation	Strategy (NLS)	Thorndike and Lorge's
Dolch's sight words	Organs of speech	word list
Labial sounds	Palatal sounds	

Debate and polarisation of opinions about the terminology

Some commentators argue that the word 'rule' is a misnomer when applied to English spelling. *Chambers Twenty-first Century Dictionary* (1999) defined a rule as 'a general principle, regulation, standard, guideline or custom'. One of the most hotly debated issues is the very use of the word 'rule' when applied to spelling. The English language is constantly changing, with new words borrowed and the meanings of others evolving and changing. The word 'rule' falls into this category. The modern use of the word 'rule' associates it with law and order. Rules, regulations and laws often include statements about what is, or is not, permissible. Phrases like 'as a rule', 'golden rule', 'breaking the rules' and 'bending the rules' imply that 'rules are rules' in common parlance.

Others suggest that there are almost no spelling rules that can be applied universally. They cite the evidence of the exceptions to the rules as a justification for their claims that English does not follow 'rule, rhyme or reason'.

Pedants have exercised their influence and it has become increasingly common to use the word 'generalisations' when considering words which follow certain spelling conventions, principles or structure. Some say that a spelling rule should apply to a large number of words. However, the rule saying 'when the prefix "all" (which is spelt "al") is added to another syllable it has only one "l"' results in the following small number of words: albeit, also, altogether, almost, almighty, already, always, although. The speller also has to remember that there is an exception to this generality which is, when 'all' is combined with 'right', it makes 'all right' as in 'my spellings are all right'. They can also be used in informal writing to make 'alright' as in 'it is alright to use this spelling'. (Authorities such as Burchfield 1996 argue for 'all right' in both senses.) This rule neatly demonstrates some of the speller's dilemmas. Those who dismiss rules as more trouble than they are worth could use this example in justification.

Influential upholders and supporters of the concept of rules

Adams (1990) gave her seal of approval and support to the use of rules when she proclaimed that 'whatever we may call them and however unreliable they may be, phonic generalisations are essentially rules'. On this side of the Atlantic, Crystal (2002) nailed his colours to the mast and gave his support to the teaching of spelling rules. The phenomenal success of *Eats, Shoots & Leaves* (Truss 2003), a book about 'formulating the clear rules' of punctuation which was at the top of the bestseller list for weeks, perhaps shows that many of the British public still want to know about for example 'the 17 rules of the comma'.

The National Literacy Strategy (NLS) appears to have settled the issues surrounding nomenclature for schools and children in the UK when it ordained that pupils should 'investigate and learn spelling rules' (DfEE 1998). It hedged its bets and later advocated the teaching of 'spelling conventions and rules' to pupils of 7 to 8 years in Year 3, and it recommended that pupils of 9 to 10 years in Year 5 should 'investigate and learn spelling rules'. The NLS gave examples of individual rules, but did not give an overall number for spelling rules. It included examples of rules as well as copious examples and guidelines about what spelling instruction should be given, when it should be given, and how and why it should be given. The National Strategy Key Stage 3 (DfEE 2001a) gave its stamp of approval and pointed out that 'there are no perfect spelling rules, but there are conventions that can help pupils to make informed choices, and English spelling is regular enough to repay systematic teaching'. It cited Crystal's (1995) *The Cambridge Encyclopedia of the English Language* as endorsement. Crystal declared of spelling that 'few attempts are made to explain what it is they have learned. They are not generally told why spellings are as they are.' English spelling has a framework and a structure. There are many guidelines which can be used to classify spelling patterns and conventions, and generalisations which can be used to formulate a set of rules.

Why did spelling rules evolve?

From the time of the Reformation during the reign of Henry VIII, the English language became more important as ecclesiastical power was slowly eclipsed in Tudor England. The Coverdale Bible (1535) was the first recognised translation of the Bible into English. During the Elizabethan Age around twelve thousand new loan words were incorporated into English from over fifty different languages. Not surprisingly people needed to know what these 'new' words meant, how to pronounce them and how they could be spelt. The gap in the market was filled by Robert Cawdrey's *Table Alphabeticall* (1604), which was the first published English dictionary. Later other dictionaries were produced with a prime objective to explain 'hard words'. They also placed great emphasis on the correct pronunciation of words. However it would be incorrect to say that spelling was routinely haphazard at this period. It was not consistent, as can be seen for example in the original folio versions of Shakespeare's plays. He spelled his own name variously throughout his lifetime as Shakespere, Shakspear, Shakspere, Shagspere. Such variations may have occurred in print because typesetters used inconsistent spellings to make words longer or shorter in order to achieve a straight (in modern terms 'justified') right-hand edge for the type area (Essinger 2006).

Samuel Johnson is usually credited with standardising English spelling. His *Dictionary of the English Language* was published in 1755 after nine years of preparation. His aims were threefold: to standardise pronunciation, to define words accurately and to give the correct fixed spelling of words. He urged his readers 'not to disturb upon narrower views . . . The orthography of their fathers'. His work became the standard reference for spelling. Subsequently disputes about the spelling of a word could be settled by consulting Johnson's dictionary.

Noah Webster was the other great lexicographer of the eighteenth century. His aims were also threefold: to standardise spelling, pronunciation and grammar for the American people. British English was gradually replaced by American English. His *Grammatical Institute of the English Language*, later known as the *American Speller and the Blue-Backed Speller*, was first published in 1783 and *An American Dictionary of the English Language* (1828) became the standard reference in the US.

Hanna et al. (1971) gave what some would consider a patriotic opinion and others would argue a biased view when they stated that Webster's 'was considered superior to Dr Johnson's British dictionary' because:

- Dr Johnson's definitions were gleaned primarily from literary sources; Webster's were based on current usage.
- As compared with Dr Johnson, Webster included many more scientific and technical terms.
- Webster's etymological entries were more extensive and more accurate than Dr Johnson's.

This declaration of American independence from British English had its origins in these polarised opinions. Each nation has continued to follow its preferred chosen path and to develop rules and generalisations for its language.

During the nineteenth and twentieth centuries there were many attempts to reform spelling in the US and UK because there was a perception that English spelling was difficult. Some argued that this was because of its mongrel parentage and its habit of intermarriage with other languages. According to Horn (1969), of the five hundred most frequently used words in English 354 were spelled irregularly, and these were mostly Anglo-Saxon words. Various attempts were made to identify these words, for both reading and spelling purposes. In the 1930s an interest developed in word frequency and usage, leading eventually to Thorndike and Lorge's (1944) list of thirty thousand basic words. But, as Hanna et al. (1971) pointed out, 'the method of teaching and learning was unchanged – each word was attacked as an independent unit to be memorised by rote'.

At the same time there was a reawakening of interest in matching the sounds of the language to the letters of the alphabet, because English is an alphabetically based system. However some commentators said that, because there were so many irregularities, matching sounds to symbols was not very reliable.

Lists were devised to identify the most commonly used words, and these were graded in difficulty as well as by length of word. One of the most famous of these was Dolch's (1939) lists of high-frequency words used in texts.

Lists of high-frequency and medium-frequency words for reading and spelling have become a focal point in the National Literacy Strategy Framework for Teaching in schools. The lists were drawn from a number of sources such as Carroll et al. (1971), Reid (1989) and Huxford (1994), according to Beard (1998).

Crystal (2002) widened the debate about statistical analysis of frequency of words used in English. He drew up a list of the twenty most frequently occurring words in British English. He divided the words into written and spoken words, which is an important distinction for teachers and learners, particularly for those learning to read and write.

The twenty most frequently used words in English

	Written English [adults] (newspapers)	Spoken English [adults] (conversation)	Spoken English [5-year-olds]	Written English [5-year-olds]
1	the	the	I	a
2	of	and	you	the
3	to	I	it	I
4	in	to	the	play
5	and	of	to	is
6	a	a	a	and
7	for	you	that	to
8	was	that	and	my
9	is	in	one	house
10	that	it	no	in
11	on	is	on	go
12	at	yes	got	on
13	he	was	in	this
14	with	this	what	with
15	by	but	do	went
16	be	on	this	are
17	it	well	my	am
18	an	he	yes	it
19	as	have	oh	at
20	his	for	there	some

Source: Crystal (2002)

HANDY HINT

The most universally understood English words are: 'pizza', 'sex', 'taxi'

Seminal studies resulting in the classification of rules and generalisations

Author, title, date	Database	Key findings
T. Clymer, *The Utility of Phonic Generalisations in the Primary Grades* (1963)	2600 Words based on four basal readers and *Webster's New Collegiate Dictionary*	• There are 'five general types of generalisations including vowels, consonants, endings, syllablisation, miscellaneous relationships'. • There are 121 different generalisations. • Narrowed these down to 45 phonic generalisations.
P.R. Hanna, J.S. Hanna, R. Hodges R. and E.H. Rudolf, *Phoneme–grapheme correspondences as Cues to Spelling Improvement* (*Stanford Spelling Study*) (1966)	17,000 based on Thorndike and Lorge's (1944) list derived from 18 million words of text; *The Merriam Webster New International Dictionary* (1957)	• 'Four fifths of the phonemes contained in the words comprising the traditional spelling vocabulary of the elementary school child approximate the alphabetic principles in their letter representations.' • There are 225 generalisations and their reliability is dependent on the number of exceptions. • 84 per cent of words are spelled according to a regular spelling pattern. • 3 per cent of words are irregular and their spelling unpredictable (the so called 'odd-bods').
A. Gillingham and B. Stillman, *Remedial Training for Children with Specific Disability in Reading, Spelling and Penmanship* (fifth ed.) (1956)	Not available	• Rules should be taught only to pupils capable of applying them. • They should be taught generalisations. • Certain spelling conventions are crystallised into rules. • Sixteen key spelling rules.
E. Carney, *A Survey of English Spelling* (1994)	Based on Thorndike and Lorge (1944), Brown University list, Lancaster-Oslo list, *Analysis of Present Day Theatrical Language* (1966–72), *American Heritage Dictionary*	• There are 225 rules, divided into: • 'core' rules which will include default rules and rules which deal with important divergent spellings'. • 'Minor' rules which contribute 5 per cent or less to the successful prediction of phonemes in words. • 'Marginal' rules which contribute less than 2.5 per cent to the successful prediction of phonemes in words.

PRACTICAL SUGGESTIONS FOR THE BASIC SKILLS APPRENTICES NEED BEFORE LEARNING RULES

The following is a review and a succinct overview of what spellers need to know and learn and includes guidelines for the sequence for teaching skills.

Spellers should be able to recognise the 26 letters of the alphabet and be able to write these in upper-case, in lower-case, in printed form and in manuscript form, including printed and cursive forms a *a* A. These must be established to a level of mastery which requires frequent practice.

The alphabet is a code where the letters are used to match the sounds. Spellers need to know that letters have sounds called phonemes. Carnine (1976) showed that children who had been taught letter–sound correspondences were able to correctly identify letters on 79 per cent of occasions whereas those who had insufficient practice and experience could achieve only 38 per cent accuracy. In the English language there are 44 phonemes, which are the sounds we hear in speech. Some sounds can be spelled with different letters. /f/ can be spelt with 'f' fan; 'ff' cliff; 'ph' phone; 'gh' laugh. Each will need specific teaching. The easier and more frequently used examples are taught first. Later the more difficult spellings are taught.

Some letters have different sounds which often depend on the letter next to them. The position also has significance. Sounds of letters can vary depending on whether the letter is at the beginning, middle or end of a word.

Explicit teaching needs to be given about the two kinds of letters, consonants and vowels. The vowels are a, e, i, o, u and the consonants are all the other letters in the alphabet. Consonants can be made in different parts of the mouth:

- The labial consonants are made by the lips such as the sounds /b/ /m/ /p/.
- The palatal consonants are the sounds made by touching the hard palate such as /c/ /j/ /s/ /z/.
- The velar consonants are the sounds made by raising the back of the tongue towards the soft palate such as /g/ /k/ /w/.
- The alveolar consonants are the sounds made by the tip of the tongue when it touches behind the upper front teeth such as /d/ /l/ /n/ /r/ /s/ /z/.
- The dental consonants are the sounds made when the teeth touch the lower lip such as /f/ /v/ /th/.

Vowels can be divided into short vowels which say their sounds and long vowels which say their names. The concept that long vowels such as the long /ē/ sound can be spelt in many different ways will need explicit teaching over a period of weeks and months. It can be a recipe for disaster, particularly for poor spellers, to introduce all the alternative ways to spell, for instance, the long /ē/ sound as a spelling concept in one lesson.

Regular spellings should be learned first, and when they have been mastered the irregular commonly used words and the alternative spellings can be learned. For those with poor visual memory this is an important consideration.

Different categories of rules

Essential rules are at the foundation of literacy and include basic knowledge such as that every word and each syllable must have one vowel sound.

Major rules stipulate for example that digraphs and blends stay together when words are divided into syllables, for example 'crash/ing'.

There are several kinds of minor rules which are used frequently. Rules can be categorised because they involve high-frequency words with highly regular spellings: words ending in 'y', change 'y' to 'i' before adding 'es' in the plural: 'baby' – 'babies'; 'copy' – 'copies'. Other rules involve low-frequency words and are highly regular: words ending in 'y' keep 'y' before adding the suffix 'ing', 'ist', 'ish': carrying; 'copyist'; 'babyish'. Others have low frequency and low regularity. Others have high frequency and low regularity: 'one; once'.

Finally there are 'core rules', which Carney (1944) describes as rules 'with a very heavy workload'.

Classification of rules and generalisations

The companion volume *Activities for Successful Spelling* (Ott 2007b) includes photocopiable worksheets, puzzles, word searches and dictations for learning and teaching spelling. The big picture includes knowing and remembering the names, shapes and the 44 sounds of all the letters as well as:

- individual letters
- adding prefixes and suffixes
- pluralisation
- syllables
- recognising word patterns
- words within words

The consonant sounds

Treiman's (1993) work confirmed that 'phonemes that have many possible spellings are harder than phonemes that have few spellings'. This is an important consideration, and therefore rules and phonemes with many examples are usually a priority when choosing what to teach.

Rules for spelling soft 'c' sound

'c' says /s/ at the beginning, middle and end of words when the next letter is 'e', 'i', 'y'. This is often referred to as 'soft' 'c' sound:

cent	century
city	circle
cycle	cylinder
face	mice
office	service

In Clymer's (1963) list the soft 'c' rule worked for 96 per cent of words. The exception was 'ocean'.

Rules for spelling 'f' sound

/f/ sound can be spelt with 'f' at the beginning of a word:

> face fish fog

'ff' at the end and middle of a word after a short vowel:

> staff   cliff   cuff
> muffin   office   suffix

'ph', usually in words borrowed from Greek, can be used at the beginning, middle or end of words:

> phobia   phone   phrase
> alphabet   prophet   dolphin
> autograph paragraph photograph

'gh' at the end of words:

> cough laugh rough

Exception: 'sapphire'

Rules for spelling hard 'g' sound

/g/ sound can be spelt with 'g' at the beginning, middle and end of words. This is often referred to as the 'hard' 'g' sound.

> gap   god   gun
> bingo   cargo   tango
> bag   fog   rug

'gu' at the beginning of a word.

> guard guess guide

'gh' at the beginning of a word.

> ghastly ghetto ghost

'gg' in the middle of a word:

> giggle goggle haggle

Exception: 'egg' and compound nouns such as 'eggbeater', 'eggshell'

Rules for spelling soft 'g' sound

'g' says /j/ at the beginning, middle and end of words when the next letter is 'e'; 'i'; 'y'. This is often referred to as the 'soft' 'g' sound.

gem	gin	gym
angel	danger	magic
stage	image	village

Exceptions: words having both hard and soft 'g': 'gadget'; 'gelignite'; 'gorgeous'

Rules for spelling 'j' sound

/j/ sound can be spelt with 'j' at the beginning and middle of words:

jam	job	jug
conjure	injure	major

'g' at the beginning of words:

gypsy   giro   gymnast

'ge' at the end of words with a long vowel and magic 'e':

cage   stage   huge

words with a vowel digraph:

gouge   stooge

Words with a consonant before the /j/ sound:

barge   binge   lounge

'dge' at the end of words with a short vowel:

dodge   hedge   judge

Exception: 'raj', which is borrowed from Sanskrit

Rules for spelling 'k' sound

/k/ sound can be spelt with 'c' at the beginning and middle of words when the next letter is 'a', 'o', or 'u'. This is often referred to as the 'hard' 'c' sound:

camp	coal	cub
dictate	locate	vacate

Exception: 'calcium' which has a hard 'c' at the beginning of the word and a soft 'c' in the middle 'k' at the beginning of words:

> key   king   karma (borrowed from Sanskrit)

'kh' at the beginning and end of words:

> khaki   khan   sheikh (borrowed from Persian and Arabic)

'ch' at the beginning, middle and ends of words (borrowed from Greek):

> chemist   choir   Christmas
> orchestra orchid   school
> eunuch   monarch stomach

Exceptions: 'gecko' is borrowed from Malay; 'loch' is Scottish

'k' at the end of a word with a consonant or a vowel digraph:

> bank   pink   monk
> oak   cheek   peak

'x' at the end of a word says /ks/:

> box   fox   mix

Exceptions: 'wok' is borrowed from Chinese and 'trek' from Afrikaans

'ke' if there is a long vowel and magic 'e':

> rake   bike   coke

'ic' if the word has two or more syllables:

> attic   music   panic

'cc' in the middle of words:

> accept   account   access
> broccoli   hiccup   occupation

'que' at the end of words (borrowed from French):

> antique   cheque   mosque

'qu' at the beginning and middle of words (borrowed from French):

> quay   queue   quiche
> conqueror   liquor   mosquito

Rules for spelling 's' sound

/s/ sound can be spelt in a number of different ways.
's' at the beginning, middle and end of words:

sand	sin	sun
basin	insert	poster
bonus	chorus	minus

'c' at the beginning of words (soft 'c' words):

cell   circus   cygnet

'sc' at the beginning, middle and end of words:

scent	science	scissors
abscess	fascination	muscle
acquiesce	convalesce	luminescence

'ss' at the middle and end of words with a short vowel and one consonant:

assess	classic	gossip
boss	kiss	fuss

Exceptions: 'bus'; 'has'; 'his'; 'gas'; 'is'; 'plus'; 'pus'; 'us'

'ps' at the beginning of words (borrowed from Greek):

psalm   psychiatry   psychology

'ce' at the beginning, middle and end of words:

cent	cereal	century
deceit	December	descent
dance	price	voice
advice	licence	practice	(when they are used as nouns)

'se' at the end of nouns:

house	mouse	tense
advise	license	practise	(when used as verbs)

'sw' at the beginning of words saying /s/:

sword

'st':

    castle   fasten   wrestle

'sch':

    schism   school   schooner

Rules for spelling 'v' sound

/v/ sound is spelt with 'v' at the beginning and middle of words:

    van   vest   video
    reveal revile revise

Exceptions: No English words end in 'v' except 'spiv', which is a colloquialism 'Rev.' which is an abbreviation for reverend; and 'rev', which is a colloquialism for increasing the speed of an engine.

've' is the usual spelling for /v/ sound at the end of words:

    gave serve five

'ov' is used to spell /uv/ sound:

    glove love shove

Rules for spelling words with 'w'

/w/ sound is spelt with 'w' at the beginning, middle and end of words:

    wax   wig   wolf
    coward power shower

When 'w' is followed by 'a' it is spelt 'wa' and usually says /wo/.

    wasp wash swan

When 'w' is followed by 'ar' it is spelt 'was' and says /wor/:

    dwarf ward swarm

When 'w' is followed by 'er' it is spelt 'wer' and says /wer/:

    word work world

Exceptions: 'one'; 'once'; 'suede' (borrowed from Anglo-Saxon and French)

Rules for spelling words with 'y'

'y' is sometimes a consonant and sometimes a vowel.
'y' when it is a consonant says /y/ at the beginning of words:

    yap   yellow   yolk

'y' when it is a vowel says /ī/ at the end of a word:

    cry   fly   spy

English words do not usually end in 'i'.

Exceptions: 'maxi'; 'taxi'; 'mini' (abbreviations). 'Ski' is borrowed from Norwegian; 'macaroni' and 'ravioli' are borrowed from Italian 'Bikini' is borrowed from the name of an atoll in the Marshall Islands in the Pacific; 'kiwi' from Maori; 'khaki' from Urdu.

/ī/ sound in the middle of a word can say /ī/ but it is spelt with 'y':

    nylon   style   tyre

'y' when it is a vowel can say /ē/ at the end of a word:

    baby   copy   happy

The Heavenly Twins rule

Rules for spelling words with 'q'

'q' and 'u' always go together and say /kw/ at the beginning of words:

    queen   quiz   quick

A mnemonic to remember this rule is to call them the conjoined twins because they stay together and are inseparable.

Double consonants

Knowing when to double consonants is a recurring problem for many spellers. Fowler (1926) asserted that letter doubling was a most frequent source of misspelling in English. The problem is compounded because, when two of the same consonants are side by side in a word, only one consonant is heard in standard speech. Clymer (1963) examined 334 words and found this was true for 99 per cent of words.

Begin to learn about doubling consonants with one-syllable words.

The Bossy Miss Flossy and the Lovely Miss Lizzy Rule

Words with one syllable and one short vowel ending with 'f', 'l', 's', 'z' double the final consonant:

'ff'   **'ll'**
cliff staff stuff   dull hill spell

Exception: 'pal'

'ss'
class miss fuss

Exceptions: 'gas'; 'has'; 'his'; 'is'; 'plus'; 'pus'; 'this'; 'thus'; 'us'

'zz'
jazz fizz fuzz

Exceptions: fez; quiz

The Double or Drop Dead Rule

How to deal with consonants in the middle of words with two syllables.

If you can hear the consonant at the beginning of the second syllable – keep it:

bobbin funny summer

If you cannot hear the consonant at the beginning of the second syllable – drop it:

betting colder gladly

If the first syllable has a short vowel and one consonant, double the consonant before adding an ending:

rabbit tennis puppet

Exceptions: 'cabin'; 'rebel'; 'robin'

If there is a short vowel and a consonant, double the consonant before adding the ending 'le':

battle little muddle

If there is a consonant digraph or consonant blend (cluster) at the end of the first syllable, do not double:

buckle castle thistle

If there is a long vowel or a vowel digraph, do not double:

people   bible   noodle

If the nasal sounds (assimilations) 'm' and 'n' are followed by 'b', 'd', 'g', 'k', 'p', 't', do not double:

bumble	jumble	tumble
bundle	candle	handle
angle	jungle	uncle
example	sample	temple
gentle	mantle	

See the suffixing rules (p. 182) for further discussion and examples on doubling consonants.

Some prefixes such as 'ad'; 'il'; 'im'; 'in'; 'ir' double the consonant to make them easier to pronounce:

adduce   illegal   irresponsible   immovable   innumerate

Consonant digraphs are two consonants making one sound. They can occur at the beginning, middle or ends of words.
   The most common are

/sh/   /ch/   /th/   /wh/   /ph/   /gh/

They can cause problems for those with poor phonemic awareness. /sh/ and /ch/ can be confused, particularly at the ends of words.

Rules for spelling /sh/ sound

/sh/ can be spelt with 'sh' in the initial, medial and final position:

'sh'
shed	ship	shop
dashing	fishing	pushing
cash	dish	rash

'ti'
addition   examination   station

'ci'
special   official   suspicion

'si'
mansion   pension   tension

's'
insure   sugar   sure

'ss'
issue   mission   tissue

'ce'
crustacean   herbaceous   ocean

'ch' at the beginning, middle and ends of words (borrowed from French):

champagne   chateau   chef
brochure   machine   parachute
creche   moustache   quiche

'sch'
schedule   schnapps   schnitzel (the latter two borrowed from German)

'sci'
conscience   conscious (borrowed from Latin)

'si'
Asian

'su'
closure   pressure

'ti'
Egyptian

'xi'
anxious

Rules for spelling /ch/ sound

/ch/ sound can be spelt differently depending on whether it is at the beginning, middle or end of a word:

'ch'
chip   chop   chum
arching   crouching marching
inch   munch   tench

If there is a consonant before the /ch/ sound it takes 'ch':

bench   church   munch

If there is a short vowel before the /ch/ sound it takes 'tch':

> itch   patch   stitch

Exceptions: 'duchess'; 'much'; 'ostrich'; 'rich'; 'sandwich'; 'such'; 'which'

If there is a vowel digraph before the /ch/ sound it takes 'ch':

> coach   reach   touch

> **'ṱ'**
> tube   tuna   tune

> **'ture'**
> future   nature   picture

The vowel sounds

Vowels are the most important letters, not least because every word has to have at least one vowel sound. Vowels are the most frequently misspelt letters. The short vowels are more often confused, according to the research findings of Ehri et al. (1987). They established that the short vowel /ĕ/ and /ĭ/ sounds are the most often confused. Post et al.'s (1999) research showed that 'more errors were made on the short vowels than on the long vowels for both vowel identification and spelling' on a study made of 164 children of 7–10 years. Kreiner and Gough (1990) 'showed that spellers make more errors on schwa [unstressed] vowels than on unambiguously pronounced vowels'.

Schlagal (1992) found evidence that children are often 9 to 10 years old before they master vowel spellings. According to Snowling et al. (1991), some pupils with dyslexia have persisting struggles with the spelling of vowel sounds, some because of poor auditory perception, others because of poor visual memory as well as a failure to internalise spellings for automatic recall, despite repeated exposure to the word.

Sawyer et al. (1999) conducted a study of the spelling errors made by a hundred dyslexic pupils of 7–15 years. They divided the errors made from 2,863 words into thirteen different categories: 2,025 errors were recorded and analysed. 'The category containing the greatest proportion of errors was vowel substitutions (805 errors 39.75 per cent).'

Reading books with controlled vocabularies to reinforce short vowel sounds should then be introduced (Ott 2007b). When consonant–vowel–consonant (cvc) words have been mastered, two-syllable words with closed syllables and the short vowel pattern can be taught.

Rules for spelling short vowels

Short vowels say their sounds.

A useful mnemonic to help remember the short vowels is: 'the vowel men met

a n
e lephant
i n
o range
u nderwear'

When this is accompanied with a picture of an elephant so attired (Ott 2007b) it is also a useful visual prop to remember that the short vowels are:

ă ĕ ĭ ŏ ŭ

This abstract information can be enlivened for the learner by creating characters and giving the Short Vowel Men names such as Mr Andy, Mr Eddie, Mr Iggy, Mr Ollie and Mr Ugly, who can also be turned into glove puppets. There are many commercially produced card games and software resources for teaching the short vowels (www. betterbooks.com; www.crossbow.education.com; www.sen.uk.com).

Time needs to be spent on learning the individual sounds: discriminating between different sounds as well as matching similar sounds in words. This can be done initially as an oral exercise and with the inclusion of games and activities such as using white-boards, phonic fans, spiral-bound flipcharts and word wheels to reinforce sounds. Written activities should be introduced as soon as possible for individual spellings to enhance multi-sensory learning. Games and puzzles can be used to reinforce and learn individual vowel sounds. Gradually discrimination exercises between the individual sounds, as well as identification of 'odd one out' using short vowels, can be used. This can be reinforced with dictation of sentences, as well as by reading activities using reading books with controlled vocabularies which match the sound currently being taught. Oral, aural and visual skills can be enhanced by looking at the target word, saying it aloud, spelling it, writing it and reading it back. In other words using the simultaneous-oral-spelling method (S-O-S) is the classic multi-sensory spelling method to help develop spelling knowledge and skills.

Rules for spelling vowels in open syllables

Long vowels say their names.

Begin by teaching the long vowel in an open syllable and give each a keyword such as:

ā   acorn
ē   emu
ī   iris
ō   oboe
ū   uniform

The 'Long Vowel Men' can also be given names such as:

Mr Aaron, Mr Egor, Mr Ivan, Mr Owen, Mr Uri

HANDY HINT

Nouns are more concrete and are easier to remember than verbs (which are more abstract) when used as keywords or as examples.

Practice needs to be given with high-frequency words with one open syllable:

be he me we
I   go no so

The concept of 'y' as a vowel should then be introduced. It can generate words such as:

by cry dry try why

Words with two open syllables and regular spelling with a clear sound-to-symbol can then be introduced for spelling and reading purposes such as:

hē/ro; jū/dō; pō/lō; sō/lō; zē/rō

Words with a closed syllable and ending in an open syllable are also useful for 'controlled' use of long vowels.

Using such examples ensures that the novice spellers do not experience spelling difficulties, because they have the security of being asked to spell only words that can be mapped to the spelling code which says that long vowels say their names. This helps to develop confidence and lessens the chance of error.

Words with two syllables and a closed and open syllable include:

bĭn/gō; hĕl/lō; lŏt/tō; măn/gō; mĕn/ū

How to spell magic 'e' words

Magic 'e' (sometimes called mute or silent 'e'), should be tackled as a spelling concept when the consonants and the short and long vowels have been taught. It can be introduced earlier as a reading concept because it occurs frequently in many reading books. The letter 'e' is the most frequently used in the English language.

The concept of a 'magic "e"' is used to create the impression that something magical happens when 'e' is used at the end of a word with a vowel and consonant preceding it.

Magic Mrs 'e' casts a spell on the letters, and when she does, she makes the vowel say its name but she keeps quiet and says nothing (Ott 1997):

mǎt	māte
pĕt	Pēte
pǐn	pīne
mŏp	mōpe
cŭb	cūbe

Carney (1994) gives a percentage for the occurrence of magic 'e' in words with long vowel spellings.

hǎt	hāte	38%
mĕt	mēte	3%
pŏp	pōpe	40%
cŏd	cōde	16%
tŭb	tūbe	17%

Many children initially struggle to know when to use 'e' at the end of words but most spellers eventually learn to do so. However, for those with dyslexia magic 'e' can be an ongoing source of difficulty because of their poor phonemic skills arising from their inability to tune their ears into sounds and to match these to the letters that represent them.

Vowel digraphs

Long vowels need to be taught individually. Generations of schoolchildren have been helped to remember how to spell long vowel sounds by the following rhyme:

> When two vowels go walking
> The first vowel does the talking
> And usually says its name.

For example:

> trāīn; wēēd; bōāt

This generalisation has been shown to be of limited value because of the number of exceptions as well as the percentages of reliability. Clymer (1963) showed that long /ē/ sound when spelt with 'ea' had 377 exceptions such as 'chief' and a utility of 45 per cent. Carney (1994) gives text frequencies for spellings. He argues that the percentages quoted should be restricted to function words (nouns) and he does not include 'articles, demonstratives, pronouns, auxiliary verbs, conjunctions and prepositions'. Personal names, place names and trade names are not used in his examples because their spelling can be unique and are sometimes coined by the author. This is an important point and should be pointed out to all spellers, particularly those who have a tendency to spell phonetically. In an age where visual images surround us in advertisements, television or on products it can compound or reinforce 'illegal' spelling. Those who think that 'beans' and 'means' are spelt as in 'Beanz Meanz Heinz' or that 'quick' is spelt as in 'Kwik Fit' tyres are not usually helped by exposure to impermissible spellings. However, there has been a proliferation of this kind of spelling as a result of the rapid expansion of the use of text messaging, which uses abbreviations and phonemic shorthand such as books for 'U2' read.

Rules for spelling long /ā/ sound

'a'
acorn   navy   stable
(used at the end of an open syllable)

'a-e'
ape   gate   phrase
dictate   lemonade   mistake
(used with magic 'e')

'ae'
aerial   aerobics   aerosol

'ai'
brain   rain   stain
(used in the middle of words)

and at the end of two-syllable words:
complain   explain   retain

'ay'
hay   play   stay

It is also used at the end of words
betray   defray   portray

'age'
page   rage   wage
cottage   image   manage

'é'
blasé   rosé   soirée (borrowed from French)

'ei'
eight   neighbour   veil

'eigh'
eight   freight   weigh

'ea'
break   great   steak

'ey'
grey obey they

'et'
ballet bouquet chalet (borrowed from French)

Exceptions: 'brae' (borrowed from Scots Gaelic); 'sundae'; 'gaol'; 'gauge'

Rules for spelling long /ē/ sound

'e'
be she we
(used at the end of an open syllable)

ego   event evict
demon legal   pecan
(used at the end of an open syllable)

'e-e'
here   mete
athlete complete delete
(used with magic 'e')

'ea'
cheat heat neat

'ee'
beef green sheep
coffee (borrowed from Turkish) toffee

'ei'
conceive perceive receipt

The 'i' before 'e' rule except after 'c' and when it rhymes with 'weigh'

This is the most frequently quoted spelling rule and incidentally often the only one many people are able to easily recall (often incompletely). Most words use 'ie'.

'ie'
field priest shield

Exceptions: 'caffeine'; 'protein'; 'seize'

'ei'
ceiling deceit receive

Exceptions: 'ancient'; 'glacier'; 'science'

'ei' is used for long /ā/ sound:

eight freight reign
heir   veil   vein

It does however have exceptions which Adams (1990) notes. She suggests memorising the following rhyme, which neatly summarises the rule and can be used as an aide-memoire.

HANDY HINT

'i' before 'e'
Except after 'c'
Or when sounded as 'a'
As in neighbo[u]r and weigh.
Either, neither, leisure and seize
Are four exceptions,
If you please.

Carney (1994) on the other hand felt that 'the more closely one looks at that supreme and for many people solitary, spelling rule, the more peculiar it seems'.

'eo'
people

'ey'
abbey honey key

'ay'
quay

'ae'
anaemia leukaemia archaeology (borrowed from Greek)

'i'
macaroni ravioli spaghetti (borrowed from Italian)

Exceptions: 'anti'; 'mini'; 'maxi'; 'semi'; 'taxi' (abbreviations)

'ie'
field niece piece
birdie calorie lingerie (the latter two words borrowed from French)

'i-e'
machine prestige regime

'is'
ambergris verdigris vis-à-vis (borrowed from French)

'it'
esprit (borrowed from French)

'oe'
amoeba   foetus   phoenix (derived from Greek)

'y'
army   lady   pony
funny   happy   mummy

Rules for spelling long /ī/

'i'
idol   iris   ivy
biology   minus   library
(used at the end of an open syllable)

'i'
child   kind   mild
(used in words with a short vowel spelling but a long vowel sound)

'i-e'
five   drive   mile
(used with magic 'e')

'ie'
die   lie   tie

'ei'
either   height   sleight
eider (borrowed from Icelandic)
eisteddfod (borrowed from Welsh)
poltergeist (borrowed from German)

'igh'
high   sigh   thigh

'ight'
light   might   tight

'y'
cry   defy   sky
(used at the end of words)

cycle   nylon   python
hybrid   hydrogen   hyena (borrowed from Greek and Latin)

'y-e'
pyre   type   tyre

'ye'
bye   dye   rye

'ui'
disguise   guide

Rules for spelling long /ō/ sound

'o'
obey   odour   oral
disco   solo   zero
avocado domino potato
(used at the end of an open syllable (borrowed from Aztecan, Italian and Spanish))

'oa'
boat   goat   soap

'o-e'
home   mole   note
camisole   casserole   profiterole (borrowed from French)
(used with magic 'e' words)

'oe'
hoe   oboe   toe

'eau'
bureau   chateau   plateau (borrowed from French)

'eo'
yeoman   video

'ew'
sew

'au'
mauve

'ou'
boulder   mould   shoulder

'ough'
dough   though

'ow'
crow   grow   slow
arrow   pillow   yellow

'o'

hold   sold   told

(used in words with a short vowel spelling but a long vowel sound)

Exceptions: 'bungalow'; 'cloche'; 'gauche'; 'imbroglio' (borrowed from Gujarati, French, Italian)

Rules for spelling long /ū/ sound

'u'

unicorn   uniform   university

guru   ormolu (borrowed from Sanskrit, French)

future   human   pupil

(used at the end of open syllables) (32 per cent of long /ū/ words are spelt with 'u')

'u-e'

huge   rule   use

(used in magic 'e' words)

'ue'

clue   glue   true

'ui'

fruit   juice   cruise

'ie'

adieu   lieu   view (borrowed from French)

'eau'

beauty

'eu'

feud   Europe   rheumatism

'ew'

brew   crew   yew

'oe'

canoe   shoe

'oo'

boot   food   moon (39 per cent of long /u/ words are spelt with 'oo')

bamboo   cuckoo   shampoo (borrowed from Malay, French, Hindi)

'ou'

group   soup   youth

caribou   marabou   sous-chef (borrowed from French Canadian; French)

Exceptions: 'do'; 'to'; 'two'; 'through'; 'who' (borrowed from Anglo-Saxon)

Dealing with the 'schwa' vowels

The schwa sound is the unstressed vowel that appears twice in 'butter'. Spelling this vowel in unstressed syllables is notoriously difficult, particularly for those with dyslexic difficulties, and such words appear on many lists of hard-to-spell words. Kreiner and Gough (1990) showed that 'spellers make more errors on schwa vowels than on unambiguously pronounced vowels'. The NLS (2001) Spelling Bank included:

alcohol	holiday	Saturday
astronomy	January	secretary
benefit	jewellery	separate
consonant	lemonade	similar
corporal	journalist	signature
dandelion	lettuce	skeleton
definite	locomotive	telephone
describe	margarine	television
fattening	mathematics	vegetable
February	medicine	
geography	miniature	
grammar	parallel	
history	parliament	

Hints for learning 'spelling demons'

Fry et al. (1984) listed some notorious examples of difficult vowel sounds, including 'accommodate; aisle; conscientious; lieutenant; muscle; noticeable; pneumonia; receipt; sergeant; unnecessary; vacuum; yacht'. Ehri (1997) added 'bargain; chocolate; excellent; lettuce; pigeon; terrace; tennis; vengeance'.

The Fernald spelling method as already described is a useful way to tackle these 'odd-bod' spellings.

Mnemonics can be devised to help such as 'You get vegetables at the table' to help remember the unsounded 'e', or 'A good secretary can keep a secret'. The 'spelling pronunciation' and syllable division can also be used: /con/ /son/ /ant/; /math/ /e/ /mat/ /ics/.

Pointing out words within words raises awareness of certain letters: 'lemon' and 'ade', 'tele' and 'phone'.

Word derivations and knowledge of the meaning of affixes, including what Henderson (1985) calls base words, helps to 'hold the spelling constant' for words. This strategy works well for those with good verbal skills and for those spellers who are at the conventional spelling stage.

confide – confident
divide – division
local – locality
medal – medallion
medicine – medical
pedant – pedantic
repeat – repetition
serene – serenity

HANDY HINT

Justification for teaching spelling rules was confirmed by Boder's (1973) study of pupils with dyslexia, which established that those who knew spelling rules made fewer errors and that their errors were good phonetic approximations making it easier to comprehend their meaning. Those who did not know or were unable to remember the spelling rules made bizarre attempts at some of the spelling.

Guidelines for teaching rules and conventions as recommended in the National Literacy Strategy

The National Literacy Strategy's *Spelling Bank* (DfEE 1999c) recommends teaching spelling conventions (rules) as follows:

- *'Tell the children the objective.'* Discuss and demonstrate the rule, verbalise and agree on a definition. The wording should be copied down for learning and revision, for example: '/ī/ or /ē/ sound at the end of a word often means that the word ends in "y"'.
- *'Introduce a set of relevant words.'* These can be given as a computer print out or can be gathered from a dictionary. They can be stored in the pupil's 'spelling log', in other words a personal dictionary.
- *'Ask the children to sort the words and identify patterns.'* These can be listed as word families in the pupil's spelling log.
- *'Help the children to hypothesise and test their ideas.'* Generate further examples to demonstrate the rule.
- *'Explain the principle behind the pattern, if appropriate.'* This could apply to the morpheme 'ed' for the past tense or 'es' for plural of nouns.
- *'Practise the convention.'* This can be done by using the words in sentences, by dictation and by games and workbooks such as Ott 2007a.
- *'Explore and extend e.g. exceptions, variations, application.'* This can be done during the text level work when reading during the Literacy Hour, and the words relating to the spelling convention currently being studied can be highlighted, underlined, copied into the spelling log and added to the pupil's spelling journal.

Adams (1990) pointed out that 'neither for the expert nor the novice can rote knowledge of the abstract rule in and of itself, make the difference. Practice, experience and frequent exposure to the rule using many examples in reading and writing is essential for mastery.' Adams (1990) delivers a forceful and important message that 'like arithmetic without application, phonics [including spelling] without connected reading amounts to useless mechanics'. The DfES (2003) responded to the Brooks Report and stated that 'phonics is an essential component within the pursuit [teaching reading] but other aspects of teaching and learning which play an equally critical role must not be neglected'. The NLS Key Stage 3 (DfEE 2001a) suggests that pupils use a personalised booklet which they call a 'Spellofax' which 'enables pupils to build a cumulative record of their learning through a sequence of "Spelling Challenges" and it can become a point of reference across the curriculum'.

This can be made using a small alphabetical pocket-sized Filofax. It can include examples of spelling rules, frequently misspelt words, hints and strategies, a crib sheet with subject spellings, spelling demons, 'odd-bod' spellings, a summary of the ten Commandments of Plurals and the seven 'Absolutely Super Suffixing' rules checklists and mnemonics.

Checklists for the best options for spelling consonant sounds

Consonants

Name/sound	Beginning	Middle	End
'b' says /b/	bag	cabin	nib
'c' says /c/	cat	picnic	music
	cot		
	cup		
'd' says /d/	dog	ladder	pod
'f' says /f/	fan	coffee	laugh
	phone	elephant	
'g' says /g/	gun	figure	pig
	ghost	giggle	egg
'h' says /h/	hut	behave	
	who		
'j' says /j/	jump	danger	page
	gin	project	bridge
	gem		
	gym		
'k' says /k/	king	chicken	bank
	chemist	acknowledge	duck
		antique	trek
			walk
'l' says /l/	lamp	pillow	wheel
			bell
'm' says /m/	man	common	palm
			lamb
			column
			paradigm
'n' says /n/	net	dinner	inn
	pneumonia		
	mnemonic		
	knife		
'p' says /p/	pig	puppet	cap
'q' (u) says /kw/	queen		
'r' says /r/	rat	carrot	purr
	rhyme	mortgage	
	wren		
's' says /s/	sun	missile	bus
	cent	castle	case
	city		class

Name/sound	Beginning	Middle	End
	c̲ycle		hou̲s̲e
	p̲s̲alm		
	s̲c̲ience		
	s̲word		
	s̲c̲heme		
't' says /t/	t̲ap	but̲t̲on	hat̲
	t̲hyme		
'v' says /v/	v̲an	vi̲v̲id	spiv̲
			fiv̲e
'w' says /w/	w̲itch	no̲body	o̲ne
	w̲hale		
'x' says /ks/	x̲-ray	ac̲c̲ess	fox̲
	ex̲it		
'y' says /y/	y̲ak	yoy̲o	
'z' says /z/	z̲ebra	raz̲or	quiz̲
		daz̲z̲le	jaz̲z̲
		scis̲s̲ors	

Checklist for the best options for spelling short and long vowels

Short vowels

Name	Beginning	Middle	End
'a' says /ă/	ăpple	hăt	Formică
		bănană	
'e' says /ĕ/	ĕgg	bĕd	
		thrĕad	
		saĕd	
		lĕisure	
'i' says /ĭ/	ĭgloo	lĭp	rentĕd
		bŭilding	womĕn
		bŭsiness	
'o' says /ŏ/	ŏrange	fŏx	squăd
'u' says /ŭ/	ŭmbrella	bŭn	gallŏp
		lŏve	
		toŭgh	

Long vowel sounds

Name	Beginning	Middle	End
'a' says /ā/	ācorn	hālo	plāy
	ēight	gāte	mistāke
	āerosol	trāin	ballēt
		rēign	obēy
		brēak	strāīght
'e' says /ē/	ēmu	scēne	shē
		mēat	athlēte

continued

Long vowel sounds (continued)

Name	Beginning	Middle	End
		bēer	coffēe
		fiēld	macaronī
		cēiling	quāy
			donkēy
			babȳ
'I' says /ī/	īvy	mīle	tīe
		nīght	skȳ
		tȳpe	recognīse
	ēye	chīld	
		gūide	
		nōte	
o says /ō/	ōpen	bōat	discō
		hōme	windōw
		shōulder	tōe
		sōld	dōugh
			gatēau
'u' says /u/	ūniform	tūbe	zōo
		vīew	stēw
		grōup	glūe
		Ēurope	shōe
		bōot	

Vowel-consonant – digraphs

Name	Beginning	Middle	End
'ar' says /ar/	ārm	fārm	burglār
'er' says /er/	ērror	fērn	sistēr
'ir' says /ir/	īrksome	bīrth	sīr
'or' says /or/	order	lord	meteōr
'ur' says /ur/	ūrn	būrn	fūr
		bīrd	stīr

Vowel diphthongs

Name	Beginning	Middle	End
'ou' says /ou/	ōur	hōuse	
'ow' says /ou/	ōwl	cōw	
'oy' says /oi/	ōyster	tōy	enjōy
'oi' says /oy/	ōil	vōice	

SUMMARY AND CONCLUSIONS

1 David Crystal (2002), considered by many to be one of the foremost authorities on the English language in Britain, and with an international reputation for his contribution to the study of the English language, boldly proclaimed that 'the suggestion that English spelling is fundamentally chaotic seems to be nonsense'. He argues that it is not that spelling is difficult but that 'children are rarely taught to spell but are just given lists of words to learn off by heart and in order to understand the spelling system of English children need to be given reasons why the spellings are as they are'. To spell well, children need to learn rules.

2 Spelling conventions, rules and generalisations have evolved throughout history because of expediency for printers, and practicality for users, when new words are encountered in spoken and written forms. This has resulted in about nine hundred new words in the English language each year: many of these are compounds of existing words, some are brand names, others are technical coinages for new inventions and some are borrowed from abroad.

3 The English language does not have a legislative body such as the Académie Française to make pronouncements about what is linguistically permissible. Samuel Johnson's and Noah Webster's dictionaries were accepted as the founts of knowledge about spelling, pronunciation and meaning. The *Oxford English Dictionary* (*OED*) took 71 years to prepare. It first appeared in twelve volumes in 1928 and, according to the editor James Murray, it included all possible words 'on historical principles from earliest records from AD 740 which resulted in a corpus of 616,500 word forms'. The second edition consists of twenty volumes.

   Webster's *New International Dictionary*, eighth edition, known as W3 when published in 1961, contained half a million words and is the most comprehensive dictionary of American English despite the criticisms about its 'permissive' style which included entries such as 'ain't'. They are now regarded as 'the standard work on British English spelling and "the ultimate authority on the English language"'.

4 A corollary to the search to improve reading standards was the development of lists of the most commonly used sight words, such as the pioneering work of Edward Dolch. From this Theodore Clymer developed a list of 45 'generalisations for spelling'. 'Words thus systematically arranged stand a chance by being recalled, when a list quickly fades from memory' according to Gillingham and Stillman (1956).

5 The gold standard for spelling rules and generalisation is to be found in the work of Hanna et al. (1971). Its pre-eminence is assured because it succeeded with the aid of technology in providing indisputable evidence that English has a predictable and rule-based spelling system, with 86 per cent of spellings being regular. This was a nail in the coffin of the disbelievers who argue that the spelling of the English language is chaotic.

6 Spelling rules and conventions can be used like a road map to chart spelling boundaries. When they are internalised they can generate confidence and guide the speller through the spelling jungle. Bos and Reitsma (2003) conducted a study on the effectiveness of various spelling strategies and exercises and concluded that 'rules are beneficial for children with spelling problems' and 'that rules can serve as a scaffold for the children and make children more aware of the presented spelling problem'.

7 Learning about spelling rules, Ehri (1997) contended, 'may be a first step. But if it is not internalised as part of working knowledge, then it remains outside the system.' This is why using a personalised spelling 'Spellofax' which includes the wording of the rule is essential for frequent revision and reinforcement to establish mastery for many spellers.

8 There should be consistency in the terminology. The language should be clear and unambiguous and as succinct as possible. These are particularly important considerations for those with word retrieval, word naming and working memory difficulties, including many dyslexic learners.

9 It is not the explicit recall of the rule that is the priority. It is the understanding of the underlying principles, and the skill to apply the knowledge. When teaching those with dyslexia it is important initially to choose rules that are mostly consistent and have few exceptions – the more examples that can be generated the better.

10 Some rules have to be mastered at the early stages of literacy, and should be matched to the cognitive skills and learning style of the individual learners. Skills need to be developed and built up over time, practised in meaningful contexts and honed with repeated experience such as when proofreading or by referring to the checklists for spelling options for personal writing. The more advanced rules, including perhaps the minor rules, can be learned later, just as rules involving technical or specialist vocabulary can be learned when the pupil has the underlying skills, knowledge and knowhow to handle these.

11 How Affixes Provide Signposts and Enhancement of Skills

- Why the study of the history of words is a key to a treasure trove of spelling knowledge and understanding
- Why root words are important basic building blocks for word study
- Checklists of useful root words
- Prefixes: an overview
- Checklist of prefixes
- Practical suggestions for teaching prefixes
- The role of grammar and its influence on suffixes
- Checklist of suffixes
- The 'Seven Seriously Super Suffixing' rules
- The 'Seven Absolutely Fabulous' rules for suffixes
- Practical suggestions for teaching suffixes
- Summary and conclusions

Keywords

Affixes	Etymology	Root words
Analytic phonics	Grapheme	Spelling pronunciation
Antonyms	High-frequency word	Suffixes
Borrowed words	Morpheme	Synthetic phonics
Comparative forms of adjectives	Morphology	Word class
	Phoneme	Word webs
Euphony	Prefixes	

Why the study of the history of words is a key to a treasure trove of spelling knowledge and understanding

Awareness of the etymology of words, which includes the study of the origins and use of Greek and Latin prefixes, suffixes and root words, enhances skills, promotes understanding of word meanings and generates many new words.

Prefixes

anti (against) Greek   antibiotic
circa (around) Latin   circulation

Suffixes

ology (study of) Greek   biology
phobia (excessive fear of) Latin   arachnophobia (fear of spiders)

Root words

cycl (circle) Greek   bicycle
loc (place) Latin   locate

Understanding of the derivation and meaning of affixes and root words makes them easier to learn to pronounce, to spell and to remember. Brown (1947) established that 60 per cent of words in printed texts were derived from Latin and Greek words. Otterman (1955) conducted an experiment on 12–13-year-olds which included learning about word origins. After thirty ten-minute lessons, the pupils were better at spelling and understanding the meanings of the words when they had been taught the meaning and the derivation of the words studied. Hanna et al. (1971) pronounced that 'knowledge of morphemes including affixes makes it possible to spell thousands of words'.

HANDY HINT

The spelling of suffixes is mostly consistent. Recognition of the spelling patterns, particularly of the most commonly used suffixes, is primarily a visual skill for normal spellers. Good spellers deduce this, but poor spellers need explicit teaching and rehearsal.

This was confirmed by a study conducted by Carlisle (1987), who compared morphological knowledge of learning-disabled 14-year-old dyslexics with 9- and 11-year-old normal spellers. She found that the former group's ability to spell 'derived forms was equivalent to 4th Graders' and their knowledge of 'morphemes equated to 6th Graders'. Henderson (1985) argues that younger children have difficulty spelling 'ed' because they are inclined to match it to the sound it makes. When meaning takes precedent over sound, as with the correct spelling of 'ed', 'meaning will be found to play the dominant role in spelling'. Many older dyslexic pupils continue to use sound rather than grammatical knowledge as their main spelling strategy, which is why phonetic spelling is a persisting characteristic of the condition.

Why root words are important basic building blocks for word study

A root word is the basic element of a word. It is sometimes described as a stem or base word (DfEE 2001b). It is often a word in itself. Root words can also take prefixes and or suffixes and then make a new word. 'Latin roots can be identified in 50–60 per cent of the words in any English dictionary' according to Cox and Hutcheson (1988). Familiarity and a working knowledge of the structure and function of these boosts decoding and encoding skills, as well as helping to generate a wider vocabulary. Henry (1988) asserted that 'the power in learning Latin roots lies in the fact that more are completely "regular", in other words they are spelt as they are sounded'. These can be noted and recorded in a personalised spelling log book or 'Spellofax' (DfEE 2001b) for further use.

Graphic organisers using a computer package such as *Inspiration* (www.iansyst.co.uk) can be used to make tree diagrams and mind maps, which are an excellent resource, particularly for strong visualisers.

The root 'duct' (*ducere* 'to lead', Latin) can have affixes added to make the following words:

Prefixes	Suffixes	Prefixes and suffixes	
ab**duct**	**duct**s	ab**duct**ed	
	ducted		
aque**duct**			
con**duct**		con**duct**or	con**duct**ing
		con**duct**ed	
de**duct**		de**duct**s	de**duct**ed
		de**duct**ing	
in**duct**	in**duct**ion	in**duct**ed	
instr**uct**	instr**uct**ed	instr**uct**ing	
obstr**uct**	obstr**uct**ing	obstr**uct**ion	
	obstr**uct**ed		
via**duct**			

Checklist of useful root words

Latin

Root	Word origin	Meaning	Examples
audi	audio	hear	audible, audience, audition
ann	annus	year	anniversary, annual, annuity
cede	cedere	to yield/admit	antecedent, precede, recede
clud	cludere	to shut	exclude, occlude, inclusion
cred	credere	to believe	creditor, credence, incredible
loc	locus	place	allocate, dislocate, located
man	manus	hand	manipulation, manual, manuscript
port	portare	to carry	deportation, import, portable
sci	scire	to know	conscious, science, scientifically
sign	signum	mark	insignia, signal, signature
spec	spectare	to see	inspection, spectacles, spectator

continued

struct	struere	to assemble/build	construction, destruction, structure
terr	terra	land/earth	extraterrestrial, territory, terrain
urb	urbs	city	suburban, urbane, urbanisation
vict	vincere	to conquer	invincible, victor victorious
vid	videre	to see	evidence, television, videophone
viv	vivere	to live	revival, survivor, vitamin
vol	volo	to wish/willing	involuntary, malevolent, volunteer
volv	volvere	to roll	evolution, devolved, revolution
vor	vorare	to eat/devour	carnivorous, herbivore, voracious

Word webs such as that shown below can be generated manually or electronically to illustrate and learn about meanings, pronunciation, usage and spelling of roots, prefixes and suffixes. They help to take away the fear of long words for poor spellers and poor readers. Using colour makes them more memorable. Using a word web will be more memorable if the root word is highlighted, or a different font is used.

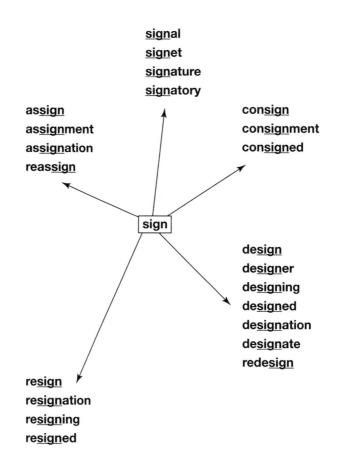

Greek

Root	Word origin	Meaning	Examples
aero	aer	air	aerial, aerobics, aerosol
arch	arche	power	archbishop, oligarchy, monarch
bio	bios	life	biography, biopsy, bionic
crat	cratos	power	aristocrat, bureaucrat, democrat
chron	chrono	time	chronic, chronical, chronology
cycl	kyklos	ring/circle	bicycle, cyclone, encyclopaedia
dem	demos	people	democracy, demagogue, demographer
epi	epi	upon	epicentre, epidemic, epilogue
gen	genos	race/kind	genealogy, genocide, progeny
gram	gramma	something written	grammar, monogram, telegram
graph	graphos	someone who writes/draws	autographical, photograph, telegraph
hydr	hydr/hydro	water	dehydration, hydroelectricity, hydrant
path	pathos	feeling	empathy, pathetic, sympathetic
phon	phone	sound/voice	phonics, telephone, saxophonist
photo	photo	light	photogenic, photography, photosynthesis
poli	polis	city	cosmopolitan, metropolitan, police
phys	physis	nature	physics, physiology, physique
psych	psyche	mind	psychology, psychiatrist, psychopathic
scop	skopein	look at	microscope, stethoscope, telescope
therm	therme	heat	thermal, thermometer, thermostat

These word lists are based on *The Key Stage 3 National Strategy Literacy Progress Unit Spelling* (DfEE 2001b). The root words have been chosen to demonstrate that affixes can be added at the beginning and ends of words, rather than to give lists of every variation possible.

HANDY HINT

The following root words can be used to generate many examples:

form   duct   port   rupt   sign   struct   tend

HANDY HINT

Many more words can be generated from these roots with the use of a dictionary of etymology, games (including computer programs), worksheets, puzzles and texts which use these keyword spellings in meaningful contexts as well as by using cloze procedures for prose passages with the keyword spellings missing (see Ott 2007).

Prefixes: an overview

According to Crystal (2002) 'There are over 100 common prefixes and suffixes in English'. These can be used singly or in combination, and, as many schoolchildren delight in discovering, 'antidisestablishmentarianism' is an example of what can be done with prefixes and suffixes when seeking new words as well as knowing how to spell them.

A prefix is a letter or a group of letters that go at the beginning of a word, usually changing the meaning of the word. The NLS (DfEE1998) defines it as 'a morpheme which can be added to the beginning of a word, to change its meaning; such as in-finite; in-conclusive; in-edible'.

HANDY HINT

The following are the most frequently used prefixes according to Becker et al.'s (1980) analysis of 26,000 high-frequency words:

com con de dis ex im in or pre pro re un

The initial objective should be to show how prefixes work. Their usefulness can be explained, illustrated and followed by examples. Use root words such as 'form'; 'port'; 'tend'. Brainstorm to generate new words orally, and try to make as many different words as possible. Use colour for the prefixes to heighten the visual impact when they are written.

HANDY HINT

The *Oxford Spell It Yourself Dictionary* lists over eight thousand root words, which are highlighted in bold, and gives the derivations.

Graphic organisers and computer packages enhance and clarify understanding, as well as enabling pupils to improve their spelling skills. Prefixes can be taught by using a spelling dictionary such as the *Oxford Colour Spelling Dictionary* or the *Oxford Quick Spelling Dictionary* (www.oup.com) or Geddes and Grosset (1997), *Dictionary of Spelling*. Pupils can choose a prefix such as 'mis' and then find and write down as many words as they know the meaning of already. They might then on another occasion be asked to find six 'mis' words they do not know the meaning of: they could look up the meaning in the dictionary and add these to their personal spelling file or log or 'Spellofax'.

Another useful activity is to take the prefix 'anti' and ask pupils to look it up in the dictionary. There is an additional feature associated with the spelling of 'anti' words. Some words have the anti joined to the root word – anticlimax; anticlockwise; antidepressant. Some words have the anti hyphenated – anti-aircraft; anti-inflammatory; anti-rust. There is an even longer dictionary list of words with 'un' as a prefix.

HANDY HINT

***Chambers Twenty-first Century Dictionary* (1999) has an alphabetical list of over a hundred 'anti' words ranging from anti-apartheid to anti-Zionist. Reading the words and then choosing a top twenty list of personal favourites can be fun as well as instructional, and improves vocabulary skills.**

HANDY HINT

Prefixes such as the following are often used to form antonyms:

> **de   dis   mis   re**

They generate many examples.

Pupils can compete to see who can find the most examples. This could be done as a paired spelling activity. The better speller could be delegated to writing the examples on a personal whiteboard. It can also be done with the help of the teacher or a teaching assistant.

Pupils enjoy being asked to read an article and then to rewrite it so as to change the meaning to the negative by using prefixes. Editorials in a newspaper can be studied. Then as a writing task pupils can be asked to put a circle around words with a prefix. Computer graphics can be used to illustrate high-frequency prefixes such as 'anti', and, the more outlandish the examples, the more memorable. These illustrations could be laminated and used in a variety of card games such as Snap and Pelmanism. Prefixes used as antonyms such as 'maxi' and 'mini' are also suitable for a number of activities and can be visually striking such 'as a mini-skirt and a maxi-skirt'. There are commercial products such as games available for sorting and matching prefixes and root words.

Checklist of prefixes

Latin

Prefix	Meaning	Examples
ab	from	abandon, absolve, abstain
ac	towards	accede, accelerate, acclivity
ambi	on both sides	ambidextrous, ambiguity, ambivalent
ante	before	antenatal, ante-post, anteroom
circa	around	circulation, circumference, circumlocution
co	among	coeducational, co-exist, cohabiting
contra	against	contraception, contradictory, contraflow
de	down/opposite	deflates, detoxification, devalue
dis	lack of	disabled, disapproval, disinterest
inter	among	interaction, intercom internet
non	not	non-alcoholic, non-stick, non-smoking
omni	all	omnibus, omnipotent, omnivorous
per	through/by means	perforation, perennial, pervade
post	after	postgraduate, post mortem, postscript
re	again	recapture, remake, retake
retro	backwards	retrocede, retrograde, retrospection
sub	under	submarine, subcontractor, subterranean
super	above	superglue, superpower, superstore
trans	across	transatlantic, transfer, transcribe
ultra	beyond	ultimatum, ultrasound, ultraviolet
uni	one/single	uniformity, unisex, unison

Greek

Prefix	Meaning	Examples
a	not/without	apathy, abortion, aversion
aero	air	aerobics, aeroplane, aerosol
ana	backwards/again	anachronism, anagram, anathema
anti	from/against	antipathy, antipodes, antonym
auto	self	autograph, automatic, automation
dys	bad/difficulty	dyscalculia, dyslexia, dyspraxia
ex	out	excavation, excerpt, exhale
hetero	one or the other	heterogeneous, heterosexual
hydro	water	hydrofoil, hydrogen, hydrotherapy
hyper	excessive	hyperactivity, hyperbole, hypermarket
hypno	sleep	hypnosis, hypnotherapy, hypnotism
hypo	under	hypochondriac, hypodermic, hypothermia
meta	between/among	metacarpal, metamorphosis, metaphor
micro	little	microclimate, microlight, microphone
mono	single	monologue, monoplane, monosyllabic
optic	seen/visible	optical, optician, optometry
peri	around	peripatetic, peripheral, periscope
photo	light	photocopy, photography, photostat
poly	many	polychrome, polygamy, polyglot
syn	with/together	synchronism, syndicate, syndrome
tele	far/far off	telephone, telescopic, televise

Anglo-Saxon

Prefix	Meaning	Examples
a/ab	without	abode, afloat, aghast
afore	before/previously	aforesaid, aforementioned, aforethought
all	all things considered	almighty, altogether, always
be/bi	about/all around	bedecked, bedevilled
by	next to/besides	byroads, bystander, byword
fore	before/beforehand	forecast, forego, forehead
mid	middle	middlemost, midriff, midwife
mis	wrongly/badly	Misfire, misfit, mislay
out	out/openly	outlandish, outlaw, outward
over	above/beyond	overdo, overrun, overstep
self	self	self-assurance, self-fulfilling, self-willed
un	not	unbearable, uncleanness, unfolding
up	upper	upright, uphill, upward
wel	competent/skilful	welcome, wellspring, well-wisher
with	away/back	withdraw, without, withstand

Prefixes associated with numeracy

Prefix	Meaning	Origin	Examples
bi	twice	Latin	bicycle, bisect, biplane
cent/centi	hundred	Latin	centimetre, centenary, century
circu	around	Latin	circle, circumference
dec	ten	Greek	decade, decimal, decagon
di	twice/double	Greek	diagonal, diameter dissect
equi	equal	Latin	equiangular, equidistant, equilateral
hecto	hundred	Greek	hectare, hectolitre, hectometre
iso	equal	Latin	isobar, isometric, isosceles
macro	great	Greek	macrocosm, macroeconomics, macroscopic
magni	great	Latin	magnificent, magnitude, magnum
mega	big	Greek	megabyte, megahertz, megaton
micro	little	Greek	microcosm, microfiche, micrometer
mil	thousand	Latin	millimetre, millennium, milligram
nonus	ninth	Latin	nonagenarian, nonagon, nonary
pent	five	Greek	pentagon, pentagram, pentathlon
peri	around	Greek	perimeter, periodic, periscope
poly	many	Greek	polygon, polygraph, polytechnic
quad	four	Greek	quadratic, quadrilateral, quadruple
septa	seven	Latin	septennial, septet, septuagenarian
tri	three	Greek	trice, triangle, trigonometry

PRACTICAL SUGGESTIONS FOR TEACHING PREFIXES

Use multi-sensory learning methods and match spelling strategies to individual learning styles.

Begin by learning the meaning of individual prefixes using keywords preferably already in the individual's vocabulary. This acts as a marker for their spelling. Use a tripartite multi-sensory approach which includes the use of visual memory. For example when learning to use the prefix 'extra', say the word and its meaning. For those who find it difficult to spell 'extra' use the spelling pronunciation to accentuate the letters. Others find it helpful to divide and count the two syllables ex/tra. Write the word. Then write the following words:

extracurricular **extra**ordinary **extra**terrestrial **extra**vagant

Colour code, highlight or use a different font to differentiate the prefix from the root word. This helps to ensure that 'a' is not omitted. Drawing attention to the word's Latin origin helps to establish that 'extra' means 'outside', 'beyond'. It is essential to bring it to the pupil's attention that 'extra' is a spelling pattern of a chunk of letters which are cemented together when saying the word and when learning to spell it. Doing this uses a multi-sensory approach to learning prefixes.

The prefix 'well' sometimes drops 'l' when it is added to a root word:

welcome   **wel**fare

When 'well' is used before the noun it qualifies in a compound word, it keeps 'll' and is hyphenated:

well-behaved (child)   **well**-educated (person)
well-groomed (girl)   **well**-informed (student)
well-known (person)   **well**-known (personality)
well-read (teenager)   **well**-timed (arrival)

When 'well' is used after the verb it qualifies in a compound word it is not hyphenated ('it was well balanced'):

well balanced
well bred
well dressed
well informed
well matched
well spoken

When 'well' is used in idiomatic phrases It is hyphenated:

well-done (satisfactory)
well-heeled
well-knit
well-wisher
well-stacked
well-wisher

When 'il' is used before a root word beginning with 'l', the 'l' appears twice:

illegal   **il**legible   **il**legitimate   **il**liberal
illogical **il**luminate   **il**lusion   **il**lustration

When 'il' is used as an adjective to make a compound adjective, the 'l' is doubled and the word is hyphenated:

ill-advised   **ill**-equipped
ill-mannered   **ill**-treated
ill-bred   **ill**-humoured

When '*im*' is used as a prefix before a word beginning with 'm' the word has double 'mm':

immaterial **imm**aturity **imm**ediate **imm**ensely   **imm**ersion
immigrant   **imm**inent   **imm**obile   **imm**oderate **imm**unise

When '*in*' is used as a prefix before a word beginning with 'n' the word has a double 'nn':

innards **inn**ate **inn**er **inn**ermost **inn**ings
innocent **inn**ocuous **inn**ovative **inn**uendo **inn**umerable

When '*ir*' is used as a prefix before a word beginning with 'r' the word has a double 'rr':

irreconcilable **irr**edeemable **irr**efutable **irr**egular **irr**elevant
irreligious **irr**emovable **irr**eplaceable **irr**itable **irr**itation

Euphony

Some words would be difficult to pronounce if certain prefixes were added to them. The last letter of the prefix is sometimes changed to harmonise with the first letter of the root word. This makes it easier to roll the word off the tongue and is known as euphony. Examples include the following prefixes:

Prefix	Root word	Examples
ad	fair	affair
	tend	attend
con	lect	collect
	lege	college
dis	ficult	difficult
	minish	diminish
in	mediate	Immediate
	movable	immovable
ob	fend	offend
	press	oppress
sub	port	support
	pose	suppose

Some prefixes are spelt differently, depending on the first letter of the root word to which they are being added.

'cent' is used before a vowel; 'centi' is used before a consonant:

centrifugal **cent**urion **cent**ury
centigrade **cent**ilitre **cent**ipede

'dec' is used before a vowel; 'deci' is used before a consonant:

decade **dec**athlon **Dec**ember
decibel **dec**imal **dec**imate

The role of grammar and its influence on suffixes

A suffix is a letter or a group of letters that go at the end of a root word, usually changing the usage of the word. The NLS (DfEE 1998) defines it as a 'morpheme which is added to the end of a word'. There are two main categories. Inflectional suffixes changes the tense or status of the word from present ('talk') to past ('talk-ed'), or from singular ('clown') to plural ('clown-s'). Derivational suffixes change the word class, for example turning a verb into a noun – 'walk', 'walker' – and turning a noun into an adjective – 'logic', 'logical'.

Crystal (2002) pointed out that English grammar has fewer than a dozen types of regular endings (and a few irregular ones). The most frequently used include:

• Regular plurals adding 's'	pen – pens
• Genitives denoting possession or ownership	cat's paw
• Past tense of verbs adding 'ed'	talk – talked
• Past participles of verbs adding 'ed'	I look – I have looked
• Present tense of verbs adding 'ing'	read – reading
• The third person singular adding 's'	I talk – he talks
• The contractions adding 'n't'	can not – can't
	shall not – shan't
• The degree of adjectives adding 'er', 'est'	hot – hotter – hottest

An illustration such as the 'friend' word web (opposite) (Adapted from Hasenstab et al. (1994), cited in Mather and Roberts (1995) helps to demonstrate grammatical processes. They can be generated manually or electronically using software such as *Kidspiration* or *Inspiration* (www.dyslexia.com). Use of colours makes them more effective, particularly for strong visualisers.

The following are the most frequently used suffixes according to Becker et al. (1980):

'al'	'ble'	'ate'	'ant'	'ed'	'en'	'er'	'ent'	'ise'/'ize'	'ist'
'ing'	'ive'	'ition'	'ic'	'ful'	'ly'	'less'	'ment'	'ness'	'ous [y]'

British publishers use both '-ise' and '-ize' for verb endings, and in many words either spelling is correct. The '-ise' system is easier for beginners to learn, since there are only two exceptions, 'size' and 'prize' in the value sense, whereas in the '-ize' system there are still many common words that must be spelt '-ise'. The same applies to '-iser', '-ising', '-isation' etc.

Some suffixes denoting verb tenses:

's'	'ed'	'en'	'ing'
walks	looked	brighten	cooking
likes	mended	frighten	running
happens	talked	tighten	snatching

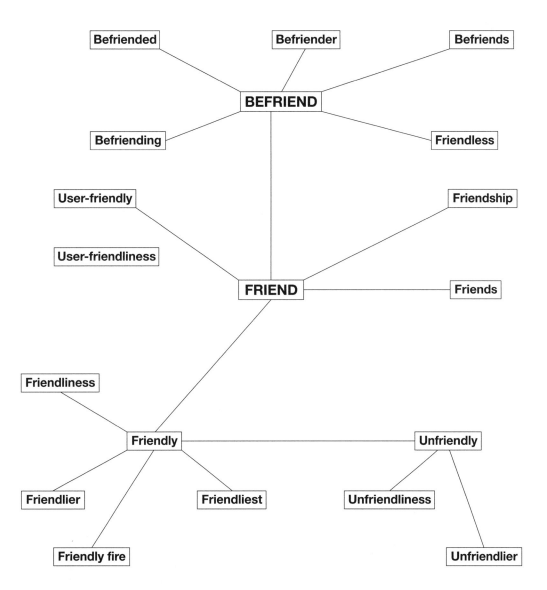

How affixes provide signposts to spelling and prenunication

Some suffixes denote grammatical properties. Word classes (colloquially known as parts of speech) include the following.

Verbs	Adverbs	Nouns	Adjectives
age manage	**ly** quickly	**ant** assistant	**able** favourable
ate decorate	**er** happier	**ard** drunkard	**ant** pleasant
en widen		**ee** employee	**al** cultural
er discover		**er** singer	**ary** customary
ify justify		**er** painter	**ible** possible
ise advertise		**ess** actress	**ic** historic
ize equalize		**hood** knighthood	**ine** feminine
		ian politician	**ish** childish
		ine heroine	**ive** creative
		ism communism	**like** childlike
		ist guitarist	**less** aimless
		ment enjoyment	**ory** peremptory
		ness slowness	
		ology radiology	

Suffixes used to make comparative and superlative forms of adjectives are 'er' and 'est'.

Positive	Comparative	Superlative
tall	tall**er**	tall**est**
quick	quick**er**	quick**est**

Checklist of suffixes

Latin

Suffix	Meaning	Examples
able	knowledge/power	capable, fashionable, payable
age	collection/set of	baggage, orphanage, wreckage
al	related/action of doing	arrival, parental, departmental
ate	like/related to	affectionate, compassionate, passionate
ee	person who is or has something	absentee, employee, payee
ese	related to a country/place	Burmese, Chinese, Japanese
ess	female of type/class	duchess, lioness, tigress
ian	relating/similar to	beautician, optician, musician
ism	ideas/principles	alcoholism, feminism, socialism
ist	believer in	anarchist, novelist, tourist
ive	quality/feeling	creative, effective, emotive
ol	derived from	alcohol, ethanol, methanol
ose	possession of a certain quality	bellicose, morose, verbose
osis	condition	hypnosis, metamorphosis, psychosis
ous	quality/character	adventurous, jealous, marvellous, zealous
tude	disposition/state of mind	attitude, gratitude, solitude
ure	action/process	displeasure, leisure, seizure

Greek

Suffix	Meaning	Examples
ism	beliefs/principles/prejudices	agnosticism, pacifism, vandalism
ide	chemical/compound	chloride, fluoride, peroxide
ite	group	anthracite, dynamite, granite
itis	name of disease/condition	appendicitis, conjunctivitis, tonsillitis
ology	science/word/reason	ecology, biology, neurology
phobia	fear	agoraphobia, claustrophobia, xenophobia

Anglo-Saxon

Suffix	Meaning	Examples
ed	denotes past tense of verbs	looked, talked, rented
en	denotes past participles of verbs	broken, fallen, written
er	someone who does something	baker, singer, teacher
est	superlative degree of adjectives	funniest, hottest, sunniest
ful	inclination to do something	forgetful, graceful, merciful
hood	state or condition of being in	childhood, fatherhood, priesthood
ing	denotes present tense/present participle of verbs	driving, loving, running
ish	slightly/fairly	babyish, reddish, fiftyish
le	names of tools/diminutives	handle, kettle, thimble
less	smaller size/lacking	breathless, homeless, tasteless
like	similar/resembling	ladylike, lifelike, warlike
ly	used to form adverbs/manner of	happily, quickly, slowly
ness	quality/condition	greediness, kindness, ugliness
ship	position/rank	apprenticeship, premiership, scholarship
ward	direction of/towards	forward, homeward, upward

The 'Seven Seriously Super Suffixing' rules

To teach spelling rules and strategies when adding suffixes (Ott 2007)

Revise, rehearse and reinforce definitions and concepts of the following: short and long vowels, roots, prefixes, vowels, consonants, digraphs, blends, syllables, suffixes beginning with consonants, suffixes beginning with vowels. Do this orally, aurally and visually with worksheets and sentences in meaningful contexts, and by using games and computer programs. The DfEE (2001b) support materials have many excellent suggestions for making and playing games to enhance skills. They use visual organisers to connect different word forms which then allows the child to formulate a statement which they then add to a 'conventions frame' which acts like a spelling rule. The element of 'self-discovering' of the rule has many pedagogic advantages.

Suffixing Spelling Rule One: The One – One – One Rule

Words with one syllable, one short vowel and ending in one consonant double the consonant before adding a suffix beginning with a vowel.
    Suffixes beginning with vowels include:

    er   ed   est   en   ing   ish   ous   y

Suffixes beginning with consonants include:

    ful   less   ly   ment   ness   some

Root words with suffixes:

    fat   fatter   fatted   fattest   fattening   fatty
    slip   slipper   slippiest   slipping   slippy   slippage   slippiness

Exceptions:

   If the root word ends in a long vowel do not double the final consonant:

    blow   blower   blowed   blowiest   blowing   blowy
    wait   waiter   waited   waiting

If the root word ends in a consonant digraph, do not double the final consonant:

    wish   wished   wishing   wishy-(washy)
    punch   puncher   punchiest   punched   punching

If the root word has two or more syllables and if the second syllable is stressed and has one vowel and one consonant, double the consonant before adding an ending beginning with a vowel:

    prefer   preferred   preferring
    occur   occurrence   occurred   occurring

Suffixing Spelling Rule Two: The Lazy 'e' Rule (a)

Drop 'e' before adding a suffix beginning with a vowel.
Root words with suffixes:

    joke   joker   joked   joking   joky
    stone   stonier stoniest   stony   stoned   stoning

The following are exceptions because they keep 'e' before adding a suffix beginning with a vowel.

    acre   acreage
    canoe   canoeing

dye	dyeing
hoe	hoeing
mile	mileage
shoe	shoeing
singe	singeing
tinge	tingeing
toe	toeing

Suffixing Spelling Rule Three: The Lazy 'e' Rule (b)

Keep 'e' before adding a suffix beginning with a consonant.

name	nameless	namely	namelessly	namelessness
use	useful	useless	usefulness	uselessly

Exceptions: Drop 'e' although adding a suffix beginning with a consonant in the following:

awe	awful
due	duly
nine	ninth
true	truly
subtle	subtly
whole	wholly

Suffixing Spelling Rule Four: The Lazy 'e' Rule (c)

Keep 'e' in words with root words ending in 'ce' and 'ge' when adding the suffixes able, ade, ous. This is because of the pronunciation conventions of soft 'c' and soft 'g'.

'able'

change	changeable
charge	chargeable
knowledge	knowledgeable
manage	manageable
notice	noticeable
pronounce	pronounceable
service	serviceable
trace	traceable

'ade'

orange	orangeade

'ous'

advantage	advantageous
courage	courageous
outrage	outrageous

Suffixing Spelling Rule Five: The 'y' rule (a)

Change 'y' to i before adding suffixes including 'al', 'ance', 'ed', 'er', 'est', 'ful', 'hood', 'ness'.

'al'
ceremony – ceremonial
memory – memorial
testimony – testimonial

'ance'
ally – alliance
apply – appliance
defy – defiance

'ed'
cry – cried
empty – emptied
supply – supplied

'er'
fry – frier
dry – drier
try – trier

'est'
busy – busiest
cosy – cosiest
tiny – tiniest

'ful'
beauty – beautiful
fancy – fanciful
mercy – merciful

'hood'
hardy – hardihood
likely – likelihood
lively – livelihood

'ness'
dreary – dreariness
tardy – tardiness
weary – weariness

Exceptions

'ly'
dry – dryly
shy – shyly
sly – slyly
spry – spryly
wry – wryly

'ness'
dryness
shyness
slyness
spryness
wryness

In some of these words either 'i' or 'y' is acceptable.

Suffixing Spelling Rule Six: The 'y' Rule (b)

Keep 'y' when adding the suffixes 'ing', 'ish', 'ist'. This is because two 'ii's do not go together in English spelling.

'ing'
dry – drying
carry – carrying
clarify – clarifying
hurry – hurrying
try – trying

'ish'
baby – babyish

'ist'
copy – copyist

Exceptions: 'skiing', 'taxiing'

Suffixing Spelling Rule Seven: The 'y' Rule (c)

Keep 'y' if there is a vowel before 'y' when adding a suffix:

key   keyed   keying   keys
employ   employable   employee   employed   employing   employs

Exceptions: These drop 'y' from the root word before adding a suffix:

day	daily
gay	gaily
lay	laid
pay	paid
say	said
slay	slain

The 'Seven Absolutely Fabulous' rules for suffixes

Some experienced practitioners tackle the following frequently used suffixes on an individual basis, before teaching the 'Seven Seriously Super Suffixing' rules, because they have a high frequency in texts and occur at the early stages of developing literacy skills. 'ate', 'ed', 'er', 'ing', 'ion', 'ly', 'y'.

They are useful and helpful for all spellers but especially for older dyslexic pupils. They include the following 'Absolutely Fabulous' rules:

1   Rules for adding the suffix 'ate'
2   Rules for adding the suffix 'ed' to verbs
    'ed' never says /ed/. It can say:

/t/	/d/	/id/
walked	thanked	mended
cooked	handed	rented

3   Rules for adding the suffix 'er'
4   Options for spelling the /shun/ sound include the following:

cean	ocean
cheon	luncheon
cian	magician
cion	suspicion
sci	conscience
shion	fashion
sion	division
ssion	possession
tion	addition
xion	crucifixion

5   Rules for adding the suffix 'ing' to root words
6   Rules for adding the suffix 'ly'
7   Rules for adding suffixes to root words ending in 'y'

PRACTICAL SUGGESTIONS FOR TEACHING SUFFIXES

When deciding what to choose for a spelling list for poor spellers, frequency of use must always be a key consideration and a priority.

HANDY HINT

Drawing the speller's attention to the fact that the most common way to spell the /shun/ sound is by using 'tion' is a priority. This can then be used to generate over five hundred words such as 'nation', 'station'.

A golden rule for choosing words for spelling lists for individuals with dyslexia is to teach the regular spellings first. Later the irregular spellings may be taught, often on another occasion, depending on the individual's degree of dyslexia. Some very poor spellers can be severely challenged to learn regular spellings, even those that follow a particular pattern or rule, with 100 per cent reliability. Furthermore, irregular spellings such as the 'odd-bods' totally confuse them even after repeated exposure and huge amounts of time and effort. They are often not committed to long-term memory for automatic recall, particularly in writing situations.

Some rules more than others, such as the one-one-one rule, repay careful study because they are used so frequently and from an early stage of spelling development.

The language included in the definition of rules needs constant revision and rehearsal, particularly for those with word naming and word retrieval difficulties. Always use examples to illustrate the application of the rule, so that the individual has a concrete target word to act as a trigger when they want to apply a rule. Good visualisers will be able to recall the spelling pattern in their mind's eye when they use it when proofreading. Those with an ability and the skills to spell by analogy will use this strategy: for example, they may say that the /e/ sound at the end of 'baby' is spelled like 'daddy'.

When proofreading it is often useful to target a specific suffixing rule, such as checking that the past tense of the verb which takes 'ed' has been spelt correctly. This for example could be part of a S-M-A-R-T target in an IEP.

Posters with examples of the checklists can be displayed on classroom walls. Laminated mats taped to the desk can be referred to during writing tasks.

The suffixing rules can be entered in the individual's spelling file, log or 'Spellofax'. They should be encouraged to refer to it, and to add further examples for personal use, for example when to use 'el' or 'le'.

HANDY HINT

Most words which end in /l/ sound are spelt with 'le'. There are some high-frequency words pronounced as /l/ but spelt with 'el' which should be learned using the 'look, say, cover, write, check' method to commit them to memory for instant recall. They include the following:

angel	kennel
barrel	label
channel	mussel
funnel	parcel

The words learned for today's test are forgotten by next week, unless they are used in meaningful contexts and are frequently rehearsed and revised over a period of weeks. If spellings are to become internalised and part of the dyslexic speller's sight vocabulary to be recalled automatically, frequent repetition is necessary.

HANDY HINT

'Keep using the spellings you have learned or you will lose them' is a useful maxim for individual words, but is essential for remembering spelling rules.

The National Literacy Strategy (DfEE 2001b) advocated using the 'self-discovery' approach and recommended asking the pupil to generate and write a rule to match a worksheet when they have completed it. For some pupils with dyslexia this may be too difficult because of their underlying expressive language and word naming difficulties. When to use 'ar', 'er', 'or' is a source of confusion for many spellers. Phenix (1996) suggested using as a mnemonic the old nursery rhyme 'Tinker, tailor, soldier, sailor, rich man, poor man, beggarman, thief'. This illustrates three different ways to spell an ending which appears to denote the same thing – a person who does a job. Words derived from Latin such as 'author' or 'orator' use 'or'. Words derived from Greek such as 'astronomer' or 'photographer' tend to use 'er'. Words derived from French such as 'conqueror' or 'surveyor' tend to use 'or'.

'ar'	'er'	'or'
beggar	butcher	actor
burglar	carpenter	doctor
bursar	farmer	director
friar	grocer	inventor
registrar	plumber	professor
vicar	waiter	supervisor

The use of colour is very effective when teaching and learning affixes. The root word can be written in green, the suffixing in red and the prefix in blue. This is helpful for good visualisers. It is useful to use colour when rewriting a passage using prefixes as antonyms. Another effective use of colour is to highlight the letters that are doubled. This is particularly effective on a computer.

Using a dictionary and playing a game to see who can find the most words for 'phobias' is amusing and instructional. For example an 'a–z' of words such as 'arachnophobia' (a fear of spiders) to 'zoophobia' (a fear of animals) works well as a paired spelling activity and equally well on a computer.

Games such as Snap or Bingo can be used to reinforce skills and to raise awareness of affixes and roots in words.

The DfEE (2001a) support material for Phonics includes a helpful suggestion for a game adding suffixes which it calls Double or Drop? It involves making cards with suffixes and a whiteboard with five categories marked as follows:

Do not double the consonant	Double the consonant	Drop the 'e'	Irregular words	Not sure

There are also many computer programs available for learning and using affixes (see Chapter 14 in this volume.

SUMMARY AND CONCLUSIONS

1   A basic understanding of the structure of language, including the anatomy of words, is a worthwhile investment in time and effort. Dissecting words and getting down to the bare bones, as with identifying the root words can help to heighten consciousness of basic spelling elements. Those with good visual skills learn by grafting on affixes and by memorising these word patterns. Strong verbalisers with good language skills deepen their understanding of word structure and spelling when using and learning the meanings of Anglo-Saxon, Greek and Latin derivatives. Ehri (1997) endorsed the practice of 'distinguishing spelling of words in terms of their origins whether Anglo-Saxon or Greek, as well as learning patterns associated with each origin to constitute systematic knowledge' and cited Henry's research (1988) in support of her argument. For those who have kinaesthetic skills, the use of multi-sensory strategies can help to compensate for poor visual skills and poor phonological skills by dividing words into roots, prefixes and suffixes, and then synthesising these words when reading and spelling.

2   Specific knowledge and understanding of affixes helps to take away the fear of spelling long words, many of which follow a reliable sound-to-symbol match.

3   Making and using a task analysis of what prefixes do repays time and effort.

4   Adding prefixes to words that follow some clear-cut guidelines and rules is worthwhile. Stauffer (1969) identified the fifteen prefixes 'that accounted for 82

per cent of the words listed in Thorndike and Lorge's *The Teacher's Word Book of 30,000 Words Most Frequently and Widely Used in General Reading for Children and Young People'* (1944) as:

ab ad com de dis en ex in (into) in (not)
mis pre pro re sub un

5 Suffixes carry out many important tasks, including grammatical and syntactic functions.

6 The rules for adding suffixes are clear-cut, specific, reliable and frequently used. The study of these pays handsome dividends for spellers. Evidence for their importance can be found in QCA's (2004) evaluation of children's performance in the English test results in the 2003 National Curriculum Assessments at Key Stage 2. It gave the results for the twenty words on the test. 'Eleven words in the test assessed knowledge of prefixes and suffixes.' The following are the six most difficult words on the test and the percentage who spelled them correctly:

effortless	45.1%
knowledge	42.8%
participate	33.5%
rehearsed	28.8%
thoroughly	15.8%

The report indicated that 'while most children achieving Level 3 can correctly spell a number of words which are inflected or have prefixes or suffixes, they still make a significant number of errors in those areas, suggesting that some children are not necessarily fully aware of word structure or how to use this to help them spell'.

7 It is important to match spelling instruction to individual learning styles, to stages of development and to curricular needs. The younger pupil or the older severely dyslexic pupil may find it advantageous to learn how to add 'ed' to words. Older pupils may need help with subject specific vocabulary. Science students will need to understand and spell Greek and Latin affixes.

8 Understanding and applying spelling strategies when using affixes lightens the load, particularly for poor spellers. It empowers all learners and leads them to discover ways and means of expanding their use of language. It enhances vocabulary, and breaks down long or difficult words into manageable steps by providing a roadmap with clear signposts for their spelling, which is a key consideration when enhancing spelling skills.

12 Using Segmentation as the Backbone of Literacy

- • Why the explicit teaching of syllables is necessary
- • At what age can syllables be taught?
- • Practical suggestions for oral activities to teach segmentation skills
- • Essential terminology needed to understand syllable division, strategies and techniques
- • Practical suggestions for learning and using syllable division
- • Guidelines for multi-sensory strategies for syllable division
- • Step-by-step processes and useful tips to learn and use syllable division
- • How to be in 'CLOVER' with syllable patterns
- • The characteristics of the six major syllable patterns
- • Guidelines when choosing words for syllable division practice based on word frequency
- • Teaching principles to 'promote active learning' with suggestions to develop understanding and know-how
- • Summary and conclusions

Keywords

Accent	Digraphs	Split vowel digraphs
Analogy	Diphthongs	Syllable
Assimilations	Letter strings	Syllable division line
Blends	Macron	Trigraphs
Breve	Monosyllable	Vowel
Consonants	Onset	Vowel digraphs
Consonant digraphs	Polysyllable	
Diacritical marks	Rime	

Why the explicit teaching of syllables is necessary

A significant number of readers and many spellers find long words hard to pronounce and spell, and many perceive them as daunting, difficult and challenging. 'A student's ability to identify a syllable is basic to his reliable pronunciation of multi-syllabic English words' (Cox 1980). Bateman's (1965) research cited by Cox and Hutcheson (1988) showed that 'the lower the reader's aptitude for recognising words, the more crucial is the need for specific instruction and extensive practice in the use of scientific formulas for dividing and pronouncing longer words – for understanding and using the structure of written English'.

To teach syllable division effectively it is necessary to consider the age of the individual, background knowledge and stage of development in spelling skills. It is important to establish awareness and knowledge about syllables as an oral activity before using them in written work. The content of lessons needs to be carefully structured and sequential; explicit teaching is necessary for individual strategies. Each process needs to be broken down into progressive steps which require frequent repetition, rehearsal and revision.

One of the biggest stumbling blocks when learning about syllables is remembering the associated terminology. Many individuals with dyslexia have difficulties with expressive and receptive language, including word retrieval and word naming difficulties. Their needs should be a prime consideration when teaching vocabulary and definitions. The way forward is to use clear, accurate and consistent wording in all definitions.

Definitions can be memorised by using crib cards for the vocabulary, using index cards or the computer, thus using a multi-sensory approach to match individual learning styles. They can also be added to the personal 'Spellofax'.

At what age can syllables be taught?

Pre-school children are sensitive to rhyme and rhythm in spoken language. Liberman et al. (1974) established that 4-year-old children can tap out and recognise syllables in words when they are presented orally. An ability to do this is now recognised as an important precursor of literacy. Ferreiro and Teberosky (1982) showed that when children first become aware that speech sounds can be matched to print they do so with the help and knowledge of syllables. Treiman and Zukowski (1991) conducted an experiment with children between the ages of 5 and 7 years, and found that most children are good at segmenting spoken words into syllables. However, Balmuth (1982) established that it is more difficult to identify syllables when reading than when listening. When awareness of syllables has been established orally, children can then learn to recognise the onset, which is the initial consonant and consonant cluster in a syllable, and the rime, which is the vowel and final consonant(s) of the syllable. Using the rime part of the word '-et' in 'pet' is easier to read than 'pe-' in 'pet'.

Many researchers, including Treiman (1985) and Goswami (1986), have studied the implications of an understanding of onset and rime for children when they are learning to read and found that the use of analogy is an important skill for readers and can be taught. Brown and Watson (1991) found that it was also helpful for spelling.

Children can then progress to being taught to identify and use individual phonemes such as /r/ /u/ /g/ and to blend these to read words. This was confirmed by Wagner and Torgesen (1987) who found that phonemic awareness appears to develop at about the age that children learn to read. Children need to work first at developing phonemic skills as an oral activity.

PRACTICAL SUGGESTIONS FOR ORAL ACTIVITIES TO TEACH SEGMENTATION SKILLS

The DfES (2001) Early Literacy Support Programme included sixty scripted lesson plans, and information about materials and resources, including whiteboards, puppets, magnetic letters, letter fans and sentence boards as well as games for the twelve-week programme to be delivered by teaching assistants. There are also many commercial resources available (see Ott 2007b).

Saying nursery rhymes and singing action songs and jingles and chants help to develop awareness and recognition of sounds (Bryant and Bradley 1985). Games can involve riddles and rhymes such as 'I saw a snake swimming in the . . . (lake)'.

The traditional way to introduce syllables as an oral activity is to ask children to say their own names. The syllables in them can be modelled by the teacher. He or she can say a name such as 'Peter', 'Diana', or 'Mohammed', then can pronounce it again, using syllables such as:

Pe/ter   Di/an/a   Mo/ham/med

Children as young as 4 to 5 years old can take turns using each other's names for this activity. The months of the year can be used to provide further practice with one-two-three-four syllable words such as saying /Jan/u/a/ry. Gradually other familiar words can be used such as:

car/rot
tom/a/to
beef/bur/ger
caul/i/flow/er

An amusing way to teach this is to ask the children to use robotic speech. They can then play games speaking in sentences which have the words in syllables. 'I am go/ing shop/ping at the su/per/mar/ket.' This is effective particularly for good verbalisers.

Clapping out syllables in words and other activities gives important feedback, particularly for kinaesthetic learners. Music and movement such as hopping and skipping can be used. The hands can be used to beat out the syllables on the thighs. Stamping one's feet is another activity to increase awareness. The children can be divided into pairs, and they can clap the syllables and rhymes on each other's laps or backs, or they can do this as a paired activity with a parent, carer or classroom assistant.

HANDY HINT

Chin-to-hand clapping of syllables is another useful multi-sensory over-learning strategy particularly for older children (Ott 2007b). The teacher models the activity first and uses this as a mnemonic device. Pupils are given a word. They repeat it aloud, giving them oral, aural and kinaesthetic

practice. They then put the back of the outstretched hand directly under their chin while keeping the forearm straight and in a horizontal position. They are then given a target word which they repeat. They are then asked to say how many times the chin touches the hand as they say the word.

Multi-syllabic words of increasing length are given for practice until pupils can finally say that 'hip/po/pot/a/mus' has five syllables, which they count each time the chin touches the hand.

This is a popular and amusing activity. An element of competition can be used by introducing progressively longer words to see who can beat Mary Poppins's record-breaking effort with 'supercalifragilisticexpialidocious'. This works well, providing the forearm and elbow are sustained in a horizontal position. Using motor memory and bodily movement is effective for kinaesthetic learners. At this stage these activities are all done orally.

Another language activity is to work with compound nouns. Say two words separately, then ask the child to put the words together to make a word such as:

bath/room baby/sit tooth/brush

Segmentation skills can be practised by asking the child to pronounce what is left if told to take away 'pop' from popcorn, 'air' from airport.

Counters can be used on a board to play a game like Bingo, to improve visual awareness of where the syllables occur, as well as increasing recognition of letter patterns in morphemes.

/daff/o/dil ham/bur/ger de/tect/ing

DfES (2001) makes much use of this idea in its support materials, including ideas for making games such as the Frame Game. Pupils are provided with a worksheet or whiteboard which is divided into boxes. The teacher says a word, and the pupil divides the word by placing a counter for each phoneme in a box. This could be adapted for use with syllables.

This is effective for good visualisers. A commercial game called 'Syllabification' (Smart Kids (UK) Ltd, www.smartkidscatalog.com) includes 100 letter chunks including prefixes, suffixes and root words and it helps 'build vocabulary and to discover that long words in English are made up of chunks'.

These oral activities with syllables should then be supplemented with awareness of onset and rimes. Finally work needs to be done with the individual phonemes at the beginning, middle and ends of words and should include blending and segmenting activities. Gradually when these skills are developed they will become part of reading activities during the word and text level of the NLS (DfEE 1998). Pupils are then ready to progress to dividing words into syllables as a spelling activity. Pupils need to have a reading age of about 7 years or above to be able to do this as a written activity.

Essential terminology needed to understand syllable division, strategies and techniques

Revise and rehearse the vocabulary and the following concepts orally:

- vowels – short and long
- digraphs
- blends
- assimilations.

This requires a structured approach using oral activities as well as worksheets, computer programs and games. Children then need to learn about the following terms.

Breve

This is derived from the Latin word *brevis* meaning 'short'. It is the code mark placed over a short or unstressed vowel to indicate that it says its sound:

/p/ŭp/   măg/nĕt   ĭn/hăb/ĭt

Macron

This is derived from the Greek word *makros* meaning 'long'. It is the horizontal code mark line placed over a long or stressed vowel to indicate that it says its name:

hē   hē/rō   rā/dī/ō

Diacritical marks

These are derived from the Greek word *diakritikos* meaning 'able to distinguish'. They are code marks written above, below or beside a letter to indicate pronunciation. They are used in dictionaries to denote pronunciation, including stress, word-division and syllabification.

- Short vowels are coded with a breve (˘):

    căt   cŏd   cŭp

- Long vowels are coded with a macron (¯):

    hē   grāīn   wēēd

- Pairs of slash marks are used to denote phonemes (sounds): /c/ /a/ /t/.
- Quote marks are used to denote letter names: 'c' 'a' 't'.
- Underlining can be used to denote digraphs, blends and assimilations.

Later as pupils progress to the more advanced forms of segmentation, it will be necessary to revise prefixes and suffixes, particularly the commonly used ones, to enable multi-syllabic words to be tackled. It is important that there is an awareness that prefixes and suffixes are cemented together as letter strings, and not separated in syllables. Revision needs to be done about the difference between phonemes and syllables.

To recognise and practise coding short and long vowels
Use the look-say-code-read approach:

wē   cŭp   ĕgg
mŭg   bȳ   hĕn

To recognise and practise underlining the blends and coding the vowels
Use the look-say-code-read approach:

tw<u>ĭ</u>n   c<u>l</u>ăp   g<u>r</u>ŭb
tw<u>ĭst</u>   c<u>r</u>ŭ<u>st</u>   c<u>r</u>ĭ<u>sp</u>

HANDY HINT

Blends stay together in a syllable. Mnemonic: The blends are like twins who always hold hands and usually stick together in a syllable.

To recognise, practise and underline the consonant digraphs
Use the look-say-code-read approach:

wĭ<u>sh</u>   gă<u>sh</u>   rĭ<u>ch</u>
<u>wh</u>ĭp   wĭ<u>th</u>   dă<u>sh</u>

HANDY HINT

Digraphs always stay together in a syllable. Mnemonic: The digraphs are inseparable like conjoined twins.

To underline the assimilations and code the vowels
Use the look-say-code-read approach:

jŭ<u>mp</u>   lŏ<u>ng</u>   wĭ<u>nk</u>
dŭ<u>mp</u>   pŏ<u>ng</u>   lĕ<u>ng</u>th

To underline blends, digraphs, assimilations and code the vowels
Use the look-say-code-read approach:

<u>str</u>ŭm   c<u>r</u>ă<u>sh</u>   <u>str</u>ĭ<u>ng</u>
<u>thr</u>ŭ<u>st</u>   <u>fl</u>ă<u>sh</u>   c<u>r</u>ĭ<u>sp</u>

For further examples see Ott (2007b).

PRACTICAL SUGGESTIONS FOR LEARNING AND USING SYLLABLE DIVISION

A syllable division line is a vertical line placed between syllables to indicate where a word can be divided for spelling and pronunciation

e/mu   ze/ro   fan/tas/tic

Syllable division should be taught first so that it is familiar as an oral activity. Syllable division knowledge, understanding and practice with written multisyllabic words helps to develop confidence and skills which can be a huge boost to those who struggle to read and spell.

Guidelines for multi-sensory strategies for syllable division

HANDY HINT

Every syllable must have a vowel. Some syllables have only one letter, which is a vowel or a vowel sound:

a/corn   ver/y

- Say the word aloud.
- Clap or count out the syllables.
- Copy out the word.
- Look at the word then insert the syllable division line.
- Underline and code the vowels.
- Mark any letter blends, clusters or affixes.
- Read the word.

Step-by-step processes and useful tips to learn and use syllable division

First, underline the vowels in the word:

g<u>o</u>b   l<u>e</u>t   m<u>ag</u>n<u>e</u>t   t<u>o</u>ns<u>i</u>l

Each syllable has only one vowel sound.

Second, put the index finger(s) of each hand on the lines under the marked vowel.

r<u>a</u>b b<u>i</u>t

When there are two consonants between the two marked vowels, the syllable division line goes between the consonants.

Third, divide the word into syllables. Read the syllables and then say the whole word. This needs practice as a reading and spelling activity. Use examples from current reading books, or during shared reading as well as worksheets (Ott 2007a) and computer packages available from www.dyslexia.com and www.sen.uk.com.

The objective is to code, divide and read two-syllable words with short vowels such as the following:

    căn/dĭd   sŭb/mĭt   pĕl/lĕt
    hĕc/tĭc   cŏb/wĕb   hăp/pĕn

When there are two consonants of the same letter, only one consonant is sounded in the accented syllable:

    pŏp/pĕt   răb/bĭt   tŭn/nĕl

There are six major types of syllables, which will be discussed below.

- closed syllables
- open syllables
- vowel–consonant 'e' syllables
- vowel–diphthong syllables
- consonant 'le' syllables
- 'r' combination syllables

Steere et al. (1971)

How to be in 'CLOVER' with syllable patterns

Schneider (1999) adapted Rome and Smith Osman's (1993) suggestion of using the word CLOVER as a mnemonic device to help remember the six types of syllable patterns:

C	Closed syllables	cot	tap	
L	Le syllables	ta/ble	ap/ple	ri/fle
O	Open syllables	be	po/lo	i/de/a
V	Vowel teams (digraphs/diphthongs)	train	speed/ing	play/ed
E	E Silent -e (magic 'e')	gate	pipe	rope
R	R-controlled vowels	col/lar	act/or	paint/er

It is important to be aware 'that it is the rime – the vowel and what follows – that defines the syllable type' (Stanback 1982).

The characteristics of the six major syllable patterns

Closed syllables

Closed syllables end in a consonant and have a short vowel.

This can be taught by using the Closed Syllable Room (Fig. 9) as a mnemonic (Ott 1997). Mr Consonant closes the back door. The vowel men are shut in and we can only hear their sounds.

Figure 9

Closed syllables end in a consonant and have a short vowel sound. This can be reinforced in a multi-sensory way to match individual learning styles. Ask for a volunteer to go outside the classroom door. Tell them to close the door behind them and to wait until they are called back inside. Meanwhile the other children talk quietly to one another. Call the volunteer back and ask him what the class were talking about. He will say he could not hear what exactly was being said because the door was closed. This little sketch helps to establish the concept of closed syllables. Pupils need practice in recognising closed monosyllables and polysyllabic words during reading and as a spelling activity. This can be rehearsed using worksheets as follows:

To recognise and divide words with closed syllables and consonant digraphs for reading and spelling purposes.

The sequence of steps to follow is as follows:

1 Look at the word.
2 Underline the digraph.
3 Code the vowels.
4 Divide the word with a syllable division line.
5 Place the index fingers of each hand under each vowel on either side of the syllable division line.
6 Read the word.

dŏl/p<u>h</u>ĭn ăn/t<u>h</u>ĕm ŏr/c<u>h</u>ĭd
wŏr/<u>sh</u>ĭp măr/<u>sh</u>ăl păn/t<u>h</u>ĕr

HANDY HINT

Remember! Digraphs, like conjoined twins, are inseparable.

The consonant digraphs are inseparable and stay together in one syllable. Vowel digraphs and diphthongs are also indivisible and stay together in the same syllable as in:

con/cēal hā<u>w</u>/thorn pō<u>i</u>/son

To recognise, practise and divide words with closed syllables and consonant blends

HANDY HINT

Remember! The blends are twins who hold hands and usually stick together in a syllable.

Use the 'look-underline blends-code-divide-fingers-read' strategy:

ĭm/<u>pr</u>ĕss pĭl/grĭm hŭm/<u>dr</u>ŭm
dăn/<u>dr</u>ŭff ĭn/<u>stĭ</u>ll ĕm/<u>bl</u>ĕm

Prefixes and suffixes follow a different convention and stay together as letter clusters, strings and patterns. This is why basic knowledge and understanding of the commonly used affixes is essential. Gillingham and Stillman (1956) illustrated this with the following examples:

cĭr/cŭm/spĕct
en/trŭst
mĭs/spĕll

Open syllables

Open syllables end in a vowel and have a long vowel. This can be taught by using the Open Syllable Room (Fig. 10) as a mnemonic (Ott 1997). Mr Long Vowel opens the door. When we look in we can see the Vowel Men and we can call them by their names. Open syllables therefore end in a vowel and say their names. Ask for a volunteer to go outside the classroom door. Tell them to leave the door open. Then ask the pupils to talk among themselves. Then recall the volunteer to the class and ask them to tell you what the others were talking about. This re-enactment will help to establish that open syllables end in a vowel and the vowel says its name. This will need reinforcing over time in reading and writing situations. It can be rehearsed using worksheets as follows.

Figure 10

To recognise, practise and divide words with open syllables for reading and spelling purposes

Use the 'look-underline the vowels-divide-code-fingers-read' strategy:

sō/lō gȳ/rō hā/lō
grā/vȳ nā/vȳ bā/bȳ

Words of two syllables can also have a mixture of closed and open syllables which can occur in either order.

To recognise, practise and divide words with open and closed syllables

Use the 'look-underline the vowels-divide-code-fingers-read' strategy. (It is useful now to indicate the type of syllable – open (o) closed (c) – on the line below the word.)

ū/nĭt hū/măn tī/gĕr
o /c   o / c   o /c

tĕm/pō lŏt/tō bĭn/gō
c / o   c / o   c / o

dĭp/lō/măt   ăc/rō/băt
c / o / c   c / o / c

Vowel–consonant 'e', v–e (magic 'e') syllables

The DfEE (2001) calls this a split vowel digraph.

Revise and rehearse the mnemonic ditty which says: 'When Magic Mrs 'e' comes knocking at the back door of the Vowel Men's room she says, "Who's there?" The Vowel Men are polite and say their names, but she keeps quiet.'

Magic Mrs 'e' makes the vowels say their names but she keeps quiet.

căp	cāpe
hĕr	hēre
pĭn	pīne
cŏd	cōde
cŭb	cūbe

To recognise, practise and code words with magic 'e' syllables for reading and spelling purposes

Use the 'look-underline the vowels-divide-code-fingers-read' strategy:

rōbe spīne scāre
 v–e   v–e   v–e

mĕm/brāne ĭm/pēde cŏn/clūde
  c /   v–e c / v–e   c /   v–e

To recognise, practise and divide words with magic 'e' syllables for reading and spelling purposes

Use the 'look-underline the vowels-divide-code-fingers-read' strategy:

rē/tīre dē/cīde dē/mūre
 o/ v–e   o/ v–e   o/ v–e

prō/mōte rē/qūire rē/vīse
 o/ v–e   o/ v–e   o/ v–e

Vowel digraphs/vowel diphthong syllables (also known as 'vowel team' syllables)

Revise and rehearse the concept that when two vowels are next to each other they make one sound in a vowel digraph. When two vowels are next to each and when they glide together and blend, they make a vowel diphthong.

HANDY HINT

Vowel digraphs and vowel diphthongs are regarded as one vowel sound and stay together in a syllable.

To recognise, practise and divide words with vowel digraphs and vowel diphthongs when reading and spelling

Use the 'look-underline vowel-divide-code-fingers-read' strategy:

> flo͞at   clau͞se   clo͞wn
> tre͞at   che͞ek   be͞at

Consonant 'le' syllables

These are found at the end of words and include:

> ble   cle   fle   gle   kle   ple   tle   zle

HANDY HINT

Remember the fable of Greedy Myrtle and Tom-Tom the piper's son, which shows that that 'e' at the end of 'le' letter clusters is dumb and does not say a thing. 'Tom-Tom the piper's son saw Greedy Myrtle at the <u>table</u> ready to gob<u>ble</u> his app<u>le</u> pie. She was struck dumb when he set his Rottweiler at her an<u>kle</u> (Ott 2007b).'

To recognise, practise and divide words with 'le' syllables

Use the 'look-underline the final three letters-divide-code-fingers-read' strategy. Remember the mnemonic 'The final 'le' syllable vowel which has been 'struck dumb' and does not say a thing because of Greedy Myrtle'.

> gŏb/<u>ble</u>   tā/<u>ble</u>   mā/<u>ple</u>
> crā/<u>dle</u>   căn/<u>dle</u>   hăn/<u>dle</u>

The 'r' combination syllables (vowel – consonant 'r' syllables)

These are made by adding 'r' to the vowels including the following:

> ar   er   ir   or   ur

These syllables can be at the beginning, middle or end of words.
Sometimes the vowel is short as is in 'mĭr/rŏr' or long as in 'sīr/ĕn'.

HANDY HINT

The suffixes 'ar', 'er', 'or' say /ĕr/. Remember the mnemonic 'Mother Superi<u>or</u>, a superi<u>or</u> schol<u>ar</u>, met a horrible murder<u>er</u> who got rid of <u>her</u>.'

To recognise, practise and divide 'r' combination syllables

'ar'

ăr/rŏw   ăr/tĭst

căr/pĕt   tăr/gĕt

călĕn/dăr   rĕg/ŭ/lăr

'er'

ĕr/ōde   ĕr/rŏr

fĕrn   tĕrm

drī/vĕr   sĭs/tĕr

'ir'

ĭr/rī/gāte   ĭr/rĕg/ū/lăr

dĭrt   shĭrt

'or'

ŏr/dĕr   ŏr/phăn

ăc/tŏr   dŏc/tŏr

'ur'

ŭr/chĭn   ŭr/gĕnt

bŭrst   hŭrt

Final stable syllables

To these six main types of syllable should be added what Cox (1980) calls 'final stable syllables,' so called because they are spelling patterns that stay together. They include the following suffixes:

tion   sion   ture   age   ain   ise   ite   ique   esque

Guidelines for choosing words for syllable division practice based on word frequency

For practitioners and individuals who seek ways to lighten the load and to simplify and find ways to 'spell successfully', Stanback's (1992) analysis of a frequency-based vocabulary merits further consideration. It is a tour de force for both the length and breadth of her corpus of words. From the 17,602 words based on Hanna et al.'s (1966) list, as well as Caroll et al.'s (1971) *Word Frequency Book List*, she obtained the following results about the frequency of use of the six major syllable patterns as well as identifying rime families. This establishes the order in which syllables should be taught. Stanback's (1992) analysis of occurrence of syllable types is shown on the following page.

Type of syllable	Number of occurrences in 17,602 words	Per cent distribution
Closed	18,644	43.3
Open	12,419	28.9
Silent 'e'	2,876	6.7
Vowel -r	4,397	10.2
Vowel team	4,092	9.5
Consonant -le –re	613	1.4

Teaching principles to 'promote active learning' with suggestions to develop understanding and know-how

This approach to teaching syllable and segmentation skills is linked to the NLS Key Stage 3 recommendations in *Literacy Progress Unit Phonics* (DfEE 2001), which says that the teaching should 'promote active learning'. The NLS advice is quoted and guidelines for the practical implementations are shown in italics.

Remember
'Identification of prior knowledge and key objectives'

Revise and rehearse key concepts such as the vowels a, e, i, o, u with the mnemonic 'The Vowel Men met an elephant in orange underwear', or use the Vowel Rap tune (DfES 2001).

Model
'Teacher demonstration of process'

Use the board, an overhead projector, an interactive white board or a computer package to demonstrate syllable division and coding strategies. The use of colour is very effective for this.

Try
'Shared explanation through activity'

Re-enact the sketch with Mr Consonant closing the door and shutting in the Vowel Men, to illustrate that closed syllables end in a consonant and have a short vowel

Apply
'Scaffolded pupil application of new learning'

Find examples when doing shared reading. Use them to construct spellings and make antonyms, for example when doing shared writing. Further examples can be found and made with the help of a dictionary or computer when doing independent work during the Literacy Hour.

Secure
'Consolidation through discussion/activity'

Revise during the plenary session of the Literacy Hour. Rehearse the newly learned concept or process, such as learning how to spell the plural of nouns ending in 'y'. Rehearse the rules. Use in extended writing activities and for spelling activities including spelling tests (see Ott 2007b).

SUMMARY AND CONCLUSIONS

1   Learning about syllables is a progressive skill which initially develops from oral activities. Good oral skills are the foundations for the successful use of syllabification: 'as children learn to read and spell they acquire a broader base of knowledge' (Treiman 1997).

    The NLS (DfEE 1998) recommends that children should be taught 'to discriminate orally, syllables in multi-syllabic words using children's names and words from their reading e.g. dinosaur, family, dinner, children. Extend to written forms and note syllable boundary in speech and writing.' A multi-sensory approach can be used to enhance awareness. These skills can be practised, revised and used with a variety of activities including games, worksheet, computer packages and writing activities.

2   There is a common perception that polysyllabic words are difficult to read and write. Those who have difficulties with phonological skills, including breaking words into parts and blending these to make words, do find longer words more challenging, often because of poor processing of sounds resulting from short-term and working memory deficits.

3   Explicit teaching of segmentation skills is necessary. Oral activities including, first, syllables, second, onset and rimes and, third, phoneme segmentation should be taught. The reverse hierarchy should be taught for beginner readers, including synthetic phonics first, then analogy and later syllables.

4   The terminology has to be mastered so as to be available automatically for use when skills and strategies are practised.

5   The six major syllable patterns can be recalled with the acronym CLOVER. There are, however, many exceptions. Examples of syllable division are not always consistent or reliable, some dictionaries, etc. divide words according to how they are spoken, others according to how they are spelt. Stanback (1992) points out that 'linguists do not agree on syllable boundaries, and dictionary divisions are often unsuitable for teaching reading'.

6   The target words used for practice should be relevant and appropriate to the learners' needs and current skills, and should be used in meaningful contexts.

7   Knowing, understanding and using syllable strategies are invaluable tools in the toolbox of all spellers, because they help to simplify spelling and reading for all spellers, but most importantly for dyslexic and poor spellers because they cut down words into smaller and more manageable pieces.

13 A Roadmap for Short Cuts Through the Spelling Jungle

- Lessons to be learnt from the strategies good spellers use to negotiate the spelling highway
- How to manage the horrible homophones happily
- Signposts to chart the speller through the homophone jungle
- Mnemonics
- High-frequency words
- Dealing with the 'awfully awkward' apostrophe, including 'contrary contractions'
- The ten commandments for managing plurals painlessly
- How to manage to 'catch' the silent letters – the stealthy robbers
- The bare essential words to spell well for older pupils
- Summary and conclusions

Keywords

Contractions	Homonyms	Silent letters
'Greengrocer's	Inflected forms	Spelling pronunciation
apostrophe'	Mnemonics	'Spellofax'
Homographs	Plurals	
Homophones	Semantic cues	

Lessons to be learnt from the strategies good spellers use to negotiate the spelling highway

How do good spellers spell? Good spellers have established that language has sounds. By tuning in their ears to the sounds of language they have learnt that sounds make words. They know that these sounds are represented by letters with which they are familiar, because they have well-established alphabetic skills and well-developed grapheme/phoneme skills. Their good phonological skills enable them to break words down into parts and match these to the letters that represent them. They can spell words correctly because they have a mental image of how words look. They can recognise whether words are spelt correctly when they look at what they have written, and they make comments like 'that doesn't seem right', or 'it has a double "m"', or 'there is an "ight" in that word'. They have absorbed this knowledge from regularly seeing words in print. They can see words in their mind's eye and can recognise visual shapes as well as spelling patterns, including letter strings. Crystal (1995) argued that 'visual strategies can be important' when using irregular words where a phonological strategy could not work. People do sometimes rehearse spellings by writing down alternative spellings to see which 'looks right'. He concluded that 'to be a good speller we need to have both this phonological awareness (to cope with the regular spelling patterns) and a good visual awareness (to cope with the exceptions). Poor spellers lack this double skill.'

Good spellers learn by what is known as the 'dual-route theory' according to Moats (1995). They are able to use phonological and phonemic skills, and can segment words. They have knowledge of word derivations and recognise root words, prefixes and suffixes, and understand the conventions for using them when they spell. They can use analogy to compare a spelling with a word they know already.

Those who have a good visual memory can visualise words by turning them into pictures and can remember whole word spellings as well as letter clusters and letter strings. They develop a spelling vocabulary which becomes internalised, and can be recalled automatically when required for writing. Evidence for this theory has been provided by laboratory experiments which have shown that the brain works like a switchboard for words that are stored. Part of the brain remembers whole words for reading and spelling, while another part of the brain remembers speech sounds and uses these to produce the letters to spell words.

In most classrooms the majority of pupils initially learn spellings whatever the theory or methodology used to teach them, but the retention rates vary. Brooks and Weeks (1998) reported that 'results indicate that using one method alone to teach children, when their individual styles are not known, can result in lower spelling age increases than an eclectic group of [spelling] methods, one of which should suit each child in the class'. For those who have a specific learning difficulty such as dyslexia, it is essential that they are taught to use strategies which match their individual learning styles, such as phonics, spelling rules, generalisations and conventions, as well as using visualisation, analogy and mnemonics. They can learn how to use compensatory strategies to bolster skills, and to compensate for weaknesses.

Cognitive style affects learning strategies. Visual learners learn best by using their eyes, which is why they remember whole words, letter patterns, words within words, diagrams and illustrations. Auditory learners learn best by saying and hearing, and using phonemes and blends as well as breaking words into onsets and rimes and syllables. They may use mnemonic devices to help them to remember how to spell a word: for example 'island' as 'an island is land'. Kinaesthetic learners learn best by using motor memory and tactile skills with their hands. They need to write the word as well as see it and say it, which explains why using a keyboard may improve spelling for those who have good motor memory.

They know how to use a dictionary, thesaurus and spell-checker, as well as being ready to 'phone a friend' or to ask the person sitting next to them for help if they need to know how to spell a word. They remember to use their personal 'Spellofax'.

How to manage the horrible homophones happily

Homophones are words that sound the same but have different spellings and different meanings. They concluded that 'English was exceptionally burdened by them' (cited by Burchfield 1996).

These words sound the same, but when the good auditory learner uses their in-built crutch to 'sound out' the letters it often does not work. The good visualiser can remember homophones, but for those with poor visual memory they are a nightmare as well as being an on-going source of grief. A conventional spell-checker on the PC can usually sort out spelling difficulties, but it frequently fails to deal with homophones. However, the new generation of spell-checkers which include a speech option are very effective when dealing with homophones because they usually include a sentence for the target word.

Ehri (1979), as part of her ongoing research into how children learn to read and its significance for spelling, carried out an experiment using sixteen pairs of homophones including berries/buries; which/witch. She showed that when homophones were used in sentences in meaningful contexts, and were accompanied by pictures to make them more memorable, children 'who practised reading the homophones in sentences recognised the correct meanings of the different spellings better, whereas subjects who read the words in isolation were able to read the words aloud more quickly and spell them more accurately'. This is evidence to support the recommendation that learning homophones needs to be taught as a tripartite activity as meaning, spelling and reading the matching pair are taught in context and by using multi-sensory strategies.

Some individuals with dyslexia expend a large amount of time and effort learning to spell 'there'/'their'. Often when they have mastered the understanding of 'which is which' they are still challenged with the spelling. Is it 'thier'/'thrie'/'their'? It can help visualisers to be reminded that all three begin with 'the' (which can be highlighted). They can be helped with a mnemonic (Ott 2006a) such as:

> If 'their' can be a my,
> Spell it with an 'i'.

For example, we can say:

> I like <u>my</u> dog.
> I like <u>their</u> dog.

You cannot say, 'I left the dog <u>my</u>' because it does not make sense. But you can say, 'I left the dog <u>there</u>'.

Signposts to chart the speller through the homophone jungle

The following classifications of homophones are devised from Carney (1994). They are useful as an aide memoire to chart differences and similarities in spelling and meanings. Grammatical, semantic and phonological knowledge can be used as cues. The NLS (DfEE 1999) *Spelling Bank* suggests for example that 'many homophone choices are best taught as a grammatical issue such as there/their'. Use of grammatical cues helps spellers to know and understand the different forms of words – the so-called inflected forms which indicate tense, number, gender and case. Pronunciation and meaning can also be used as guidelines to distinguish homophones.

Signs for grammatical cues

/s/	/z/
brews	bruise
chews	choose
claws	clause
cocks	cox
crews	cruise
days	daze
knows	nose
prays	preys
sighs	size
teas	tees

Some verbs whose past tense ends in 'ed' say /d/ also have homophones. These are challenging spellings because they both say /d/ but are spelt 'ed':

fined/find   mined/mind

This can be a source of confusion for some who have been taught that verbs adding 'ed' say /t/ /d/ /id/. Learn first how to spell the verb which adds 'ed'. Then learn the noun using the 'look–say–cover–write–check' method.

banned	band
bowled	bold
fined	find
guessed	guest
mined	mind
missed	mist
sighed	side
stayed	staid
tied	tide

Some homophones are verbs/noun pairs. They are also quite challenging and include the following:

Verbs – take 's'	Nouns – take 'c'
advise	advice
devise	device
license	licence
practise	practice
prophesy	prophecy

HANDY HINT

A useful aide-memoire is to remember to use 'c' for nouns and 's' for verbs. Another suggestion is to use a mnemonic such as: 'My advice is that 'c' is your best device for a licence about the practice of the art of prophecy.' An illustration with the 'c' highlighted helps.

Comparative forms of adjectives and nouns ending in 'er' sometimes make homophone twins: Other confusing homophones include:

boarder	border
bolder	boulder
bridal	bridle
conker	conquer
dyer	dire
fryer	friar
grosser	grocer
higher	hire
leaver	lever
lessen	lesson
seller	cellar

They can be practised and then recognised more readily by putting them on cards with an illustration on the back, which are then used for sorting and matching games.

Signs for etymological cues

Knowledge of the history and understanding of the origins of words and how their use has evolved helps with learning and remembering their spelling. A helpful mnemonic device is to draw a picture of what the target words represent. Then put the words beside the appropriate picture. This will help good visualisers to learn to spell homophones such as 'ark'/'arc' (Fig. 11; see Ott 2007).

Figure 11

The NLS (DfEE 1999) Spelling Bank recommended that children should 'research [the] history of words to explain the origin of some homophones' spellings'. Here are some other examples:

ark	arc	Latin 'arcus' (bow/circle)
bark	barque	Latin 'barca' (small boat)
block	bloc	French 'bloc' (group)
cash	cache	French 'cache' (hiding place)
mark	marque	French 'marques' (brand/make)
mask	masque	Middle French 'masque' (hide/cover place)
peak	pique	Middle French 'pique' (sting/irritation)
scull	skull	Old Icelandic 'skalli' (bald/head)
shoot	chute	French 'chute' (fall)

The following information may be helpful, particularly for those who have good receptive language skills as well as visual skills.

HANDY HINT

Those who have good visual skills may find a mnemonic illustration helpful such as a picture of a sculler in a scull on a river beside a grave digger with a skull.

Signs for phonological cues

Articulation and pronunciation can be used to denote and highlight the differences between homophones. The use of what is sometimes called 'spelling pronunciation', which the NLS (DfEE 2001) calls 'spellspeaking', puts stress or emphasis on the 'tricky letters' for example in multisyllabic words with unstressed vowels. This can be a help to those with good auditory skills, such as when learning to discriminate between /bar/ /on/ and /bar/ /ren/

HANDY HINT

Learning can be enhanced with the use of a mnemonic illustration such as a picture of a soldier sitting by a tent in the desert in Iraq eating an ice cream for his dessert.

Letters doubled

bans	banns
baron	barren
bury	berry
canon	cannon
desert	dessert
mat	matt
medal	meddle
palate	pallet
step	steppe

Vowel sounds and spelling changes

It helps to raise awareness and to flag up differences when vowel changes occur by using colour or a different font. This will be helpful especially for those with good visual memory.

confirmation	conformation
literal	littoral
vacation	vocation
veracious	voracious

Silent letters in homophones

When learning and remembering silent letters it can be useful to use colour or different fonts as well as using the spelling pronunciation.

HANDY HINT

Mnemonics are useful such as: 'A <u>k</u>night met a <u>k</u>nave who said he <u>k</u>new how to tie <u>k</u>nots in string and <u>k</u>nows how to <u>k</u>nead bread' (an illustration would be an excellent multi-sensory strategy).

knave	nave
knead	need
knew	new
knight	night
knot	not
know	no
whether	weather
which	witch
whole	hole
wright	write	right	rite

Long vowel sounds

/ā/

brake	break
grate	great
made	maid
mane	main
pale	pail
plane	plain
sale	sail
tale	tail
wait	weight
way	weigh

/ē/

beach	beech	
flea	flee	
heal	heel	
leak	leek	
meat	meet	mete
peace	piece	
sea	see	
scene	seen	
steal	steel	
weak	week	

/ī/

die	dye	
file	phial	
giro	gyro	
liar	lyre	
pi	pie	
sight	cite	site
sign	sine	
slight	sleight	
stile	style	
tire	tyre	

/ō/

brooch	broach	
doe	dough	
groan	grown	
lone	loan	
pole	poll	
road	rode	
row	roe	
sew	so	sow
sold	soled	
yoke	yolk	
throne	thrown	
toe	tow	

/ū/

due	dew
root	route
rude	rood
through	threw
troop	troupe

Recent homophones

These include:

| program | series of tasks or operations performed by a computer |
| programme | list of proceedings or participants in an event |

| disc | audio disc as played by a disc jockey |
| disk | used to describe a hard/soft disk for a computer or a flat thin object |

Odds and ends including high-frequency confusable words

altar	alter	
be	bee	
been	bean	
by	buy	bye
fair	fare	
for	four	fore
meter	metre	
our	hour	
were	where	wear
wood	would	

The NLS (DfEE 1999) Spelling Bank lists homophones from the 'high-frequency word list' in the NLS (DfEE 1998) *Framework for Teaching*. Other suggestions for teaching and learning the homophones include the following.

HANDY HINT

'Past' and 'passed' are notoriously difficult to teach and learn. It helps to establish that 'past' refers to something that is over, finished, has been done.

The mnemonic 'At last I got *past* the traffic jam and I *passed* my driving test' can be used. This can be made more helpful with an illustration of a learner driver who has just passed the test with 'L' plates driving past a traffic jam (Fig. 16; see Ott 2007).

An alternative way to teach 'past'/'passed' is as follows. If the personal pronouns 'I', 'you', 'he'/'she', 'we', 'you', 'they' can be used in front of the word, then 'passed' is the correct spelling. 'They passed the winning post.' 'She passed me the salt.'

Figure 16

Make sets of homophones – twins or triplets words – on the computer, using a size 24 font. Then put these on index cards which can be laminated for durability. Shuffle the cards and use to play Snap or Pelmanism. Players must give the meaning of the word written on the card they pick up before they add it to their pile of cards.

In another game, the picture can be on the front of the card with the words on the back. This can be used as a paired spelling activity. The teacher, parent or learning support assistant can read the words. Players can begin by sorting and matching pictures. Later when they can spell the words they turn over the card and check the spelling of the homophone. To win the card the player must be able to match and spell both words correctly. This game can later be used as a timed activity.

HANDY HINT

It is helpful for some spellers to concentrate on learning to spell one word of the pair initially, such as 'hear'. However the pupil should be shown both words and asked to read and give the meaning of both words. This ensures that 'they know which is which, even if they have the skill initially only to spell one of the pair correctly. Decoding is an easier task than encoding. This can be reinforced with the mnemonic 'You *hear* with an *ear*'. Later 'here' can be reinforced, with the mnemonic as one of the place words: 'You go *here*, there and everywhere to *hear* your favourite musician playing.'

Worksheet activities can be used to reinforce and use the homophones correctly. Dictation is also helpful for practice and revision to reinforce the homophones. Computer printouts can be given with homophones used incorrectly. The objective is to find the errors which the spell-checker failed to spot. Do this as a proofreading exercise.

Mnemonics

Mnemonics such as the following need frequent revision and constant use to be memorised. They should be added to the personal spelling 'Spellofax'. They help to differentiate between the homophones. Strong visualisers will probably form visual images and/or remember the illustrations when using the word while those with good auditory skills will remember the sentences.

are/our

<u>A</u>re <u>r</u>ats <u>e</u>vil?

a   <u>a</u>re
r   <u>r</u>ats
e   <u>e</u>vil

<u>O</u>ur <u>u</u>niforms <u>r</u>ot.

o   <u>o</u>ur
u   <u>u</u>niforms
r   <u>r</u>ot

for/four

Foals often race for fun.

f   foals
o   often
r   race

Four old unicorns run.

f   four
o   old
u   unicorns
r   run

witch/which

The witch is taking cats home because her cat has an itch.

w   The witch
i   is
t   taking
c   cats
h   home

Which William has icy cold hands?

w   William
h   has
i   icy
c   cold
h   hands

great/grate

Great rabbits eat any time.

g   great
r   rabbits
e   eat
a   any
t   time

Greedy rabbits ate the entire lettuce patch.

g   greedy
r   rabbits
a   ate
t   the
e   entire lettuce patch

Ehri (1996) conducted a number of experiments on children of 7–9 years on a task that, like learning mnemonics, involved a 'paired associate learning approach'. She found that 'children's recall was better when the pairs were connected by verbs closely related to the first object'. This finding has useful pedagogical implications. Rohwer et al. (1967) showed that children's memory for pairs of pictures was better when meaningful connections linked the objects. Using verbs to connect the words was more effective than using prepositions or conjunctions. This explains the rationale in the choice of wording in many of the mnemonic sentences.

Marvellous mnemonics for high-frequency 'odd-bod' spellings

Mnemonics and memory strategies or devices can be used to help remember technical vocabulary, odd spellings and tricky parts of words. They can also be used to remember facts such as the days of the months of the year: 'Thirty days hath September . . .', and remember numerical sequences such as the old nursery rhyme:

> One two, buckle my shoe,
> Three, four, knock at the door

Mnemonics can be created to help remember the most difficult or troublesome spellings. In theory individuals should create their own mnemonics so that they can be personalised to make them more relevant by using personally meaningful contexts. This works for individuals, but in practice it does not work in a classroom because the teacher and the pupils need to constantly repeat and rehearse the sentences and acronyms to establish mastery and instant recall. Many dyslexic people have difficulties with recalling definitions, so consistency and conciseness in language are a crucial element for success.

HANDY HINT

Levin (1996) asserts that 'sufficient research evidence now exists to suggest that even skilled learners can become more skilled through mnemonic strategy acquisition and implementation'.

People remember in different ways, often depending on their individual learning styles. The good visualiser will be able to take a snapshot of what they want to learn, such as an index card with an 'odd-bod' spelling like 'many' written in a large font and the sentence 'Many aunts never yell' with a picture of a yelling aunt and a smiling child and aunt.

Those who have a good sense of rhyme and rhythm, which indicates good auditory skills, will find that clapping out the letters in words such as 'difficulty' or Mississippi' often helps to remember their spelling, as when saying:

> Mrs 'D' – Mrs 'I' – Mrs 'Ffi' – Mrs 'C' – Mrs 'U' – Mrs 'Lty'

'When Bessie fell off her bike she rolled down the hill and her bike whizzed past her'. An illustration will make this even more memorable (Fig. 17; see Ott 2007).

Figure 17

PRACTICAL SUGGESTIONS FOR TEACHING MNEMONICS IN A MULTI-SENSORY WAY FOR SPELLING MASTERY

To learn and remember how to spell the word 'because'

- Look at the word 'because' and highlight the letters 'au'.
- Say the word aloud.
- Spell the word aloud while continuing to look at the letters.
- Say the sentence with the mnemonic 'The elephant got stuck *because* big elephants can't always use small entrances'.
- Underline or highlight the first letters in the sentence and use them to spell the word.
- Cover the word.
- Write it down.
- Check the spelling.
- Draw a picture for the mnemonic using colour. Take a snapshot in your mind's eye of the picture.
- Practise saying the sentence with the mnemonic.
- Write the mnemonic sentence on the computer and highlight the letters 'au'. Do a print out and stick this on an index card with an illustration beside it.
- Add it to the personal collection of mnemonics which are in alphabetical order for easy reference in an index box, spelling logbook, 'Spellofax', list of personal hard-to-spell words.
- Revise the mnemonic and the spelling three days in a row, then in a week's time, then in a month's time.
- Practise it daily when doing writing assignments and when proofreading.
- Make a poster or use post-it notes which are displayed in prominent places.

Mnemonics to help remember the 'odd-bod' spellings in the NLS high-frequency lists and lighten the load for poor spellers

The words in the 'high-frequency' lists (DfEE 1998) are essential for pupils to tackle even simple texts. These words usually play an important part in holding together the general coherence of texts, and early familiarity with them helps pupils to develop pace and accuracy in reading from an early stage. Some of these words have irregular or difficult spellings. They often play an important grammatical role and are sometimes difficult to predict from the surrounding text.

Many of the words in the NLS high-frequency lists are regular and follow sound-to-symbol matches and can be spelt using synthetic phonics. The DfES (2003) drew attention to this and pointed out that 'only those that are irregular should be taught as sight words'. The irregular 'odd-bod' spellings can be challenging, and can be taught using the Fernald method or with mnemonics as an aide-memoire. Illustrations, especially in colour, are an additional help for spellers. The following are some suggestions for mnemonics for the 'Odd-bod' spellings.

all

All these children always look lovely.

a	always
l	look
l	lovely

This can also be used to remember other 'all' words:

ball	Bella	always	looks	lovely
fall	Freddie	always	looks	lovely
wall	Willa	always	looks	lovely

away

Go away, Andy wants a yoyo.

a	Andy
w	wants
a	a
y	yoyo

This can then be used to remember the rest of the 'ay' family of words:

I say Andy wants a yoyo to stay and play this way all day.

beautiful

<u>B</u>ig <u>e</u>lephants <u>a</u>re <u>u</u>sually <u>bea</u>utiful.

b	<u>b</u>ig
e	<u>e</u>lephants
a	<u>a</u>re
u	<u>u</u>sually beautiful

come

Come! Come! <u>c</u>ats <u>o</u>ften <u>m</u>iaow <u>e</u>agerly!

c	<u>c</u>ats
o	<u>o</u>ften
m	<u>m</u>iaow
e	<u>e</u>agerly

look

<u>L</u>ook at those <u>l</u>azy, <u>o</u>dd <u>o</u>ld <u>k</u>angaroos!

l	<u>l</u>azy
o	<u>o</u>dd
o	<u>o</u>ld
k	<u>k</u>angaroos

my

<u>M</u>y <u>m</u>um <u>y</u>ells at me often when I am silly.

| m | <u>m</u>um |
| y | <u>y</u>ells |

This can also be used to remember that an /ī/ or /ē/ sound at the end of a word often means that the word ends in a 'y':

> I tr<u>y</u> not to cr<u>y</u> when m<u>y</u> mum yells at our naught<u>y</u> cat.

said

She said <u>S</u>ally <u>A</u>nn <u>is</u> <u>d</u>ancing.

s	<u>S</u>ally
a	<u>A</u>nn
i	<u>is</u>
d	<u>d</u>ancing

you

You are unlucky to have a yucky old uniform.

y   yucky
o   old
u   uniform

was

She was right, wasps always sting.

w   wasps
a   always
s   sting

brother

Her brother runs over the hills everywhere regularly.

b   brother
r   runs
o   over
t   the
h   hills
e   everywhere
r   regularly

could

You could, and would and should come on, 'u' little darling.

c   come
o   on
u   'u'
l   little
d   darling

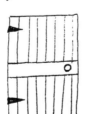

door

His door often opens regularly.

d   door
o   often
o   opens
r   regularly

first

First I'll run straight through the words.

f	first
i	I'll
r	run
s	straight
t	through the words

girl

That little girl Georgina is rather lovely.

g	Georgina
i	is
r	rather
l	lovely

half

Half of my pet hamsters always love food.

h	hamsters
a	always
l	love
f	food

house

My happy old uncle sold everything in his house at the car-boot sale.

h	happy
o	old
u	uncle
s	sold
e	everything

laugh

Don't laugh when I tell you that some old ladies always use green hot water in their baths.

l	ladies
a	always
u	use
g	green
h	hot water in their baths

love

I love old velvet everywhere on chairs.

l	love
o	old
v	velvet
e	everywhere on chairs

many

Many aunts never yell.

m	many
a	aunts
n	never
y	yell

mother

Mother has a moth.

This can be used to remember other 'oth' words:

My other brother gave my mother another box of mothballs.

new

New baby birds never eat worms.

n	never
e	eat
w	worms

night

Last night I didn't get to bed, now I'll go home tonight.

n	now
i	I'll
g	go
h	home
t	tonight

This can be used to remember other 'ight' words:

Last night I got such a fright in the bad light, when I saw that street fight. What a sight! so I'll go home tonight while it's still light.

once

Once upon a time the <u>o</u>ld <u>n</u>ever <u>c</u>hewed <u>e</u>verything because they had no teeth.

o   <u>o</u>ld
n   <u>n</u>ever
c   <u>c</u>hewed
e   <u>e</u>verything

saw

When I saw him <u>S</u>am <u>a</u>lways <u>w</u>aved.

s   <u>S</u>am
a   <u>a</u>lways
w   <u>w</u>aved

took

The burglar took a chance once <u>t</u>oo <u>o</u>ften <u>o</u>pening <u>k</u>itchen drawers.

t   <u>t</u>oo
o   <u>o</u>ften
o   <u>o</u>pening
k   <u>k</u>itchen drawers

This can also be used to remember other 'ook' family words:

> The c<u>ook</u> who t<u>ook</u> a l<u>ook</u> at a b<u>ook</u> when she should have been c<u>ook</u>ing got the sack.

want

<u>We</u> do not want an <u>ant</u> in our pants.

w   <u>we do not want an</u>
a   <u>a</u>
n   <u>n</u>
t   <u>t</u> in our pants

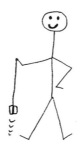

your

Your <u>y</u>oyo <u>o</u>ften <u>u</u>ses <u>r</u>ubber string

y   <u>y</u>oyo
o   <u>o</u>ften
u   <u>u</u>ses
r   <u>r</u>ubber string

High-frequency words

High-frequency words need to be learned in a systematic and structured way over time, using a multi-sensory approach. They will need to be revised and rehearsed at frequent intervals to ensure that they become part of sight vocabulary for reading and for spelling when writing. Irregular 'spelling demons' which cannot be read or spelt phonetically are another ongoing source of grief and frustration for poor spellers. They include the following:

bouquet	fiancé	react
break	guitar	rhythm
busy	heights	suede
calf	island	sugar
chauffeur	none	tongue
depot	prove	yacht

Adams and Huggins (1985)

However problems with high-frequency 'odd-bod' spellings, many of which are Anglo-Saxons words such as the notoriously difficult 'ough' words 'though', 'cough', 'through', 'bough', 'tough', as well as the 'spelling demons' can be solved electronically. Hand-held spell-checkers must be the greatest invention for many poor spellers since the appearance of the eraser, which was augmented by products such as ink eradicators. Nevertheless, as every pupil knows, good spelling is still the gold standard which must be used for good writing. Text messaging has developed a new shorthand which is often imaginative, ingenious and labour-saving, but examiners are not prepared to accept it, nor will they consider its use legitimate in examination scripts.

CASE STUDY: 'MICHAEL' (32 YEARS)

I was 7 years old when I was seen at school by an educational psychologist (EP) because '['Michael'] mishears similar-sounding words leading to confusion in conversation and his spelling is poor and he is often surprised to find out how words are spelt as he apparently never heard or said them correctly'. I had a hearing test and my hearing was satisfactory. A school report said 'Could we be expecting too much from a child who is just not very bright and is he therefore unable to cope with the work or is there some problem which is holding him back?' Meanwhile I was referred to an ear, nose and throat consultant at St Bartholomew's Hospital in London. His report said, 'no lesion exists in the actual organ of hearing'. Then I was taken to see a neurologist. His report said that I had 'real difficulty in the interpretation of sounds which he can hear and this problem includes the spoken word. When pairs of words such as "mob" and "nob", "bed" and "bet" were whispered behind his back he confused them. This also applied to non-verbal sounds he could hear but not identify: rattling of coins, ticking of a clock, striking a match, tearing of paper. He could not tap out a number of beats to reproduce the same number accurately, especially if one introduced certain rhythms into the percussion. His hearing-problem constitutes a type of dyslexia.'

I was ten and a half years old before I discovered the cause of my difficulties. I later found out that my full scale IQ is 134 on the WISC. I had a tough time at school with certain subjects because of my 'spelling and slowness at completing my work'.

I went to university, where I got a B TEC (Distinction) in Engineering and a B ENG (Honours) in Electronics and Computer Engineering.

To this day I still know that I can't spell. Here are some examples:

paddla	(paddle)
pebly	(pebbly)
fammus	(famous)
feablness	(feebleness)
ridicules	(ridiculous)
bleeaver	(believer)
discrasful	(disgraceful)
boalging	(bulging)
engament	(engagement)
sencable	(sensible)
maniging	(managing)
sincearley	(sincerely)

The spell-checker saves me from embarrassment and exposure, and without it my life would be a misery.

I subsequently found out that my mother, who is 62 years old, had many of the same difficulties as I had and she now knows that she is dyslexic. My grandfather, who is 106 years old, is one of the surviving veterans of the First World War, he has kept a daily diary for over seventy years and I am pretty sure that he experienced problems with the interpretation of sounds. He often confuses similar-sounding words even though his hearing is otherwise good.

Dealing with the 'awfully awkward' apostrophe, including 'contrary contractions'

The apostrophe is a punctuation mark which is frequently misused, particularly by poor spellers. One of the most common errors is the use of an apostrophe when a noun is plural and does not indicate possession or ownership. This is sometimes referred to as the green-grocer's apostrophe because of the frequency of the misuse of the apostrophe on notices in shops saying 'apple's – banana's – cauli's' (Burchfield 1996).

The word 'apostrophe' was initially derived from the Greek words *apostrophos* and *prosoidia* meaning to avert or turn away or the omission of a letter or a sound, and was introduced in the seventeenth century to denote possessives. The ground rules for using apostrophes include the following.

Possession

If there is one owner the apostrophe goes before the 's':

> The dog's tail
> The girl's hands

If the owner is plural the apostrophe goes after the 's':

> The lions' manes
> The boys' classroom

If the plural noun does not end in 's', add an 's' but the apostrophe goes before the 's':

> The children's clothes
> The women's hats

Collective nouns have the apostrophe before 's' because for example a 'team' is one team even if it has many players.

> The team's photograph was taken.
> The herd's vaccination was carried out by the vet.

Carney (1994) pointed out that 'names are allowed a greater deal of freedom in spelling'. This also applies to the way the apostrophe is used in names, and according to Truss (2003) 'institutions, towns, colleges, families, companies and brands have authority over their own spelling and punctuation (which is often historic), and there is absolutely nothing we can do except raise an eyebrow and make a mental note'. The convention nowadays is not to use the apostrophe in place names such as: Gerrards Cross; Golders Green; St Andrews. However there are many noteworthy exceptions such as: St John's Wood in London; St Michael's Mount in Cornwall; St Peter's Basilica in Rome. It is not usually used in the names of organisations or publications such as Barclays Bank; Harrods; Lloyds TSB, but Lloyd's of London use it. Trade names follow their own conventions (source: *Chambers Twenty-first Century Dictionary*).

However *The Times* (1998) cautions users to 'beware of organisations that have variations in their house style' such as: St Thomas' Hospital; St Paul's School; Lord's Cricket Ground. Proper nouns ending in 's' can be problematic. Should another 's' be added to indicate possession or not? Burchfield (1996) recommends 's for the possessive case in English names and surnames whenever possible'. This is often ignored in modern usage. It prompted a former American Ambassador to the Court of St James, Raymond Seitz, to write to *The Times* in protest at incorrect usage. He pointed out that the Prince of Wales's official residence was St James's Palace, which is what was used in Court Circular reports, and not St James' Palace.

Exceptions include multisyllabic words that would otherwise be cumbersome or difficult to pronounce such as 'Mercedes' sports cars. Names from antiquity as in 'Hercules' labours'; 'Jesus' miracles' do not require an additional 's'. When two names are used side-by-side, the latter name only has an apostrophe when used in the possessive form such as: 'Alexander and Melanie's wedding'.

Pronouns such as 'hers', 'his', 'its', 'ours', 'theirs', 'yours', when used to denote possession do not have an apostrophe: 'Those are ours'. However, indefinite pronouns take an apostrophe:

anybody's guess
anyone's fault
in each other's pocket
everybody's name
nobody's responsibility
somebody's fault
someone's shoes.

Contractions

When words are abbreviated, an apostrophe is used to show where the letter or letters have been omitted. These short forms are called contractions and occur in informal speech. Some of these abbreviations cause problems for poor spellers, often because they are not spelt like they sound.

HANDY HINT

Write the long form of the words first, then put the abbreviation beside it. Learn the long spelling first and then look at the abbreviation, and at the same time note the letter or letters that have been omitted.

Auxiliary verbs used in contractions

are not	**aren't**
can not	**can't**
could not	**couldn't**
did not	**didn't**
does not	**doesn't**

Pronouns with auxiliary verbs used as contractions

<u>am</u>	<u>will</u>	<u>have</u>	<u>would</u>
I am – **I'm**	I will – **I'll**	I have – **I've**	I would – **I'd**
you are **you're**	you will – **you'll**	you have – **you've**	you would – **you'd**
he is – **he's**	he will – **he'll**	he has – **he's**	he would – **he'd**
she is – **she's**	she will – **she'll**	she has – **she's**	she would – **she'd**
it is – **it's**	it will – **it'll**	it has – **it's**	it would – **it'd**
we are – **we're**	we will – **we'll**	we have – **we've**	we would – **we'd**
they are – **they're**	they will – **they'll**	they have – **they've**	they would – **they'd**

The use of 'it's' and 'its' is frequently challenging. It helps if the pupil is reminded to think of the long form such as 'it is' before deciding how to spell the contracted form. 'It is a cold day' can be abbreviated to 'It's a cold day'. 'The cat cut its paw' cannot be changed to 'The cat cut it's (it is) paw'.

HANDY HINT

The most confusable are:

It is	it's	(its)
who is	who's	(whose)
you are	you're	(your)

Substitute 'it is' for 'it's' when in doubt and see if this makes sense. Do likewise for 'who's' and 'you're'.

Apostrophes

Apostrophes are used in abbreviations such as 'o'clock'; 'fish 'n chips'; 'huntin', 'shootin' and 'fishin'. When abbreviations are used in the possessive case they take an apostrophe: 'MPs' votes'; 'VIPs' lounge': 'NCOs' uniforms'. Many words are now used in the abbreviated form without the apostrophe originally used to indicate how influenza became flu; refrigerator, fridge; telephone, phone.

Plurals

An apostrophe is used for plurals of single letters such as 'Mind your p's and q's' or 'Don't forget to dot the i's and cross the t's'. An apostrophe is sometimes used in some dates and numbers: 'the swinging 60's' or 'the naughty 90's'.

The ten commandments for managing plurals painlessly

Plurals of nouns can be a challenge and need to be taught and learned. The use of plurals is not straightforward or trouble-free. The rules and generalisations for making plurals can be classified as follows.

The first commandment of plurals

The most common way to make a word plural is to add 's'

's'			
pen	pens	friend	friends
car	cars	teacher	teachers

Some plurals say /z/ 'boys'; 'paws' but are always spelt with 's'.

Words ending in 'ful' add 's' to 'ful':

cupful	cupfuls
mouthful	mouthfuls
teaspoonful	teaspoonfuls

The second commandment of plurals

Words ending in 's', 'x', 'z', 'ch', 'sh', add 'es'.

's'

atlas	atlases
glass	glasses
kiss	kisses

'x'

box	boxes
fox	foxes
mix	mixes

'z'

buzz	buzzes
quiz	quizzes
topaz	topazes

'ch'

church	churches
peach	peaches
witch	witches

'sh'

crash	crashes
dish	dishes
wish	wishes

Exception: nouns ending in 'ix' or 'ex' add 'ces' or 'es' depending on the sense:

appendix	appendices	appendixes
index	indices	indexes
matrix	matrices	matrixes

The third commandment of plurals

Words ending in 'f' or 'fe' change 'f' to 'v' and add 'es':

'f'

calf	calves
half	halves
leaf	leaves

'fe'

curve	curves
knife	knives
life	lives

Exceptions: some words ending in 'f' just add 's':

belief	beliefs	handkerchief	handkerchiefs
chef	chefs	proof	proofs
chief	chiefs	puff	puffs

Exception: some words ending in 'f' cannot make their minds up. Sometimes they change 'f' to 'v' and add 'es'; at other times they just add 's':

	'ves'	's'
dwarf	dwarves	dwarfs
hoof	hooves	hoofs
scarf	scarves	scarfs

The fourth commandment of plurals

Words ending in 'y' change 'y' to 'i' and add 'es':

'y'

city	cities	penny	pennies
copy	copies	story	stories
daisy	daisies	try	tries

Exception: words with a vowel before the 'y' just add 's':

abbey	abbeys	holiday	holidays
boy	boys	jersey	jerseys
chimney	chimneys	trolley	trolleys

The fifth commandment of plurals

Many nouns ending in 'o' add 's' in the plural; others add 'es':

- Nouns adding 's': 'sofas', 'yo-yos'.
- Nouns associated with music add 's': 'pianos', 'cellos'.
- Nouns borrowed from other languages add 's': 'patios', 'pizzas'.
- Nouns ending in two vowels add 's': 'kangaroos', 'zoos'.

Words ending in 'o' which add 's' in the plural:

's'

avocado	avocados
disco	discos
Eskimo	Eskimos
kilo	kilos
manifesto	manifestos
photo	photos
radio	radios
solo	solos
soprano	sopranos
stereo	stereos
stiletto	stilettos
zero	zeros

Words ending in 'o' which add 'es' in the plural:

'es'

buffalo	buffaloes
cargo	cargoes
domino	dominoes
echo	echoes
hero	heroes
negro	negroes
potato	potatoes
tomato	tomatoes
veto	vetoes
volcano	volcanoes

Exceptions include words borrowed from Italian which add 'i' in the plural:

graffito	graffiti
virtuoso	virtuosi

Exceptions: some words ending in 'o' cannot make their minds up. Sometimes they add 's'; at other times they add 'es'. Publishers and printers have varying styles. However, more add 's' especially those connected with music.

	's'	'es'
banjo	banjos	banjoes
halo	halos	haloes
innuendo	innuendos	innuendoes
mango	mangos	mangoes
memento	mementos	mementoes
mosquito	mosquitos	mosquitoes
motto	mottos	mottoes
torpedo	torpedos	torpedoes

The sixth commandment of plurals

Some words are always plural:

arms (weapons)	crossroads	pants	slacks
barracks	forceps	pincers (tool)	suds
bellows	glasses (spectacles)	pyjamas	thanks
binoculars	headquarters	remains	tights
braces	jeans	scissors	tongs
clippers	knickers	series	trousers
clothes	means	shears	tweezers
corps	measles	shorts	

The seventh commandment of plurals

Some nouns do not change in the plural when considered as a group:

aircraft	plaice
bison	poultry
cannon	salmon
chickenpox	sheep
cod	smallpox
deer	spacecraft
grouse	swine
hovercraft	trout
mackerel	whiting
people	youth

The eighth commandment of plurals

Some compound nouns add 's' to the first word; others add 's' to the second word:

's' added to the first word:

brother-in-law	brothers-in-law
chief-of-staff	chiefs-of-staff
commander-in-chief	commanders-in-chief

court-martial	courts-martial
father-in-law	fathers-in-law
hanger-on	hangers-on
maid-of-honour	maids-of-honour
mother-in-law	mothers-in-law
looker-on	lookers-on
passer-by	passers-by
runner-up	runners-up
sister-in-law	sisters-in-law

'**s' added to the second word:**

by-law	by-laws
by-way	by-ways
drive-in	drive-ins
lay-by	lay-bys
part-timer	part-timers
play-off	play-offs
sit-in	sit-ins
stand-by	stand-bys
take-off	take-offs
tie-up	tie-ups

The ninth commandment of plurals

Old English words (words that have survived from Anglo-Saxon times) follow their own rules and have little 'rhyme or reason':

child	children	man	men
die	dice	mouse	mice
foot	feet	ox	oxen
goose	geese	tooth	teeth
louse	lice	woman	women

Some Old English words have both regular and irregular plurals:

brother	brothers	brethren
cloth	cloths	clothes
die	dies	dice
pea	peas	pease
penny	pennies	pence

The tenth commandment of plurals

Words borrowed from other languages often form their plurals according to the rules of the original language:

Latin

alga	algae
alumnus	alumni
bacterium	bacteria
crisis	crises
crocus	crocuses
curriculum	curricula
datum	data
fungus	fungi
formula	formulae
gladiolus	gladioli
larva	larvae
medium	media
nebula	nebulae
radius	radii
referendum	referenda
stoma	stomata
stratum	strata

Greek

crisis	crises
criterion	criteria
hypothesis	hypotheses
oasis	oases
parenthesis	parentheses
phenomenon	phenomena
schema	schemata
synopsis	synopses
thesis	theses

French

beau	beaux
bureau	bureaux
chateau	chateaux
gateau	gateaux
plateau	plateaux

Plurals of these French words in English are now often made by adding 's'.

Exceptions: some words borrowed from foreign languages can't make their minds up and can be spelt either way in the plural, sometimes with a difference in meaning:

antenna	antennae	antennas
appendix	appendices	appendixes
cactus	cacti	cactuses
formula	formulae	formulas
fungus	fungi	funguses
memorandum	memoranda	memorandums
syllabus	syllabi	syllabuses
terminus	termini	terminals

How to manage to 'catch' the silent letters – the stealthy robbers

HANDY HINT

It is useful to be reminded that 'the silent letters steal away the sounds of certain letters so you do not hear them when you say the words'. Good visualisers would respond to an illustration of a burglar with a tote bag on his back with the letter emblazoned on it (Ott 2007).

Silent letters can be a painful reminder that there has to be a variety of approaches used when learning to spell. Spellers need to establish which spelling strategy they should use for individual spelling tasks. For instance, someone who relies on using just phonic methods will find it hard to spell words where a sound is not pronounced. When dealing with silent letters in spellings, visual tactics such as the Fernald method are helpful, other spellers may find the multi-sensory 'look-say-cover-write-check' method more helpful. Mnemonics can be used and perhaps linked to the word's derivation. Colour coding helps others. Using a different font to highlight the silent letter in a computer printout is another useful strategy. Using the spelling pronunciation jogs the memory of spellers when words have unstressed schwa vowels in syllables

/an/i/mal/   /bus/i/ness   /di/no/saur

Checklist of words with silent letters

Silent 'a'
aisle

Silent 'b'
bomb	climb	comb	debt
doubt	dumb	lamb	numb
thumb	tomb	subtle	

Silent 'c'
descent	scissors
discipline	sceptre
science	scythe

Silent 'd'
handkerchief
Wednesday

Silent 'g'

campaign	design	diaphragm	gnarled
gnash	gnat	gnaw	gnome
neighbour	reign	sign	

Silent 'gh'

alight	bought	bright
brought	caught	dough
fright	hight	knight
light	night	right
sight	tight	

Silent 'h'

diarrhoea	exhaust	exhibit
honest	honour	hour
khaki	loch	lough
rhubarb	rhinoceros	rheumatism
rhythm	rhyme	yoghurt

Silent 'i'
marriage
miniature
parliament

Silent 'k'

knapsack	knave	knead	knee
knew	knife	knight	knit
kneel	knob	knock	knoll
knot	know	knowledge	knuckle

Silent 'l'

alms	calf	calm	chalk	folk
half	palm	psalm	salmon	stalk
talk	walk	yolk		

Silent 'm'
mnemonic

Many never ever spell mnemonic correctly because it is a demonic word.

Silent 'n'

autumn   damn
column   hymn
condemn   solemn

Mnemonic: At the end of the autumn term we have many nice treats such as Halloween.

Silent 'p'

cupboard   pneumatic   pneumonia
psalm   pseudo   psoriasis
psychedelic   psychiatry   psychic
psychology   ptarmigan   receipt

Silent 'r'

February
library

Silent 's'

island

Silent 't'

castle   chestnut
depot   debut
listen   mortgage
thistle   whistle

Silent 'u'

guinea   guild
guilt   guilty
guise   guitar

Silent 'w'

answer   playwright   sword
who   whole   whom
wrap   wrath   wreathe
wreck   wreckage   wren
wrench   wrestle   wretched
wriggle   wrinkle   wrist
write

The bare essential words to spell well for older pupils

Busy teachers have been helped when deciding which words to teach by the NLS (DfEE 2001) *Framework for Teaching English* which provides spelling lists for pupils in Years 7, 8 and 9. It includes useful subject spelling lists which will be the backbone of spelling for most pupils' writing.

Some suggestions for mnemonics for older pupils

arithmetic	A rat in Tom's house might eat Tom's ice cream.
believe	I believe you will never tell a lie.
chocolate	Owen was late because he ate all the chocolate.
daughter	Her daughter always uses granny's hats at every race meeting.
parallel	Parallel has three parallel 'l's
people	People eat old potatoes luckily especially when they're baked.
Saturday	Saturday is 'u-r' day for having fun.
separate	Separate the food in case a rat eats it.
sincerely	I sincerely hope I can trust you since I rely on you.
soldier	Soldiers die regrettably in battle.
Wednesday	Wednesday is a never eat sweets day.
women	Women often have many men friends.

Common homophones and confusions

advise/advice	affect/effect	allowed/aloud
bought/brought	braking/breaking	choose/chose
cloth/clothe	complement/compliment	conscience/conscious
course/coarse	defuse/diffuse	our/are
pour/pore	practise/practice	quiet/quite
reign/rein	sites/sights	source/sauce
threw/through	to/too/two	toe/tow

Spelling demons

This list of frequently misspelt words is adapted from Fowler (Burchfield 1996), Crystal (1997) and Schott (2002).

1	absence	2	abscess
3	accessible	4	accidentally
5	acclaim	6	accommodation
7	affected	8	alleged
9	aluminium	10	apparatus
11	Arctic	12	barbecue
13	because	14	beetle
15	beginning	16	believe
17	benefited	18	bibliography
19	biscuit	20	broccoli
21	business	22	calendar
23	character	24	cemetery
25	century	26	collectable
27	commitment	28	committee
29	connoisseur	30	conscientious
31	consciousness	32	corroborate
33	curriculum	34	decaffeinated
35	definitely	36	desert

37	desiccated	38	diarrhoea
39	disappearance	40	drunkenness
41	ecstasy	42	embarrassment
43	entrepreneur	44	existence
45	exuberance	46	fascination
47	February	48	fictitious
49	forty	50	forfeit
51	fourteenth	52	fulfilment
53	geography	54	grammar
55	guarantee	56	guerrilla
57	harassment	58	hiccough
59	hindrance	60	holocaust
61	idiosyncrasy	62	immediately
63	inoculation	64	independent
65	indispensable	66	illegal
67	inefficient	68	ingredients
69	intelligence	70	interesting
71	intermittent	72	jealousy
73	knowledgeable	74	liaise
75	liquefy	76	manoeuvre
77	mayonnaise	78	medieval
79	Mediterranean	80	meringue
81	millennium	82	minuscule
83	mischievous	84	misspelt
85	mistletoe	86	mnemonic
87	mortgage	88	museum
89	necessary	90	neighbour
91	nightmare	92	obsession
93	obsolescent	94	obstacle
95	occasionally	96	omelette
97	originally	98	parallel
99	parliament	100	perseverance
101	picnicking	102	physically
103	prescription	104	preliminary
105	presumptuous	106	principle
107	privilege	108	pursue
109	questionnaire	110	quotient
111	raspberries	112	realistically
113	reference	114	remembrance
115	restaurant	116	rhyme
117	salary	118	scientifically
119	separate	120	signature
121	simile	122	successfully
123	surreptitiously	124	temperature
125	temporary	126	tendency
127	thermometer	128	thirtieth
129	transferred	130	truly

131	twelfth	132	tyranny
133	unnecessary	134	until
135	usage	136	vaccination
137	vacuum	138	vigorous
139	Wednesday	140	zealot

SUMMARY AND CONCLUSIONS

1   Good spelling develops easily for some but, like many skills, including academic skills, it can be improved with practice and experience. To spell well, spellers need to use a combination of spelling methods, different strategies and a variety of techniques. For those for whom these skills do not come easily or naturally, such as dyslexic people, it is necessary to spend more time and to give explicit teaching of spelling and of compensatory strategies.

2   Homophones are notoriously difficult for many spellers, but are a persisting source of anguish and frustration for poor spellers, especially for those with under-functioning visual skills. There are strategies and ways around the problems, ranging from mnemonics to rhymes to jingles, as well as short cuts including using spell-checkers and graphics. However, many spell-checkers do not always spot errors of meaning.

3   The 'odd-bod' spellings are confusing and Crystal (2002) blames them for the popular misconception that English spelling is highly irregular. The problem, however, is that many of the 'high-frequency' words have irregular spellings. But on an optimistic note he added that 'there are only 400 everyday word[s] in English whose spelling is wholly irregular'. Hanna et al. (1966) established that from 17,000 of the most frequently used words in English 14 per cent were 'irregular'; 86 per cent follow the regular sound/symbol rules.

4   The misuse of the apostrophe is well documented, including the so-called green-grocer's apostrophe where there is confusion between the possessive case for nouns and plural nouns: 'apple's and orange's'.

5   Pluralisation is a multifaceted challenge, but there are clear-cut guidelines for spellers. Knowledge and understanding of the principles help.

6   Silent letters are perceived by many as a severe test of spelling knowhow. However there are a number of hints that help lighten the load for all spellers, including those with dyslexia.

7   There are many ways to learn these 'nuisance' spellings. It helps learners if they remember to use their eyes, ears, hands and lips and some of the methods suggested in Chapter 8, which match individual learning styles as learners follow the roadmap through the spelling jungle.

14 How Information and Communications Technology (ICT) has Revolutionised Living and Learning for those with Dyslexia

- Is the computer the greatest and most successful means of mass communication ever invented?
- What can technology do to lighten the load for those who struggle to acquire literacy?
- Guidelines when choosing hardware and software for those with dyslexia and dyspraxia
- How CD-ROMs can be used to enhance skills
- Evidence of the 'before-and-after' effect of the spell-checker
- Why the word-processor is a 'writer's best friend'
- Is the computer a 'copper-bottomed' solution to writers' difficulties?
- Why spell-checkers are boon companions for all spellers particularly poor spellers
- How and why text messaging has revolutionised communication
- Popular computer packages to empower learners and spellers
- Summary and conclusions

Keywords

Information and Communications Technology (ICT)	Internet Multimedia software	Speech recognition and screen-readers (SRS)
Interactive whiteboard	QWERTY keyboard	Text messaging

Is the computer the greatest and most successful means of mass communication ever invented?

The computer has been acclaimed as one of the greatest inventions of the many technological marvels of the twentieth century. It ranks beside television as one of the most influential communication instruments ever devised, and has made global mass communication a reality. Its impact on universal literacy can be put on a pedestal beside Johann Gutenberg's printing press. It has literally changed the world and its influence is as strong and unstoppable as Caxton's printing press was for the English language.

What can technology do to lighten the load for those who struggle to acquire literacy?

All computers carry out a huge range of basic functions. They can be programmed to carry out a multiplicity of tasks in schools, homes and in the workplace including the following:

- word processing
- graphics
- spreadsheets
- faxing
- databases
- desktop publishing
- e-mailing
- internet
- multimedia use
- video conferencing

Guidelines when choosing hardware and using software for those with dyslexia and dyspraxia

Considerations include the choice of type size. The vertical height of the type is measured in points and which can range from 4 to 48 point. The normal font size is 12 point. Poor readers find small print challenging. Space between individual letters makes for greater clarity and makes it easier to keep and find one's place on the line. Many individuals with dyslexia and dyspraxia find 14-point type easier to read and work with, particularly when they have to proofread documents. Double line spacing also makes it easier to read text, particularly when editing and revising work.

Typeface styles – of which there are many, such as Arial, Times New Roman, Helvetica – are a matter of choice. However, some find certain type styles more difficult to read than others. Like everybody else, dyslexic people find a typeface with serifs – the short lines across the ends of arms and stems of letters – easier for sustained reading. Times New Roman is an example.

Smythe (1996) conducted a small study among 57 adolescent students and found 'no preference in typeface'. Styles such as Comic Sans that match cursive writing 'a' and 'g' help. Word lists and spelling options on spell-checkers should be given in lower-case rather than upper-case letters because they are easier to read.

The colour of paper should be considered because there is anecdotal evidence that some people with visual difficulties find black print on white paper more difficult to read and easier on coloured paper. It is useful to experiment to find an optimum colour such as cream or yellow paper. The background colour of the computer screen as well as the colour of the print can also be adjusted for those who experience visual stress or colour preferences. Some people may experience less eyestrain if they use a white font on a blue screen, or a darker screen with a lighter font. Others find highlighted or greyed text easier and more comfortable to read.

Desktop PCs come with a standard 15-inch or 17-inch screen, but are also available in 18, 19 and 22 inches. Larger screens are helpful, particularly for those with poor eyesight or poor visual perception. The popular AlphaSmart Neo is used in many schools and can display six lines of text. This can be reduced to two lines if a very large font is easier to read. Some machines, including laptops, have screens that can be adjusted for light and colour. These are important considerations because some individuals, such as those who have scotopic sensitivity syndrome, are more or less sensitive to variations in light and colour. Such adjustments cut down on eyestrain for those who work for long periods. Just as the size of font and the space between words and lines are a key consideration when choosing printed texts for poor readers, so too is choice of computer screen. Cost and the compatibility of school and home computers are other priorities.

Keyboards come in different shapes and sizes. The BigKeys LX has keytops four times the size of normal (www.r-e-m.co.uk). The size of the keyboard is important when choosing laptops and pocket-size handheld spell-checkers and personal digital assistants (PDAs) which are miniature handheld computers. This is because those with poor visual discrimination or poor fine motor skills such as those with dyspraxia find small keyboards more challenging. If the keys are very small, like those on some palm models, they can be difficult to use particularly for someone with poor co-ordination. Other PDAs do not have a keyboard: instead the user writes on a touch screen using a stylus. Some users find using a stylus challenging because of poor fine motor skills. They require manual dexterity and an additional mental effort to operate. The outcome is that secretarial aspects of the writing task may distract from the content. This also applies to some portable PCs, including some laptop models. Some PDAs also have a speech option, which is useful for hearing words pronounced, particularly homophones and confusable words, and for making spelling lists, noting homework details, learning vocabulary, taking notes or recording a lecture. The alarm can be set as a reminder for lessons and appointments, which is helpful for those with poor organisational skills and poor short-term memory.

Touch-typing is one of the most valuable and transferable skills pupils can be taught and should be a compulsory teaching requirement for all pupils with specific learning difficulties. It requires a systematic structured approach to teach it. There are a number of teaching packages on the market such as Touch-type Read and Spell, which is a multi-sensory teaching package linked to the phonics programme *Alpha to Omega*, Hornsby et al. (1999). Typing Instructor Deluxe includes instruction games and tests. For some students it is a slow procedure to learn to touch-type because they may have sequencing difficulties. This is why it is important to have a picture of the keyboard always visible on the screen. Others learn quickly and easily using packages such as Mavis Beacon which is a self-help package which suits those with good kinaesthetic skills. Because touch-typing is a motor skill it must be practised regularly to become established. Unfortunately, often not enough time is available owing to the restraints of the curriculum requirement. Time is not allocated nor is there the knowhow among staff in some schools for teaching and learning this life-enhancing skill. Pupils with special educational needs benefit from being able to word-process quickly and efficiently, using their eyes and fingers automatically, rather than using the 'hunt and peck' approach using two fingers to search for letters and having constantly to look at the screen which is also time-consuming when typing. Touch-typing when it has become an automised skill becomes the 'servant not the master' of the writer and frees up mental energy for thinking about the contents, editing and the organisation of what is being written (www.dyslexic.com).

The mouse is the tool which is clicked to give commands to the computer. Underneath the mouse is a sensor, which moves the cursor on the screen. When pointed on the screen the cursor selects items from, for example, the toolbar. This consists of icons, which are chosen by a click of the mouse button. It can also signal an action, such as starting a video sequence. It is important to be aware that some individuals, such as those with directionality difficulties and dyspraxic difficulties, may take longer to learn how to use a mouse than others. They have to remember what a single click does, what a double click does, or what happens when the mouse is dragged to the correct place, then held down. A touchpad can be used instead. These movements involve fine motor skills as well as eye–hand co-ordination. It is also important to be aware that there are left-handed keyboards on the market which are helpful for left-handed users. Mice can also be configured for left-handers.

HANDY HINT

According to a survey about left-handedness conducted by the Consumers Association (*Which* 2000), 'our users liked the left-handed keyboard, with five out of the six saying it suited them better than a right-handed one' and 'it felt more natural and was quicker and easier to use'.

Speech recognition software comprises software programs that allow users to speak to the computer. The words spoken are converted to text, which then appears on the screen. They are a boon for those who have good speaking skills but poor spelling skills. They can play back what has been said, which helps those with poor working memory skills and is particularly useful for proofreading. Kurzweil 3000 (www.sightandsound.co.uk) is one of the most popular (and most expensive) programs. Talking word-processors, which read aloud words as they are typed help those with poor short-term memory. Some programs such as Write Out Loud (www.donjohnston.co.uk) have a wordbank facility, which lists frequently used words on the screen and reduces the amount of typing. Dragon Naturally Speaking 8 (www.dyslexic.com) is an alternative option. Texthelp (http://www.texthelp.com) Read & Write GOLD is another package that reads speech back, has a phonetic spell-checker and gives meanings for homophones as well as audible definitions and sentences to help choose the correct option. Another useful facility is what it calls Logs: this records spelling mistakes by date and type, and is useful for teacher and learner for revision and reinforcement. It can read text that has been scanned, enlarges the font and permits the use of different colours on the screen, and can be used to read documents from the Internet. There are two kinds of speech options available. Synthesised speech, which is robotic speech, can be irritating for some; others find it helpful. However, for spelling packages where sound-to-symbol match is important, digitised speech is the other option available and is often preferable. It uses a human voice. It requires 128MB of RAM as well as a sound card and speakers. It also requires time and assistance to train the computer to recognise the user's voice. It has a phonetic dictionary and thesaurus, and offers help with homophones and syllables.

Olson et al. (1997) conducted a number of studies about 'the remediation of dyslexia using talking computers for [a period of] ten years'. Their research showed that the greatest gains were made 'with intensive training in phonological awareness, taught by teachers using guided discovery activities off the computer, and practised by children on computers'. Their research on the use of speech recognition technology showed that it is best used to develop discrete skills, including word-processing. Speech recognition technology lightens the load for those writers who are chronically poor spellers, or for those who have poor motor skills, because all the words dictated appear on the screen correctly spelt. It circumvents the obligation to be able to access the keyboard, and it becomes a means to an end, rather than an end in itself, for many users.

The World Wide Web (www) was developed by an Englishman, Tim Berners-Lee. He originally developed a program to allow researchers to cross-reference their research publications. Documents are stored on Web pages and can be cross-referenced to other pages with hyperlinks. When connected to the Internet, on payment to a provider of online services, the user can access information stored by the Web-servers. Establishing what is available about a chosen subject or topic can be done by logging on to a search engine. This feature of the Web is highly popular, particularly for students and researchers. Many schools and colleges are now on-line. The government has made it part of its education policy to ensure that all schools are on-line. The day-to-day uses of the Internet are increasing all the time, whether it is the teacher who wants to buy a textbook on line or a parent who wants to look at facilities offered by a future school for their child. The school's website will probably include a copy of its SATs results, Ofsted inspection report and other details about the curriculum and extracurricular activities it provides. Others incorporate chatrooms which include discussion forums and information from users about resources and helpful ideas. The following are useful websites: www.bda-dyslexia.org.uk; www.dyslexiaaction.org.uk; www.dfee.gov.uk.

E-mail (electronic mail) is used to send and receive messages via telephone lines or radio waves round the globe. Its speed is its greatest advantage. It is also relatively inexpensive to transmit messages in comparison to sending letters by post, or in comparison to the price of a phone call. Some e-mailers use a cryptic style, and punctuation conventions more lax than in other forms of writing, which may help those who have difficulties with these skills. Personal users can pick up messages in their own time. Pupils can e-mail homework to their teacher for marking. Details of homework which may have been forgotten or lost can be obtained by e-mailing a friend. Parents can be contacted quickly and easily if they are on-line. Some people who have dyslexia find it difficult to remember e-mail addresses, not least because of the precise nature of the punctuation. Addresses can, however, be copied for later use.

Floppy disks or CDs need to be labelled and dated, and kept in a storage system. This can be challenging for those who have poor organisational skills. All work can be stored on the hard disk. Individual pieces of work, such as course and revision notes, can be stored on floppy disks or CDs. This is important as a back-up system in case the computer crashes. Pupils need to be aware that computers can sometimes crash. This occurs when the computer stops working, and sometimes the information or documents are not retrievable. This is why all users should be encouraged to make back-up copies of important documents, such as coursework or projects, on floppy disks and to label these clearly (as well as keeping hard copy).

Disks can be taken to school or college to use there. They can be sent or received by individuals for personal or business use. A manuscript of a book can be submitted to a publisher by e-mail. Those who have organisational problems will find that having their work stored on a computer makes the retrieval and use of the information much easier. Files get lost and essays sometimes disappear when required for revision. Details for bibliographies can be filed alphabetically, and retrieved at the flick of a switch.

Those who are strong visualisers can be helped to remember spellings when they see the words on screen. Kinaesthetic learners remember spellings because they have a good tactile memory and their fingers remember the letter patterns. Spelling packages which are designed to practise spelling, as well as spell-checkers, help to reinforce spellings for some as well as lessening the sense of frustration others experience when they write. Multimedia packages also help strong visualisers, when for instance they use a CD-ROM, because they can see illustrations beside the words.

Auditory learners can be helped by hearing the spellings, if using a multimedia package while they type.

How CD-ROMs can be used to enhance skills

CD-ROM software programs store computer data on disks. They can include text, graphics, speech, pictures, sound and video. They are user-friendly, and include many different methods and means to gather knowledge and information.

Some programs contains video clips of significant events, involving world affairs and historic events: seeing and hearing the names and events makes them easier to remember, for example for those with word retrieval or word naming difficulties, and eliminates difficulties associated with spelling.

Virtual reality tours can show the contents as well as the layout of world-famous buildings and landmarks, which is helpful for history or geography students. They help to put flesh on the skeletons of our ancestors, so that we can better understand them and their environment. The vocabulary and terminology associated with these can be stored by learners for later use.

Timelines put significant events in history in chronological order. These make it easier to remember dates and events, when the names are correctly spelt, for someone who has difficulties with sequential and working memory.

Animation turns complex scientific data into reality. Those who have good kinaesthetic skills will find that watching a science experiment being carried out helps when they later want to write an explanation, or when they have to carry out an operation such as wiring an electric plug. Seeing, hearing and typing spellings is more effective than just trying to remember words by rote. It is much easier to remember the names of the planets of the solar system if the planets can be shown as they orbit the sun, and the spelling is available for easy reference.

Subjects and topics can be researched by using the Oxford Pop-up CD-ROM for reference, just as when using a printed version of *Encyclopaedia Britannica* (www.eb.com). Files can be kept, copied or downloaded for reference and used in essays or projects.

Using packages such as Kidspiration or Inspiration (www.dyslexia.com; www.r-e-m.co.uk) helps to create Mind Maps™ which organise ideas or information using words, colour, pictures and symbols when brainstorming. Other forms of graphic organisation such as word-webs, which enhance memory when writing, are particularly useful for strong visualisers. They can be installed in the low-cost AlphaSmart Neo (www. alphasmart.co.uk). However it is important to remember individual learning styles. When learning, for example, about suffixing rules the spelling is more memorable when pupils see the syllables and hear them, while looking at an illustration as they read the word using multi-sensory learning.

Evidence of the 'before-and-after' effect of the spell-checker

The following alphabetic poem was written by a severely dyslexic 10-year-old boy, 'Terry', and shows what a wonderfully creative imagination he has, and how, when he was unencumbered by having to 'watch out' for his spellings, he could write vividly and humorously. He did the first draft unaided. He then did the corrections next day with support from his mother and with help from the spell-checker. He commented, 'I can't write and think about spellings [at the same time] and the spell-checker puts the words I want to use out of my head.'

An Alphabet Menagerie

A	Apse ambel aimlesley		A	is for Apes who amble aimlessly
B	Bares broze for berees		B	is for Bears who browse for berries
C	Cobra koil for the cill		C	Is for Cobras who coil for the kill
D	Dogs bake loudly		D	is for Dogs who bark loudly
E	Elefantets stomp wildly		E	is for Elephants who stomp wildly
F	Fols frisk and folow there mofers		F	is for Foals who frisk and follow their mothers
G	Gorillas danse stilesly		G	is for Gorillas who dance stylishly
H	Hippos burp like angre pigs		H	is for Hippos who burp like angry pigs
I	Inects get sqoshoshed eesley		I	is for Insects who get squashed easily
J	Jaguars stark you like cats		J	is for Jaguars who stalk you like cats
K	Koala bears eat ucoluptus allday		K	is for Koala bears who eat eucalyptus all day
L	Lions rove like hippos burp		L	is for Lions who roar like hippos burp
M	Monkeys are chater boks		M	is for Monkeys who are chatterboxes
N	Newts swim round lick littel dots		N	is for Newts who swim round like little dots
O	Octopus wave goodbye all day which there tentlecrawes		O	is for Octopus who waive goodbye all day with their tentacles
P	Parrots our grte copecats		P	is for Parrots who are great copycats
Q	Quails fli arowned and rule the ski		Q	is for Quails who fly around and rule the sky
R	Rattlesnakes rattle and role all day		R	is for Rattlesnakes who rattle and roll all day
S	Seals flop around on the sand		S	is for Seals who flop around on the sand

T	Tarantula's terize they're fictm's	T	is for Tarantulas who terrorise their victims
U	Unicorns like joysting	U	is for Unicorns who like jousting
V	Voles dig down wholes	V	is for Voles who dig down holes
W	Whales hav wotroles in there top end	W	is for Whales who have waterholes in their top end
X	Noa had a sige on the arc dore saying no exit	X	is for Noah who had a sign on the ark door saying no exit
Y	Yaks have long necks you cood tiy a roap to	Y	is for Yaks who have long necks you could tie a rope to
Z	Zebras our good crosing plases.	Z	is for Zebras who are good crossing places

Why the word-processor is a 'writer's best friend'

The cut and paste facility which moves text from one part of a document to another is efficient and time-saving. It allows difficult or long words to be typed in only once and then they can be copied everywhere else in the document. It is a favourite option for those who find scientific terminology very difficult to spell. The delete facility makes editing easier, especially for those who have sequencing difficulties.

The print preview facility allows the changes made to be seen on the screen before doing a printout of the document. It is a saver of time and paper.

Those who have speech recognition software can have what they have written read back to them. This is helpful for those who have sequencing difficulties, or a tendency to omit words. It is an invaluable asset when they proofread a document. Generations of schoolchildren spent long hours rewriting work because perhaps of 'careless spelling errors' or 'messy untidy writing ' or 'crossings out'. Others had comments written on their work such as 'You did not write enough' or 'Please rewrite this for homework' written at the bottom of a piece of work. Other unfortunate pupils suffered the indignity of having their' unacceptable work' ripped out of their exercise book and torn up in front of the class. Dyslexic pupils often wrote very little because they were unable to spell the words they wanted to write. Adam, aged 13, said 'I only use words I know I can spell'. Another pupil said, 'when I write I am a bit like a juggler. I struggle to keep the handwriting, spelling and punctuation balls in the air. I usually fail because I have to also think about what I am going to say, so I often drop one of the balls.'

Those who are dyspraxic are often criticised and judged harshly for the appearance of their work, which can include illegible, messy writing. When their work is done on the computer it can be assessed for content and ideas. This removes the sense of failure and is highly motivating and uplifting.

The spell-checker and grammar checker correct mistakes at the touch of a button for many uses. Some dyslexic users have difficulties with spell-checkers. TechDis (2003) found that 30 per cent of spelling errors were not corrected. James and Draffan (2004) conducted a study about the accuracy of spell-checkers for dyslexic users. They concluded that the correct word should appear at the top of the list of suggestions.

Word-processing frees up thoughts, emotions and knowledge of those who are unfairly handicapped in the writing stakes when they have to write manually. It also helps to improve vocabulary and expressive language skills. A thesaurus is a great ally, for example for someone who wants to use the word 'obnoxious' and knows that it means 'nasty' but cannot spell it.

The Franklin Collegiate Speaking Dictionary and Thesaurus (British spelling) and *The Franklin Speaking Language Master* (US spelling) provide speech feedback, which is a help for many dyslexic users.

Microsoft Word has an 'auto correct' facility which will automatically correct commonly misspelt words when the computer is given the instruction to spell a word such as 'dyslexia' throughout the whole of the document. The user can opt for British English over American English spelling, which avoids forms such as 'color' for 'colour'. One's own most frequently misspelt words can be added to the dictionary.

The ultimate reward, when proofreading has been completed, is seeing a print-out of work which is neat and pristine. Seeing the ecstatic expression on the face of someone who has struggled with literacy and observing their pride in 'being just like everyone else' when their written work is evaluated is a joy for all involved.

Those who have poor decoding reading skills, or who read very slowly or who have poor comprehension skills, can use a package such as Text-EASE which will read the text they type back to them. This allows them to keep pace with most of their peers. It allows them to focus on content rather than on the mechanical aspects of decoding text.

Those who have poor word retrieval or word naming skills can use a predictive word processing package such as Co: Writer PredicIT or Prophet. Pen Friend and textHELP have prediction facilities (www.dyslexic.com). It offers pupils a choice of words to help finish 'sentences that are grammatically correct, even if they use phonetic spelling. For 'The Plough is a kstl [of stars]', the options read aloud were:

1 castle
2 costly
3 kestrel
4 kettle
5 constellation

TextHELP's Read & Write GOLD claims to be the 'one stop solution' for reading and writing because it can read back text, correct phonetic spelling errors, help with homophones, record persistent errors and has a dictionary, thesaurus and word prediction facility all in one software package.

Listening to what they have said on a voice-activated package helps some students to pick up errors such as omitting words in their writing. This is because some find it very challenging to proofread for their own errors: they tend to 'read' what they wanted to say rather than what appears on the screen.

The printer allows all documents to be downloaded. Some individuals find it difficult to proofread on screen, just as some individuals find it difficult to use a dictaphone to communicate their ideas. The strategy used should match individuals' preferred learning style. They can proofread on a hardcopy, and then add the corrections on screen. Those who have good auditory skills will find listening to a talking spell-checker useful when learning and using spellings. The *Franklin Speaking Homework Wiz* (www.dyslexic.com) reads the suggestion list aloud and gives definitions, and the words can be written in cursive style. It uses American English spelling. The look of sheer elation on the face of writers who see a 'clean' page of writing, when they have previously suffered the indignity of seeing their work covered in red ink when their mistakes were corrected, is a sight to melt the heart.

Copies can be made of work for storage or display. Classroom displays for visitors, school open days and school inspections by Ofsted can be transformed by the marvels of what can be produced with the help of technology. All children can have examples of their work on display in the classroom. This does wonders for self-esteem and pride, and being just like everyone else is a boost for sometimes battered egos.

The computer can be useful for a host of classroom tasks. Spreadsheets can be produced for work during the Numeracy Hour. Labels with the subject names spelled correctly can be made for exercise books and files. There are a range of software products available for maths such as Numbershark 3, Mathmania, Maths Workshop (www. dyslexic.com).

Graphics can be used in many cross-curricular activities, such as when writing about a geography field trip or writing up a science experiment, and when using different writing genres such as an advertisement or playscript.

Colour printers have many additional advantages (the only restraint in using is them is the prohibitive cost of the ink cartridges). Colour is useful when teaching spelling, for example when making acronyms such as when teaching mnemonics for the 'odd-bods' and the 'high-frequency' irregular spellings as well as for highlighting word patterns. Silent letters become more memorable and less easy to forget, especially for strong visualisers, if they are highlighted in red.

The computer cuts down on the physical effort involved. Kraynak (1995) commented that 'the biggest timesaving feature of computers is that you never have to retype'.

CASE STUDY: 'NEIL' (35 YEARS)

Just because you can't spell doesn't mean to say that you can't write. I am now most fortunate that I have a PC and a PA so that my clients never know I can't spell. The great irony for me is that, despite my dyslexia, I now write for a living. I write speeches, papers and letters for people that are helping the charities that I work for, so I regularly write for Dukes, Marquises, senior politicians, etc., and I often think of the English teachers over the years who told me that I can't write – well I can and I am being well paid for it.

The National Curriculum puts great emphasis on computer literacy and on the use of ICT in all subject areas. School budgets have been increased to take account of the increased costs of providing sufficient resources to meet the needs of all pupils. A survey conducted in 2004 by the Qualifications and Curriculum Authority (QCA 2005) showed that 46 per cent of lessons in primary schools used ICT and 32 per cent in secondary schools. The *National Literacy Strategy* (DfEE 1998) makes few explicit references to the use of ICT at the word and sentence work level. However it recommends its use, particularly when teaching writing skills. It can be tailor-made, for example when teaching and learning about non-fiction writing, and when implementing genre theory (Martin 1989). This theory was developed as a result of the realisation that good writing follows certain conventions and processes. Writing frames or scaffolds can be made for these, such as templates for letters or reports. There are a number of excellent computer packages available for this, such as desktop publishing packages to produce reviews, letters, pamphlets, school newsletters and advertisements. These include Kidspiration, which is a 'visual learning tool which produces maps and diagrams and also has an audio feature. Write: Outloud 'allows pupils to hear what they say while writing it'. 'Hugo', aged 11, created this advertisement (Fig. 18) on his computer when he was learning about persuasive writing.

Figure 18

Interactive whiteboards provide portable hardware and software to record, play back, print and share information including e-mail and the Internet. In the classroom they can be used for presentations, brainstorming and instruction. For instance letters or affixes can be colour-coded or highlighted with an electronic pen. Then these can be omitted and the pupils can be asked to fill in the missing letters. Pictures can be used as visual cues. When the spelling appears, it can then be erased and the pupil is asked to write the word. This can be reinforced with a voice saying the letters as pupils proofread what they have written. Printouts can be saved and filed in a personal 'Spellofax'.

Is the computer a 'copper-bottomed' solution to writers' difficulties?

Great optimism and inflated expectations often pepper discussions about the merits and potential for improvement in individuals' writing skills when word-processing is used. A number of studies have been conducted on whether word-processing improves the quality of pupils' writing. Beard (2000) reviewed a large number of research studies and cited Peacock's (1992) review of fifty research projects, which established that a 'large majority found no difference in the writing quality of writers using word processors when compared to the writing quality of writers using pen and paper'. None the less these findings are at variance with anecdotal evidence from users. The polarisation of opinions and the counter-arguments have arisen because both sides are talking about different aspects of writing. Good writing requires skill, understanding, knowledge and knowhow about writing processes and different writing forms. It is dependent on cognitive skills and an understanding of the basic writing principles. Good writers also need to be able to deal with the mechanics of writing such as spelling, grammar, punctuation and presentation. The word-processor can be used to make the secretarial aspects of writing easier as well as taking away much of the physical effort. It can also provide models and outlines, but the ideas, feelings, opinions and facts expressed are still the writer's own, and these require mental effort and knowhow from the writer. The computer has an infinite storehouse of information but to use this an individual has to personally access and understand it. Human intelligence is still mightier than cyber intelligence.

CASE STUDY: 'WILLIE' (32 YEARS)

I was about seven years old when I was asked in my first class at Prep school to name the four seasons. I replied that they were 'the Flat [Racing], National Hunt, rugby and cricket'. I was so embarrassed and later teased about my answer. The Headmaster quoted it in his speech on Speech Day. The computer has helped me. I find the spell-checker invaluable and I could never have won the Martin Wills Young Writers Award for the best original racing article without one. However I still had to endure a painstaking apprenticeship when I learned how to write.

Why spell-checkers are boon companions for all spellers, particularly poor spellers

People sometimes fantasise about what they would rescue if their house was burning down and they were woken by the fire alarm, or what they would choose to take to a desert island as the participants do on the popular radio show *Desert Island Discs*. Many individuals with dyslexia would now try to salvage their PC or their laptop because 'I cannot imagine what my life would be like without it, particularly the spell-checker'.

Most word-processing packages now come with a spell-checker. There are different models available, including ones that make a bleep when an error has been made. Many find this intrusive and distracting. It is therefore useful to be able to switch off the spell-checker until the document has been completed.

Word for Windows has an in-built dictionary which can be activated when the spell button is clicked, or it can be selected from the Toolbar menu under 'spelling'. When an error is made, a red wavy line appears under the error in the document. The Spelling Dialog Box appears on the screen. It can identify:

- spelling errors
- incorrect capitalisation
- repetition of words
- incorrect use of hyphens.

Then it gives the option to 'change to' with the target word. It also gives a list of further suggestions. The user can then ignore the prompt, change or add the target word. Words with a green wavy line are possible grammar errors. The only snag is that the user needs to be able to read the suggestions offered, which unfortunately some individuals are unable to do. The way forward now is the talking spell-checker.

A particularly user-friendly option for the dyslexic speller who has a tendency to misspell the same word such as friend as 'freind' is to click 'Change All' so that Word automatically makes the substitution without bothering the user every time (Gookin 1996). Another very useful option for those who make persistent errors with words such as 'thay' for 'they' or 'becos' for 'because' is to use the Word Auto Correct tool, which acts like a fairy godmother and changes all the 'wrongs' to 'rights'. However Gookin (1996) adds a note of caution: 'Spell checking doesn't fix things other than finding rotten words and offering suggested replacements.'

Many users say that having a spell-checker means that they can use the word they want to rather than having to restrict their choice of vocabulary to a word they know they can spell.

Other spell-checkers underline or highlight errors which can be corrected when the document is completed. This is a great asset for all writers, because even the most competent writers do sometimes make typographical errors as a result of a slip of a finger. The naked eye often will miss these, but a spell-checker will identify them. Many poor spellers, particularly those who have dyslexic difficulties, always work with the spell-checker turned off. This is because they lose their train of thought and forget what they want to say because of their working memory difficulties. They also find it difficult to process too much information simultaneously. They do not have enough 'mental space' to cope with too many proceses simultaneously, often because of poor working memory skills.

Spell-checkers with a facility to add a personal list of persistent 'hard spellings' are very useful. Words can be added to the customised dictionary and should include personal names and names of places or subject jargon that may not otherwise be recognised by the spell-checker.

Talking spell-checkers have added another dimension to spelling correctly. Some of the homophones can be picked up through this facility. TextHELP Read & Write GOLD 'provides colour coding of the confusable words and suggests possible alternatives and audible definitions and sample sentences'.

The spell-checker can spare the poor speller public embarrassment and humiliation by allowing the user to produce documents that are error-free. There is much anecdotal evidence from users of how they have 'narrow escapes' from potentially disastrous situations such as sending their CV to an employer with two spelling errors. Other candidates have reported that they made spelling mistakes when they filled in their UCAS forms. They were saved from probable rejection by using the spell-checking facility.

> ## CASE STUDY: 'RICHARD' (28 YEARS)
>
> My job involves writing letters to people about health issues. I work for a large drug manufacturing company. I am always making spelling mistakes despite using the spell-checker. They are usually spotted by a colleague before the information goes out to clients. My worst mistake was when I wrote 'DOES' on a questionnaire being sent out by the company to twenty thousand people about the correct 'DOSE' to take of a product. If it had gone out I would probably have been sacked on the spot.

Asking a dyslexic speller to check his or her spelling by using a dictionary can be the final straw, particularly for those with sequencing difficulties, and for those who are unable to remember the order of the letters in the alphabet. It is often a time-wasting activity, and some dictionaries, such as the shorter dictionaries used in classrooms, do not include root words with the endings 'ed' or 'ing'. So a speller's query about whether the final consonant should be doubled, or the 'e' at the end of the root word dropped, is left unanswered. Electronic dictionaries such as the Franklin models are very useful when individuals are not using a computer, and some can read the words and definitions aloud.

How, when and why do spell-checkers sometimes fail writers?

Spell-checkers are little use when those who have low literacy levels are unable to read the options offered to correct their mistakes. This problem can now be circumvented with the use of speaking options. Conventional spell-checkers do not always identify homophones when they are used incorrectly whereas a speaking dictionary would. Spell-checks pick up only non-existent words. They do not pick up wrong words if they would be correctly spelled in another context. The following are examples taken from the work of 12-year-old 'Tony':

> 'We had to keep a dairy' (We had to keep a diary).
> 'Are friends were coming to tee' (Our friends were coming to tea).
> 'We where at home' (We were at home).
> 'It was a great derision' (It was a great decision).
> 'I bought a pencil and pen to school' (I brought a pencil and pen to school).
> 'I didn't know witch way to go' (I didn't know which way to go).

This problem can now be resolved by using packages which include a speech feedback facility and often give sample sentences to illustrate the correct usage.

Some individuals' spelling is so poor that the computer is unable to recognise the words. Some individuals find using the spell-checker very difficult, and they work very slowly, particularly with some small hand-held versions with a small font. The following is a witty reminder of the limitations and shortcomings of the spell-checker:

A cautionary spell-checker's 'tail'

Eye have a spelling chequer
It came with my pea sea
It plainly marques four my revue
Miss Steaks eye kin knot sea.

Eye strike a key and type a word
And weight four it two say
Weather eye am wrong oar write
It shows me strait a weigh.

As soon as a mist ache is maid
It nose bee fore two long
And eye can put the error rite
Its rare lea ever wrong.

Eye have run this poem threw it
I am shore your pleased two no
Its letter perfect all the weigh
My chequer tolled me sew
The Times Magazine (2000)

Pocket spell-checkers

These are becoming widely available, and prices have dropped just as calculator prices did. Here are some questions to ask when choosing a handheld spell-checker (Ott 1997):

- Is the keyboard clear and easy to read?
- Does it use the QWERTY keyboard layout?
- Does the screen have a clear display?
- Is there a large enough word list? 70,000 should be the minimum.
- Can it help with homophones, for example giving meanings and using them in sentences?
- Can it deal with words that do not have the correct initial letters? Capitals are more difficult to use.
- Does it have a facility to add a list of personal misspellings?
- How long does the battery last?
- Does it turn itself off when not in use?
- Does it use upper-case or lower-case letters?
- How does it cope with phonetically spelled words?
- Can word families be used for different purposes?
- Can it deal with the addition of prefixes and suffixes to root words?
- Is the font size large enough to read easily?
- Does it have a speech option?
- Does it have a thesaurus which is also useful for cross-referencing meanings?
- Is the case durable and strong enough?

Speech recognition (SR) software is seen by many dyslexic useres as the ultimate solution to the problems of those with reading, writing or spelling problems as well as those with poor fine motor skills. The technology has improved over the years and it has become easier to use. The talking spell-checker has been compared to using a magic wand because it can instantly change what is wrong and make it right.

How and why text messaging has revolutionised communication

Text messaging is yet another innovative means of communication. It has become universally popular, particularly among young people, and has spawned its own language in response to the technology. In Britain over a billion text messages are sent each month on mobile phones. One of the reasons for their huge popularity is that they are cheap and accessible to the increasing millions of people worldwide who carry mobile phones. There have been reports in the media of people texting messages from the top of mountains and lives being saved as a result of a text from the middle of oceans and deserts. They have been acclaimed by many people and have become the 'normal means' of communication for large sections of the population.

In order to say as much as possible with a restricted number of characters, many text messages

- aim to shorten words to the bare minimum
- use acronyms for longer words or phrases
- use single letters or numbers, for example 'u' for you; '4' for for.

The use of acronyms has been around for a long time as a form of abbreviation. Their use in text messaging has become a language in itself. Reports by GCE and GCSE examiners on national tests showed that a text messaging style of spelling was used by some candidates in their examination scripts. This led to concerns being raised that spelling would suffer as a consequence. This cryptic laissez-faire approach to spelling is a great boost for dyslexic writers because many of them already spell phonetically. Spelling phonetically has become acceptable and is often the norm when texting.

As long ago as the 1780s Noah Webster was asserting that 'it is quite impossible to stop the progress of language – it is like the course of the Mississippi the motion of which is at times scarcely perceptible yet even it possesses a momentum quite irresistible. Words and expressions will be forced into use in spite of all the exertions of all the writers in the world' (cited in Gowers 1973). Shakespeare's legacy to the English Language survives intact but is Hamlet's soliloquy about to be rendered as '2B or nt 2B'?

> 2B or nt 2B – dats DQ, ? Tz noblr in D mnd 2 sufr D slingzNROs of RtrAjs 42n
> Or 2 tk Rms vs C O trbis N by opOzng Nd thm? 2 di 2 slEp – No mr: N by a slEp
> 2 sA we Nd D hRt-Ak Nd K n@rl shox Th@z flshz air2, tz a consum8n Devtly
> 2B wishd. 2 di 2 slEp, 2 slEp, pchRnz 2 drEm. Ah derz D rb

> To be, or nor to be – that is the question.
> Whether 'tis nobler in the mind to suffer
> The slings and arrows of outrageous fortune
> Or to take arms against a sea of troubles,

And by opposing end them. To die, to sleep –
No more: and by a sleep to say we end
The heartache and the thousand natural shocks
That flesh is heir to. 'Tis a consummation
Devoutly to be wished. To die, to sleep;
To sleep, perchance to dream. Ay, there's the rub.

Popular computer packages to empower learners and spellers

Keates (2000), speaking from her experience as a parent of a dyslexic son, as a teacher of ICT, and former chairperson of the British Dyslexia Association's (BDA) computer committee, sounded a note of caution when she said that 'clever marketing often delivered by professionals can be very persuasive and can make software a panacea' [for spellers' difficulties]. She reviewed many of the well-known programs for literacy and stated that 'I very rarely use spelling programs because in my opinion, it is an incorrect use of ICT merely to do skills and drills work'. On the other hand many teachers find that the spelling packages have an important role to play in teaching literacy, particularly to adults who may have previously failed using conventional methods.

There are three different types of packages, which include 'practice' packages for reinforcing and rehearsing skills. They often use the computer for revising and overlearning skills, particularly at the end of a lesson where playing a game has often been seen as a reward for hard work. A game is also a great motivator, particularly for those with a competitive streak, when they can keep a record of their scores and aim to beat their scores next time they play the game. It can be used as a carrot for the less than enthusiastic learner who will feel less challenged by the endlessly patient computer, which also allows them to work at a pace they feel comfortable with. In the classroom such packages have many uses. They can also be used by parents and for homework.

Computer packages for teaching and reinforcing spelling

Starspell 2.3 Fisher Marriott (www.fishermarriott.com)	• Games with spelling exercises • Word lists linked to the NLS • Uses 'look-say-cover-write-check' strategies • Good-quality speech when sentences are read aloud in context-related sentences • Suitable for 7–16+ years
Wordshark 3S (www.wordshark.co.uk)	• 37 different games • Word lists based on *Alpha to Omega*, NLS and KS3 • Used with SEN pupils and brings 'greater benefit to spelling' than reading • Suitable for 4–14 years

Teaching packages linked to dyslexia programmes

Units of Sounds Multimedia Version 3 (www.LDAlearning.com)	• Emphasis on the auditory channel for developing listening skills because 'spelling comes from sound' (Moss 2000) • The CD-ROMs have a strong visual element • It has a spelling programme including 40 dictation passages • Used by Dyslexia Institute-trained teachers

'General' support packages for SEN pupils

TextHELP! Read and Write www.texthelp.com	• Reads text aloud • Has a word prediction facility • Has a phonic spell-checker and support for homophones • Can pronounce and break words up into syllables
Clicker 4 / Crick Software www.cricksoft.com	• On-screen keyboard • Has a grid with letters, words, phrases and pictures which can be inserted in a document • Useful for those with language difficulties and poor motor skills

Some recommended CD-ROMs

Title/publisher	Subject	Age	Key Stages
Wordshark 3/White Space	literacy	5–14	1–3
Clicker 4/Crick	literacy	4–11	1–2
Textease 2000 V.5/Softease	ICT	6–14	1–3
Numbershark/White Space	numeracy	6–14	1–3
My World 3/Semerc	cross-curriculum	3–14	1–3
Starspell 2.2./Fisher-Marriott	literacy	5–13	1–3
Infant Video Toolkit/2Simple	ICT	4–7	1–2
Junior Viewpoint/Logotron	ICT	7–14	2–3
LessonMaker Junior Infant/Edutech	ICT	5–11	1–2
IEP Writer 2 with five Databases/Learn How	sch adm	4–90	1–4

The British Dyslexia Association also recommends for literacy: Gamz Player (www.gamzuk.com); the Catch Up project CD-Rom (www.dyslexic.com).

SUMMARY AND CONCLUSIONS

1   ICT is now an indispensable part of the fabric of everyday life. It has become as commonplace as the motorcar or the telephone became in the twentieth century. Industries and businesses would collapse without computers. Computer literacy is now ranked side-by-side with basic literacy and is now regarded as an essential skill for employees.

2   The information superhighway, electronic mail and texting are integral parts of the technological revolution that has taken place.

3   People will still read books, and handwritten communication will still be a feature of people's lives. But the computer will complement, augment and enhance all forms of written communication, not least because of its speed, efficiency and ability to store and retrieve documents and information.

4   The computer has changed for ever the prospects and lifestyle of those who previously would have been marginalised in society because they could not read, write and spell too well. It has been hailed as the great liberator because it can free users from a lifetime of low literacy. However, Hutchins (2003), a pioneering champions of the use of ICT for dyslexic people in the UK, still maintains that 'ICT does not actually give equal opportunities – users have to learn so much about how to use their computers to achieve the same as their peers do more easily'. This includes the ability to word-process more quickly than they can write by hand.

5   Assistive technology is a great leveller and has put the world of words at the fingertips of all who want to read and write, even when they lack the physical skills to do so. The Disabilities Discrimination Act 1995 (DDA) and the Special Educational Needs and Disabilities Act 2001 (SENDA) became legally binding from September 2002 in all the educational establishments. The onus is on the education provider not to treat individuals with disabilities 'less favourably' and to make 'reasonable adjustments' for them.

6   The computer has opened the door to academia and employment for many who would in the past not have been able to write a handwritten letter of application – or, if they could do so, would have had their application rejected because of poor spelling and writing. Poor spelling was for long regarded as a mark of ignorance or poor education and was often considered to be self-inflicted. Today judgements tend to be made about what people say and how they say it when they communicate. The technology takes care of the secretarial aspects of the writing. The content and ideas are still the writer's own.

7   Many schoolchildren's lives have been revolutionised by the use of technology. School work has changed and so too has the way children are taught. The use of ICT is part of the National Curriculum.

8   The spell-checker has at last made spelling the servant not the master of the writer. None the less, all writers need spelling knowledge and understanding if they are to use spoken and written language effectively and efficiently. Fine ingredients and state-of-the-art kitchens do not in themselves result in good cooking. The master chef knows, understands and uses experience and skills to produce well-cooked food; so too the good writer. 'Computers and computer software will not solve dyslexia' (Keates 2000). The computer, particularly the use of speech recognition software, is a powerful tool that can enhance skills, boost morale and enrich the lives of learners, and is a powerful partner when used by those who have been taught to manage dyslexia and spelling successfully.

Appendix

PHONICS QUIZ

1 What are the vowels?
2 What are the short vowels?
3 What are the long vowels?
4 What are the consonants?
5 What are digraphs, and where do they occur in words?
6 What are the two different types of digraphs, and can you give examples of each?
7 Can you give seven different consonant digraphs with an example of each?
8 What are trigraphs?
9 Can you define and give three examples of blends?
10 Can you give examples of three consonant blends which can be used at the beginnings and ends of words?
11 What is a consonant cluster?
12 What are assimilations, and can you give six examples?
13 Can you define and give six examples of diphthongs?
14 What are phonemes, and what is phonemic awareness?
15 How many phonemes are there in the English language?
16 What is a syllable?
17 What must a syllable have? Can you give an example of words with one, two, three, four and five syllables?
18 How are syllables divided?
19 Where does the syllable division line usually occur in words with two consonants in the middle of two-syllable words?
20 What exceptions are there to this generalisation? Can you explain why?
21 How many types of syllable are there?
22 What are closed syllables? Give examples of one, two and three closed-syllable words.
23 What are open syllables? Give examples of one, two and three open-syllable words.
24 Name and give examples of the six main categories of syllable.
25 What are diacritical marks?
26 What does soft 'c' say?
27 When does 'c' say /s/? Give three examples.
28 What does hard 'c' say? Give examples.
29 What does soft 'g' say?
30 When does 'g' say /j/? Give three examples.

31 When does 'g' say the hard sound /g/? Give examples.
32 Can you say how many different ways the /k/ sound is spelt at the end of a word? Give examples.
33 How are words derived from Latin or Greek spelt when they have a hard 'c' sound? Give three examples.
34 Can you identify a unique feature about the letter 'q' in the word 'Iraq'?
35 Can you name a letter which can be a semi-vowel? Give four examples and reasons for this.
36 Can you identify and give two examples for the different sounds 'y' makes?
37 Can you explain and give two examples for the spelling of words saying the /i/ sound but which end in a 'y'? Can you think of six exceptions to this rule?
38 Can you explain what is unique about the word 'spiv'?
39 What is a prefix? Explain its main function and give two examples.
40 How do you usually spell a word with a short vowel ending in 'f', 'l', 's' or 'z'? Can you think of one example as well as an exception, for each?
41 Can you think of three different ways 'w' affects the sounds of letters that follow it and give two examples?
42 How many different ways are there to spell the /j/ sound at the end of a word? Can you give two examples of each?
43 What effect has 'magic 'e'' on vowels and can you give an example for each of the vowels?
44 How many ways can the /shun/ sound be spelt and can you give an example of each?
45 What is the most frequently used letter in the English language?
46 How many functions does the letter 'e' perform? Give three examples of each of these.
47 What are morphemes? Give two examples of 'free' and 'bound' morphemes.
48 What are affixes? Give three examples of different usage.
49 What is a suffix? What is its main function? Give three examples.
50 How many major rules are there for adding suffixes to words?
51 What is a root word? Give three examples?
52 What do the letters i.t.a. stand for?
53 Who invented i.t.a.?
54 What are phonics?
55 What are phonetics?
56 What is meant by the phonic teaching method?
57 What is phonology?
58 What is phonological awareness?
59 What are graphemes?
60 What are synthetic phonics?
61 What are analytic phonics?
62 What are onsets? Give three examples.
63 What are rimes? Give three examples.
64 What approximate percentage of words in the dictionary have Latin roots?
65 Which two letters are never found in English words derived from Latin?
66 How many different ways can the /f/ sound be spelt? Give two examples of each.
67 How many different ways are there for spelling the /s/ sound? Give three examples of each.

68 How many different ways are there for spelling long /ē/ sound? Give two examples of each.

69 How many ways can verbs ending in 'ed' be pronounced? Give an example of each.

70 Can you name the seven most commonly used suffixes?

71 What are the four most frequently used consonants in the alphabet?

72 Can you give, with an example of each, the sixteen different ways to spell long /o/ sound?

73 Can you name the most commonly used rime stems?

74 How many words can be generated from the list of the 37 most commonly used rimes?

75 What are 'schwa' vowels? Explain why they are difficult to spell and give three examples.

76 What is the most common way to spell the short /ĭ/ sound? Give examples of seven other ways it is spelt.

77 How many ways can the long /ī/ sound be spelt? Can you give an example of each?

78 What are the five different ways to spell the /or/ sound and can you give an example of each?

79 Can you give seven major stumbling blocks for spellers?

80 How many words of two or three letters can be made by someone who can recognise and write 13 letters (including vowels)?

81 Can you name 10 words ending in /ō/ sound but which are spelt with 'oe'

82 Which 25 words are the most frequently mis-spelt by primary school children?

83 How many phonemes are there in the following words?

pen   dash   fox   catch

depth   shrub   train   speed

84 Are there differences in how words are divided into syllables in dictionaries?

85 How many phonemes are there in 'exit'? Say what they are.

86 How many phonemes are there in 'Christmas'? Say what they are.

87 What are the second and third most frequently used letters in English?

88 How many examples are there of words spelt with 'ei' in English?

89 Can you give eleven examples of words spelt with 'ei'?

90 Can you name three English words that have no corresponding rhyming words?

91 What is the 'NATO' alphabet?

92 Name three of the most universally understood words in the world?

93 What is the most commonly spoken word in over 700 languages?

94 What do the letters VAKT stand for?

95 What famous Irish born playwright left a bequest for a new alphabet which would match the 44 English sounds to letters to represent these?

96 What are linguistic reading books?

97 State two features the following words have in common.

does   one   said

98 Who wrote the first published book on dyslexia and what nationality was he?

99 Who is commonly regarded as the patriarch of the dyslexia movement?

100 By common consent the first working definition of specific developmental dyslexia was published by the World Federation of Neurologists in 1968 when under the chairmanship of a British neurologist. What was his name?

ANSWERS TO THE PHONICS QUIZ
(Alternative examples are acceptable.)

1 The vowels are 'a' 'e' 'i' 'o' 'u' and sometimes 'y', as in 'cry', 'baby' and 'type'.
2 Short vowels say their sounds:

ă   ăpple
ĕ   ĕlephant
ĭ   ĭnk
ŏ   ŏrange
ŭ   ŭmbrella

3 Long vowels say their names:

ā   ācorn
ē   ēmu
ī   īron
ō   ōpen
ū   ūnIform

4 The consonants are 'all the other letters in the alphabet – other than the vowels'.
5 Digraphs are two letters making one sound. They can occur at the beginning, middle or ends of words.
6 (a) Vowel digraphs are two vowels making one sound vowel.

/ā/   tr/āi/n
/ē/   w/ēe/d
/ī/   p/īe/
/ō/   g/ōa/l
/ū/   tr/ūe/

(b) Consonant digraphs are two consonants making one sound.

/s̄h/   /s̄h/op   da/s̄h/ing   wi/s̄h/

7 /ch/   /ch/ip
  /ck/   du/ck/
  /sh/   /sh/ip
  /wh/   /wh/ip
  /th/ voiced   /th/umb
  /th/ unvoiced /th/is
  /ph/   /ph/one
  /gh/   lau/gh/

8 Trigraphs are three letters making one sound:

/tch/   ma/tch/
/dge/   ju/dge/

9 Blends are letters found next to each other in a word. They sound separately but quickly and retain their distinct sounds which blend when pronounced: 'bl' blot; 'cr' crab; 'dr' drum.

10 'sk'   <u>sk</u>ip   ri<u>sk</u>
   'sp'   <u>sp</u>ot   cri<u>sp</u>
   'st'   <u>st</u>op   ru<u>st</u>

11 A consonant cluster is another term for a blend. It is used in NLS (1998) materials. These groups of letters can occur at the beginning, middle and ends of words. They stay together in syllables, which is an important guideline for pronunciation and for syllable division:

<u>sk</u>in;   ri<u>sk</u>/ing;   du/<u>sk</u>/y.

12 Assimilations are sounds made down one's nose. They are sometimes called nasal sounds. Only two letters make their sounds down one's nose. They are /m/ and /n/. These sounds are sometimes assimilated by the adjacent letter sounds. They occur at the end of words as well as in root words to which suffixes can be added:

/nch/   bu<u>nch</u>   cru<u>nch</u>/ed
/nd/   ba<u>nd</u>   la<u>nd</u>/ing
/ng/   ri<u>ng</u>   si<u>ng</u>/er
/nk/   i<u>nk</u>   li<u>nk</u>/ing
/nt/   re<u>nt</u>   ve<u>nt</u>/ed
/mp/   ju<u>mp</u>   cra<u>mp</u>/on

13 Diphthongs are two vowels found next to each other in a word which glide together when pronounced. They count as one vowel in a syllable. They include:

/aw/   dr/aw/
/ew/   gr/ew/
/oi/   b/oi/l
/ou/   gr/ou/p
/ow/   c/ow/
/oy/   t/oy/

14 Phonemes are the smallest units of sound in a language. In alphabetic languages these sounds are matched to the letters which represent them when reading and writing. Phonemic awareness is an explicit understanding and ability to discriminate between individual sounds and to recognise the differences between initial, medial and final phonemes in words. It is also an ability to identify, manipulate, segment and blend individual phonemes, including consonants and vowels in words when reading and spelling, as in /p/ /i/ /g/ and /r/ /u/ /g/.

15 Most authorities now agree that there are 44 sounds in the English language. The National Literacy Strategy (DfES 2001) stated that 'there are approximately 44 phonemes in English represented by 26 letters in about 140 letter combinations'.

16 A syllable is used to segment words into parts and is often described as a 'beat'.

17 A syllable must have one vowel sound, as in the following one, two, three, four and five syllabled words:

```
dish               (1)
pup/ pet           (2)
but/ ter/ cup      (3)
mag/ nif/ i/ cent  (4)
en/ thu/ si/ as/ tic  (5)
```

18 Syllables are divided with a syllable division line, as in 'Sep/tem/ber'.

19 The syllable division line usually occurs between the two consonants in 85 per cent of words, as in 'rab/bit'.

20 Words with digraphs or blends do not follow the above generalisation. These letters stay together and are never divided. The syllable division line therefore occurs at the end of the second consonant. Suffixes and prefixes are separate syllables, as in 'gosp/el' and 'patch/es'

21 There are two main types of syllable: monosyllables which have one syllable, and polysyllables which have two or more.

22 Closed syllables end in a consonant and have a short vowel sound, as in these one, two and three closed-syllable words:

```
pĕn    pĕn / cĭl   pĕn / cĭl / ĭng
 c      c / c       c / c / c
```

23 Open syllables end in a vowel and have a long vowel sound, as in the following one, two and three open-syllable words:

```
sō     pō / lō   rō / dē / ō
 o      o / o     o / o / o
```

24 The six main categories of syllable are:

```
closed                ten / nis
open                  ze / ro
vowel-consonant – e   cake
diphthong             boat
consonant l-e         ta / ble
r- combination        teach / er
```

25 Diacritical marks are code marks which are written above, below or beside a letter to indicate its pronunciation, as in a dictionary. Short vowels are coded with a breve (˘). Long vowels are coded with a macron (¯), as in trŭmpĕt and zērō.

26 Soft 'c' says /s/.

27 'c' says /s/ when the next letter is an 'e', 'i' or 'y'.

cent   city   cycle

28 Hard 'c' says /k/ when it is followed by 'a', 'o' or 'u'.

cat   cot   cup

29 Soft 'g' says /j/.
30 Soft 'g' says /j/ when the next letter is 'e', 'i' or 'y'.

gem   ginger   gypsy

31 Hard 'g' says /g/ when the next letter is 'a', 'o' or 'u'.

game   god   gun

32 These are the six different ways to spell the /k/ sound:

- words with a short vowel take 'ck'.

  black

- If there is a consonant before /k/ it takes 'k'.

  bank

- If there is a vowel digraph before the /k/ sound it takes 'k'.

  cloak

- If there is a long vowel and magic 'e' it takes 'k-e'.

  duke

- Some words of two or more syllables take 'c'.

  music

- Words borrowed from the French take 'que'.

  antique

33 Words borrowed from Greek or Latin are spelled with 'ch' as in:

ache   choir   echo   (Greek)
anchor   chemist   school   (Latin)

34 There is a well known and often quoted spelling rule which says that the letter ' q' is always followed by 'u', as in: 'quick', 'queen' and 'request'. However, words borrowed from other languages do not follow this rule, which accounts for the spelling of Iraq.

35 The letter 'y' is sometimes known as a semi-vowel because it can be used as a consonant or as a vowel:

fly   lady   tyre   yo-yo

36 The letter 'y' has three different sounds:

- When 'y' is a consonant it says /y/ yell, yellow
- When it is a vowel it sometimes says /i/

  type   gyro
  spy   try

- When it is a vowel it can also say /ē/

  army   copy

37 There is a spelling rule which says that English words do not usually end in 'i'. They
usually use the letter 'y' instead: 'cry' and 'sky'. The exceptions are usually borrowed
from other languages or they are abbreviations:

'ski' is borrowed from Norwegian
'ravioli' is borrowed from Italian
'bikini' is borrowed from name of an island in the Marshall Islands in the Pacific
'khaki' is borrowed from Urdu and Persian
'taxi' is an abbreviation of taxicab
'maxi' is an abbreviation of maximum

38 'Spiv' is the only English word that ends in 'v'. There is a spelling rule which says
there is always an 'e' after 'v' at the end of words such as 'five' and 'cove' because of
magic 'e'.

39 A prefix is a letter or a group of letters added to the beginning of a root word. It
usually changes the meaning of a word:

'un'   unwell   unfit
're'   recharge   retake

40 Words with a short vowel ending in 'f', 'l', 's' or 'z' double the final consonant:

stiff   bell   miss   jazz (*examples*)
if   pal   bus   quiz (*exceptions*)

41 The /o/ sound after 'w' is spelt with an 'a', as in 'wasp' and 'swan'. The /or/ sound
after 'w' is spelt with 'ar', as in 'war' and 'swarm'. The /er/ sound after 'w' is spelt
with 'or', as in 'word' and 'work'.

42 There are five different ways of spelling the /j/ sound at the end of a word, including
the following:

- words with a short vowel take 'dge'

  badge   hedge

- If there is a consonant before the /j/ sound it takes 'ge'

  barge   charge

- If there is a vowel digraph or diphthong it takes 'ge'

  gouge   stooge

- If there is a long vowel and magic 'e' it takes 'g-e'

  page   wage

- Some words take 'age' or 'ege'

  cottage   college

43 Magic 'e' makes a vowel long and says its name, but 'e' is silent:

hăt   hāte
mēt   mēte
rĭp   rīpe
nŏt   nōte
tŭb   tūbe

44 The /shun/ sound may be spelt in ten different ways including:

'cean'   ocean
'cheon'   luncheon
'cian'   politician
'cion'   suspicion
'sci'   conscience
'shion'   cushion
'sion'   television
'ssion'   possession
'tion'   station
'xion'   crucifixion

45 The letter 'e' is the most frequently used letter in the English language.
46 The letter 'e' has three main functions which are as follows:

- It changes short vowels into long vowels:

  răt rāte;   pĭp pīpe;   cŏd cōde

- It keeps 'c' and 'g' soft:

  centre ice   cycle
  genre   gin   gym

- It helps to distinguish plural from visually similar words

  pleas   please
  hows   house
  brows   browse

47 Morphemes are the smallest meaningful parts of a word. 'Free' morphemes are words in themselves such as 'box' and 'tap'. 'Bound' morphemes are attached to a word and include prefixes, suffixes, plurals and comparative adjectives:

<u>mis</u>	<u>mis</u>take	<u>mis</u>represent
'ed'	walk<u>ed</u>	fill<u>ed</u>
'es'	box<u>es</u>	glass<u>es</u>
'er'	quick<u>er</u>	slimm<u>er</u>

48 An affix is a letter or a group of letters that can be added to a root word. It can be used at the beginning and end of a word or both beginning and end.

    <u>d</u>eport   port<u>er</u>   <u>r</u>eport<u>ing</u>

49 A suffix is a letter or a group of letters added to the end of a root word. It usually changes the use of the word:

'ing'	sing<u>ing</u>	runn<u>ing</u>
'est'	fast<u>est</u>	hott<u>est</u>
'ed'	look<u>ed</u>	talk<u>ed</u>

50 There are seven major rules.

51 A root is the main part or stem of a word. It can stand alone. It can also take a prefix, suffix as well as a prefix and a suffix:

    'form'   de<u>form</u>   <u>form</u>ing   re<u>form</u>er

52 i.t.a. is an acronym for the Initial Teaching Alphabet which was an alphabet of 44 lower-case letters each of which had one sound. It was devised to simplify the teaching of reading to beginners.

53 i.t.a. was invented by Sir James Pitman in 1959. It was based on his grandfather Sir Isaac Pitman's 'phonicprint' called Fonotypy and on the Nue Spelling of the Simplified Spelling Society.

54 Phonics involves teaching reading and spelling by sounding out the individual letter sounds, then blending the sounds to pronounce a word when reading and segmenting the letter sounds when spelling, as in /m/ /a/ /t/.

55 Phonetics is the study of human speech. It describes the speech sounds made by speakers when using both receptive and expressive language. It includes the study of how speech is articulated.

56 The phonic method teaches reading and spelling by sounding out the individual phonemes in a word then blending and synthesising these to pronounce a word when reading and segmenting the phonemes when spelling.

57 Phonology is the study of the sound system and of speech including the sound/symbol correspondences in relation to meaning. It also includes the rules governing the combination of sounds in a given language.

58 Phonological awareness is an ability to recognise, analyse and manipulate sound segments in words including segmenting syllables and affixes. It includes an ability to use and understand alliteration and rhyme.

59 Graphemes are the letters of the alphabet used to represent the phonemes (speech sounds). A grapheme can be a single letter 'o' in cot or a group of letters 'ough' 'though'.

60 Synthetic phonics is used to sound out the individual phonemes in a word and then blend these when reading and segment them when spelling, as in /p/ /i/ /g/ and /c/ /r/ /a/ /sh/.

61 Analytic phonics uses whole words usually with a consistent sound/symbol match and breaks words into chunks called onsets and rimes to read and spell, as in /m/ /at/ and /br/ /ick/

62 Onsets are the initial consonant/consonants in a word, as in <u>h</u> am <u>ph</u> one <u>str</u> ing

63 Rimes are the vowels and final consonant/consonants in a word.

    cr <u>ab</u>   pr <u>ay</u>   l <u>ight</u>

64 Approximately 50–60 per cent of words (depending on the word count) in the dictionary are derived from Latin.

65 The two letters never found in English words derived from Latin are 'k' and 'w'.

66 There are four different ways of spelling the /f/ sound. They are:

'f'	fish	deaf
'ff'	cliff	staff
'ph'	phone	siphon
'gh'	cough	laugh

67 There are eight different ways of spelling the /s/ sound:

'c'	<u>c</u>edar	<u>c</u>ider	<u>c</u>ycle
's'	<u>s</u>and	<u>s</u>un	ga<u>s</u>
'sc'	<u>sc</u>are	<u>sc</u>ent	<u>sc</u>ript
'se'	hor<u>se</u>	mou<u>se</u>	ca<u>se</u>
'ss'	bo<u>ss</u>	mi<u>ss</u>	go<u>ss</u>ip
'st'	apo<u>st</u>le	ca<u>st</u>le	thi<u>st</u>le
'ps'	<u>ps</u>alm	<u>ps</u>yche	<u>ps</u>ychologist
'sw'	<u>sw</u>an	<u>sw</u>ord	<u>sw</u>ordfish

68 There are thirteen different ways to spell long /ē/ sound including the following:

'ae'	an$\overline{ae}$mia	encyclop$\overline{ae}$dia
'ay'	qu$\overline{ay}$	
'e'	$\overline{e}$go	z$\overline{e}$ro
'ea'	$\overline{ea}$r	t$\overline{ea}$m

'ee'	ēērie	wēēk
'e-e'	ēvē	athlētē
'ey'	kēy	trollēy
'ei'	wēird	recēipt
'ie'	fīēld	shīēld
'eo'	pēōple	thēōry
'oe'	ōēstrogen	fōētus
'i'	maxī	minī
'it'	esprīt	

69 /ed/ at the end of a verb can be pronounced in three ways /t/ /d/ /id/:

walked   jammed   rented

70 The most commonly used suffixes are:

'ed'   'ing'   'y'   'ate'   'er'   'ion'   'ly'

71 The most frequently used consonants are 'n', 't', 'd' and 's'.

72 Long /o/ sound can be spelt as follows:

'o-e'	mōlē
'o'	ōld
'ow'	bōwl
'oa'	cōal
'oe'	tōē
'ol'	fōlk
'ou'	sōul
'ow'	crōw
'ew'	stēw
'ough'	dough
'au'	māūve
'oo'	brōōch
'eo'	yēōman
'om'	cōmb
'eau'	chatēāū
'oh'	ōh

73 The most commonly used rime stems in single syllable words are as follows:

ack	all	aim	ale	ame	an
ank	ap	ash	ate	aw	ay
eat	ell	est	ick	ide	ight
ain	ake	at	ice		
ill	in	ine	ink	ip	ir
ock	oke	op	ore	or	uck
ug	ump	unk			

74 Approximately 500 words can be derived from these 37 rimes.

75 The 'schwa' vowels are vowel sounds that occur in unstressed (unaccented) syllables. Because they cannot be heard separately, they are sometimes called murmur vowels which makes them difficult to spell: 'col/our', 'fam/ous' and 'so/fa'.

76 The most common way to spell the short vowel /ĭ/ sound is with an 'i' as in 'b/ĭg' and 'd/ĭg'. It occurs in 97 per cent of words. According to Barry (1994). It can also be spelt as follows:

'y'	mȳth
'e'	prētty
'u'	lettūce
'ui'	būild
'o'	wōmen
'ie'	sīeve
'ei'	forfēit

77 Long /ī/ can be spelt in the following fourteen ways:

'ai'	āisle	'igh'	nīght
'ay'	āȳe	'oi'	chōir
'I'	chīld	'y'	skȳ
'ei'	nēither	'ye'	rȳe
'ey'	ēȳe	'i-e-'	pīnē
'ic'	īce	'ty'	tȳpe
'ie'	pīe	uy	būȳ

78 The /or/ sound can be spelt in the following five ways:

'or'	nōrth
'ore'	stōrē
'our'	mōurn
'oor'	dōor
'ar'	wārd

79 The major stumbling blocks for poor spellers include the following:

- 'schwa' vowels
- silent letters
- phonemes that can be spelt in different ways
- knowing when to double letters
- 'odd-bods' that do not follow spelling rules or conventions
- words derived or borrowed from other languages
- homophones (pronounced the same but having different meanings and spellings)

80 Someone who can recognise and write 13 letters can generate 39 words.

81 The words ending in /ō/ but spelt 'oe' are:

doe floe foe hoe oboe mistletoe roe sloe toe woe

82 The 25 most commonly misspelt words among primary school children are:

their, too, there, they, then, until, our, asked, off, through, you're, clothes, looked, people, pretty, running, believe, thought, and, beautiful, it's.

83 pen   p/ /e/ n/   (3)
     dash   /d/ /a/ /sh/   (3)
     fox   /f/ /o/ /k/ /s/   (4)
     catch   /c/ /a/ /tch/   (3)
     depth   /d/ /e/ /p/ th/   (4)
     shrub   /sh/ /r/ /u/ /b/   (4)
     train   /t/ /r/ /ai/ /n/   (4)
     speed   /s/ /p/ /ee/ d/   (4)

84 British dictionaries often denote syllable division according to how words are pronounced. American dictionaries often divide words according to the syllables. Linguists and lexicographers follow different conventions.

85 There are five phonemes in 'exit': /e/ /k/ /s/ /i/ /t/.

86 There are seven phonemes in 'Christmas': /k/ /r/ /i/ /s/ /m/ /a/ /s. (The letter 't' is silent.)

87 The second most frequently used letter in English is 't' and 'a' is the third.

88 There are eleven words spelt with 'ei' in English.

89 Examples of words spelt with 'ei' are: ceiling, perceive, receipt, receive, received, receiving, receivable, receivability, receivableness, receiver, receivership

90 There are no rhyming words for the words 'orange', 'purple', 'month'.

91 The NATO alphabet is a set of names used by the military and police forces in radio communication to identify individual alphabet letters such as 'C' for Charlie; 'T' for tango.

92 Pizza, sex, taxi.

93 'Papa'.

94 VAKT stands for visual, auditory, kinaesthetic and tactile. They describe the multi-sensory teaching of literacy.

95 Bernard Shaw.

96 Linguistic reading books use only words that have a consistent sound/symbol (phoneme/grapheme) match.

97 They are high frequency words and they have irregular spellings.

98 James Hinshelwood, a Scot.

99 Doctor Samuel Orton.

100 Doctor Macdonald Critchley.

Glossary and Key Terminology

ABC reading and spelling method involves spelling the word aloud while saying the names of the letters of the alphabet. This was used to teach and learn reading and spelling.

Accent is the emphasis or stress put on a particular syllable, word, phrase or sentence when it is spoken, sometimes used in printed text to indicate pronunciation: 'butterfly', 'Decem'ber', 'spi'der'. It also applies to marks on letters such as acute or grave accents.

Acquired dyslexia occurs as a result of damage to the brain which can be caused by a cerebrovascular accident such as a stroke, head injury or by a brain tumour. There are four types with varying symptoms and specific features: deep dyslexia, phonological dyslexia, surface dyslexia and word-form-Deterine syndrome dyslexia (Ott 1997).

Additional Literacy Support (ALS) was a government-sponsored initiative which was part of the National Literacy Strategy. Its purpose was to give additional support to pupils at Key Stage 2 who had not attained certain targets and who had fallen behind in literacy. It was to be delivered in small groups using a set of structured materials which included scripted lessons. Teachers and teaching assistants had a key role in delivering ALS.

Affix is a letter or a group of letters added to the beginning or the end of a root word to form another word. It is called a prefix at the beginning of a word and a suffix at the end of a word.

Alliteration is used when two or more words, phrases or sentences begin with the same initial sound such as 'She sells seashells by the seashore'.

Alphabet is derived from the Greek word *alphabetos* which combines *alpha* and *beta*, the first two letters in the Greek alphabet. It is a set of letters, characters or symbols which are used to denote the sounds in language when it is written. The alphabetic principle was invented in West Asia and the first alphabet was the North Semitic alphabet from which all later alphabets evolved.

Alveolar sounds are made by putting the tip of the tongue in the ridge behind the upper front teeth, as when saying /t/ or /d/ sounds.

Amalgamation theory (Ehri 1986) is a hypothesis that spelling and reading are 'like circuits on a switchboard' (Moats 1995). Reading and spelling are interconnected and complementary and depend on a knowledge of sounds, grammar, word origins, spelling patterns and letter order (Ehri 1997).

Analogy is used to compare something already known to something new such as the similarity between a pair or a group of words when reading or an inference that two or more words with similar spelling will be similar in pronunciation. It can be used to decode words not already in the reader's sight vocabulary. If a similar word to the target word is known it can be used as a model for spelling words of similar word patterns such as 'found', 'round', 'sound' by changing the initial consonant or consonants to generate a word family. Bowey and Hansen (1994) found that analogising was more common in older pupils than in beginners because it requires remembering related spelling patterns in sufficient detail to make the analogy. Stanback (1992) argued that 'dyslexics may not spontaneously make analogies unless their attention is directed to words with common rimes and they are provided with oral reading and especially spelling practice in learning rimes'.

Analytical errors are made when an individual attempts to match a word from visual memory to a particular word pattern such as spelling 'nite' for 'night' 'because it rhymes with bite'.

Analytic phonics describes a method of using whole words with a consistent sound–symbol match then breaking these words into segments or 'chunks' and focusing on the parts as an aid to reading and spelling. The words can be broken down into the 'onset', which is the initial consonant or consonant, and the 'rime' which includes the vowel and the final consonant or consonants (Ott 1997). This is sometimes described colloquially as the 'word family' approach. The NLS puts great emphasis on rhyme, rhythm and alliteration activities in initial literacy. This emphasis on oral activities and language games reflects the evidence from international studies which showed that 4-year-olds can understand the concept of syllables as an oral activity. Five-year-olds can understand onset and rime as an oral activity. Many individuals have assumed that these oral skills can be applied to these same activities when beginning to read and write. The evidence from international research showed that the contrary is true. Torgerson et al. (2006)

found that it was the root cause of the fierce arguments which have raged about whether beginner readers should be taught analytic or synthetic phonics first.

Antonyms are words which mean the opposite of each other: 'entrance–exit'; 'big–small'.

Assimilations are sounds made down one's nose. The sound made by one letter influences the articulation of the other letter. There are only two letters that make such sounds, 'm' and 'n'. These are sometimes called nasal sounds when they are joined to other consonants such as:

| /ng/ ring | /nk/ ink | /nd/ sand |
| /nt/ tent | /nch/ bunch | /ngth/ length |

'At risk' is used to describe children who are predisposed to learning difficulties because of emotional, behavioural, psychological, physical, biological or genetic factors.

Auditory perception is an ability to understand and make sense of sounds which are heard. It includes an ability to recognise as well as to differentiate between phonemes, blends, syllables and words as well as environmental or mechanical sounds. Difficulties are not attributable to hearing loss or to soft or loud sounds.

Auditory skills relate to listening skills. Those with good auditory skills learn best by using sounds and syllables when spelling and by listening to conversations, discussions, tape recordings and lectures.

Automaticity is a term applied to skills such as reading and writing and includes motor skills which when learned become internalised and effortless and can be used immediately when required. Individuals with dyspraxia have problems with developing automaticity with gross and fine motor skills, including the muscles involving the lips, tongue, mouth and soft palate to produce speech sounds and words as well as skills perfomed by the fingers, hands and toes and skills performed by the arms, legs and feet. Researchers such as Nicolson and Fawcett (1990) showed that individuals with dyslexia have problems developing automaticity with skills. This is linked to the cerebellum in the brain.

Behavioural psychology is a theory for learning behaviour which is dependent on heredity, on environment and on conditioning. It was based initially on the work of Burrhus Frederic Skinner. From his hypothesis a theory was developed that 'language learning was the result of the process of habit formation' (McArthur 1992). This later resulted in a core curriculum of what pupils needed to know and learn resulting in a National Curriculum (1988, 1995) in countries such as Britain.

Blends are two consonants found next to each other. They sound separately but quickly to make one sound in a syllable or a word. They are sometimes called consonant clusters and can occur at the beginning, middle or ends of words:

s<u>k</u>	<u>sk</u>ip	ba<u>sk</u>et	ca<u>sk</u>
s<u>t</u>	<u>st</u>op	cru<u>st</u>y	ru<u>st</u>
s<u>p</u>	<u>sp</u>it	li<u>sp</u>ed	wa<u>sp</u>

Borrowed words The word 'borgian' is an Old English word meaning to borrow or to lend. McArthur (1992) argues that 'borrowing is a major aspect of language change, but the term itself is a misnomer: it presumes repayment'. There are 'loan words' from over 350 languages used in English. The most common sources for English are Latin, Greek, French and Anglo-Saxon. 'About fifty per cent of our words came from Latin, the language of the Romans; ten to twelve per cent from Anglo-Saxon, the native language of ancient England' according to Steere et al. (1971).

Breve is derived from the Latin word 'brevis' meaning 'short'. It is the code mark placed over a short or unstressed vowel to indicate that it says its sound: 'pŭp', 'măgnĕt', 'ĭnhăbĭt'.

Cerebellar deficit theory is a hypothesis about the function of the cerebellum, which is the main part of the hind brain and lies underneath the cerebrum. It is responsible for motor skills including precise timing and co-ordination of the muscles and postural stability including balance and muscle tone. Fawcett and Nicolson (2001) conducted a number of studies on deficits related to the cerebellum and found that the dyslexic groups' skills were 'less well automaticised, not only for literacy but also for other tasks' and they showed symptoms of 'cerebellar abnormality' and 'cerebellar dysfunction' including a 'lack of co-ordination and impaired timing of rapid pre-planned, automatic movements' which they ascribed to an 'automatisation deficit hypothesis'.

Cerebral dominance is a theory used to describe the superiority of one side of the brain which controls major functions. The brain is divided into two hemispheres, left and right. Each side performs different functions, and up to seventeen regions are involved when a dyslexic subject reads. The left hemisphere controls the right side of the body and the language centres for most individuals and is regarded as the dominant side for most people. The right hemisphere controls the left side of the body and the centres controlling rhythm, artistic, spatial and creative skills.

'Chinese' spelling style describes spellers who 'rely heavily on word-specific associations, between each word and its associated pronunciation' (Baron and Strawson 1976). In other words they spell by analogy and by using word patterns.

Cloze is derived from the word 'closure'. It is used to describe a procedure whereby a missing word in a sentence or missing letters in a word are chosen from a supplied list of optional words to complete the sentence or word. It is sometimes used to test reading comprehension.

Clymer's list of phonic generalisations (1963) consisted of 121 generalisations. They were devised from a list of 2,600 words which were later refined to 45 spelling conventions to help a 'child unlock the pronunciation of unknown words'.

'Code emphasis' reading method teaches the relationship between letters and sounds. It uses the alphabetic code to teach explicit decoding skills including phonics. Pupils decodes the letters they see. They match these to the sounds when they sound out an unknown word when reading. They encode the sounds they hear when they match these to the letters when spelling.

Cognition describes mental processes such as perception, memory, learning and thinking which enable people to process knowledge and information.

Cognitive abilities are mental skills which enable a person to know, be aware, to think, to reason, to criticise and to be creative. They are often measured using IQ tests.

Cognitive style refers to the way a person habitually thinks, organises, retains, presents and processes knowledge and information.

Co-morbid is the simultaneous existence of two or more unrelated conditions or disorders. 'Co-existence' or 'co-occurring' are considered more precise terms, as in the case of dyslexia and dyspraxia.

Comparative forms of adjectives are used when describing and comparing two or more nouns. There are three degrees: positive, comparative and superlative. Regular forms: big – bigger – biggest. Longer adjectives of two or more syllables use 'more' or 'most': beautiful – more beautiful – most beautiful. Irregular forms: bad–worse–worst.

'Compensated' dyslexics are those whose problems have been identified and who have received learning support. They may have overcome earlier reading and writing difficulties but retain other characteristics including difficulties with short-term and working memory, sequencing and processing at speed.

Consonants are the letters in the alphabet other than the vowels. They are sounds made by using the different organs of speech such as the lips, nose, teeth and tongue.

Consonant digraphs are two consonants which make one sound. 'Digraph' is derived from the Greek word *di* meaning 'twice' and *graphe* meaning 'mark' and it can occur at the beginning, middle or end of words: /ch/ /ck/ /gh/ /ph/ /sh/ /th/ /wh/ – shop, crashing, fish.

Contractions are short forms of words when letters or groups of letters are omitted from words. An apostrophe is used to denote the omitted letters: do not–don't; cannot–can't; will not–won't.

Core spelling rules are the basic rules such as that every word must have a vowel or vowel sound.

Criterion-reference tests measure a pupil's performance or standard of attainment in specific skills or tasks such as a test using a phonics checklist or a test of times tables. The National Curriculum SATs are criterion-referenced to measure skills and knowledge.

Decoding is an ability to look at the visual representation of the letters and to pronounce and read a word by matching the symbols to their sounds.

Derivation is the source or origin of a word and is a 'process by which the forms and meanings of words change over centuries' (McArthur 1992). Some more complex words are formed from less complex words: pure, purify, purification, purity. Other words have affixes added to them such as 'tele' in 'telescope', 'telescopic', derived from the Greek words *tele* meaning 'far', *skopos* meaning 'seeing' and *ikos* meaning 'characteristic'.

Developmental psychology is based on Piaget's theory that children develop intellectually at different stages and at different speeds. The child should therefore be guided through a process of discovery at each of the stages of development. This enables the individual to develop and proceed to the next stage of development.

Developmental stages in the theory of learning to spell evolved from the stages in cognitive development. Read (1971) conducted a pioneering study of how children develop spelling skills. Henderson (1985), Moats (1995) and Ehri (1997) described the characteristics and main features of the child's spelling at each of what they called 'phases', 'stages' or 'levels' in the development of spelling skills.

Diacritical marks are derived from the Greek word *diakritikos* meaning 'able to distinguish'. They are code marks written above, below or beside a letter to indicate pronunciation. They are used in dictionaries to denote pronunciation including stress, word-division and syllabification. Short vowels are coded with a breve (˘): căt, cŏd, cŭp. Long vowels are coded with a macron (¯): hē, gr ā̄ n, w ē̄ d. Slash marks can be used to denote letter sounds: /c/, /a/, /t/. Quotation marks can be used to denote letter names: 'c', 'a', 't'

Dictionary is a book which contains a list of words, usually in alphabetic order. It gives meanings. Some give guidance on pronunciation, spelling, word class, etymology, usage, punctuation and grammatical forms.

Differentiation is a term used in the *Special Educational Needs Code of Practice* DfES (2001a) when the statutory requirements of the National Curriculum are considered. It may mean reducing the content of the curriculum, such as giving a different spelling list of words to learn, or giving additional time to carry out assignments such as in exams. It may allow the use of ICT to access the course materials. It may provide learning support by a learning support assistant or teaching assistant either in the classroom or in a one-to-one situation. 'Differentiation of learning activities within the primary curriculum framework will help schools to meet the learning needs of all children' is the rationale.

Digraphs are two consonants or two vowels making one sound: s<u>h</u>ip, da<u>sh</u>, trā̄n, wē̄d.

Diphthong is derived from the Greek word *diphthonggos* meaning 'double sound'. It occurs when two vowels are side by side and glide together when pronounced in rapid succession, as in bōil, mōon, hōuse. 'w' and 'y' are regarded as vowels when used in words such as: stew̄, roȳal.

Direct instruction teaches a specific skill, for example cursive handwriting, using a handwriting programme during a specific handwriting lesson using carefully sequenced and structured materials. It sets goals and provides adequate time to attain these. It monitors and provides feedback until the skill is mastered.

Discrepancy criteria scores indicate the difference between the pupil's current attainment scores and his or her potential as predicted by IQ test scores. Tests such as the Wechsler Objective Reading Dimensions (WORD) (Wechsler 1993), which is often used in conjunction with the Wechsler Intelligence Scale for Children 111 UK (WISC 111uk) test battery (Wechsler 1992), has a table for such scores. The WORD test includes a test of basic reading, spelling and reading comprehension. This test also includes a predictive score which is used to ascertain how well literacy scores match ability as calculated from the overall IQ score on the test. Critics such as Stanovich and Siegel (1994) and Siegel and Himel (1998) argue that using the discrepancy criteria may result in some achieving children not being identified as dyslexic because of the test design which affects those with short-term memory, language difficulties and cultural differences and may result in depressed scores.

Those who have experience of working with individuals with dyslexia will testify how significant knowing the ability (IQ) and the attainment levels of the individual are for both diagnosis and remediation. Discrepancies between scores on reading and spelling scores and IQ play a significant part and are often useful when predicting or establishing whether someone has a specific learning difficulty. They also influence the type of provision made for the pupil, such as whether or not he or she is statemented. Thomson (2001) maintained that 'the relationship between attainment and intelligence' is statistically and conceptually valid and that 'the discrepancy between predicted and observed' attainments in reading and spelling must be linked to IQ.

Dolch's sight words (Dolch and Buckingham 1936) were lists of 'high-frequency' words compiled to teach children to read and included words with irregular spellings.

Double-masked (blind) randomised placebo-controlled trials (RCT) are used to establish which treatment or intervention is the most effective. Subjects are divided into two groups, a treatment group and a control group. Each group is for example allocated dyslexic pupils, chosen at random. The intervention being studied is given to the treatment group and not to the control group. The duration and quality of help are matched, for example the controls are taught using a spelling package on the computer while the treatment group is taught using Fernald's spelling strategy to evaluate their effectiveness for teaching spelling. The data are then analysed to establish which intervention was most effective.

Dyscalculia 'is a condition that affects their ability to acquire arithmetical skills. Dyscalculic learners may have difficulty understanding simple number concepts, lack an intuitive grasp of numbers and have problems learning number facts and procedures. Even if they produce a correct answer or use a correct method, they may do so mechanically and without confidence' (DfES 2001b).

Dyslexia is derived from the Greek words *dys* meaning 'difficult' or 'bad' and *lexis* meaning 'language'. It indicates a difficulty with receptive and expressive language in both its written and spoken forms. Dyslexia is a constitutional difficulty which is often hereditary. Individuals with dyslexia may have difficulties with reading, writing, spelling and oral language. It also involves difficulties with memory, sequencing, organisation, processing speed and motor skills.

Dysplasias are a form of scarring found on brain tissue during invasive procedures during brain surgery or post-mortem examinations.

Dyspraxia is derived from the Greek words *dys* meaning 'difficult' or 'bad' and *praxis* meaning 'practice' or 'action'. It is used to describe people who have a difficulty planning and carrying out non-habitual motor skills (Ayres 1972). They have 'an impairment in the ability to perform familiar or unfamiliar motor skills' with automaticity. It is now sometimes described as development co-ordination disorder (DCD). Kaplan et al. (1998) indicated that 50 per cent of dyslexic people also have features of dyspraxia.

Ectopias are abnormal growths on the brain which are sometimes described as brain warts.

Electroencephalography (EEG) uses scalp electrodes to detect electrical activity generated by neurons in the brain. These changes can be recorded graphically and the brain waves can be reviewed on a printout so that the response to, for instance, speech sounds can be analysed.

Encoding is an ability to match the sounds of a spoken word to the letters that represent them when writing.

Etymology tells the history of words. It studies the origins and development of words. It gives explanations for the spelling and pronunciation of words as well as for how they have changed throughout history.

Euphony is derived from the Greek word *euphonia* meaning 'well sounding'. It refers to modifications of word forms to make them flow off the tongue more easily and easier to pronounce, particularly in running speech: 'an egg' instead of 'a egg'; 'impossible' instead of 'inpossible'.

Explicit teaching implies that specific skills are taught and that each step in acquiring a skill is taught specifically and in a structured sequence. It also involves modelling by the teacher as well as practice and support while the skill is being acquired.

Fernald's spelling method involves the word being written in cursive writing by the teacher, who pronounces it slowly. The pupil repeats the word while looking at it and then highlights tricky letters. Then he or she traces over the word with a finger. Then he or she turns over the paper and writes the word from memory using cursive writing. Then he or she turns back the paper and checks what he or she has written against the original.

Free writing is sometimes also referred to as expressive writing and refers to children's spontaneous writing about a topic which they are 'free' to write, in any way they choose, including ideas and choice of vocabulary. It is often used for diagnostic purposes, for example when testing writing speed to establish the number of words written per minute (wpm) and when making a miscue analysis of spelling errors.

Grapheme is derived from the Greek word *graphe* meaning 'writing'. It is a letter or a group of letters used to represent a single phoneme. There are 130 in English.

Headword is the word that appears at the top of the page in a dictionary. The first word on the page appears at the top left side and the last word on the page appears at the top right side.

Hieroglyphics (derived from the Greek words *hieros* meaning 'sacred' and *glyphein* meaning 'to carve') were symbols used in ancient Egypt to denote words. They were frequently used in temples.

High-frequency words are those most commonly used in writing and reading and are derived from a variety of sources. *The NLS: Framework for Teaching* (DfEE 1998) produced two lists of high-frequency words comprising 45 words and 150 words to be learned because 'these words usually play an important part in holding together the general coherence of texts and early familiarity with them will help pupils get pace and accuracy into their reading at an early stage'.

Holoalphabetic is a pangram sentence which includes all the letters of the alphabet: 'The quick brown fox jumped over the lazy dog.'

Homographs are words that are spelt the same but have a different sound and a different meaning, such as *lead* (to show or guide) – *lead* (metal): 'Susan will lead you to your car'; 'Luke collects lead soldiers'.

Homophones are words that sound the same but have a different spelling and a different meaning, such as *to* – *two* – *too*: 'I go to school'; 'We have two cars'; 'Tim was too hot'.

Homonyms are words that are spelt the same and have the same sound but have different meanings such as *pole* (north/south – ends of the earth or a native of Poland) – *pole* (piece of wood/metal): 'We watched a programme about a trip to the North Pole'; 'The horse jumped over the wooden pole'.

Hornbooks first appeared in about 1450 (Diack 1965). They were made from a sheet of paper in a wooden frame that was protected by a see-through sheet of horn. They were often mounted on a handle or paddle which could be used to hold them aloft such as when used in a classroom.

They usually included the alphabet, numbers and some prayers.

Horn's spelling method is known as the 'look-say-cover-write-check' method. Pupils look at the words and note the letter. They then say the word aloud and write the word while saying the letter names. Then they cover the letters and write the word from memory. Finally they check what they have written.

Ideograms or ideographs are signs or symbols used to convey an abstract concept, such as a wavy line denoting electric current.

Individual Education Plan (IEP) is a document drawn up by those who teach a pupil with special educational needs, as defined by the *SEN Code of Practice* (DfES 2001a). It should include strategies and short-term targets for individual pupils which are 'different from or additional to those' in place for their peers. The targets should be specific, measurable, achievable, relevant and time-related (SMART) targets (Lloyd and Berthelot 1992). '[It] should provide clear guidance and evidence of provision for the individual's special needs. [It should be] an easily accessible means of monitoring progress across the curriculum for all involved in teaching the pupil.'

Inflected forms are words which change in form to denote tense, number, gender or case: 'comes'–'coming'–'came'; 'box–boxes'; 'actor–actress'.

Information and communications technology (ICT) describes the use and study of various technologies to communicate, store, process and transmit information. It is a statutory requirement of the National Curriculum and a compulsory element of Initial Teacher Training. Pupils are required to use a range of equipment including computers and software in different areas of the curriculum.

Intelligence Quotient (IQ) is the result of the subscores on a standardised intelligence test which are expressed as a ratio of mental age to chronological age, multiplied by 100 to give a figure for intelligence as measured on the test. There are two types of IQ tests: 'open' tests which may be administered by teachers, and 'closed' tests which may be administered only by appropriately qualified psychologists.

Interactive whiteboards are large touch-screen monitors connected to a computer to allow users to interact with the content. They can be used with projectors.

International Phonetic Alphabet (IPA) is a 'conventionalised system of letters and symbols used to represent or record all the speech sounds of every language' (McArthur 1992). It has been used by linguists as an aid to pronunciation. The symbols are based on the Roman alphabet and it also reverses or inverts Roman or Greek letters.

There are symbols for 58 consonants, 27 vowels, 15 other consonant sounds and dozens of diacritical marks to indicate the pronunciation of speech sounds.

Invented spellings are so called because spellers make up their own spellings for words they do not know or remember how to spell in the conventional way. Examples of this are often found in the work of children who attempt to write before they have had formal literacy teaching. They are characterised by attempts to make correspondences between the sounds perceived by children in words they hear such as 'chb' for tube.

Keyword is a word that sums up the contents of a passage. In the context of this book it applies also to a word that is consistently used to help recall a letter–name–sound association. The keyword 'apple' could be used to practise saying 'a–apple', while looking at a picture of an apple and then saying the sound /ă/.

Key stage is a term used in the National Curriculum (QCA 1999) to describe different age groups.

Foundation	Reception (R)	(4–5 years)
Key Stage 1	year 1	
	year 2	(5–7 years)
Key Stage 2	year 3	
	year 4	
	year 5	
	year 6	(8–11 years)
Key Stage 3	year 7	
	year 8	
	year 9	(12–14 years)
Key Stage 4	year 10	
	year 11	(15–16 years)

Attainment targets known as 'levels' set out the 'knowledge, skills and understanding that pupils of different abilities and maturities are expected to have by the end of each key stage'.

Expected range of levels for the majority of pupils	Expected [average] attainment levels for the majority of pupils at the end of the key stage	
Key Stage 1	Level 1–3	Age 7	2
Key Stage 2	Level 2–5	Age 11	4
Key Stage 3	Level 3–7	Age 14	5/6

Source: QCA (1999)

Kinaesthetic skills relate to using physical skills involving motor memory and touch. Motor skills apply to gross-motor skills involving the arms, neck, trunk and legs. Fine motor skills apply to the fingers, hands and speech muscles. Kinaesthetic learners learn by a sensation of movement either by using the muscle memory in their fingers, hands and arms when carrying out an activity such as skywriting, tracing, copying or word-processing spellings or by doing a project, a science experiment, making a model, writing notes or using computer packages or CD-ROMs.

Labial sounds are made by the lips such as when saying /b/, /p/ and /f/, /v/.

Language is a system of communication involving speech and writing allowing one user to transmit meaning to another. Spoken language is made by using the mouth, nose, throat and lungs. There are two forms. Receptive language involves the understanding of spoken language when listening and reading. Expressive language involves the use of spoken language to convey meaning and understanding when speaking and writing.

Learning literally means understanding and knowing how to do something. To a student of psychology it means more than this: it means focusing on the processes by which something is committed to memory so that the learner becomes proficient.

Learning skill is an ability or expertise acquired naturally or developed over time as a result of training and practice.

Learning strategy is a set of processes used to learn a task or skill. It can be used and developed to improve or optimise learning.

Learning style refers to the way individuals process, remember and recall information and facts. There are four main pathways to learning: oral, visual, auditory and kinaesthetic. There are many means of assessing someone to establish their preferred learning style. Some measures are controversial and lack scientific evidence of validity. Using the preferred learning style is now regarded as the most effective and efficient way of learning. The significance for teachers and learners is that we learn best when teaching and learning matches the individual's strongest sense. This has been linked to Howard Gardner's theory of multiple intelligences (1983). He argues that individuals have different strengths and abilities. This has now been substantiated by research which shows that the different hemispheres of the brain are responsible for different functions. Knowing about learning theory and how we learn and 'thinking about thinking' enhances all learning. One-size teaching does not fit all students' learning.

Learning style inventories are often derived from the work of Dunn and Dunn (1978). They are questionnaires which establish whether individuals are primarily visual, auditory, verbal or kinaesthetic learners.

Letter string is a sequence of letters that remain together in words. Letter strings are sometimes called word patterns or word families: igh in 'fight'; ough in 'brought'; our in 'colour'.

Lexicographers are compilers and editors of dictionaries who study the history and meaning of words.

Linguistics is derived from the Latin word *lingua* meaning 'tongue'. It is the scientific study of the structure of language including the principles and how these affect humans. It also studies the links between languages. Phonetics is regarded as the scientific study of the speech sounds in language and is an intrinsic part of linguistics.

Liquid sounds are the sounds made by the letters 'l' and 'r'.

Loan words are 'given' from one language to another. English has given French 'babysitter' and Italian has given English 'pizza' (which, after 'taxi' and 'sex', is the most widely known and recognised word in the world).

Logograms and logographs are symbols used to denote a word or phrase in languages such as Chinese. They are also used for scientific notation and for road signs: for example a picture of a man with a spade could be used to denote roadworks.

Longitudinal study is a scientific study of the same subjects conducted over a protracted period. For example children can be tested at age 4, 8 and 12 to compare development or progress.

Long-term memory is an ability to hold for a long period of time information which can later be recalled and used. There are two types. Episodic memory involves visual and sensory images such as the smell of onions frying triggering memories of a first visit to the seaside aged 5 and a visit to a burger bar. Semantic memory involves general knowledge and language.

'Look-and-say' method of reading teaches the pupil to recognise whole words. It is primarily a visual approach. It was used in reading schemes which had controlled vocabularies of 'sight words' which were memorised. These words were often reinforced and practised by using flash cards and with reading schemes with controlled vocabularies.

Macron is derived from the Greek word *makros* meaning 'long'. It is the horizontal code mark line placed over a long or stressed vowel to indicate that it says its name: hē; hē/rō.

Magnetic resonance imaging (MRI) is a brain-imaging technique using a scanning machine that can convert the signals it receives into a video display. It enables users to examine the structure of the living brain and to study brain function when it is engaged in a cognitive process.

Magnocellular deficit theory The magnocellular pathway and parvacellular pathway relate to the two visual pathways used to see. Livingstone et al. (1991) first used the word in relation to specific developmental dyslexia (SpLD). 'Magnocellular' is derived from *magno* meaning 'great' or 'large' and *parva* meaning 'small' or 'lesser'. The magnocellular pathway is responsible for new information or changes in the visual field and the parvacellular pathway is responsible for fine details in the visual field. Both functions work in tandem. The magnocells are large neurons in a system which Stein et al. (2001) note are 'responsible for timing sensory and motor events'. They argued that weaknesses in the visual magnocellular system results in 'visual confusion of letter order and poor visual memory for orthography'. Evans (2001) reviewed the literature and found 'evidence for a [magnocellular] deficit' in cases of dyslexia but 'it seems that, although visual factors can contribute to some of the reading errors, they do not play the major causal role in dyslexia'. Stein et al. (2001) argued from the studies they had conducted that in some subjects 'the visual magnocellular system is impaired' and that it 'impacts on reading'. But 'it is not immediately obvious how the magnocellular system contributes to reading'.

Major spelling rules are rules that have a high frequency and a high level of reliability.

Maturation lag is derived from the Latin word *maturare* meaning 'to ripen'. It describes a delay in development. 'Lag' implies growing or developing more slowly and consequently gradually falling behind. It presupposes that there is a predetermined growth rate for physical and cognitive functions. It can be applied to children with a delay in a particular ability or skill such as speech or motor skills. For some this is a temporary delay which initially may lead to a diagnosis of a learning disability and of special educational needs. Other children fail to reach milestones for their age and ability, and experience permanent disabilities. Some children with dyslexia and dyspraxia have a developmental delay in the acquisition of skills. Many outgrow these earlier difficulties; others have long-lasting and persisting specific difficulties with skills.

'Meaning emphasis' reading method is used to teach reading to beginners by focusing primarily on words which are connected to text for meaning. Children are assumed to learn about alphabetic principles by reading for meaning. The prime focus is using texts that can be read quickly and easily so that unknown words can be deciphered easily. Contextual cues help a student to guess words rather than having to attempt to decode words by sounding them out letter-by-letter.

Metacognition is derived from the Greek words *meta* meaning 'alongside' or 'co-existent' and *gnosco* meaning to 'understand' or 'the process of understanding'. Metacognition skills are an ability to take control of one's own thinking processes to study and understand how we think and the processes involved in thinking. This self-awareness involves knowing what to learn and how to remember, as well as an awareness of one's personal strengths and weaknesses.

Mind Map™ is a registered trademark (Buzan 1993). It is a visual representation of thoughts, words and ideas such as an essay plan or notes from a textbook or lecture which is illustrated by hand or with a word-processor. Computer packages are available to help create the illustrations.

Minor spelling rules are rules that do not have a high frequency.

Miscue analysis involves examining errors recorded during testing with standardised tests and/or errors recorded when reading aloud and then using these diagnostically. Errors are scrutinised then analysed and categorised. It developed from the supposition that readers use phonological, semantic or syntactic 'cues' when reading to decode text. The 'miscue' can provide evidence about underlying strengths and weaknesses. Reading errors can provide information about the stage of development reached as well as the strategies being used either correctly or incorrectly. They can also be used to analyse spelling errors made in tests in personal writing.

Mnemonic is derived from the Greek word *mnemonikos* meaning 'memory' or 'mindful'. It is associated with Mnemosyne, the Greek goddess of memory. It is a memory device used to help remember facts, words, phrases or sentences. The sentence 'never eat shredded wheat' helps the learner to recall that the points of the compass are: North, East, South and West. Mnemonics can be used to remember the letters used to spell a word: 'big elephants can't always use small exits' helps to remember how to spell 'because'. The initial letters of the target words can be recalled by repeating the sentence. Rhymes can also be used: 'you hear with an ear'.

Monosyllable is derived from the Greek word *monos* meaning 'single'. It is a word with one syllable: 'cat'; 'cot'; 'cup'.

Morpheme is derived from the Greek word *morphe* meaning 'form'. It is the smallest meaningful part of a word and can be a prefix, suffix, plurals: 'mis', 'ing', 'es'. There are two kinds, 'free' and 'bound' morphemes. Free morphemes are found in words that are entities in themselves such as 'cup', 'walk'. Bound morphemes are so called because they are attached to words and cannot be used alone, such as 's' in 'cups' or 'ed' in 'walked'.

Morphology is the study of the structure of words and how this affects spelling and the use of words including prefixes and suffixes. It also includes the study of word formation and letter patterns.

'Morphophonological' errors were so called by Moats (1995). They apply to affixes such as 's', 'ed', 'ing', 'il', 'im', 'ir'.

Motor skills apply to muscular movements. Gross motor skills apply to the large muscles involving the arms, legs, body and neck. Fine motor skills apply to the fingers, hands and the speech muscles of the tongue.

Multi-media software includes animation, colour, pictures, sound, text and video which can be used interactively.

Multiple intelligences theory is a hypothesis put forward by Howard Gardner (1983) who argued that intelligences consist of different abilities and skills and that each ability has its individual characteristics. These included visual/spatial, logical/ mathematical, musical/rhythmic, bodily/ kinaesthetic, interpersonal, intrapersonal, verbal/linguistic and naturalistic intelligences. The locations for these functions may be situated in different parts of the brain.

Multi-sensory learning uses the eyes, ears, lips and the hands simultaneously: the eyes to look at the words, the lips to pronounce the word, the ears to listen to the word and the hand to write the word, thus incorporating all the learning pathways to the brain to optimise learning.

National Literacy Strategy (NLS) was a government initiative to raise national standards in reading, writing, speaking and listening. The Department for Education and Employment (DfEE 1998) published non-statutory guidelines to meet a national target for all pupils to become literate for children from Reception to Year 6 Key Stage 1 and Key Stage 2. The objectives were set out in the *Framework for Teaching*, which was a reference document for classroom teachers. It gave a detailed analysis as well as guidance for the implementation of the Literacy Strategy in schools and day-to-day guidance for the implementation of the Literacy Hour which was structured to include word-level work, sentence-level work and text-level work. The objectives for each of these were subdivided for each term of a 36-week school year from Reception Year to Year 6. These were to be taught as follows: '15 minutes whole class teaching using shared text work including reading and spelling'; '15 minutes whole class work which is focused on word work or sentence work including systematic, regular and frequent teaching of phonological awareness, throughout Key Stage 1'; 20 minutes group and independent work such as guided reading with a group of individual pupils as well as guided writing which includes different aspects of writing processes which can be completed by other pupils working independently';

10 minutes known as the plenary session when teaching points are reviewed, revised and feedback is given to pupils'. Key Stage 3 National Strategy was introduced in 2001 (DfEE 2001).

National Numeracy Strategy (DfEE 1999b) describes what is to be taught at each key stage and sets out a yearly programme and key objectives for each year. A lesson of 45–60 minutes should include: oral work and mental arithmetic; teaching activity; plenary work to summarise key facts. It includes five strands: numbers and the number system; calculations; solving problems; measures, shape and space; handling data.

Neurolinguistics studies the brain's involvement in language development and how the brain controls speaking, listening, reading and writing.

Neuro-linguistic programming (O'Connor and Seymour 1990) was devised to identify individuals' preferred learning style and to use this information to develop learning strategies to match visual, auditory or kinaesthetic styles. An example of an informal approach is to ask an individual who is sitting in an upright position to think about an object such as his house and then ask, 'How many windows have curtains that you can see from the front of the house?' The objective is to identify the visual strategies they use, by observing the direction their eyes move to when they think about the windows. The hypothesis to the diagnostic eye-movement diagram is that visual learners will lift their head and turn their eyes upwards as if they are looking at the windows as they count them in their mind's eye. Auditory learners will turn aside and turn their eyes to the side as they try to count out the numbers. Kinaesthetic learners will turn the eyes downwards and may trace out the number with the fingers. Neuro-linguistic programming uses a strongly visual approach to learning.

Non-word reading and spelling is the use of pseudo-words used to assess underlying phonological and phonemic skills. Rack et al. (1992) identified a non-word reading deficit in individuals with dyslexia.

Norm-referenced tests are standardised on a widely distributed population and can be used to compare the performance of pupils of the same age, locally and nationally.

Ocular motor factors involve the eyes. The brain is responsible for controlling the muscles that move the eyes and help them to sustain focus. The eyes need to be fully co-ordinated to have normal vision.

'Odd-bod' spellings (Ott 1997) are irregular spellings including words where there is poor sound-to-symbol match. They can include silent letters and words borrowed from other languages. Words derived from Anglo-Saxon are a prime source. They also include words which do not have rhyme words: 'orange', 'pint'.

Onset is the initial consonant or cluster of consonants of letters in words: d̲(og), ch̲(ap), str̲(ing).

Organs of speech are the parts of the body used in speech production such as the tongue, mouth, nose, lips and teeth. They each make sounds which depend on the movement of each organ. Sounds can be classified by where they are made and how they are articulated.

Orthography is derived from the Greek words *ortho* meaning 'correct' and *graphein* meaning 'to write'. It is the correct or customary everyday spelling of a word. It also involves studying the spelling to check the correct shape of the letters and the correct order of the letters.

Paired reading is undertaken with a beginner reader and a skilled reader. They read a text simultaneously. The teacher praises and supports the effort. Gradually, as the pupil becomes more confident, he or she can read alone.

Paired spelling method This is undertaken with a partner. The teacher says the word aloud and the pupil echoes this. They look at the word together and the teacher writes the word. The pupil says the word again and writes it. Then he or she reads what he or she has written and says it. Then he or she writes the word again quickly. The teacher praises the pupil's effort.

Palatal sounds are made by raising the back of the tongue towards the soft palate such as when saying /k/, /g/.

Pangram is a sentence or verse containing all the letters of the alphabet. This is sometimes described as a holoalphabetic sentence. It is is derived from the Greek word *holos* meaning 'whole' because it uses all the letters of the alphabet: 'The five boxing wizards jumped quickly.'

Pedagogy is derived from the Greek word *paidagogos* meaning 'teacher'. It includes an understanding of science and the principles and methods of teaching.

Percentiles show the percentage of pupils nationally of a similar age or age range (for example 9 years 0 months to 9 years 4 months) who would score at the same level, or below, on standardised tests. Thus a percentile of 96 shows that 96 per cent of individuals score at the same level or below while only 4 per cent score more highly.

Perception is the process whereby information from the five senses is organised and interpreted to become meaningful, often from previous experiences. Auditory perception is an ability to recognise and distinguish between sounds spoken and heard and includes blending, discrimination, memory segmenting, sequencing and phonological awareness. Visual perception is an ability to recognise and distinguish between letters, numbers and geometric patterns, pictures and designs, and includes visual discrimination, memory and awareness of wholes or parts of letter words and patterns. Motor perception is an ability to co-ordinate fine and gross motor movements and includes a sense of directionality and orientation. Kinaesthetic perception is an ability to use body and muscle movement and includes recognition and identification of the function of different parts of the body.

'Phoenician' spelling style describes spellers who 'rely heavily on the rules' according to Baron and Strawson (1976). This includes matching the sounds (phonemes) to the letters (graphemes) that represent them.

Phoneme is derived from the Greek word *phonema* meaning 'uttered sound'. It is the smallest unit of sound that changes the meaning of one spoken word from another: 'c', 'b', 'f' before 'at' makes /b/ /a/ /t/, /c/ /a/ /t/, /f/ /a/ /t/. In the past there was an ongoing debate about the exact number of phonemes in English. The number has varied between 33 and 44. There is now a general consensus (DfEE 1998) that there are 44 phonemes in the English language. There are over 70 letter or letter combinations to represent the sounds in speech and there are approximately 140 letter combinations illustrated within words (DfEE 1999a).

Phonemic awareness is the ability to judge the relationship of sounds *within* words, receive the whole and identify the parts, including the explicit awareness of 'phoneme-sized segments of spoken words' (Borstrom and Elbro 1997) and an ability to understand phoneme segmentation. Lindamood et al. (1997) described phonemic awareness 'as an ability to identify individual sounds and their order within words – to divide a whole word into parts'. The child must have an awareness of the individual sounds in words in oral language. This can be difficult to learn without explicit teaching, primarily because in speech many sounds are co-articulated and sounds elide, such as /l/ /e/ /ng/ /th/ in 'length'.

Phonemic decoding is an ability to use the alphabetic principle for the sounds represented by letters and, by blending these individual phonemes, to read the words they represent and, by segmenting the individual phonemes, to spell the word.

Phonetic errors are made when there is mismatch between the phonemes and the letters that represent them. They can occur at the beginning, middle or end of words: 'cet' for get; 'cot' for cut; 'boks' for box.

Phonics involves teaching reading and spelling by sounding out the individual letter sounds, then blending and synthesising the sounds to pronounce the word when learning to read (Ott 1997). It is used to segment the letters when spelling a word. There are two phonic methods – analytic phonics and synthetic phonics. The analytic method teaches the child to look at whole words and break them into chunks when reading. The synthetic method teaches the child to look at the individual letter sounds then to blend them into a whole word and pronounce it when reading. The NLS (DfEE 2001a) Literacy Progress Unit: Phonics stated that 'phonics consists of the skill of segmentation and blending, knowledge of the alphabetic code and understanding of the principles which underpin how the code is used in reading and spelling'. It did not give specific guidance on the use of synthetic or analytic phonics, which is perhaps a reflection of the polarisation of opinions associated with the teaching of phonics among educational professionals resulting in the so-called phonic 'wars'. It did however, strongly recommend the use of systematic phonics. The Rose (2006) Review recommended teaching systematic, synthetic phonics from the age of 5 using a multi-sensory approach.

Phonograms are the letters that represent individual sounds such as the common elements in word families: 'ight' in 'bright', 'fight', 'might'. Phonographic

writing systems use a character for each sound.

Phonological awareness is an ability to recognise, analyse and manipulate different sounds such as 'bun', 'pun', 'fun'. Liberman and Shankweiler (1985) said that 'phonological awareness is the explicit awareness of the sound segments in words'. The National Literacy Strategy (DfEE 1998) defined it as 'an awareness of sounds within words – demonstrated by the ability to generate rhyme, alliteration, and in segmenting and blending component sounds'.

Phonological decoding is an ability to translate printed words into sounds when for example reading aloud or repeating oral information. This can be tested using a non-word repetition test such as Gathercole and Baddeley (1996) or a non-word reading test such as Crumpler and McCarty (2004).

Phonological errors are made when there is a mismatch between knowledge of word parts such as syllables, affixes, blends and vowel digraphs, for example 'rember' for remember; 'lookt' for looked; 'crips' for crisps; 'tran' for train.

Phonology is the study of the sound system and the speech sounds in relation to meaning, including the syllables and the phonemes produced. It also involves the rules governing the combination of sounds in a given language.

Piaget's cognitive development theory describes Jean Piaget's study of 'how children think and how their thinking changes as they mature'. He asserted that children go through four stages in the development of intelligence: the sensorimotor stage (0–2 years) when the child reacts with the environment and learns through sensory or motor experience; the pre-operational stage (2–7 years) when the child tends to think about how things seem rather than by logical principles: they can use symbols and language to interact and learn about the environment; the concrete operational stage (7–11 years) when the child performs operations with the use of concrete objects; the formal operational stage (11–15 years) when the child can reason using statements and think about hypothetical situations and deal with abstract ideas to solve problems. The teacher needs to identify which stage the child has reached to guide and help the child to move on to the next stage (based on Gross 1996). Teaching can be tailored to the existing knowledge of the individual child or adult learner.

Pictograms and Pictographs are pictures or symbols used to denote objects or geographical features in picture writing.

Plurals are two or more of something or someone: 'cars', 'pupils', 'we', 'themselves'.

Polysyllable is derived from the Greek word *polys* meaning 'many' or 'much'. It denotes a word with more than one syllable:

'mag/net', 'fan/tas/tic',
'dis/mem/ber/ment'.

Positron-emission tomography (PET) scans are used to assess activity in brain tissue. They use radiation to measure metabolic activity of tissues in the brain.

Prefixes are letters or groups of letters added to the beginning of a root word which usually change the meaning of the word: 'conform'; 'deform'; 'misform'.

Pre-readers are children who have not received any formal reading instruction.

Primary National Strategy (DfES 2006) The National Literacy Strategy and the National Numeracy Strategy were combined and are known collectively as the Primary National Strategy.

Processing speed deficits indicate difficulties in interpreting language at the speed at which it is presented such as when doing a spoonerism task. It also applies particularly to information in sequential form such as a digit span task.

'Progressive education' movement was 'an education system which placed greater emphasis on the needs and activities of the individual child than traditional forms of teaching and which usually involved greater freedom of choice, activity and movement. Stressing social as well as academic development' (*Chambers Twenty-first Century Dictionary* 1999).

Psycholinguistics studies language and the mind and the relationship between language and mental processes.

Psychometric tests such as the Wechsler Intelligence Scale for Children (WISC) are used for psychological measurements.

Quartile is a term used to denote how a dictionary can be divided into approximately four sections. It cuts down having to leaf through the whole dictionary and speeds up research when the user knows what letters are in each of the quartiles. The mnemonic 'Elephants Move Slowly in Zoos' helps to remember which letter each section ends in:

A–E: first quartile; F–M: second quartile; N–S: third quartile; T–Z: fourth quartile.

Quotients are calculated by dividing an attainment score by chronological age. Quotients can be devised to include an age allowance. For example scores can be used to compare children within one month of each other, thus showing that a child with scores below average for the class may in fact have an average score for children of the same precise age.

QWERTY keyboard is so called because these are the letters on the top line of keys on a standard keyboard.

Rapid automised theory (RAN) Denckla and Rudel (1976) established that children with dyslexia had problems processing language at speed. They devised a test for tasks which involved the child having to give as quickly as possible the names of 50 stimuli, such as digits, letter names, colours, objects.

Raw scores are established when the total number of correct answers in a test is counted. These can be converted to standardised scores when the test is norm-referenced.

Reading The word is derived from the Anglo-Saxon *rǣdinge* meaning to extract meaning from written or printed language. The reader needs to recognise words quickly and fluently to be able to concentrate on the meaning of text. 'Silent reading' is done privately while 'reading aloud' is reading orally, usually to an audience. The NLS (DfEE 1998) advocated 'shared reading' which is done with a common text and often with a 'big book'. Pupils and teacher study and read specific features of grammar to learn about specific features of grammar and language. This allows poor readers to access more demanding texts with adult support. 'Guided reading' takes place when groups of children matched for reading ability read from individual copies of a common text. Key Stage 1 pupils are helped to identify 'hard' words before embarking on silent reading of a text of 'greater richness and complexity than they would otherwise be able to read'.

Reading age gives age-equivalent scores and measures reading attainment on a norm-referenced test and compares results with children of a similar chronological age. Results are given in years and months. Sometimes teachers and parents assume that reading and spelling ages should equal chronological age. However, these results are often considered unreliable because one word read can be equivalent to three months in the norms for 7-year-olds, whereas two words differentiate between the norms for 16-year-olds and 24-year-olds when using for example the TOWRE (Torgenson et al. 1999) according to Backhouse and Morris (2005).

Regular spellings are words that can be spelled by using phonological skills, in other words using the grapheme/phoneme approach. Irregular 'odd-bod' words (Ott 1997) have to be memorised using a visual approach.

Rhyme occurs when two or more words have the same ending sound.

Rime is the vowel and final consonant(s)in a word: 'b(ack)', 'cr(ime)', 'str(ong)'. Rimes can also be single sounds: 'fr(ee)', 'sh(e)', 'd(ay)'. Goswami (2002) pointed out that 'rime' is used because multisyllabic words have more than one 'rime'; 'mountain' and 'fountain' rhyme but each has two rimes, 'ount' and 'ain'. 'Mountain and 'counting' do not rhyme but they do have the same initial rime, 'ount'.

Root words (sometimes described as base words) are words which can stand alone or have a prefix, suffix or both added to make other words: 'form'; 'reform'; 'formed'; 'performing'.

Rote memory is used to memorise something by heart, without necessarily understanding it, such as times tables, formulas or words of a song.

Scaffolding is a term derived from the work of Vygotsky, who advocated that the apprentice learner should be supported by the expert practitioner who guides and supports the learner with practical assistance.

Schwa vowels are unstressed vowel sounds which occur in unaccented syllables such as /u/ in 'circus', /a/ in 'sofa', /er/ in 'discover', /or/ in 'forget', /ous/ in 'famous', /tion/ in 'instruction'. They have been shown to be the source of most errors for spellers (Kreiner and Gough 1990). The word is borrowed from the Hebrew *shěwā* meaning emptiness.

Segmentation skill is an ability to break words into individual phonemes, /m/ /a/ /n/, into speech sounds /ch/ /i/ /p/, and into syllables: 'trum/pet'.

Semantics deals with the study of meaning in language including sentences and words.

Semantic cues are derived from the meanings of words, phrases or sentences which help the reader to guess or make sense of unfamiliar words when reading.

SEN Tribunals were set up under Section 333 of the Education Act 1996. They are independent bodies which review complaints or disputes between parents and local education authorities (LEAs) with regard to decisions made about assessments and statements made about children with special educational needs (SEN).

Short-term memory is a temporary mental storage facility and is used to hold a small amount of sensory information in one's mind for a period of several seconds while the information is processed and interpreted to allow the individual to carry out an intellectual task such as remembering a telephone number or recognising a picture.

Sight words are whole words which are instantly recognisable because all the letters have been memorised in long-term memory. Decoding or encoding strategies are not used because they can be read rapidly, effortlessly and automatically within one second from memory.

Silent letters are not sounded when words are pronounced: 'knife', 'psalm', 'wrist'.

Simultaneous oral spelling (S-O-S) involves saying the word aloud, spelling the word orally, while simultaneously writing the word naming letters (see p. 100). It is the classic Orton–Gillingham spelling method.

Skywriting involves using an outstretched arm and the index finger of the dominant hand to trace letters in the air. It can be used to develop motor memory of letter shapes and spelling patterns. It is particularly useful for those with a kinaesthetic preferred learning style.

Special Educational Needs (SEN) According to the Education Act 1996 'a child has a learning difficulty if he or she (a) has a significantly greater difficulty in learning than the majority of children of the same age. (b) Has a disability which either prevents or hinders the child from making use of educational facilities of a kind provided for children of the same age in schools within the area of the local authority.'

Special Needs and Disability Act (2001) SENDA was developed from the Disability Discrimination Act (1995) and applies to all aspects of discrimination against disabled pupils. It is illegal to treat disabled individuals 'less favourably' and establishments must make 'reasonable adjustments' to accommodate and provide for pupils with learning disabilities. The Disability Rights Commission is responsible for overseeing that the Code of Practice for Schools and Post-16 pupils is implemented.

Specific developmental dyslexia is, according to the World Federation of Neurology, a 'disorder manifested by difficulty in learning to read despite conventional instruction, adequate intelligence and socio-cultural opportunity. It depends on fundamental cognitive disabilities which are frequently constitutional in origin' (Waites 1968). With the advent of neuroimaging techniques, more is known about the condition. More recent definitions such as the BDA's highlight the fact that abilities and weaknesses often co-exist. Dyslexia is a 'combination of abilities and difficulties which affect the learning process in one or more of reading, spelling and writing. Accompanying weaknesses may be identified in areas of speed of processing, short-term memory, sequencing, auditory and/or visual perception, spoken language and motor skills' (Peer 2001).

Specific learning difficulty (SpLD) The term is frequently used as a synonym for dyslexia. Pumfrey and Reason (1991) sent out questionnaires to educational psychologists. Among the questions asked were: whether they found the term 'specific learning difficulty' useful in their professional work; whether they found 'dyslexia' useful in their professional work; whether they considered the two terms synonymous. Of the 882 completed questionnaires 87.4 per cent opted for SpLD as a useful term, 30.5 per cent opted for dyslexia as a useful term, and 22 per cent considered the two terms synonymous. The results of a national enquiry of 1989, *Specific Learning Difficulties, Dyslexia – Challenges, Responses and Recommendations* (Pumfrey and Reason 1991) when submitted to the Department of Education acknowledged that 'the DES takes the view that under the Education Act 1981, the precise name used to describe a child's learning difficulties is not important'. There was acceptance that some children do have specific learning difficulties but none of the 'eminent committees' who advised the DES 'recommended the adoption of the term 'dyslexia'. Deponio (2004) argues that 'the term "specific learning difficulties" has taken on a wider meaning' and should be used as an 'umbrella term' because it now refers to children who 'display discrepancies across their learning' because of 'dyspraxia/developmental co-ordination difficulties, specific language impairment and the attention deficit disorders'.

Specific learning disability The US government's United States Education for All Handicapped Children Act, Public Law 94–142, was a landmark for legislation about 'learning disability' which it defined as 'a disorder in one or more of the basic psychological processes involved in understanding or using language, spoken or written which may manifest itself in an imperfect ability to listen, think, speak, read, write, spell or do mathematical calculations'. It was reflected in subsequent legislation including the US government's Individuals and Disabilities Education Act 1997 (IDEA), which states: 'The term "specific learning disabilities" means those children who have a disorder in one or more of the basic psychological processes involved in understanding or in using language, spoken or written, which disorder may manifest itself in imperfect ability to listen, think, speak, read, write, spell or do mathematical calculations'; 'a severe discrepancy exists between the student's apparent *potential for learning* and his or her low level of achievement'.

Spelling involves saying or writing the correct letters in a word. According to the NLS (DfEE 2001) it 'is a letter-by-letter process which involves a set of conscious choices not required in reading'.

Spelling age measures spelling attainments on a norm referenced test and compares the results with children of a similar chronological age. The age-equivalent scores are usually recorded in years and months. Critics regard it as a crude measurement of attainments because the 'age-equivalents become less appropriate as the age of the testee increases, since the rate of development of skills and attainments lowers'. Non-professionals regard it as a means of comparing pupils' achievement with their peers'.

Spelling conventions are generally accepted practices or customs.

Spelling error categorisation can be used to provide a snapshot of knowledge of spelling as well as pinpointing what needs to be taught, for example: phonemic knowledge – sound-to-symbol matches; phonological awareness – sounds within words; orthographic knowledge – individual letters or word patterns; morphemic knowledge – prefixes and suffixes; sight vocabulary – such as the high-frequency irregular spellings. When spelling error analysis is used effectively it can play a significant role in the diagnosis of dyslexia by establishing the existence of a 'pattern of difficulties'.

Spelling generalisations are processes or examples that can be applied to a wide range of individual words when spelling.

Spelling patterns are groups of letters that are consistently used and have a large number of representations such as 'ight'; 'ough'. The 'ight' pattern can be used to generate the spelling of 90 words (Stanback 1992).

Spelling pronunciation uses an exaggerated pronunciation or stresses a sound such as a silent letter or a syllable. A mnemonic can be used to help recall the letters, for example sounding the silent letters: 'He knew when he knelt on his knees [that] he had a knife in his knitted knickers' (Mudd 1997) or 'Wed/nes/day'.

Spelling quotients are used to compare the performance of children on a standardisation sample of pupils of a similar chronological age. They allow a comparison to be made of how an individual pupil performs in relation to the national average.

Spelling rules are general principles and guidelines which may include exceptions to the rule.

Spelling skill is an ability or expertise to spell words easily and accurately and to use them automatically when required in writing. It can be acquired naturally as well as developing as a result of learning, experience and practice.

Spelling stages refers to a progression in the development of spelling skills. There is a consensus of opinion that there are four stages in spelling development.

Spelling strategy is a chosen method to learn and remember spelling using one or all of the senses including the eyes, ears, hands and lips. Choice will often depend on the individual's preferred learning style.

Spelling styles imply that learners have preferred methods of learning. Those who sound out words and match these to the letters that represent them are sometimes called 'Phoenician' spellers and have good auditory skills. Those who take a snapshot of a word and recognise whole words and spelling patterns are called 'Chinese' spellers and have good visual memories (Baron and Strawson 1976).

'Spellofax' is 'a pupil workbook [notebook or file] which enables pupils to build a cumulative record of their learning [as well as] through a sequence of "spelling challenges" and it can become a point of future reference across the curriculum' according to the NLS (DfEE, 2001).

Split vowel digraphs are two vowels which are split by a consonant but make one vowel sound, such as: 'a–e' tāpe; 'e–e' hēre; 'i–e' pīpe; 'o–e' rōpe; 'u–e' tūbe. They are usually known colloquially as the 'magic "e"' or 'silent "e"' or 'mute "e"'.

Standard deviation scores denote the spread of scores from the mean (average) score. If on a standardised test the mean score is 100, a standard deviation is usually 15 points on educational or IQ tests. Dunn et al. (1997) pointed out 'that irrespectively of the difficulty of the test, about 68 per cent of the national average will have a standardised score within one standard deviation (15) points of the average (between 85 and 115) and about 95 per cent will have a standardised score within two standard deviations (30 points) of the average (between 70 and 130)'. Most human attributes appear to be distributed in what is known as the 'bell-shaped curve' of probability. (See Fig. 19, from Thomson 2001.)

Standardised scores are calculated from the raw score test results and compare a pupil's performance with that of other pupils nationally of exactly the same age in years and months. This explains why someone with a higher raw score may obtain a lower standardised score than a pupil who is younger. It is a better indication of attainment; and also provides a means of comparing how an individual's performance deviates from the national average score. The mean score is 100 and the nearer the pupil is to this, the nearer he or she is to the average for the age group.

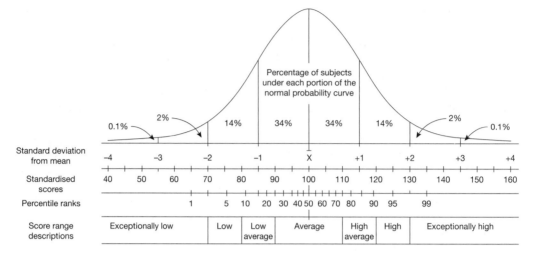

Percentage of subjects under each portion of the normal probability curve

Figure 19

Another use of standardised scores is to make comparisons with scores obtained on other tests such as IQ tests.

Standardised spelling tests have been developed from testing a large representative sample of pupils. A scale of average scores is worked out from these results which can then be used to compare performance and attainment levels with other pupils of a similar age and nationally. Standardised tests should produce the same results whenever they are administered because they have been trialled on large cross-sections of individuals from a wide social background and over a wide geographical area. Goulandris (1996) pointed out that 'standardised tests help us to decide whether a child is only somewhat poorer (as a rule of thumb 9 months below the mean) or significantly below its peers (more than 18 months if the child is less than 8-years-old or 24 months or more from 8 years onwards)'.

Stanford Spelling Study was set up with financial backing from the US government (Hanna et al. 1966). More than seventeen thousand of the most frequently used words in English print were analysed for their sound/symbol regularities. The results showed that English spelling is not as irregular as critics suppose. 'An important fact demonstrated by the study is that the number of so-called spelling demons scattered throughout our writing system is relatively small (above 3 per cent of the core vocabulary falling into this category).' They added that 'in sum, certain words do contain rare, even unique, spellings of phonemes, and such words need to be mastered by whatever means available to the pupil'.

Stanines This term is derived from 'standard' and 'nine'. It is used to subdivide standardised scores into nine bands or divisions called standard nine scores. Standardised scores can range from 60 to 140. Stanines range from 1 to 9: stanine 1 is very low; stanines 2, 3 are below average; stanines 4, 5, 6 are average; stanines 7 and 8 are above average; stanine 9 is very high.

Statement is a document issued by a local education authority (LEA) after a child has been assessed and is found to have significant special educational needs. It describes these needs and lists the appropriate provision for the child. Large numbers of appeals were made to SEN Tribunals by parents to obtain official recognition and appropriate support for the child. The Special Educational Needs Code of Practice (DfES 2001) states that 'Children who demonstrate features of moderate, severe or profound learning difficulties, such as dyslexia or dyspraxia, require specific programmes to aid progress in cognition and learning'.

Strategy is a long-term plan for procedures and can include a blueprint for teaching and learning.

Strephosymbolio is a term coined by Samuel Orton to describe an 'instability in recognition and recall of the orientation of letters and order of letters in words' (J.L. Orton 1966).

Stress is a term used in linguistics to denote where the emphasis is put on a syllable when it is pronounced: 'alien'; 'begonia'; 'petunia'.

Structural linguistics studies the underlying patterns and catalogues the linguistic elements and structures in language. It was developed from the work of Ferdinand de Saussure. Leonard Bloomfield (1933) was its main proponent, and in his book *Language* he argued that 'the analysis appropriate to a particular language must be inferred from its own structure'. He broke down language analysis using a formulaic approach as used in his reading books *Let's Read*. He argued that children need to be taught about language in a structured way. Noam Chomsky opposed this and argued that language is an innate ability which explains why children develop and use complex grammatical structures. Linguistic analysis analyses mental operations.

Suffixes are letters or groups of letters that are added to the ends of root words, usually changing their use and meaning. There are two forms of suffixes. Inflectional suffixes show changes in meaning and grammatical features such as

plurals, tense, comparison of adjectives: 'cats', 'talking', 'fattest'. Derivational suffixes make new words and change meaning: 'catflap', 'catwalk', 'catnap'.

Syllable is a beat. Chambers (1996) states that it is 'a segment of a spoken word consisting of one sound or of two or more sounds such as a single unit of speech [a phoneme]'. It must have one vowel sound. Most syllables also have consonants but some syllables just have a vowel: 'ō/pĕn', 'gŏb/lĕt', 'făn/tăs/tĭc'.

Syllable division line is a slash or vertical line placed between syllables to indicate where a word can be divided for spelling and pronunciation: 'i/de/a', 'ze/ro', 'fan/tas/tic'. Linguisticians and lexicographers follow different conventions for syllable division.

Syllabograms are syllabic symbols used to represent syllables in the small units of pronunciation in writing, as in Japanese *kana*.

Syntax is the ordering of words in a sentence and the grammatical rules that apply to it.

Synthetic phonics is derived from the Greek words *synthetikos* meaning 'skilled at putting together' and *thesis* meaning 'playing'. When used in linguistics and for teaching and learning phonics it applies to the sounding out of individual phonemes from left to right and then blending them together to help pronounce a word, such as when reading. The converse is involved when segmenting the individual phonemes to match the sounds when spelling (Rose 2006). This method is sometimes described colloquially as the 'sounding out' or the 'code emphasis' approach. The use of the term 'synthetic' can be a source of confusion because of the semantic issues involved since the common meaning of the word 'synthetic' is something artificial or insincere.

Systematic phonics gives explicit direct teaching of letter/sound correspondences by following a clearly structured and cumulative programme of phonics which helps to develop skill in identifying and spelling words not recognised automatically (see Ott 2007).

Theory is derived from the Greek word *theoria* meaning 'contemplation' or 'speculation'. It examines underlying principles and gives explanations for causes.

Thorndike and Lorge's (1944) word list This was a database derived from 18 million words of text published in *The Teacher's Word Book* of thirty thousand words. This word count was frequently used when looking at spelling statistics, particularly when considering frequency of use, and was very influential in deciding what vocabulary to include in children's spelling and reading books.

Tracking exercises were devised to practise left-to-right scanning of letters and words on lines of text.

Transparent languages are languages which have a clear sound-to-symbol match such as Finnish, Italian, Spanish or Greek. This makes pronouncing words and learning to read and spell easier. There are fewer unique or irregular spelling patterns than for example in English. Language orthographies are described as transparent (shallow) when a letter is pronounced the same way wherever it occurs in a word. In opaque (deep) languages such as English, French or Polish letters can be pronounced in different ways.

Visual discrimination is an ability to detect the differences in shape, size and conformation of letters and objects.

Visual memory is an ability to recall or retain a mental picture of a letter, word or object including its shape, length and the orders of letters in a word.

Visual sequential memory is the ability to recall a series of letters or objects in the order they were presented. It involves orientation as well as sequences (Ott 1997). It is an essential skill for the competent reader and speller and helps to develop

instant, automatic recall of words resulting in a sight vocabulary for reading and for spelling when writing.

Visual skills include an ability to remember by seeing and being able to turn these details into pictures including their colour in the mind's eye. It is related to spatial abilities which include patterns for shapes and word patterns. Some students learn best by looking at spellings. They can 'video' the word and recall the image when they spell it. They learn by using diagrams, pictures, videos, Mind Maps and CD-ROMs.

Visual stress is a term describing the effect of distortions in print or flicker on computer monitors; sensitivity to colour including font and paper; sensitivity to light including fluorescent lighting. It is often described as Meares-Irlen syndrome.

Vowel The term is derived from the Latin word *vocalis* meaning a letter representing uninterrupted voice or breath. They are the letters 'a', 'e', 'i', 'o' and 'u'. 'y' is sometimes used as a vowel, as in 'cry', 'baby', 'type'. Vowel sounds are made with an open mouth and there is no contact with the lips, teeth or tongue. There are two kinds of vowels – short and long. Short vowels say their sounds and long vowels say their names. Every word must have a vowel and every syllable must have a vowel sound. Some vowels are unstressed in normal pronunciation and are known as 'schwa' vowels: 'fam/i/ly', 'tel/e/phone'.

Vowel digraphs are two vowels making one sound: 'dream', 'seed', 'soap'.

Vygotsky's zone of proximal development (ZPD) Vygotsky (1962 and 1978) showed that tasks can be divided into different levels of difficulty. He explained how very difficult tasks will be beyond the ability of the individual's capacity and that simple tasks will be too easy for the individual. The middle way is when a task is neither too easy nor too difficult for the individual.

Learning is best done when it is in the zone of proximal development which is the distance between someone's development level and the level they can achieve with the help and support of someone more capable than themselves.

Whole language movement developed from the philosophy that reading is linked to oral and written language (Lerner 2000). Goodman (1986), one of its main architects, opined that children should be immersed in books from an early age. He argued that reading skills developed naturally and that it was not necessary to learn phonic rules. Reading is a process in which the reader picks and chooses information to predict and decode meaning just as in speech. It therefore was not necessary to teach sound–symbol relationships formally. These would be acquired naturally by frequent exposure to good literature. This 'psycho-linguistic guessing game' method works for some children, but many pupils need explicit teaching of decoding skills including phonics to enable them to crack the code.

'Whole word' reading method had its beginnings in the nineteenth century in the US. Children were given books with good illustrations and encouraged to memorise and recognise whole words rather than systematically decoding the letters. It became popular in the UK with the publication of The Happy Venture Readers (Schonell and Serjeant 1939) reading scheme and the Janet and John (O'Donnell and Munro 1949) scheme. This later became known as the 'look-and-say' reading method. Others called it the 'look-and-guess' method. It became the most popular reading method for schools in the UK by the 1960s. It worked well for good visualisers but was disastrous for those with poor visual perception and poor visual skills including pupils with dyslexia. Critics called it the Chinese method because they likened reading whole words to reading logographs.

Word class is a grammatical term to describe words that belong to the same parts of speech. The *NLS Framework for Teaching – Glossary of Terms* (DfEE 2002) states that 'the main word classes are verb, noun, adjective, adverb, pronoun, determiner, preposition and conjunction'.

Word family comprises words with the same pattern of letters, known as the rime, but with a different initial consonant or consonants, known as the onset.

Word recognition is an ability to recognise and pronounce written words as well as understanding their meaning. It results in automaticity when reading which enhances comprehension.

Word webs are diagrammatic representations of words using affixes with root words which show how new words can be generated by adding prefixes and suffixes.

Working memory is correlated to short-term memory. It involves holding a piece of information in mind to or from which another piece of information can be added or subtracted. In other words two things are done at once. It can include auditory memory, motor memory, visual memory and semantic memory. It is used, for example, when saying multiplication times tables, keying in a PIN number at a cash machine, remembering a personal car number plate or saying a digit span in reverse order and in non-word repetition tasks. It is a classic cause of difficulty in dyslexia. It accounts, for example, for a tendency to omit syllables or affixes from words when reading, writing or saying polysyllabic words and for difficulties with sequencing tasks.

Bibliography

Chapter 1

Barnhart R.K. (ed.) (1988) *Chambers Dictionary of Etymology*. Chambers Harrap Publishers Ltd, Edinburgh

Baugh A.C. (1957) *A History of the English Language* (fourth edition). Appleton-Century-Crofts, New York

Bragg M. (2002) *The Adventure of English*. Television documentary, LWT, December

Bragg M. (2003) *The Adventure of English*. Hodder & Stoughton, London

Bruck M. (1987) 'The adult outcomes of children with learning disabilities'. *Annals of Dyslexia*, 37: 252–263

Burchfield R.W. (ed.) (1996) *The New Fowler's Modern English Usage* (third edition). Clarendon Press, Oxford

Byers S. (1998) Report in *The Times*, 7 January, on keynote address at an international congress for school effectiveness in Manchester

Carney E. (1994) *A Survey of English Spelling*. Routledge, London

Chambers (1999) *Chambers Twenty-first Century Dictionary*. Robinson M. and Davidson G. (eds). Chambers Harrap Publishers, Edinburgh

Collins (1999) *Collins English Dictionary*, Millennium edition. Words of the Century. Harper Collins Publishers, Glasgow

Coote E. (1596) *The English Schoole-Maister*. Ralph Jackson and Robert Dextar, Company of Stationers, London

Cox A.R. and Hutcheson L. (1988) 'Syllable division: A prerequisite to dyslexics' literacy'. *Annals of Dyslexia*, 38: 226–242

Crystal D. (1995) *The Cambridge Encyclopaedia of the English Language*. Cambridge University Press, Cambridge

Crystal D. (1997) *English as a Global Language*. Cambridge University Press, Cambridge

Crystal D. (2002) *The English Language* (second edition). Penguin Books Ltd, London

Daily Mail (2003) 'The joy of text'. 4 March

Daily Mail (2004) 'The year of the chav'. 19 October

Daily Telegraph (2000) 'Exam body tell pupils to spell like Americans' (Lightfoot J.). 25 November

DfEE (2001) *Literacy Progress Unit. Key Stage 3 National Strategy: Spelling*. DfEE Publications, London

Ehri L.C. (1997) 'Sight word learning in normal readers and dyslexics'. In Blachman B. (ed.) *Foundations of Reading Acquisition and Dyslexia*. Lawrence Erlbaum Associates, Mahwah, NJ

Essinger J. (2006) *Spellbound: The Improbable Story of English Spelling*. Robson Books, London.

Franklin B. (1768) 'A scheme for a new alphabet and a reformed mode of spelling' (first published in 1768). In Bigelow J. (ed.) *Franklin's Works* vol. IV (1887–1888). G.P. Putnam's Sons, New York and London

Gardner J.L. (1973) *Reporting Glory*. Charles Scribner's Sons, New York

Havelock E. (1986) *The Muse Learns to Write*. Yale University Press, New Haven and London

Horn E. (1969) 'Spelling'. In Ebel R.L. (ed.) *Encyclopedia of Educational Research* (fourth edition). Macmillan, New York

International Dyslexia Association (1998) www. interdys.org

Johnson S. (1755) *A Dictionary of the English Language*. Strahan, London

Lennox C. and Siegel L.S. (1994) 'The role of phonological and orthographic processes in learning to spell'. In Brown G.D.A. and Ellis N.C. (eds) *Handbook of Spelling: Theory, Process and Intervention*. John Wiley & Sons, Chichester

McArthur T. (ed.) (1992) *The Oxford Companion to the English Language*. Oxford University Press, Oxford

Man J. (2000) *Alpha Beta: How our Alphabet Changed the Western World*. Headline Book Publishing, London.

Mulcaster R. (1582) *The First Part of the Elementarie Which Entreath Chefelie of the Right-Writing of Our English Tung*. Thomas Vautroullier, London.

Nist, J. (1966) *A Structural History of English*. St Martin's Press, New York.

Palmer S. (2000) *A Little Alphabet Book*. Oxford University Press, Oxford.

Quirk C.R., Greenbaum S., Leech G. and Svartvik J. (1985) *A Comprehensive Grammar of the English Language*. Longman, London

Reid Lyon G., Schaywitz S.E. and Shaywitz B.A. (2003) 'Defining dyslexia, comorbidity teachers' knowledge of language and reading: A definition of dyslexia'. *Annals of Dyslexia*, 53: 1–14

Salter R. and Smythe I. (eds) (1997) *The International Book of Dyslexia*. World Dyslexia Network Foundation London and European Dyslexia Association, Bedford

Scragg D.G. (1974) *A History of English Spelling*. Manchester University Press, Manchester

Simplified Spelling Society (2003) *Aims and Objectives of the Simplified Spelling Society*. www.Spelling Society.org

Terban M. (1998) *The Scholastic Dictionary of Spelling*. Scholastic Inc., New York

TES (2002) 'Delete text message style say examiners'. *The Times Educational Supplement*. 16 August

The Times (2000a) 'English spelling falls out of favor' (O'Leary J.). 25 November

The Times (2000b) '"Sulfur and fetus". Standardisation of scientific spelling might do no harm'. 25 November

Upward C. (1992) *Cut Spelling: A Handbook to the Simplification of Written English by Omission of Redundant Letters*. The Simplified Spelling Society, Birmingham

Upward C. (2003) *American Spellings for British Schools? A Submission from the Simplified Spelling Society to the School Curriculum and Assessment Authority (SCAA)*. www.Spelling Society.org

Venezky R.L. (1976) 'Notes on the history of English spelling'. *Visible Language*, 10: 351–365

Venezky R. (1980) 'From Wester to Rice to Roosevelt'. In Frith U. (ed.) *Cognitive Processes in Spelling*. Academic Press, London

Warfel H.R. (1936) *Noah Webster, Schoolmaster to America*. Macmillan, New York

Webster N. (1783) *A Grammatical Institute of the English Language, Part 1*. Hudson and Goodwin, Hartford, CT

Webster N. (1789) 'The reforming of spelling'. In *Old South Leaflets*, VIII, No. 196. Directors of the Old South Work, Boston, NJ

Chapter 2

Adams M.J. (1997) 'The great debate: Then and now'. *Annals of Dyslexia*, 47: 265–276

Bear D.R., Invernizzi M., Templeton S. and Johnston F. (2000) *Words Their Way: Word Study for Phonics, Vocabulary and Spelling Instruction*. Merrill, Columbus, OH

Beard R. (1998) *National Literacy Strategy. Review of Research and Other Related Evidence*. DfEE Publications, Sudbury

Blakemore S.-J. and Frith U. (2005) *The Learning Brain: Lessons for Education*. Blackwell Publishing Ltd, Oxford

Boder E. (1973) 'Developmental dyslexia: A diagnostic approach based on three atypical reading-spelling patterns'. *Developmental Medicine and Child Neurology*, 15: 663–687

Bosman A.M.J. and Van Orden G.C. (1997) 'Why spelling is more difficult than reading'. In Perfetti, C.A. Rieben and Fayol M. (eds) *Learning to Spell: Research, Theory and Practice Across Languages*. Lawrence Erlbaum Associates, Mahwah, NJ

Bradley L. and Bryant P. (1983) 'Categorising sounds and learning to read: A causal connection'. *Nature*, 301: 419–421

Bradley L. and Huxford L. (1994) 'Organising sound and letter patterns for spelling'. In Brown G.D.A and Ellis N.C. (eds) *Handbook of Spelling: Theory, Process and Intervention*. John Wiley & Sons, Chichester

Brand V. (1985) *Spelling Made Easy*. Egon Publishers Ltd, Baldock

Caithness J. (1997) 'To this day I cannot recite the alphabet'. *ISIS Bulletin*, London

Chasty H. (1990) 'The challenge of specific learning difficulties'. In Hales G. (ed.) *Meeting Points in Dyslexia*. BDA, Reading

Cox A.R. (1978) 'The Samuel T. Orton Award for 1997: A Response' *Bulletin of the Orton Society*, 28: 5–7

Cripps C. (1988) *A Hand for Spelling*. LDA, Wisbech

Dejerine J. (1892) 'Contribution à l'étude anatomo-pathologique et clinique des différentes variétés de cécité verbale'. *Mémoires de la Société de Biologie*, 4: 61–90

Denckla M.B. and Rudel R.G. (1976) 'Rapid "automatized" naming (RAN): Dyslexia differentiated from other learning disabilities'. *Neuropsychologia*, 14: 471–479

Denckla R., Dunn K. and Price G.E. (1996) *Learning Style Inventory*. Price Systems Inc., Lawrence, KS

DfEE National Literacy Strategy (1999a) *NLS Training Modules YR and Y1*. DfEE, London

DfEE National Literacy Strategy (1999b) Spelling Bank: *List of Words and Activities for the KS2 Spelling Objectives*. DfEE, London

DfEE National Literacy Strategy (2001) *Key Stage 3 Literacy Progress Unit – Spelling*. DfEE, London

Ehri L.C. (1980) 'The development of orthographic images'. In Frith U. (ed.) *Cognitive Processes in Spelling*. Academic Press, London

Ehri L.C. (1986) 'Sources of difficulty in learning to spell and read'. In Wolraich M.L. and Routh D. (eds) *Advances in Developmental and Behavioural Pediatrics*, 7. JAI Press, Greenwich, CT

Ehri L.C. (1997) 'Learning to read and learning to spell are one and the same, almost'. In Perfetti C.A., Rieben L. and Fayol M. (eds) *Learning to Spell: Research, Theory and Practice Across Languages*. Lawrence Erlbaum Associates, Mahwah, NJ

Ellis A.W. (1993) *Reading, Writing and Dyslexia: A Cognitive Analysis*. Lawrence Erlbaum Associates Ltd, Hove

Frith U. (1980) 'Unexpected spelling problems'. In Frith U. (ed.) *Cognitive Processes in Spelling*. Academic Press, London

Frith U. (1997) 'Brain, mind and behaviour in dyslexia'. In Hulme C. and Snowling M. (eds) *Dyslexia: Biology, Cognition and Intervention*. Whurr Publishers, London

Galaburda A.M.(1989) 'Ordinary and extraordinary brain development: Anatomical variation in developmental dyslexia'. *Annals of Dyslexia*, 39: 67–79

Galaburda A.M. (ed.) (1993) *Dyslexia and Developmental Neurobiological Aspects of Extra-Ordinary Brains*. Harvard University Press, Cambridge, MA

Galaburda A.M. and Kemper T.L. (1979) 'Cyto-architectonic abnormalities in developmental dyslexia: A case study'. *Annals of Neurology*, 6: 94–100

Galaburda A.M., Sherman G.F., Rosen G.D., Abioitiz F. and Geschwind N. (1985) 'Developmental dyslexia: Four consecutive patients with cortical anomalies'. *Annals of Neurology*, 18, 222–233

Gardner H. (1983) *Frames of Mind: The Theory of Multiple Intelligences*. Basic Books, New York

Gentry J.R. (1982) 'An analysis of developmental spelling in GYNS At WRK'. *The Reading Teacher*, 36: 192–200

Geschwind N. (1982) 'Why Orton was right'. *Annals of Dyslexia*, 32: 13–30

Geschwind N. and Levitsky W. (1968) 'Human brain: Left–right asymmetries in temporal speech region'. *Science*, 161: 186–187

Gillingham A. and Stillman B. (1956) *Remedial Training for Children with Specific Language Disability in Reading, Spelling and Penmanship* (fifth edition). Educators Publishing Service Inc., Cambridge, MA

Given B.K. and Reid G. (1999) *Learning Styles: A Guide for Teachers and Parents*. Red Rose Publications, St Annes on Sea

Head H. (1926) *Aphasia and Kindred Disorders of Speech*. Macmillan, London

Henderson E. (1981) *Learning to Read and Spell: The Child's Knowledge of Words*. Northern Illinois University Press, Dekalb, IL

Hilton C. and Hyder M. (1997) *GCSE English Spelling and Vocabulary*. Letts Educational, London

Hinshelwood J. (1917) *Congenital Word-Blindness*. H.K. Lewis, London

Hiscock M. and Kinsbourne M. (1987) 'Specialization of the cerebral hemispheres: Implications for learning'. *Journal of Learning Disabilities*, 20 (3): 130–143

Hutchins, J. (2003) Personal Communication.

Knight D.F. and Hynd G.W. (2002) 'The neurobiology of dyslexia'. In Reid G. and Wearmouth J. (eds) *Dyslexia and Literacy: Theory and Practice*. John Wiley & Sons, Chichester.

Larsen J.P., Høien T., Lundberg I. and Odegaard H. (1990) 'MRI evaluation of the size and symmetry of the planum temporale in adolescents with developmental dyslexia'. *Brain and Language*, 39: 289–301

Lundberg I., Frost J. and Petersen O.-P. (1968). 'Effects of an extensive program for stimulating phonological awareness in pre-school children'. *Reading Research Quarterly*, 23: 263–284

Miles E. and Miles T.R. (1994) 'The interface between research and remediation'. In Brown G.D.A. and Ellis N.C. (eds) *Handbook of Spelling: Theory, Process and Intervention*. John Wiley & Sons, Chichester

Moats L.C. (1995) *Spelling: Development, Disability and Instruction*. York Press, Baltimore, MD

Nicolson R.I. and Fawcett A.J. (1990) 'Automaticity: A new framework for dyslexia research'. *Cognition*, 35: 159–182

O'Connor J. and Seymour J. (1990) *Introducing Neuro-Linguistic Programming*. Thorsons, London

Orton J.L. (1966) 'The Orton–Gillingham approach'. In Money J. (ed.) *The Disabled Reader: Education of the Dyslexic Child*. Johns Hopkins Press, Baltimore, MD

Orton S.T. (1931) 'Special disability in spelling'. *Bulletin of the Neurological Institute of New York*, 1: 159–192

Orton S.T. (1937) *Reading, Writing and Speech Problems in Children*. Norton, New York

Orton S.T. (1989) *Reading, Writing, and Speech Problems in Children and Selected Papers*. PRO-ED, Austin, TX

Ott P. (1997) *How to Detect and Manage Dyslexia: A Reference and Resource Manual*. Heinemann Educational Publishers, Oxford

Peer L. (2001) 'Dyslexia and its manifestation in the secondary school'. In Peer L. and Reid G. (eds) *Dyslexia: Successful Inclusion in the Secondary School*. David Fulton Publishers, London

Peters M.L. and Smith B. (1993) *Spelling in Context*. NFER-Nelson, Windsor

Read C. (1971) 'Pre-school children's knowledge of English phonology'. *Harvard Educational Review*, 41: 1–34

Rosen G.D., Sherman G.F. and Galaburda A.M. (1993) 'Dyslexia and brain pathology. Experimental animal models'. In Galaburda A.M. (ed.) *Dyslexia and Development: Neurobiological Aspects of Extra-Ordinary Brains*. Harvard University Press, Cambridge, MA

Scheerens J. (1992) *Effective Schooling: Research, Theory and Practice*. Cassell, London

Schlagal B. (2001) 'Traditional, developmental, and structured language approaches to spelling: review and recommendations'. *Annals of Dyslexia*, 51: 147–176

Schonell F.J. (1932) *Essentials in Teaching and Testing Spelling*. Macmillan and Co. Ltd, London

Shaywitz S., (2003) *Overcoming Dyslexia: A New and Complete Science-based Program for Reading Problems at any Level*. Alfred A. Knopf, New York

Shaywitz S.E., Shaywitz B.A., Pugh K.R., Fulbright R.K., Constable R.T., Mencl W.E., Shankweiler D.P., Liberman A.M., Skudlarski P., Fletcher J.M., Katz L., Marchione K.E., Lacadie C., Gatenby C. and Gore J.C. (1998) 'Functional disruption in the organization of the brain for reading in dyslexia'. *Proceedings of the National Academy of Sciences*, 95: 2636–2641

Snowling M.J. (1981) 'Phonemic deficits in developmental dyslexia'. *Psychological Review*, 43: 219–234

Snowling M.J. (1994) 'Towards a model of spelling acquisition: The development of some component skills'. In Brown G.D.A. and Ellis N.C. (eds) *Handbook of Spelling: Theory, Process and Intervention*. John Wiley & Sons, Chichester

Stanback M. (1980) 'Teching spelling to learning disabled children: Traditional and remedial approaches to spelling instructions'. In Neuman E. (ed.) *Research Review Series*, Volume 3. New York: Teachers College, Columbia University: Research Institute for the Study of Learning Disabilities

Templeton S. and Morris D. (2000) 'Spelling'. In Kamil M.L., Mosenthal P.B., Pearson P.D. and Barr R. (eds) *Handbook of Reading Research*, 3: 525–543. Lawrence Erlbaum Associates, Mahwah, NJ

Thomson M. (2003) 'Monitoring dyslexics' intelligence and attainments: A follow-up study'. *Dyslexia: An International Journal of Research and Practice*, 9 (1): 3–17

Treiman R. (1993) *Beginning to Spell: A Study of First-Grade Children*. Oxford University Press, New York

Waites L. (1968) 'Dyslexia International World Federation of Neurology: Report of research group on developmental dyslexia and world illiteracy'. *Bulletin of the Orton Society*, 18: 21–22

Wolf M. and O'Brien B. (2001) 'On issues of time, fluency, and intervention'. In Fawcett A. (ed.) *Dyslexia Theory and Good Practice*. Whurr Publishers, London

Wylie R.E. and Durrell D.D. (1970) 'Teaching vowels through phonograms'. *Elementary English*, 47: 787–791

Chapter 3

Adams M.J. (1990) *Beginning to Read: Thinking and Learning about Print*. MIT Press, Cambridge, MA

Adams M.J., Foorman B.R., Lundberg I. and Beeler T. (1997) *Phonemic Awareness in Young Children: A Classroom Curriculum*. Paul Brookes Publishing Co., Baltimore, MD

Badian N.A. (1995) 'Predicting reading ability over the long term: The changing roles of letter naming, phonological awareness and orthographic processing'. *Annals of Dyslexia*, 45: 79–96

Brooks G. (2003) *Sound Sense: The Phonics Element in the National Literacy Strategy – A Report to the Department for Education and Skills*. University of Sheffield

Burchfield R. (1981) *The Spoken Word: A BBC Guide*. BBC, London

Caithness J. (1997) 'To this day I cannot recite the alphabet'. *ISIS Bulletin*, London

Chall J.S. (1967) *Learning to Read: The Great Debate*. McGraw-Hill, New York

Denckla M.B. and Rudel R.G. (1976) 'Rapid automatised naming (RAN): Dyslexia differentiated from other disabilities'. *Neuropsychologia*, 14: 471–479

DfEE (1998) *The National Literacy Strategy. Framework for Teaching*. Department for Education and Employment, London

Ehri L.C. (1997) 'Learning to read and learning to spell are one and the same, almost'. In Perfetti C.A., Rieben L. and Fayol M. (eds) *Learning to Spell: Research, Theory and Practice Across Languages*. Lawrence Erlbaum Associates, Mahwah, NJ

Ehri L. and Wilce L. (1987) 'Does learning to spell help beginners learn to read words?' *Reading Research Quarterly*, 22: 47–65

Feitolson D. and Goldstein Z. (1986) 'Patterns of book ownership and reading in young children in Israeli school-oriented and nonschool-oriented families'. *Reading Teacher*, 39: 924–930

First Steps (1997) *First Steps, Oral Language, Reading, Writing and Spelling Developmental Continuum Book (4) and Resources Books (4)*. Rigby Heinemann, Port Melbourne, Victoria

Havelock E. (1986) *The Muse Learns to Write*. Yale University Press, New Haven and London

Hodges R.E. (1977) 'In Adam's fall: A brief history of spelling instruction in the United States'. In Robinson H.A. (ed.) *Reading and Writing Instruction in the United States: Historical Trends*. International Reading Association, Newark, DE

Holdaway D. (1979) *The Foundations of Literacy*. Ashton Scholastic, Sydney

Hoole C. (1660) *A New Discovery of the Old Art of Teaching School*. Andrew Crook, London

James A. and Draffan E.A. (2004) *The Accuracy of Electronic Spell Checkers for Learners*. www.dyslexic.com/database/articles/spellcheckeraccuracy

Landerl K., Wimmer H. and Frith U. (1997) 'The impact of orthographic consistency on dyslexia: a German–English comparison'. *Cognition*, 63: 315–334

McArthur T. (ed.) (1992) *The Oxford Companion to the English Language*. Oxford University Press, Oxford

Man J. (2000) *Alpha Beta: How our Alphabet Changed the Western World*. Headline Book Publishing, London

Mason J.M. (1980) 'When do children begin to read: An exploration of four year old children's letter and word reading competencies'. *Reading Research Quarterly*, 15: 203–227

Masonheimer P.E. (1982) *Alphabetic Identification by Spanish Speaking Three to Five Year Olds.* Unpublished manuscript. University of California, Santa Barbara, CA

Mathews M.M. (1966) *Teaching to Read, Historically Considered.* University of Chicago Press, Chicago, IL

Maxwell C. (2005) *Dictionary of Perfect Spelling* (revised ed.). Barrington Stoke Ltd, Edinburgh

Moseley D.V. (1993) 'From theory to practice: Errors and trials'. In Brown G.D.A. and Ellis N.C. (eds) *Handbook for Spelling: Theory, Process and Intervention.* John Wiley & Sons, Chichester

Moseley D. (1995) *Ace Spelling Dictionary* (second ed.). LDA, Wisbech.

National Reading Panel (2000) *Report of the National Reading Panel Teaching Children to Read: An Evidence-based Assessment of the Scientific Research Literature on Reading and its Implications for Reading Instruction: Reports of the Subgroups National Institute of Child Health and Human Development.* NIH Publications No. 00–4754. Government Printing Office, Washington, DC

OED (1989) *The Oxford English Dictionary.* Simpson J.A. and Weiner E.S.C. (eds) Oxford University Press, Oxford

Ott P. (1997) *How to Detect and Manage Dyslexia: A Reference and Resource Manual.* Heinemann Educational Publishers, Oxford

Pitman J. and St John J. (1969) *Alphabets and Reading.* Pitman, London

Read C., Yun-Fei Z., Hong-Yin N. and Bao-Qing D. (1986) 'The ability to manipulate speech sounds depends on knowing alphabetic writing'. *Cognition*, 24: 31–44

Rose J. (2006) *Independent Review of the Teaching of Early Reading.* www.standards.dfes.gov.uk/rosereview

Rowe K. (2005) *Teaching Reading: The Final Report of the National Inquiry into Teaching Literacy.* Australian Government, Canberra

Saussure F. de (1916) *Cours de Linguistique Générale.* Mauro T. de (ed.). Payot, Paris

Schott B. (2002) *Schott's Original Miscellany.* Bloomsbury Publishing plc, London

Shankweiler D. and Liberman I.Y. (1972) 'Misreading: A search for causes'. In Kavanagh J.F. and Mattingly I.G. (eds) *Language by Eye and Ear: The Relationship Between Speech and Reading.* MIT Press, Cambridge, MA

Tinker M.A. (1931) 'The influence of form or type on the perception of words'. *Journal of Applied Psychology*, 16: 167–174

Treiman R. (1993) *Beginning to Spell: A Study of First-Grade Children.* Oxford University Press, New York

Waites L. (1980) 'Sense of direction, the arrow and the alphabet'. *Annals of Dyslexia*, 30: 277–283

Whale A. (2001) Personal communication

Chapter 4

Adams M.J. (1990) *Beginning to Read: Thinking and Learning About Print.* MIT Press, Cambridge, MA

Adams M.J. (1997) 'The great debate: Then and now'. *Annals of Dyslexia*, 47: 265–276

Adams M.J., Foorman B.R., Lundberg I. and Beeler T. (1988) *Phonemic Awareness in Young Children: A Classroom Curriculum.* Paul Brookes Publishing Co. Inc., Baltimore, MD

American Psychiatric Association (1994) *Diagnostic and Statistical Manual for Mental Disorders* (fourth edition). American Psychiatric Association, Washington, DC

Anderson R.C. (1994) 'Afterword' in Adams M.J. *Beginning to Read: Thinking and Learning About Print.* MIT Press, Cambridge, MA

Audit Commission (2002) *Statutory Assessment and Statements of SEN: In Need of Review.* Audit Commission, London

Ball E.W. and Blachman B.A. (1991) 'Does phoneme awareness training in kindergarten make a difference in early word recognition and developmental spelling?' *Reading Research Quarterly*, 26 (1): 49–66

Balmuth M. (1992) *The Roots of Phonics* (2nd ed.). York Press, Baltimore, MD

Barber M. (1999) 'Foreword' to *The National Literacy Strategy: Additional Literacy Support.* DfEE, London

Barry C. (1994) 'Spelling routes (or roots or rules)'. In Brown G.D.A. and Ellis N.C. *Handbook of Spelling: Theory, Process and Intervention.* John Wiley & Sons, Chichester

Beard R. (1998) *National Literacy Strategy: Review of Research and Other Related Evidence.* DfEE Publications, Sudbury

Becker W., Dixon R. and Anderson-Inman L. (1980) *Morphographic and Root Word Analysis of 26,000 High Frequency Words.* University of Oregon, College of Education, Eugene, OR

Bevan F.L. (1857) *Reading Without Tears.* Hatchards, London

Blachman B.A. (1997) 'Early intervention and phonological awareness: A cautionary tale'. In Blachman B.A. (ed.) *Foundations of Reading Acquisition and Dyslexia: Implications for Early Intervention.* Lawrence Erlbaum Associates, Mahwah, NJ

Bond G.L. and Dykstra R. (1967) 'The cooperative research program in first-grade reading instruction'. *Reading Research Quarterly*, 2: 5–142

Bos M. and Reitsma P. (2003) 'Teachers' expectations about the potential effectiveness of spelling exercises'. *Annals of Dyslexia*, 53: 104–127

Bramley W. (1995) *Units of Sounds, Stages 1, 2, 3.* Dyslexia Institute, Staines.

Brooks G., Pugh A.K. and Schagen I. (1996) *Reading Performance at Nine*. National Foundation for Educational Research, Slough

Brooks P. and Weeks S. (1998) *Individual Styles in Learning to Spell: Improving Spelling in Children with Literacy Difficulties and All Children in Maintained Schools*. Research Report No. 754, Department of Education and Employment. HMSO, Norwich

Carnine D.W. (1976) 'Similar sound separation and cumulative introduction in learning letter–sound correspondence'. *Journal of Educational Research*, 69: 368–372

Chall J.S. (1967) *Learning to Read: The Great Debate*. McGraw-Hill, New York

Chall J.S. (1997) 'Are reading methods changing again?' *Annals of Dyslexia*, 47: 257–263

Chall J.S. and Popp H.M. (1996) *Teaching and Assessing Phonics. Why, What, When, How: A Guide for Teachers*. Educators Publishing Service Inc., Cambridge, MA

Chambers (1999) *Chambers Twenty-first Century Dictionary*. Chambers Harrap Publishers Ltd, Edinburgh

Cox A.R. (1980) *Structures and Techniques: Multisensory Teaching of Basic Language Skills*. Educators Publishing Service, Inc. Cambridge, MA

Cox A.R. and Hutcheson L. (1988) 'Syllable division: A prerequisite to dyslexics' literacy'. *Annals of Dyslexia*, 38: 226–242

Cox C.B. and Dyson A.E. (1969) *Fight for Education*. The Critical Quarterly Society, London

Cunningham A.E., Perry K.E., Stanovich K.E. and Stanovich P.J. (2004) 'Disciplinary knowledge of K-3 teachers and their knowledge calibration in the domain of early literacy'. *Annals of Dyslexia*, 54: 139–167

Dale N. (1900–1902) *The Dale Readers*. Philip, London

Daniels J.C. and Diack H. (1954) *Learning to Read*. The News Chronicle, London

Daniels J.C. and Diack H. (1960) *The Royal Road Readers*. Chatto and Windus, London

DeFries J.C. (1991) 'Genetics and dyslexia: An overview'. In Snowling M.J. and Thomson M. (eds) *Dyslexia: Integrating Theory and Practice*. Whurr Publishers, London

DfEE (1995) *English in the National Curriculum*. Department for Education and Employment, London

DfEE (1998) *The National Literacy Strategy: Framework for Teaching*. DfEE Publications, London

DfEE (1999) *The National Literacy Strategy Additional Literacy Support Module 4*. Department for Education and Employment, London

DfEE (2001a) *The National Literacy Strategy: Phonics. Progression in Phonics: Material for Whole-class Teaching*. Department for Education and Employment, London

DfEE (2001b) *Key Stage 3 National Strategy: Literacy Progress Unit, Phonics*. Department for Education and Employment, London

DfES (2001) *The National Literacy Strategy Phonics (with CD-ROM): Progression in Phonics*. Department for Education and Skills, London

DfES (2003) *DfES Response to the March 2003 Phonics Seminar and Professor Greg Brooks' Report*. www.dfes.gov.uk

Denckla M.B. and Rudel R.G. (1976) 'Rapid "automatized" naming (RAN): Dyslexia differentiated from other learning disabilities'. *Neuropsychologia*, 14: 471–479

Ehri L.C. (1980) 'The development of orthographic images'. In Frith U. (ed.) *Cognitive Processes in Spelling*. Academic Press, London

Ehri L.C. (1997) 'Learning to read and learning to spell are one and the same, almost'. In Perfetti C.A., Rieben L. and Fayol M. (eds) *Learning to Spell: Research, Theory and Practice Across Languages*. Laurence Erlbaum Associates, Mahwah, NJ

Ehri L.C., Wilce L.S. and Taylor B.B. (1987) 'Children's categorization of short vowels in words and the influence of spelling'. *Merrill-Palmer Quarterly*, 33 (3): 393–421

Elkonin D.B. (1973) 'USSR'. In Downing J. (ed.) *Comparative Reading*, 551–580. Macmillan, New York

Ernst and Young (1993) *Literacy, Education and Training: Their Impact on the UK Economy*. Ernst and Young, London

Fassett J.H. (1922) *The Beacon Readers*. Ginn, London

Fernald G.M. (1943) *Remedial Techniques in Basic School Subjects*. McGraw-Hill, New York

Flesch R. (1955) *Why Johnny Can't Read. And What You Can Do About It*. Harper Row, New York

Frith U. (1997) 'Brain, mind and behaviour in dyslexia'. In Hulme C. and Snowling M (eds) *Dyslexia: Biology, Cognition and Intervention*. Whurr Publishers, London

Frith U. (2002) 'Culture, the brain and dyslexia'. In Hjelmquist E. and Euler C. von (eds) *Dyslexia and Literacy*. Whurr Publishers, London

Fromkin V. and Rodman R. (1993) *An Introduction to Language*. Harcourt Brace Janovitch, Fort Worth, TX

Fry E. (1994) *Phonics Pattern: Onset and Rhyme Word Lists*. Laguna Beach Educational Books, Laguna Beach, CA

Gillingham A. and Stillman B.W. (1956) *Remedial Training for Children with Specific Disability in Reading, Spelling and Penmanship* (fifth edition). Educators Publishing Service Inc., Cambridge, MA

Goodman K.S. (1986) *What's Whole in Whole Language: A Parent–Teacher Guide*. Heinemann, Portsmouth, NH

Goswami U. (2002) 'Phonology, reading, development, and dyslexia: A cross-linguistic perspective'. *Annals of Dyslexia*, 52: 141–163

Hanna P.R., Hanna R.E., Hodges R.E. and Rudorf E.H. (1966) *Phoneme–grapheme Correspondences as Cues to Spelling Improvement*. US Office of Education, Government Printing Office, Washington, DC

Henderson E. (1985) *Teaching Spelling*. Houghton Mifflin Company, Boston, MA

Hickey K. (1992) *Dyslexia: A Language Training Course for Teachers and Learners*. Dyslexia Institute, Staines

Hinshelwood J. (1917) *Congenital Word-Blindness*. H.K. Lewis, London

Horner P. (1986) 'The development of reading books in England from 1870'. In Brooks G. and Pugh A.K. (eds) *Studies in the History of Reading*. National Foundation for Education Research, Slough

Hornsby B. and Shear F. (1993) *Alpha to Omega* (fourth ed.). Heinemann Educational, Oxford

House of Commons (2004) *Transcript of Oral Evidence. Teaching Children to Read*. House of Commons Education and Skills Committee. www.publications.parliament.uk

House of Commons (2005) *Teaching Children to Read*. House of Commons Education and Skills Committee. The Stationery Office, London

Johnston R. and Watson J. (2005). *The Effects of Synthetic Phonics Teaching on Reading and Spelling Attainment. A Seven Year Longitudinal Study*. The Scottish Executive Central Research Unit, Edinburgh

Kingman Report (1988) *Report of the Committee of Inquiry into the Teaching of English Language*. DES, London

Kreiner D. and Gough P. (1990) 'Two ideas about spelling: Rules and word-specific memory'. *Journal of Memory and Language*, 29: 103–118

Labour Party (1997) *New Labour: Because Britain Deserves Better*. Election Manifesto, Labour Party, London

Lerner J. (2000) *Learning Disabilities: Theories, Diagnosis and Teaching Strategies*. Houghton Mifflin Company, Boston, MA

Liberman I.Y. and Liberman A.M. (1990) 'Whole language vs Code emphasis: Underlying assumptions and their implications for reading instruction'. *Annals of Dyslexia*, 40: 51–76

Liberman I. and Shankweiler D. (1985) 'Phonology and the problems of learning to read and write'. *Remedial and Special Education*, 6: 8–17

Lundberg I., Frost J. and Petersen O.-P. (1988) 'Effects of an extensive program for stimulating phonological awareness in preschool children'. *Reading Research Quarterly*, 23 (3): 263–284

McCutchen D., Harry D.R., Cunningham A.E., Cox S., Sidman S. and Covill A.E. (2002) 'Reading teachers' knowledge of children's literature and English phonology'. *Annals of Dyslexia*, 52: 207–228

Man J. (2000) *Alpha Beta: How our Alphabet Changed the Western World*. Headline Book Publishing, London

Miles T.R., Wheeler T.J. and Haslum M.N. (2003) 'The existence of dyslexia without severe literacy problems'. *Annals of Dyslexia*, 53: 340–354

Moats L.C. (1994) 'The missing foundation in teaching education, knowledge of the structure of spoken and written language'. *Annals of Dyslexia*, 44: 81–102

Moats L.C. and Foorman B.R. (2003) 'Measuring teachers' content knowledge of language and reading'. *Annals of Dyslexia*, 53: 23–45

Morais J., Cary L., Alegria J. and Bertelson P. (1979) 'Does awareness of speech as a sequence of phones arise spontaneously?' *Cognition*, 7: 323–331

Morris E. (2001) 'Preface' to *Special Educational Needs Code of Practice*. DfES, London

Morris J. (1959) *Reading in the Primary School: An Investigation into Standards of Reading and their Association with Primary School Characteristics* (National Foundation for Educational Research in England and Scotland). Newnes Educational Publishing Company Ltd, London

Morris J. M. (1986) 'Phonics: From an unsophisticated past to a linguistics-informed future'. In Brooks G. and Pugh A.K. (eds) *Studies in the History of Reading*. National Foundation for Educational Research, Slough

National Curriculum (1988) (1995) The Department for Education and Employment. HMSO, London

National Institute of Child Health Development (2000) *Report of the National Reading Panel Teaching Children to Read: An Evidence-based Assessment of the Scientific Research Literature on Reading and its Implications for Reading Instruction: Reports of the Subgroups* (NIH Publication No. 00–4754). US Government Printing Office, Washington, DC

National Literacy Strategy (1998) *Framework for Teaching*. Department for Education and Employment, London

Nicholson T. (1997) 'Closing the gap on reading failure: Social background, phonemic awareness and learning to read'. In Blachman B.A. (ed.) *Foundations of Reading Acquisition and Dyslexia*. Lawrence Erlbaum Associates, Publishers, Mahwah, NJ

Nicolson R.I. and Fawcett A.J. (2000) 'Long-term learning in dyslexic children'. *European Journal of Cognitive Psychology*, 12: 357–393

Nicolson R.J. (2001) 'Introduction developmental dyslexia: Into the future'. In Fawcett A. (ed.) *Dyslexia Theory and Good Practice*. Whurr Publishers, London

Nolan P.A., McCutchen D. and Berninger V. (1990) 'Ensuring tomorrow's literacy: A shared responsibility'. *Journal of Teacher Education*, 41: 63–72

O'Donnell M. and Munroe R. (1949) *The Janet and John Series*. Nisbet, London

Office for Standards in Education (Ofsted) (1998) *The Annual Report of Her Majesty's Chief Inspector of*

Schools: Standards and Quality in Education 1996/97. HMSO, London

Office for Standards in Education (Ofsted) (1999) *The National Literacy Strategy: An Evaluation of the First Year.* Ofsted, HMSO, London

Office for Standards in Education (Ofsted) (2003) *Teaching of Phonics: A Paper by HMI.* www.ofsted. gov.uk

Office for Standards in Education (Ofsted) (2004) *Reading for Purpose and Pleasure: An Evaluation of the Teaching of Reading in Primary Schools.* Ofsted, HMSO, London

OISEUT (2003) *Watching and Learning 3. Final Report of the External Evaluation of England's National Literacy and Numeracy Strategies.* Ontario Institute for Studies in Education, University of Toronto. Department for Education and Skills. DfES, Nottingham

Organisation for Economic Co-operation and Development and Human Resources Development, Canada (1997) *Literacy Skills for the Knowledge Society: Further Results from the International Adult Literacy Survey.* OECD, Paris

Organisation for Economic Co-operation and Development (OECD) (2000) *Measuring Students' Knowledge and Skills: The PISA 2000 Assessment of Reading, Mathematical and Scientific Literacy.* OECD, Paris

Orton Dyslexia Society (1986) 'Some facts about illiteracy in America'. *Perspectives on Dyslexia*, 13 (4): 1–13

Orton S.T. (1931) 'Special disability in spelling'. *Bulletin of the Neurological Institute of New York*, 1 (2): 159–192

Ott P. (1997) *How to Detect and Manage Dyslexia: A Reference and Resource Manual.* Heinemann Educational Publishers, Oxford

Ott P. (2007) *Activities for Successful Spelling.* Routledge, London

Pennington B.F., McCabe L.L., Smith S.D., Lefly D.L., Brookman M.O., Kimberling W.J. and Lubs H.A. (1986) 'Spelling errors in adults with a form of familial dyslexia'. *Child Development*, 57: 1001–1013

Rawson M.B. (1970) 'The structure of English: The language to be learned'. *Bulletin of the Orton Dyslexia Society*, 20: 118

Rose J. (2006) *Independent Review of the Teaching of Early Reading.* www.standards.dfes.gov.uk/rose review

Royal Mail (2003) 'Typos cost UK business over £700 million a year'. Consumer and Small Business. Press Release, Royal Mail, London

Salter R. and Smythe I. (1997) (eds) *The International Book of Dyslexia.* World Dyslexia Network Foundation and European Dyslexia Association, England

Schlagal R.C. (1992) 'Patterns of orthographic development in the middle grades'. In Templeton

S. and Bear D. (eds) *Development of Orthographic Knowledge and the Foundations of Literacy.* Lawrence Erlbaum, Hillsdale, NJ

Schonell F.J. and Serjeant I. (1939) *The Happy Venture Readers.* Oliver and Boyd, Edinburgh

Slavin R.E. (1997) 'Success for All: Implications for British Education'. Paper presented at the Literacy Task Force Conference, London

Smith F. (1978) *Understanding Reading: A Psycholinguistic Analysis of Reading and Learning to Read* (second ed.). Holt, Rinehart and Winston, New York

Stannard J. (1999) 'The phonics war is phoney'. Letters to *Times Educational Supplement.* 5 March

Stannard J. (2003) 'And then there were phonics'. *Times Educational Supplement.* 21 February

Stedman L.C. and Kaestle C.E. (1987) 'Literacy and reading performance in the United States from 1880 to the present'. *Reading Research Quarterly*, 22: 8–46

Stein M.M. (1993) *The Beginning Reading Instruction Study.* U.S. Government Printing Office, Washington DC

TES (2001a) 'Postcode lottery: Statemented pupil numbers reach record levels'. *Times Educational Supplement.* 2 November

TES (2001b) 'Unsound logic of phonics fans'. Letters to *Times Educational Supplement.* 16 November

TES (2002) 'Red tape consumes special needs millions. The Audit Commission says vulnerable children are losing out because of poor statementing'. *Times Educational Supplement.* 31 May

TES (2006) 'Boys falter at English and fail to narrow gap'. *Times Educational Supplement.* 15 September

Torgerson C.J., Brooks G. and Hall J. (2006) *A Systematic Review of the Use of Phonics in the Teaching of Reading and Spelling.* Research Report RR 711. DfES, London

Turner M. (1997) *Psychological Assessment of Dyslexia.* Whurr Publishers, London

Wimmer H. and Mayringer H. (2002) 'The reading rate deficit of German dyslexic children and surface dyslexia'. In Hjelmquist E. and Euler C. von (eds) *Dyslexia and Literacy.* Whurr Publishers, London

Wolf M. (1991) 'Naming speed and reading: The contribution of the cognitive neurosciences'. *Reading Research Quarterly*, 26: 123–141

Wylie R. and Durrell D. (1970) 'Teaching vowels through phonograms'. *Elementary English*, 47: 787–791

Chapter 5

Adams M.J., Foorman B.R., Lundberg I. and Beeler T. (1998) *Phonemic Awareness in Young Children: A Classroom Curriculum.* Paul Brookes Publishing Co., Baltimore, MD

Badian N.A. (1997) 'Dyslexia and the double deficit hypothesis'. *Annals of Dyslexia*, 47: 69–87

Badian N.A. (2001) 'Phonological and orthographic processing: Their roles in reading prediction'. *Annals of Dyslexia*, 51: 179–202

Ball E.W. and Blachman B.A. (1988) 'Phoneme segmentation training: Effect on reading readiness'. *Annals of Dyslexia*, 38: 208–225

Ball E.W. and Blachman B.A. (1991) 'Does phoneme awareness training in kindergarten make a difference in early word recognition and developmental spelling?' *Reading Research Quarterly*, 26 (1): 49–66

Bloomfield L. (1933) *Language*. Holt, Rinehart and Winston, New York

Bloomfield L. Barnhart C.L. and Barnhart R.K. (1964) *Let's Read*. Educators Publishing Service Inc., Cambridge, MA

Borstrøm I. and Elbro C. (1997) 'Prevention of dyslexia in kindergarten: Effects of phoneme awareness training with children of dyslexic parents'. In Hulme C. and Snowling M. (eds) *Dyslexia: Biology, Cognition and Intervention*. Whurr Publishers, London

Bowers P.G. and Wolf M. (1993) 'Theoretical links among naming speed, precise timing mechanisms and orthographic skill in dyslexia'. *Reading and Writing: An Interdisciplinary Journal*, 5: 69–85

Bowey J.A. and Francis J. (1991) 'Phonological analysis as a function of age and exposure to reading instruction'. *Applied Psycholinguistics*, 12: 91–121

Bradley L.L. (1987) 'Categorising sounds, early intervention and learning to read: a follow-up study'. Paper presented at the British Psychological Society London Conference, December

Bradley L.L. (1988) 'Making connections in learning to read and spell'. *Applied Cognitive Psychology*, 2: 3–18

Bradley L.L. (1989) 'Predicting learning difficulties'. In Dumont J.J. and Nakken H. (eds) *Learning Disabilities, Vol. 2: Cognitive, Social and Remedial Aspects*. Swets, Amsterdam

Bradley L.L. and Bryant P.E. (1983) 'Categorising sounds and learning to read: A causal connection'. *Nature*, 301: 419–421

Bradley L.L. and Bryant P.E. (1991) 'Phonological skills before and after learning to read'. In Brady S. and Shankweiler D. (eds) *Phonological Processes in Literacy*. LEA, London

Bradley L. and Huxford L. (1994) 'Organising sound and letter patterns for spelling'. In Brown G.D.A. and Ellis N.C. (eds) *Handbook of Spelling: Theory, Process and Intervention*. John Wiley & Sons, Chichester

Brady S. (1986) 'Short-term memory, phonological processing, and reading ability'. *Annals of Dyslexia*, 36: 138–153

Bruce D.J. (1964) 'The analysis of word sounds'. *British Journal of Educational Psychology*, 34: 158–170

Bryant P.E. and Bradley L.L. (1985) *Children's Reading Problems*. Blackwell, Oxford

Bus A.C. and van IJzendoorn M.H. (1999) 'Phonological awareness and early reading: A meta-analysis of experimental training studies'. *Journal of Educational Psychology*, 91 (3): 403–414

Catts H.W. (1989) 'Defining dyslexia as a developmental language disorder'. *Annals of Dyslexia*, 39: 50–64

Catts H.W. (1991) 'Early identification of dyslexia: Evidence from a follow-up study of speech-language impaired children'. *Annals of Dyslexia*, 41: 163–177

Chambers (2004) *Chambers Primary Rhyming Dictionary* Harrap Publishers Ltd, Edinburgh

Cherry C. (1971) *Creative Movement for the Developing Child*. Fearon Publishers, Belmont, CA

Chomsky N. (1986) *Knowledge of Language: Its Nature, Origin and Use*. Praeger, New York

Denckla M.B. and Rudel R.G. (1974) 'Rapid automatized naming of pictured objects, colours, letters and numbers by normal children'. *Brain and Language*, 3: 1–15

Denckla M.B. and Rudel R.G. (1976) 'Rapid automatized names (RAN): Dyslexia differentiated from other learning disabilities'. *Neuropsychologia*, 14: 471–479

DfEE 1998) *The National Literacy Strategy: Framework for Teaching*. Department for Education and Employment, London

Elbro C., Borstrom I. and Paterson D.K. (1998) 'Predicting dyslexia from kindergarten: The importance of distinctiveness of phonological representations of lexical items'. *Reading Research Quarterly*, 33: 36–60

Elkonin D. (1963) 'The psychology of mastering elements of reading'. In Simon B. and Simon J. (eds) *Educational Psychology in the USSR*. Routledge and Kegan Paul, London

Elkonin D. B. (1973) 'U.S.S.R.'. In Downing J. (ed.) *Comparative Reading: Cross National Studies of Behaviour and Processes in Reading and Writing*. Macmillan, London

Evans J.W. (2001) *Dyslexia and Vision*. Whurr Publishers, London

Frederickson N., Frith U. and Reason R. (1997) *Phonological Assessment Battery (PhAB)*. NFER-Nelson, London

Frith U. (1997) 'Brain, mind and behaviour in dyslexia'. In Hulme C. and Snowling M. (eds) *Dyslexia: Biology, Cognition and Intervention*. Whurr Publishers, London

Gathercole S.E. and Baddeley A.D. (1989) 'Evaluation of the role of phonological SIM in the development of vocabulary in children: A longitudinal study'. *Journal of Memory and Language*, 28: 22–213

Gathercole S.E., Willis C.S., Baddeley A.D. and Emslie H. (1994) 'The children's test of nonword repetition: A test of phonological working memory'. *Memory*, 2: 103–127

Geschwind N. (1965) 'Disconnection syndromes in animals and man'. *Brain*, 88: 237–294

Goswami U. (1994) 'Reading by analogy: Theoretical and practical perspectives'. In Hulme C. and Snowling M. (eds) *Reading Development and Dyslexia*. Whurr Publishers, London

Goulandris N. and Snowling M. (1991) 'Visual memory deficits: A plausible cause of developmental dyslexia? Evidence from a single case study'. *Cognitive Neuropsychology*, 8: 127–154

Hatcher P.J. (1994) *Sound Linkage: An Integrated Programme for Overcoming Reading Difficulties*. Whurr Publishers, London

Hatcher P.J., Hulme C. and Ellis A.W. (1994) 'Ameliorating early reading failure by integrating the teaching of reading and phonological linkage hypothesis'. *Child Development*, 65: 41–57

Johnston R. and Watson J. (2005) *The Effects of Synthetic Phonics Teaching on Reading and Spelling Attainment: A Seven Year Longitudinal Study*. The Scottish Executive Central Research Unit, Edinburgh

Katz R.B. (1996) 'Phonological and Semantic factors in the object-naming errors of skilled and less-skilled readers'. *Annals of Dyslexia*, 46: 189–208

Liberman I. (1973) 'Segmentation of the spoken word and reading acquisition'. *Bulletin of the Orton Society*, 23: 65–77

Liberman I.Y. and Liberman A.M. (1990) 'Whole language vs. code emphasis; underlying assumptions and their implications for reading instruction'. *Annals of Dyslexia*, 40: 51–76

Liberman I.Y., Shankweiler D., Fischer F.W. and Carter B. (1974) 'Explicit syllable and phoneme segmentation in the young child'. *Journal of Experimental Child Psychology*, 18: 201–212

Liberman I.Y. and Shankweiler D. (1985) 'Phonology and problems of learning to read and write'. *Remedial and Special Education*, 6: 8–17

Lie A. (1991) 'Effects of a training programme for stimulating skills in word analysis in first grade children'. *Reading Research Quarterly*, 26: 234–250

Lundberg I. (1994) 'Reading difficulties can be predicted and prevented. A Scandinavian perspective on phonological awareness and reading'. In Hulme C. and Snowling M. (ed.) *Reading Development and Dyslexia*. Whurr Publishers, London

Lundberg I. (2002) 'Twenty-five years of reading research as a basis for prediction of future development'. In Hjelmquist E. and Euler C. von (eds) *Dyslexia and Literacy*. Whurr Publishers, London

Lundberg I., Frost J. and Petersen O.-P. (1988) 'Effects of an extensive program for stimulating phonological awareness in preschool children'. *Reading Research Quarterly*, 23: 263–284

McArthur T. (ed.) (1992) *The Oxford Companion to the English Language*. Oxford University Press, Oxford

Maclean L., Bryant P. and Bradley L. (1987) 'Rhymes, nursery rhymes, and reading in early childhood'. *Merrill-Palmer Quarterly*, 33: 255–281

Mann V. (1991) 'Language problems: A key to early reading problems'. In B. Wong (ed.) *Learning about Learning Disabilities*. Academic Press, San Diego, CA

Mann V.A. and Liberman I.Y. (1984) 'Phonological awareness and future reading ability'. *Journal of Learning Disabilities*, 26: 129–157

Moats L.C. (1994) 'The missing foundation in teacher education: knowledge of the structure of spoken and written language'. *Annals of Dyslexia*, 44: 81–102

Molfese D.L., Molfese V.J., Key S., Modglin A., Kelley S. and Terrell S. (2002) 'Reading and cognitive abilities: Longitudinal studies of brain and behaviour changes in young children'. *Annals of Dyslexia*, 52: 99–119

Muter V., Hulme C. and Snowling M. (1997) *Phonological Abilities Test (PAT)*. Harcourt Assessment, Oxford

Olson D.R. (2002) 'Literacy in the past millennium'. In Hjelmquist E. and Euler C. von (eds) *Dyslexia and Literacy*. Whurr Publishers, London

Ott P. (1997) *How to Detect and Manage Dyslexia: A Reference and Resource Manual*. Heinemann Educational, Oxford

Palmer S. and Morgan M. (1998) *Tune into Sounds and The Big abc Book, Teachers' Book*. Ginn and Company, Oxford

Paulesu E., Frith U., Snowling M., Gallagher A., Morton J., Frackowiak R.S.J. and Frith C.D. (1996) 'Is developmental dyslexia a disconnection syndrome? Evidence from PET scanning'. *Brain*, 119: 143–157

QCA (2005) *Key Stage 2 Assessment and Reporting Arrangements. Qualifications and Curriculum Authority*. HMSO, London

Rack J.P., Snowling M.J. and Olsen R.K. (1992) 'The nonword reading deficit in developmental dyslexia: A review'. *Reading Research Quarterly*, 27: 29–53

Rose J. (2006) *Independent Review of the Teaching of Early Reading*. www.standards.dfes.gov. uk/rose review

Rosen M. (1991) *The Kingfisher Book of Children's Poetry*. Kingfisher Publications plc, London

Rosner J. (1999) *Helping Children Overcome Learning Difficulties*. Walker and Co., New York

Scarborough H.S. (1990) 'Very early language deficits in dyslexic children'. *Child Development*, 61: 1728–1743

Snowling M.J. (1981) 'Phonemic deficits in developmental dyslexia'. *Psychological Review*, 43: 219–235

Snowling M.J., Gallagher A. and Frith U. (2003) 'Family risk of dyslexia is continuous: Individual differences in the precursors of reading skill'. *Child Development*, 74 (2): 358–373.

Snowling M.J., Stothard S.E. and Maclean J. (1986) *Graded Non-word Reading Test*. Thames Valley Test Co., Bury St Edmunds

Stanovich K.E. (1992) 'Speculations on the causes and consequences of individual differences in early reading acquisition'. In Gough P.B., Ehri L.C. and Treiman R. (eds) *Reading Acquisition*. Lawrence Erlbaum, Hillsdale, NJ

TES (2004) 'Quote of the week: "Teaching spelling is about repetition, repetition, repetition".' *Times Educational Supplement*. 23 January

Thomson M. (2001) *The Psychology of Dyslexia: A Handbook for Teachers*. Whurr Publishers, London

Torgesen J.K. (2001) 'The theory and practice of intervention: Comparing outcomes from prevention and remediation studies'. In Fawcett, A (ed.) *Dyslexia Theory and Good Practice*. Whurr Publishers, London

Torgesen J.K., Rashotte C.A., Burgess S. and Hecht S. (1997) 'Contributions of phonological awareness and rapid naming ability to the growth of word-reading skills in second-to-fifth grade children'. *Scientific Studies of Reading* 1: 161–185

Torgesen J.K., Wagner R.K. and Rashotte C.A. (1994) 'Longitudinal studies of phonological processing and reading'. *Journal of Learning Disabilities*, 27: 276–286

Troia G.A. (1999) 'Phonological awareness intervention research: A critical review of the experimental methodology'. *Reading Research Quarterly*, 34: 28–52

Vellutino F.R. (1979) *Dyslexia: Theory and Research*. MIT Press, Cambridge, MA

Vellutino F.R. and Scanlon D. (1987) 'Phonological coding and phonological awareness'. *Merrill-Palmer Quarterly*, 33 (3): 321–363

Wagner R.K., Torgesen J.K. and Rashotte C.A. (1999) *Comprehensive Test of Phonological Processing (CTOPP)*. Harcourt Assessment, Oxford

Wolf M. (1997) 'A provisional, integrative account of phonological and naming-speed deficits in dyslexia: Implications for diagnosis and intervention'. In Blachman B.A. (ed.) *Foundations of Reading Acquisition and Dyslexia: Implications for Early Intervention*. Lawrence Erlbaum Associates, Publishers, Mahwah, NJ.

Wolf M., Bowers P. and Biddle K.R. (2000) 'Naming-speed processes, timing and reading: A conceptual review'. *Journal of Learning Disabilities*, 33: 387–407

Chapter 6

Bartlett D. and Moody S. (2000) *Dyslexia in the Workplace*. Whurr Publishers, London

Beard R. (1998) *National Literacy Strategy: Review of Research and other Related Evidence*. DfEE Publications, Sudbury

Bradley L.L. and Bryant P.E. (1983) 'Categorizing sounds and learning to read: A causal connection'. *Nature*, 301: 419–421

Brooks P. and Weeks S. (1998) *Individual Styles in Learning to Spell: Improving Spelling in Children with Literacy Difficulties and All Children in Maintained Schools*. Research Report No. 754. Department of Education and Employment, HMSO, Norwich

Brown G.D.A. and Ellis N.C. (eds) (1994) *Handbook of Spelling: Theory, Process and Intervention*. John Wiley & Sons, Chichester

Bryant P.E. and Bradley L.L. (1985) *Children's Reading Problems*. Blackwell, Oxford

Caravolas M., Bruck M. and Genesee F. (2003) 'Similarities and differences between English- and French-speaking poor spellers'. In Goulandris N. (ed.) *Dyslexia in Different Languages: Cross-linguistic Comparisons*. Whurr Publishers, London

Coffield F. (2004) *Learning Styles and Pedagogy in Post-16 Learning: A Systematic and Critical Review*. www.LSRC.ac.uk

DfEE (2001) *Key Stage 3 National Strategy. Framework for Teaching English: Years 7, 8 and 9*. Department for Education and Employment, London

Ehri L.A. (1991) 'The development of reading and spelling in children: an overview'. In Snowling M. and Thomson M. (eds) *Dyslexia: Integrating Theory and Practice*. Whurr Publishers, London

Ehri L.C. (1997) 'Learning to read and learning to spell are one and the same, almost'. In Perfetti C.A., Rieben L. and Fayol M. (eds) *Learning to Spell: Research, Theory and Practice Across Languages*. Lawrence Erlbaum Associates, Mahwah, NJ

Gentry J.R. (1982) 'An analysis of developmental spelling in GNYS AT WRK'. *The Reading Teacher*, 36: 192–200

Geschwind N. (1982) 'Why Orton was right'. *Annals of Dyslexia*, 32: 13–30

Gillingham A. and Stillman B. (1956) *Remedial Training for Children with Specific Language Disability in Reading, Spelling and Penmanship* (fifth edition). Educators Publishing Service, Cambridge, MA

Green D. (2003) 'Education targets fall short of the mark'. *The Times*. 29 January

Gross R. (1996) *Psychology: The Science of Mind and Behaviour*. Hodder & Stoughton, London

Henderson E. (1985) *Teaching Spelling*. Houghton Mifflin Company, Boston, MA

Joshi R.M., Dahlgren M. and Boulware-Gooden R. (2002) 'Teaching reading in an inner city school through a multi-sensory teaching approach'. *Annals of Dyslexia*, 52: 229–242

Landerl K., Wimmer H. and Frith U. (1997) 'The impact of orthographic consistency on dyslexia: a German–English comparison'. *Cognition*, 63: 315–334

Lennox C. and Siegel L.S. (1994) 'The role of phonological and orthographic processes in learning to spell'. In Brown G.D.A. and Ellis N.C.

(eds) *Handbook of Spelling: Theory, Process and Intervention*. John Wiley & Sons, Chichester

Lerner J.W. (2000) *Learning Disabilities: Theories, Diagnosis and Teaching Strategies*. Houghton Mifflin Company, New York

Levine M. (1994) *Educational Care: A System for Understanding and Helping Children with Learning Problems at Home and in School*. Educators Publishing, Cambridge, MA

Lie A. (1991) 'Effects of a training program for stimulating skills in word analysis in first grade children'. *Reading Research Quarterly*, 26: 234–250

Lingren S., De Renzi E. and Richman L. (1985) 'Cross-national comparisons of developmental dyslexia in Italy and the United States'. *Child Development*, 56: 1404–1417

Lundberg I, Frost J. and Petersen O.-P. (1988) 'Effects of an extensive program for stimulating phonological awareness in preschool children'. *Reading Research Quarterly*, 23: 263–284

Lyon G.R. (1995) 'Research initiatives in learning disabilities: Contributions from scientists supported by the National Institute of Child Health and Human Development'. *Journal of Child Neurology*, 10 (Suppl. 1): S120–S126

McCutchen D., Harry D., Cunningham A.E., Cox S., Sidman S. and Covill A.E. (2002) 'Reading teachers' knowledge of children's literature and English phonology'. *Annals of Dyslexia*, 52: 207–228

Moats L.C. (1994) 'The missing foundation in teacher education: Knowledge of the structure of spoken and written language'. *Annals of Dyslexia*, 44: 81–102

Moats L.C. (1995) *Spelling: Development Disabilities, and Instruction*. York Press, Baltimore, MD

Morris D., Blanton L., Blanton W.E. and Perney J. (1995b) 'Spelling instruction and achievement in six classrooms'. *Elementary School Journal*, 92: 145–162

Morris D., Blanton L., Nowacek J. and Perney J. (1995a) 'Teaching low-achieving spellers at their "instructional level"'. *Elementary School Journal*, 96: 163–177

Morris D., Nelson L. and Perney J. (1986) 'Exploring the concept of "spelling instructional level" through the analysis of error-types'. *Elementary School Journal*, 87: 181–200

National Assessment of Education Progress (2000) *The Nation's Report Card*. National centre for Educational Statistics. Washington, DC

National Working Party on Dyslexia in Higher Education (1999) *Dyslexia in Higher Education: Policy, Provision and Practice*. University of Hull, Hull

NLS (2001) *Key Stage 3 National Strategy. Literacy Progress Unit: Spelling*. Department for Education and Employment, London

OECD and Human Resources Development Canada

(HRCD) (1997) *Literacy Skills for the Knowledge Society: Further Results from the International Adult Literacy Survey (IALS)*. OECD, Paris

OECD (2001) *Knowledge and skills for life – First results from The Program for International Student Assessment (PISA) 2000*. Organisation for Economic Cooperation and Development OECD, Paris

Ott P. (2006) *Teaching Children with Dyslexia*. Routledge, London

Piaget J. (1970) *The Science of Education and Psychology of the Child*. Grossman, New York

QCA (2005) *Key Stage 2 Assessment and Reporting Arrangements*. Qualifications and Curriculum Authority, London

Rawson M.B. (1986) 'The many faces of dyslexia'. *Annals of Dyslexia*, 36: 179–191

Read C. (1970) *Children's Perceptions of the Sounds of English: Phonology from Three to Six*. Doctoral Dissertation, Harvard University

Read C. (1971) 'Preschool children's knowledge of English phonology'. *Harvard Educational Review*, 41: 1–34

Reid G. (1998) *Dyslexia: A Practitioner's Handbook*. John Wiley & Sons, Chichester

Rosenshine B. and Stevens R. (1986) 'Teaching functions'. In Wittock M. (ed.) *Handbook of Research on Teaching* (third edition), 376–391. Macmillan, New York

Schlagal B. (2001) 'Traditional developmental, and structured language approaches to spelling review and recommendations'. *Annals of Dyslexia*, 51: 147–176

Sherman G.F. (2002) 'The citation: Acceptance of the Samuel Torrey Orton Award'. *Annals of Dyslexia*, 52: 21–23

The Shorter Oxford English Dictionary on Historical Principles (1933) Onions C.T. (ed.) Oxford University Press, Oxford

Thomson M. (1991) 'The teaching of spelling using techniques of simultaneous oral spelling and visual inspection'. In Snowling M. and Thomson M. (eds) *Dyslexia, Integrating Theory and Practice*. Whurr Publishers, London

Tornéus M. (1984) 'Phonological awareness and reading: a chicken and egg problem?' *Journal of Educational Psychology*, 76 (6): 1346–1358

Treiman R. (1993) *Beginning to Spell*. Oxford University Press, New York

Treiman R. and Cassar M. (1997) 'Spelling acquisition in English'. In Perfetti C.A., Rieben L. and Fayol M. (eds) *Learning to Spell: Research, Theory and Practice Across Languages*. Lawrence Erlbaum Associates, Mahwah, NJ

Vygotsky L. (1962) *Thought and Language*. MIT Press, Cambridge, MA

Vygotsky L. (1978) *Mind in Society: The Development of Higher Psychological Processes*. Cole M., John-Steiner V., Scribner S. and Souberman E. (eds), Harvard University Press, Cambridge, MA

Wimmer H. (1996) 'The early manifestation of developmental dyslexia: Evidence from German children'. *Reading and Writing*, 8: 171–188

Chapter 7

Baron J. and Strawson C. (1976) 'Use of orthographic and word specific knowledge in reading words aloud'. *Journal of Experimental Psychology: Human Perception and Performance*, 2: 386–393

Baron J., Treiman R., Wilf J.K. and Kellman P. (1980) 'Spelling and reading by rules'. In Frith U. (ed.) *Cognitive Processes in Spelling*. Academic Press, London

Bradley L.L. and Bryant P.E. (1983) 'Categorising sounds and learning to read: A causal connection'. *Nature*, 301: 419–421

Bradley L. and Huxford L. (1994) 'Organising sound and letter patterns for spelling'. In Brown G.D.A. and Ellis N.C. (eds) *Handbook of Spelling: Theory, Process and Intervention*. John Wiley & Sons, Chichester

Brand V. (1989) *Spelling Made Easy: Multi-sensory Structured Spelling*. Egon Publishers, Baldock

Brewer E.C. (1965) *A Dictionary of Phrase and Fable* (ninth edition). Cassell and Company Ltd, London

Brooks G., Flanagan N., Henkhuzens Z. and Hutchinson D. (1998) *What Works for Slow Readers? The Effectiveness of Early Intervention Schemes*. National Foundation for Educational Research (NFER), Slough

Bruck M. (1987) 'The adult outcomes of children with learning disabilities'. *Annals of Dyslexia*, 37: 252–263

Buckingham B.R. and Dolch E.W. (1936) *A Combined Word List*. Ginn and Company, Boston, MA

Buckton C. and Corbett P. (2002) *Searchlights for Spelling*. Cambridge University Press, Cambridge

Cataldo S. and Ellis N. (1988) 'Interactions in the development of spelling, reading and phonological skills'. *Journal of Research in Reading*, 11 (2): 86–109

Chew J. (2001) Letter, *Times Educational Supplement*. 14 December

Clymer T. (1963) 'The utility of phonic generalisations in the primary grades'. *The Reading Teacher*, 16: 252–258

Coote E. (1596) *The English Schoole-Maister*. Ralph Jackson and Robert Dextar, Company of Stationers, London

Cripps C. (1984) *An Eye for Spelling*. Educational Software, Wisbech

Dale N. (1898) *On the Teaching of English Reading*. Dent, London

DfEE (1998) *The National Literacy Strategy: Framework for Teaching*. Department for Education and Employment, London

DfEE (1999) *The National Literacy Strategy, Spelling Bank. List of Words and Activities for KS2 Spelling Objectives*. Department for Education and Employment, Nottingham

DfEE (2001) *Key Stage 3 National Strategy. Year 7 Spelling Bank*. Department for Education and Employment, Nottingham

DfES (2003) *Response to the March 2003 Phonics Seminar and Professor Greg Brooks' Report*. Primary/Key Stage 3 Helpdesk, Department for Education and Skills, London

Diack J. (1965) *In Spite of the Alphabet: A Study of the Teaching of Reading*. Chatto & Windus, London

Dolch E.W. (1939) *Manual for Remedial Reading*. Ginn and Company, Boston, MA

Dolch E.W. and Buckingham B. (1936) *A Combined Word List*. Ginn and Company, Boston, MA

Ehri L. (1986) 'Sources of difficulty in learning to spell and read'. In Wolraich M. and Routh D. (eds) *Advances in Developmental and Behavioural Paediatrics*, 7: 121–195. JAI Press, Greenwich, CT

Ehri L.C. (1997) 'Learning to read and learning to spell are one and the same, almost'. In Perfetti C.A., Rieben L. and Fayol M. (eds) *Learning to Spell: Research, Theory and Practice Across Languages*. M. Lawrence Erlbaum Associates, Mahwah, NJ

Ellis A.W. (1993) *Reading, Writing and Dyslexia: A Cognitive Analysis* (second edition). Lawrence Erlbaum Associates Publishers, Hove

Fawcett A.J. and Nicolson R.I. (2001) 'Dyslexia: The role of the cerebellum'. In Fawcett A. (ed.) *Dyslexia: Theory and Good Practice*. Whurr Publishers, London

Frith U. (1976) 'How to read without knowing how to spell'. Paper presented to the British Association for the Advancement of Science, Lancaster

Gentry J. (1982) 'An analysis of developmental spelling in GNYS AT WRK'. *Reading Teacher*, 36: 192–200

Gillingham A. and Stillman B. (1956) *Remedial Training for Children with Specific Language Disability in Reading, Spelling and Penmanship* (fifth edition). Educators Publishing Service Inc., Cambridge, MA

Goodman K.S. (1967) 'Reading: A psycholinguistic guessing game'. *Journal of the Reading Specialist*, 6: 126–135

Hanna P.R., Hodges R.E. and Hanna J.S. (1971) *Spelling: Structure and Strategies*. Houghton Mifflin, Boston, MA

Henderson E. (1985) *Teaching Spelling*. Houghton Mifflin, Boston, MA

Hinshelwood J. (1917) *Congenital Word-Blindness*. H.K. Lewis and Co. Ltd, London

Hoole C. (1969) *A New Dictionary of the Old Art of Teaching School* (1660). Reprint, Scolar Press, Menston

Horn E. (1919) 'Principles of method in teaching spelling as derived from scientific investigation'. In Whipple G. (ed.) *Eighteenth Yearbook of National Society for the Study of Education*. Public School Publishing, Bloomington, IL

Huey E.B. (1908) *The Psychology and Pedagogy of Reading*. Macmillan, New York

Jastak S. and Wilkinson G.S. (1984) *Wide Range Achievement Test*. Jastak Associates, Wilmington, DE

Jensen A.R. (1962) 'Spelling errors and the serial-position effect'. *Journal of Educational Psychology*, 53: 105–109

Kavanagh J.F. and Mattingly I.G. (eds) (1972) *Language by Ear and by Eye: The Relationship Between Speech and Reading*. MIT Press, Cambridge, MA

Lennox C. and Siegel L.S. (1994) 'The role of phonological and orthographic processes in learning to spell'. In Brown G.D.A. and Ellis N.C. (eds) *Handbook of Spelling: Theory, Process and Intervention*. John Wiley & Sons, Chichester

Liberman I.Y., Rubin H., Duques S. and Carlisle J. (1985) 'Linguistic abilities and spelling proficiency in kindergarten and adult poor spellers'. In Gray D.B. and Kavanagh J.F. (eds) *Behavioural Measures of Dyslexia*. New York Press, New York

Lundberg I., Frost J. and Petersen O.-P. (1988) 'Effects of an extensive program for stimulating phonological awareness in preschool children'. *Reading Research Quarterly*, 23: 263–284

Lundberg I., Olofsson A. and Wall S. (1980) 'Reading and spelling skills in the first school years predicted from phonemic awareness skills in kindergarten'. *Scandinavian Journal of Psychology*, 21: 159–173

Miles E. and Miles T.R. (1994) 'The interface between research and remediation'. In Brown G.D.A. and Ellis N.C. (eds) *Handbook of Spelling: Theory, Process and Intervention*. John Wiley & Sons, Chichester

Moats L.C. (1995) *Spelling Development, Disabilities and Instruction*. York Press, Baltimore, MD

Montessori M. (1912) *The Montessori Method*. F.A. Stokes, New York

Morris D., Blanton L., Blanton W.E. and Perney J. (1995a) 'Spelling instruction and achievement in six classrooms'. *Elementary School Journal*, 92: 145–162

Morris D., Blanton L., Blanton W.E., Nowacek J. and Perney J. (1995) 'Teaching low-achieving spellers at their "instructional level"'. *Elementary School Journal*, 96: 163–177

Morris D., Nelson L. and Perney J. (1986) 'Exploring the concept of "spelling instructional level" through the analysis of error-types'. *Elementary School Journal*, 87: 181–200

Mudd N. (1997) *The Power of Words. Guidelines for Improving Spelling and Vocabulary*. United Kingdom Reading Association, Royston

Nicolson R.I. and Fawcett A.J. (1990) 'Automaticity: A new framework for dyslexia research?' *Cognition*, 35 (2): 159–182

Nicolson R.I. and Fawcett A.J. (1994) 'Comparison of deficits in cognitive and motor skills among

children with dyslexia'. *Annals of Dyslexia*, 44: 147–164

Olson D.R. (2002) 'Literacy in the past millennium'. In Hjelmquist E. and Euler C. von (eds) *Dyslexia and Literacy*. Whurr Publishers, London

Orton J.L. (1966) 'The Orton–Gillingham approach'. In Money J. (ed.) *The Disabled Reader: Education of the Dyslexic Child*. The Johns Hopkins Press, Baltimore, MD

Orton S.T. (1931) 'Special disability in spelling'. *Bulletin of the Neurological Institute of New York*, 1: 192

Orton S.T. (1937) *Reading, Writing and Speech Problems in Children*. W.W. Norton, New York

Ott P. (2007) *Teaching Children with Dyslexia*, Routledge, London

Palmer S. (2002) 'Phonics is not a dirty word'. *Times Educational Supplement*. 15 November

Palmer S. and Morgan M. (2003) *Big Book Spelling*. Ginn, Oxford

Patoss (2006) *Resources List* (January). Patoss, Evesham

Peters M.L. and Smith B. (1993) *Spelling Context: Strategies for Teachers and Learners*. NFER-Nelson Publishing Company Ltd, Windsor

Read C. (1971) 'Pre-school children's knowledge of English phonology'. *Harvard Educational Review*, 41: 1–34

Reid G. (1998) *Dyslexia: A Practitioner's Handbook* (second edition). John Wiley & Sons, Chichester

Schlagal B. (2001) 'Traditional, developmental and structured language approaches to spelling: Review and recommendations'. *Annals of Dyslexia*, 51: 147–176

Schneider E. (1999) *Multisensory Structured Metacognitive Instruction: An Approach to Teaching Foreign Language to At-Risk Students*. Peter Lang, Frankfurt am Main

Schonell M.A. (1932) *The Essential Spelling List*. Macmillan and Company Limited, London

Sheffield B.B. (1991) 'The structured flexibility of Orton–Gillingham'. *Annals of Dyslexia*, 41: 41–54

Smith P., Hinson M. and Smith D. (1998) *Spelling and Spelling Resources*. NASEN Publications, Tamworth

Spache G. (1940) 'A critical analysis of various methods of classifying spelling errors'. *Journal of Educational Psychology*, 31: 111–134

Stanovich K. (1992) 'Speculations on the causes and consequences of individual differences in early reading acquisition'. In Gough P., Ehri L. and Treiman R. (eds) *Reading Acquisition*. Lawrence Erlbaum, Hillsdale, NJ

Stephenson S. (1904) 'Reports of the society for the study of disease in children', *Lancet*, 4

Stephenson S. (1907) 'Six cases of congenital word-blindness affecting three generations of one family'. *The Ophthalmoscope*, 5: 482

Sweeney J. and Doncaster C. (2002) *Focus on Spelling:*

Spelling: Teacher's Guide. Harper Collins Publishers, London

TES (2002) 'Inspectors spell out bigger role for phonics'. *Times Educational Supplement.* 15 November

Torgesen J.K. (1980) 'The use of efficient task strategies by learning disabled children: Conceptual and educational implications'. *Journal of Learning Disabilities*, 13: 364–371

Treiman R. (1993) *Beginning to Spell.* Oxford University Press, New York

Webster N. (1783) *A Grammatical Institute of the English Language, Part 1.* Hartford, Hudson and Goodwin. Facsimile reprint No. 89, Scolar Press, Menston (1968)

Webster N. (1931) *The American Spelling Book.* Facsimile reprint. Bureau of Publications, Teachers College, Columbia University (1958)

Wechsler D. (1991) *Wechsler Individual Achievement Test (WISC).* Psychological Corporation, San Antonia, TX

Willows D.M. and Scott R. (1994) 'Spelling processes of the reading disabled'. In Brown G.D.A. and Ellis N.C. (eds) *Handbook of Spelling: Theory, Process and Intervention.* John Wiley & Sons, Chichester

Wilson J. (1993) *Phonological Awareness Training. A New Approach to Phonics.* Educational Psychology Publishing, University College, London

Chapter 8

Alberg J., Cook L., Fiore T., Friend M. and Sano S. (1992) *Educational Approaches and Options for Integrating Students with Disabilities: A Decision Tool.* Research Triangle Institute, Triangle Park, NC

Barber M. (1998) *The National Literacy Strategy: Additional Literacy Support.* Department for Education and Employment, London

Barraquer-Bordas L. (1993) 'Foreword'. In Galaburda A.M. (ed.) *Dyslexia and Development: Neurobiological Aspects of Extra-Ordinary Brains.* Harvard University Press, Cambridge, MA

Binet A. and Simon T. (1916) *The Development of Intelligence in Children.* Williams and Wilkins, Baltimore, MD

Black's Medical Dictionary (1995) Macpherson G. (ed.) (thirty-eighth edition). A. and C. Black (Publishers), London

Bos M. and Reitsma P. (2003) 'Experienced teachers' expectations about the potential effectiveness of spelling exercises'. *Annals of Dyslexia*, 53: 104–127

Bramley W. (1993) *Units of Sounds: Developing Literacy for Study and Work.* LDA, Wisbech

Brooks P. and Weeks S. (1998) *Individual Styles in Learning to Spell: Improving Spelling in Children with Literacy Difficulties and all Children in Mainstream Schools.* Research Report No. 754. DfEE, HMSO, Norwich

Burt C.L. (1955) 'The evidence for the concept of intelligence'. *British Journal of Educational Psychology*, 25: 158–177

Childs S.B. (1956) 'How to make spelling make sense: A new spelling curriculum'. *Bulletin of The Orton Society*, 6: 37–42

Clark L. (2001) '1,000 people were asked to find the spelling errors in the passage below'. *Daily Mail.* 18 August

Coffield F. (2005) 'Kinaesthetic nonsense'. *Times Educational Supplement.* 14 January

Coffield F., Moseley D., Hall E. and Ecclestone K. (2004) *Should We Be Using Learning Styles? What Research Has to Say to Practice.* Learning and Skills Research Centre. Learning and Skills Development Agency, London

COP (1994) *The Code of Practice on the Identification and Assessment of Special Educational Needs.* Department for Education, HMSO, London

COP (2001) *Special Educational Needs Code of Practice.* Department for Education and Skills, DfES Publications, Annesley

Cotterell G.C. (1970) 'The Fernald auditory kinaesthetic technique of teaching reading and spelling'. In White Franklin A. and Naidoo S. (eds) *Assessment and Teaching of Dyslexic Children.* Invalid Children's Aid Association, London

Cox A.R. (1980) *Structures and Techniques: Multisensory Teaching of Basic Language Skills.* Educators Publishing Service Inc., Cambridge, MA

Daniels J.C. and Diack H. (1954) *Learning to Read.* The News Chronicle, London

Dejerine J. (1892) 'Contribution à l'étude anatomo-pathologique et clinique des différentes variétés de cécité verbale'. *Mémoires de la Société de Biologie*, 4: 61–90

DfEE (1998) *The National Literacy Strategy: Framework for Teaching.* Department for Education and Employment, London

DfEE (1999) *The National Literacy Strategy: Spelling Bank. List of Words and Activities for KS2 Spelling Objectives.* Department for Education and Employment, London

DfEE (2000) *The National Literacy Strategy: Supporting Pupils with Special Educational Needs in the Literacy Hour.* Department for Education and Employment, London

DfEE (2001) *Key Stage 3 National Strategy. Framework for Teaching English: Years 7, 8 and 9.* Department for Education and Employment, London

DfES (2001) *SEN Toolkit. Department for Education and Skills.* DfES Publications, Annesley

Driscoll M. (2002) 'Why are we such poor spellers?' *The Sunday Times.* 31 March

Dunn R., Dunn K. and Price G.E. (1975) *Learning Styles Inventory.* Price Systems, Inc., Lawrence, KS

Dunn R., Dunn K. and Price G.E. (1989) *Learning Style Inventory.* Price Systems, Lawrence, KS

Dunn R. and Griggs S.A. (1989) 'Learning styles: A quiet revolution in American secondary schools'. *The Clearing House*, 63: 1

Fairweather E. (2006) 'Spelling monitor: Tired of public illiteracy? We name and shame the worst offenders'. *The Daily Telegraph*. 12 June

Fawcett A.J. and Nicolson R.I. (2001) 'Dyslexia: The role of the cerebellum'. In Fawcett A.J. (ed.) *Dyslexia: Theory and Good Practice*. Whurr Publishers, London

Fernald G.M. (1943) *Remedial Techniques in Basic School Subjects*. McGraw-Hill, New York

Flesch R.F. (1981) *Why Johnny Still Can't Read: A New Look at the Scandal of Our Schools*. Harper & Row Publishers, New York

Frith U. (1997) 'Brain, mind and behaviour in dyslexia'. In Hulme C. and Snowling M. (eds) *Dyslexia: Biology, Cognition and Intervention*. Whurr Publishers, London

Fry E., Polk J. and Fountoukidis D. (1984) *The Reading Teacher's Book of Lists*. Prentice-Hall, Englewood Cliffs, NJ

Galaburda A.M. (ed.) (1993) *Dyslexia and Development: Neurobiological Aspects of Extra-Ordinary Brains*. Harvard University Press, Cambridge, MA

Galaburda A.M. and Kempner T.L. (1979) 'Cyto-architectonic abnormalities in developmental dyslexia: A case study'. *Annals of Neurology*, 6: 94–100

Gardner H. (1983) *Frames of Mind: The Theory of Multiple Intelligences*. Basic Books, New York

Gardner H. (1987) 'The theory of multiple intelligence'. *Annals of Dyslexia*, 37: 19–35

Gentry R.J. (1997) *My Kid Can't Spell!! Understanding and Assisting Your Child's Literacy Development*. Heinemann, Portsmouth, NH

Geschwind N. (1982) 'Why Orton was right'. *Annals of Dyslexia*, 32: 13–30

Geschwind N. and Levitsky W. (1968) 'Human brain: left–right asymmetries in temporary speech region'. *Science*, 161: 186–187

Gill C.(2003) 'How dyslexia can turn out to be a route to riches'. *Daily Mail*. 6 October

Gillingham A. and Stillman B. (1956) *Remedial Training For Children with Specific Language Disability in Reading, Spelling and Penmanship* (fifth edition). Educators Publishing Service Inc., Cambridge, MA

Given B.K. and Reid G. (1999) *Informal Teacher and Parent Learning Style Inventory*. Red Rose Publications, St Anne's on Sea

Goulandris N.K. (1994) 'Teaching spelling: Bridging theory and practice'. In Brown G.D.A. and Ellis N.C. (eds) *Handbook of Spelling: Theory, Process and Intervention*. John Wiley & Sons, Chichester

Grinder M. (1991) *Righting the Educational Conveyor Belt* (second edition). Metamorphous Press, Portland, OR

Gross R. (1999) *Psychology: The Science of Mind and Behaviour* (third edition). Hodder & Stoughton, London

Hanna P.R., Hodges R.E. and Hanna J.S. (1971) *Spelling: Structure and Strategies*. Houghton Mifflin Company, Boston, MA

Hatcher P., Hulme C. and Ellis A.W. (1994) 'Ameliorating early reading failure by integrating the teaching of reading and phonological skills: The phonological linkage hypothesis'. *Child Development*, 65: 41–57

Hatcher J. and Rack J. (2002) 'SPELLIT: The first case study. Working with parents: The SPELLIT Home Support Programme'. *Dyslexia Review*, 14 (1): 10–15

Helenius P. and Salmelin R. (2002) 'Neuromagnetic correlates of impaired reading in developmental dyslexia'. In Hjelmquist E. and Euler C. von (eds) *Dyslexia and Literacy*. Whurr Publishers, London

Hinshelwood J. (1917) *Congenital Word-blindness*. H.K. Lewis, London

Hiscock M. and Kinsbourne M. (1987) 'Specialisation of the cerebral hemispheres: Implications for learning'. *Journal of Learning Disabilities*, 20 (3): 130–143

Holloway J. (2000) *Dyslexia in Focus at Sixteen Plus: An Inclusive Teaching Approach*. NASEN, Tamworth

Horn E. (1919) 'Principles of method in teaching spelling as derived from scientific investigation'. In Whipple G. (ed.) *Eighteenth Yearbook of National Society for the Study of Education Part II*: 52–57. Public School Publishing, Bloomington, IL

Horn E. (1969) 'Spelling'. In Ebel R.L. (ed.) *Encyclopedia of Educational Research* (fourth edition). Macmillan, New York

Horner P. (1986) 'The development of reading books in England from 1870'. In Brooks G. and Pugh A.K. (eds) *Studies in the History of Reading*. National Foundation for Education Research, Slough

Kolb D.A. (1976) *Learning Style Inventory: Technical Manual*. Prentice Hall, Englewood Cliffs, NJ

Larsen J.P., Høien T., Lundberg I. and Ödegaard H. (1990) 'MRI evaluation of the size and the symmetry of planum temporale in adolescents with developmental dyslexia'. *Brain and Language*, 39: 289–301

Lepkowska D. (1997) 'Record GCSE results? The teenagers of today don't even know how to shake hands'. *Daily Mail*. 28 August

Lerner J.W. (2000) *Learning Disabilities: Theories, Diagnosis and Teaching Strategies* (eighth edn). Houghton Mifflin Company, Boston, MA

Levine M.D. (1993) *PEEX and PEERAMID Assessment Batteries for Ages 6–9 and 9–16*. Educators Publishing Service Inc., Cambridge, MA

Lyon G.R. (1995) 'Learning disabilities: Past, present and future perspectives'. *The Future of Children*, 6: 24–46

Miles T.R. and Miles E. (1999) *Dyslexia: A Hundred*

Years On (second edition). Open University Press, Buckingham

Moats L.C. (1994) 'The missing foundation in teacher education: Knowledge of the structure of spoken and written language'. *Annals of Dyslexia*, 44: 81–102

Moats L.C. (1995) *Spelling: Development, Disabilities, and Instruction*. York Press, Baltimore, MD

Moats L.C. and Foorman B.R. (2003) 'Measuring teachers' content knowledge of language and reading'. *Annals of Dyslexia*, 53: 23–45

Molfese D.L., Molfese V.J., Key S., Modglin A., Kelley S. and Terrell S. (2002) 'Reading and cognitive abilities: Longitudinal studies of brain and behaviour changes in young children'. *Annals of Dyslexia*, 52: 99–119

Moore J.T. Jr (1951) 'Phonetic Elements Appearing in a Three-Thousand-Word Spelling Vocabulary'. Unpublished doctoral dissertation, Stanford University, CA

Morris J.M. (1986) 'Phonics: from an unsophisticated past to a linguistics-informed future'. In Brooks G. and Pugh A.K. (eds) *Studies in the History of Reading*. National Foundation for Education Research, Slough

Nisbet J. and Schucksmith J. (1986) *Learning Strategies*. Routledge and Kegan Paul, London

Ofsted (1999) *The SEN Code of Practice Three Years On*. Office for Standards in Education, HMSO, London

O'Brien J. (1997) *Lightening Learning*. Quantum Training Co Ltd, Old Bosham

Orton J.L. (1966) 'A history and synopsis of Orton's contribution to the theory and identification of reading disability'. In Money J. (ed.) *The Disabled Reader: Education of the Dyslexic Child*. The Johns Hopkins Press, Baltimore, MD

Orton S.T. (1937) *Reading, Writing and Speech Problems in Children*. Norton, New York

Ott P. (1997) *How to Detect and Manage Dyslexia: A Reference and Resource Manual*. Heinemann Educational Publishers, Oxford

Paulesu E., Frith U., Snowling M., Gallagher A., Morton J., Frackowiak R.S. and Frith C.D. (1996) 'Is developmental dyslexia a disconnection syndrome? Evidence from P.E.T. scanning'. *Brain*, 119: 143–157

Penfield W. and Roberts F. (1959) *Speech and Brain Mechanisms*. Princeton University Press, Princeton, NJ

Peters M.L. (1985) *Spelling: Caught or Taught – A New Look*. Routledge, London

Posner M., Petersen S., Fox P. and Raichle M. (1988) 'Localisation of cognitive operations in the human brain'. *Science*, 240: 1627–1631

Rack J. and Hatcher J. (2002) 'SPELLIT: Research summary'. *Dyslexia Review*, 14 (1): 6–10

Rawson M.B. (1987) 'The Orton trail 1896–1986'. *Annals of Dyslexia*, 37: 36–48

Riding R.J. (1991) *Cognitive Styles, Analysis and Cognitive Styles Analysis User Manual*. Learning and Training Technology, Birmingham

Riding R.J., Glass A., Butler S.R., Pleydell-Pearce C.W. (1997) 'Cognitive style and individual differences in EEG alpha during information processing'. *Educational Psychology* 17: 219–234

Riding R. and Rayner S. (1999) *Learning Styles and Learning Strategies: Understanding Style Differences in Learning and Behaviour*. David Fulton Publishers, London

Riding R.J. and Watts M. (1997) 'The effect of cognitive style on the preferred format of instructional material'. *Educational Psychology*, 17: 179–183

Rosen G.D., Sherman G.F. and Galaburda A.M. (1993) 'Dyslexia and brain pathology: experimental animal models'. In Galaburda A.M. (ed.) *Dyslexia and Development: Neurological Aspects of Extra-Ordinary Brains*. Harvard University Press, Cambridge, MA

Schlagal R.C. and Schlagal J. (1992) 'The integrated character of spelling: Teaching strategies for multiple purposes'. *Language Arts*, 69: 418–424

Schneider E. (1999) *Multisensory Structured Meta-cognitive Instruction: An Approach to Teaching a Foreign Language to At-Risk Students*. Peter Lang, Frankfurt am Main

Shaywitz S., Schaywitz B., Pugh K., Constable R.T., Mencl W.E., Shankweiler D., Liberman A., Skudlarski P., Fletcher J., Katz L., Marchione K., Lacadie C., Gatenby C. and Gore J. (1998) 'Functional disruption in the organisation of the brain for reading in dyslexia'. *Neurobiology*, 95: 2636–2641

Sheffield B.B. (1991) 'The structured flexibility of Orton–Gillingham'. *Annals of Dyslexia*, 41: 41–54

Spear-Swerling L. and Brucker P.O. (2003) 'Teachers' acquisition of knowledge and English word structure'. *Annals of Dyslexia*, 53: 72–103

Springer S.P. and Deutsch G. (1984) *Left Brain, Right Brain*. W.H. Freeman, New York

TES (2004) 'Knowledge shortfall'. *Times Educational Supplement*. 23 January

Terman L.M. (1921) In symposium: 'Intelligence and its measurement'. *Journal of Educational Psychology*, 12: 127–133

Thomson M. (1991) 'The teaching of spelling using techniques of simultaneous oral spelling and visual inspection'. In Snowling M. and Thomson M. (eds) *Dyslexia: Integrating Theory and Practice*. Whurr Publishers, London

The Times (2003) 'Reading skills at risk: Poor listening skills and teaching methods are causing a decline in literacy'. 30 January

Topping K. (1992) *Cued Spelling. Training Tape*. Kirklees Metropolitan Council, Huddersfield

Topping K. (2002) 'Paired thinking: Developing thinking skills through structured interaction with peers, parents and volunteers'. In Reid G. and

Wearmouth J. (eds) *Dyslexia and Literacy*. John Wiley & Sons, Chichester

Vernon P.E. (1969) *Intelligence and Cultural Environment*. Methuen, London

West T.G. (1997) *In the Mind's Eye: Visual Thinkers, Gifted People with Dyslexia. Computer Images and the Ironies of Creativity*. Prometheus Books, New York

White Space (2001) *Word Shark 3*. White Space Ltd, London

Yussen S.R. (1985) 'The role of metacognition in temporary theories of cognitive development'. In Forrest-Pressley D.L., MacKinnon G.E. and Waller T.G. (eds) *Metacognition, Cognition, and Human Performance*, 1: 353–384. Academic Press, Orlando, FL

Chapter 9

Barnhart R.K. (ed.) (1988) *Chambers Dictionary of Etymology*. Chambers Harrap Publishing Ltd, Edinburgh

Beers J.W. and Henderson E.H. (1977) 'A study of developing orthographic concepts among first grades'. *Research in the Teaching of English*, II: 133–148

Brand V. (1984) *Spelling Made Easy: Multisensory Structured Spelling*. Egon Publishers Ltd, Baldock

British Psychology Society (1999) *Dyslexia, Literacy and Psychological Assessment: Report by a Working Party of the Division of Educational and Child Psychology of the BPS*. British Psychological Society, Leicester

Brooks G., Gordon T. and Kendall L. (1993) *The Spelling Abilities of 11- and 15-Year Olds*. NFER, Slough

Brown G.D.A. and Ellis N.C. (1994) 'Issues in spelling research: An overview'. In Brown G.D.A. and Ellis N.C. (eds) *Handbook of Spelling: Theory, Process and Intervention*. John Wiley & Sons, Chichester

Bruck M. (1987) 'The adult outcomes of children with learning disabilities'. *Annals of Dyslexia*, 37: 252–263

Burden B. (2002) 'A cognitive approach to dyslexia: Learning styles and thinking skills'. In Reid G. and Wearmouth J. (eds) *Dyslexia and Literacy: Theory and Practice*. John Wiley & Sons, Chichester

Burt C.L. (1921) *Mental and Scholastic Tests*. King and Son, London

Campbell R. (1983) 'Writing nonwords to dictation'. *Brain and Language*, 19: 153–178

Caravolas M., Bruck M. and Genesee F. (2003) 'Similarities and differences between English- and French-speaking poor spellers'. In Goulandris N. (ed.) *Dyslexia in Different Languages: Cross-linguistic Comparisons*. Whurr Publishers, London

Chew J. and Turner M. (2003) 'Testing the tests: standards of ability and spelling'. *Dyslexia Review*, 14 (2): 23–24

Cook L. (1981) 'Misspelling analysis in dyslexia: Observation of developmental strategy shifts'. *Bulletin of the Orton Society*, 31: 123–134

Critchley M. (1975) 'Specific developmental dyslexia'. In Lenneberg E.H. and Lenneberg E. (eds) *Foundations of Language Development: A Multi-disciplinary Approach*, II. Academic Press, New York

Crystal D. (1995) *The Cambridge Encyclopaedia of the English Language*. Cambridge University Press, Cambridge

DfEE (1998) *The National Literacy Strategy: Framework for Teaching*. Department for Education and Employment, London

DfEE (1999) *The National Literacy Strategy: Framework for Teaching Spelling Bank: Lists of Words and Activities for the KS2 Spelling Objectives*. Department for Education and Employment, London

DfEE (2001a) *Key Stage 3 National Strategy Framework for Teaching English: Years 7, 8 and 9*. Department for Education and Employment, London

DfEE (2001b) *Key Stage 3 National Strategy. Year 7 Spelling Bank*. Department for Education and Employment, Annesley

DfEE (2001c) *Key Stage 3 National Strategy: Literacy Progressive Unit, Spelling*. Department for Education and Employment, Annesley

Dunn L.M., Dunn L.M., Whetton C. and Burley J. (1997) *The British Picture Vocabulary Scale Testbook* (second edition). NFER-Nelson Publishing Company, Windsor

Frith U. (1994) 'Foreword'. In Brown G.D.A. and Ellis N.C. (eds) *Handbook of Spelling: Theory, Process and Intervention*. John Wiley & Sons, Chichester

Frith U. (1997) 'Brain, mind and behaviour in dyslexia'. In Hulme C. and Snowling M. (eds) *Dyslexia: Biology, Cognition and Intervention*. Whurr Publishers, London

Frith U. (2002) 'Resolving the paradoxes of dyslexia'. In Reid G. and Wearmouth J. (eds) *Dyslexia and Literacy: Theory and Practice*. John Wiley & Sons, Chichester

Goulandris N. and Snowling M. (1991) 'Visual memory deficits: A plausible cause of developmental dyslexia. Evidence from a single case study'. *Cognitive Neuropsychology*, 8: 127–154

Hedderly R. (1995) 'Sentence completion test'. *Dyslexia Review*, 7 (2) (Autumn): 19–21

Henderson E. (1985) *Teaching Spelling*. Houghton Mifflin Company, Boston, MA

Hieronymus A.N., Linguist E.F. and France N. (1988) *Richmond Tests of Basic Skills*. NFER-Nelson, Windsor

Horn E. (1926) *A Basic Writing Vocabulary: 10,000 Words Most Commonly Used in Writing*. University of Iowa. Monographs in Education. First Series No. 4, April. University of Iowa, Iowa IA

Hornsby B. and Shear F. (1994) *Alpha-to-Omega* (fourth edition). Heinemann Education, Oxford

Johnson L.W. (1950) '100 words most often

mis-spelled by children in the elementary grades'. *Journal of Educational Research*, 44 (2): 154–155

Joint Council for General Qualifications (2005) *GCE, AEA, VCE, GCSE and GNVQ Entry Level & Key Skills Regulations and Guidance Relating to Candidates who are Eligible for Adjustments in Examinations*. Joint Council for General Qualifications, Cambridge

Kaufman A. and Kaufman N. (1985) *Kaufman Test of Educational Achievement (K-TEA)*. American Guidance Service, Circle Pines, MN

Kibel M. and Miles T.R. (1994) 'Phonological errors in the spelling of taught dyslexic children'. In Hulme C. and Snowling M. (eds) *Reading Development and Dyslexia*. Whurr Publishers, London

Larsen S.C. and Hammill D.D. (1986) *Test of Written Spelling*. PRO-ED, Austin, TX

Lloyd S.R. and Berthelot C. (1992) *Self Empowerment: How to Get What You Want From Life*. Kogan Page, London

Moats L.C. (1983) 'A comparison of the spelling errors of older dyslexic and second-grade normal children'. *Annals of Dyslexia*, 33: 121–140

Moats L.C. (1993) 'Spelling error interpretation: Beyond the phonetic/dysphonetic dichotomy'. *Annals of Dyslexia* 43: 174–185

Moats L.C. (1995) *Spelling: Development, Disabilities, and Instruction*. York Press, Baltimore, MD

Muncey J. and McGinty J. (1998) 'Target setting and special schools'. *British Journal of Special Education*, 25 (4) (December)

Muter V., Hulme C., Snowling M. and Taylor S. (1998a) 'Segmentation not rhyming. predicts early progress in learning to read'. *Journal of Experimental Child Psychology*, 71: 3–27

Muter V., Hulme C., Snowling M.J. (1998b) 'Grammar and phonology predict spelling in middle childhood'. *Reading and Writing*, 9: 407–425

Orton S.T. (1931) 'Special disability in spelling'. *Bulletin of the Neurological Institute of New York*, 1 (2): 159–192

Ott P. (1997) *Activities for Successful Spelling*. Routledge, London

Read C. (1971) 'Preschool children's knowledge of English phonology'. *Harvard Educational Review*, 41: 1–34

Sacre L. and Masterson J. (2002) *Single Word Spelling Test*. NFER-Nelson, London

Sawyer D.J., Wade S. and Kim J.K. (1999) 'Spelling errors as a window on variation in phonological deficits among students with dyslexia'. *Annals of Dyslexia*, 49: 137–159

Schlagal R.C. (1992) 'Patterns of orthographic development in the middle grades'. In Templeton S. and Bear D. (eds) *Development of Orthographic Knowledge and the Foundations of Literacy*. Lawrence Erlbaum Associates, Hillsdale, NJ

Schonell F.J. (1932) *Essentials in Teaching and Testing Spelling*. Macmillan and Company, London

Schonell F.J. and Schonell F.E. (1950) *Diagnostic and Attainment Testing*. Oliver and Boyd, Edinburgh

Scottish Council for Research in Education (1961) *Studies in Spelling*. University of London Press, London

Simon D. (1976) 'Spelling: A task analysis'. *Instructional Science*, 5: 277–302

Smith P., Hinson M. and Smith D. (1998) *Spelling and Spelling Resources*. NASEN Publications, Tamworth

Spache G. (1940) 'A critical analysis of various methods of classifying spelling errors'. *Journal of Educational Psychology*, 31: 111–134

Thomson M. (2001) *The Psychology of Dyslexia: A Handbook for Teachers*. Whurr Publishers, London

Thorndike E.L. and Lorge I. (1944) *The Teacher's Word Book of 30,000 Words*. Teachers College, Columbia University, New York

Treiman R. (1993) *Beginning to Spell: A Study of First Grade Children*. Oxford University Press, New York

Treiman R. (1997) 'Spelling in normal children and dyslexics'. In Blachman B.A. (ed.) *Foundations of Reading Acquisition and Dyslexia: Implications for Early Intervention*. Lawrence Erlbaum Associates, Mahwah, NJ

Turner M. (1997) *Psychological Assessment of Dyslexia*. Whurr Publishers, London

Turner M. and Chew J. (2003) 'Testing the tests: Standards of ability and spelling'. *Dyslexia Review*, 14 (2): 23–24

Vernon P.E. (1998) *Graded Word Spelling Test* (second edition). Hodder & Stoughton Educational, London

Vincent C. and Crumpler M. (1997) *British Spelling Test Series*. NFER-Nelson, Windsor

Vincent D. and Claydon J. (1982) *Diagnostic Spelling Test*. NFER-Nelson, Windsor

Wechsler D. (1992) *Intelligence Scale for Children* (third UK edition) (*WISC – III UK*). Harcourt Assessment, Oxford

Wechsler D. (1993) *WORD: Wechsler Objective Reading Dimension*. Harcourt Assessment, Oxford

Wilkinson G.S. (1993) *The Wide Range Achievement Test*. Jastak Associates, Wilmington, DE

Woodcock R.W. and Johnson M.B. (1989) *Woodcock–Johnson Tests of Achievement* (revised). American Guidance Service, Circle Pines, MN

Young D. (1998) *Parallel Spelling Tests* (second edition). Hodder & Stoughton Educational, London

Chapter 10

Adams M.J. (1990) *Beginning to Read: Thinking and Learning About Print*. MIT Press, Cambridge, MA

Arkell H. and Pollock J. (1973) *The Edith Norrie Letter-Case*. The Helen Arkell Dyslexia Centre, London

Barnhart R.K. (ed.) (2001) *Chambers Dictionary of Etymology* (ninth edition). Chambers Harrap Publishers, Edinburgh

Beard R. (1998) *National Literacy Strategy: Review of Research and Other Related Evidence*. DfEE Publications, Sudbury

Becker W., Dixon R. and Anderson-Inman L. (1980) *Morphographic and Root Word Analysis of 26,000 High Frequency Words*. University of Oregon College of Education, Eugene, OR

Boder E. (1973) 'Developmental dyslexia: A diagnostic approach based on 3 atypical reading-spelling patterns'. *Developmental Medicine and Child Neurology*, 15: 663–687

Bos M. and Reitsma P. (2003) 'Experienced teachers' expectations about the potential effectiveness of spelling exercises'. *Annals of Dyslexia*, 53: 104–127

Bragg M. (2002) *The Adventure of English*. Post production script. London Weekend Television (LWT) Ltd, Episodes 1–4

Burchfield R.W. (ed.) (1996) *The New Fowler's Modern English Usage*. Clarendon Press, Oxford

Carney E. (1994) *A Survey of English Spelling*. Routledge, London

Carnine D.W. (1976) 'Similar sound separation and cumulative introduction in learning letter-sound correspondence'. *Journal of Educational Research*, 69: 368–372

Carroll J.B., Davies P. and Richman B. (1971) *The Word Frequency Book*. Houghton Mifflin, New York

Chambers (1999) *Chambers Twenty-first Century Dictionary*. Chambers Harrap Publishers, Edinburgh

Clymer T. (1963) 'The utility of phonic generalisations in the primary grades'. *The Reading Teacher*, 16: 252–258

Cox A.R. and Hutcheson L. (1988) 'Syllable division: A prerequisite to dyslexics' literacy'. *Annals of Dyslexia*, 38: 226–42

Crystal D. (1995) *The Cambridge Encyclopedia of the English Language*. Cambridge University Press, Cambridge

Crystal D. (2002) *The English Language* (second edition). Penguin Books Ltd, London

Cummings D.W. (1988) *American English Spelling – An Informed Description*. Johns Hopkins University Press, Baltimore, MD

DfEE (1998) *The National Literacy Strategy: Framework for Teaching*. Department for Education and Employment, London

DfEE (1999a) *The National Literacy Strategy. Progression in Phonics: Materials for Whole-Class Teaching*. Department for Education and Employment, London

DfEE (1999b) *The National Literacy Strategy: Training Modules 4 Phonics YR and Y1*. Department for Education and Employment, London

DfEE (1999c) *The National Literacy Strategy: Spelling Bank Lists of Words and Activities for KS2 Spelling Objectives*. Department for Education and Employment, London

DfEE (2001a) *Key Stage 3 National Strategy Literacy Progress Unit: Spelling*. Department for Education and Employment, Annesley

DfEE (2001b) *Key Stage 3 National Strategy. Literacy Progress Unit: Phonics*. Department for Education and Employment, Annesley

DfES (2003) *DfES Response to the March 2003 Phonics Seminar and Professor Greg Brooks' Report*. www.dfes.gov.uk

Dolch E.W. (1939) *A Basic Sight Vocabulary of 220 Words. Providing 50%–70% of all Reading Matter*. www.finhall-demon.co.uk/dolch.htm

Dolch E.W. and Bloomster M. (1937) 'Phonic readiness'. *Elementary School Journal*, 38: 201–205

Ehri L.C. (1997) 'Learning to read and learning to spell are one and same, almost'. In Perfetti C.A., Rieben L. and Fayol M. (eds) *Learning to Spell: Research, Theory and Practice Across Languages*. Lawrence Erlbaum Associates, Mahwah, NJ

Ehri L.C., Wilce L.S. and Taylor B.B. (1987) 'Children's categorisation of short vowels in words and the influence of spellings'. *Merrill Palmer Quarterly*, 33: 393–421

Essinger J. (2006) *Spellbound: The Improbable Story of English Spelling*. Robson Books, London

Ferguson R. (ed.) (1985) *Rhyming Dictionary*. Penguin Books, London

Fowler H.W. (1996) *A Dictionary of Modern English Usage* (third edition). Oxford University Press, Oxford

Fry E., Polk J. and Fountoukidis D. (1984) *The Reading Teacher's Book of Lists*. Prentice-Hall, Englewood Cliffs, NJ

Geddes and Grosset (1997) *Dictionary of Spelling*. Children's Leisure Products Limited, New Lanark

Gillingham A. and Stillman B. (1956) *Remedial Training for Children with Specific Disability in Reading, Spelling and Penmanship* (fifth edition). Distributed by Gillingham A. Bronxville, New York

Hanna P.R., Hanna J.S., Hodges R.E. and Rudorf E.H. (1966) *Phoneme–Grapheme Correspondences as Cues to Spelling Improvement*. US Department of Health, Education and Welfare, Office of Education, US Government Printing Office, Washington, DC

Hanna P.R., Hodges R.E. and Hanna J.S (1971) *Spelling: Structure and Strategies*. Houghton Mifflin, Boston, MA

Henderson E. (1985) *Teaching Spelling*. Houghton Mifflin, Boston, MA

Henry M. (1988) 'Beyond phonics. Integrated decoding and spelling instruction based on word origin and structure'. *Annals of Dyslexia*, 38: 258–275

Horn E. (1969) 'Spelling'. In Ebel R.L. (ed.) *Encyclopedia of Educational Research* (fourth edition). Macmillan, New York

Huxford L.M. (1994) *The Spelling Book*. Stanley Thornes, Cheltenham

Kreiner D. and Gough P. (1990) 'Two ideas about spelling: Rules and word-specific memory'. *Journal of Memory and Language*, 29: 103–118

McArthur T. (ed.) (1992) *The Oxford Companion to the English Language*. Oxford University Press, Oxford

Merriam-Webster New International Dictionary of the English Language (1957) Nelson W.A. (ed.) (second edition). Merriam, Springfield, IL

Moats L.C. (1995) *Spelling Development, Disabilities and Instruction*. York Press, Baltimore, MD

NLS (2002) *The National Literacy Strategy. Framework for Teaching. Glossary of Terms*. The Standards site. Literacy.http://www.standards.dfes.gov.uk/literacy/glossary

Ott P. (1997) *How to Detect and Manage Dyslexia: A Reference and Resource Manual*. Heinemann Educational Publishers, Oxford

Ott P. (2007a) *Teaching Children with Dyslexia*. Routledge, London

Ott P. (2007b) *Activities for Successful Spelling*. Routledge, London

Otterman L.M. (1955) 'The value of teaching prefixes and word-roots'. *Journal of Educational Research*, 48: 611–616

Post Y.V., Swank P.R., Hiscock M. and Fowler A.E. (1999) 'Identification of vowel speech sounds by skilled and less skilled readers and the relation with vowel spelling'. *Annals of Dyslexia*, 49: 161–194

Reid D. (1989) *Word for Word*. Learning Development Aids, Wisbech

Sawyer D.J., Wade S. and Kim J.K. (1999) 'Spelling errors as a window on variations in phonological deficits among students with dyslexia'. *Annals of Dyslexia*, 49: 137–159

Schlagal B. (2001) 'Traditional, developmental, and structural language approaches to spelling: Review and recommendations'. *Annals of Dyslexia*, 51: 147–176

Schlagal R.C. (1992) 'Patterns of orthographic development in the middle grades'. In Templeton S. and Bear D. (eds) *Development of Orthographic Knowledge and the Foundations of Literacy*. Lawrence Erlbaum, Hillsdale NJ

Snowling M., Hulme C., Wells B. and Goulandris N. (1991) 'Continuities between speech and spelling in a case of developmental dyslexia'. *Reading and Writing*, 4: 19–31

Steere A., Peck C.Z. and Kahn L. (1971) *Solving Language Difficulties: Remedial Routines*. Educators Publishing Service Inc., Cambridge, MA

TES (2002) 'Phonics at hub of literacy drive'. *Times Educational Supplement*. 5 December

The Sunday Times (1965) 'Hints on pronunciation for foreigners'. January

The Times (1998) *Guide to English Style and Usage*. News International plc, London

The Times (2000) 'English spelling falls out of favor' (O'Leary J.). 25 November

Treiman R. (1993) *Beginning to Spell: A Study of First Grade Children*. Oxford University Press, New York

Truss L. (2003) *Eats, Shoots & Leaves: The Zero Tolerance Approach to Punctuation*. Profile Books, London

Thorndike E.L. and Lorge I. (1944) *The Teacher's Word Book of 30,000 Words*. Teachers College, Columbia University, New York

Venezky R.L. (1967) 'English orthography. Its graphical structure and its relation to sound'. *Reading Research Quarterly*, 2: 75–106

Venezky R.L. (1970) *The Structure of English Orthography*. Mouton, The Hague

Chapter 11

Adams M.J. (1990) *Beginning to Read: Thinking and Learning About Print*. MIT Press, Cambridge, MA

Barnhart R.K. (ed.) (2001) *Chambers Dictionary of Etymology* (ninth edition). Chambers Harrap Publishers, Edinburgh

Becker W., Dixon R. and Anderson-Inman L. (1980) *Morphographic and Root Word Analysis of 26,000 High Frequency Words*. University of Oregon College of Education, Eugene, OR

Brown J.J. (1947) 'Reading and vocabulary: 14 master words'. In Herzberg M.J. (ed.) *Word Study*. G. and C. Merriam, Springfield, IL

Burchfield R.W. (ed.) (1996) *The New Fowler's Modern English Usage*. Clarendon Press, Oxford

Carlisle J.F. (1987) 'The use of morphological knowledge in spelling derived forms by learning – disabled and normal students'. *Annals of Dyslexia*, 37: 90–108

Chambers (1999) *Chambers Twenty-first Century Dictionary* Chambers Harrap Publishers, Edinburgh

Cox A.R. and Hutcheson L. (1988) 'Syllable division: A pre-requisite to dyslexics' literacy'. *Annals of Dyslexia*, 38: 226–242

Crystal D. (2002) *The English Language* (second edition). Penguin Books Ltd, London

DfEE (1998) *The National Literacy Strategy. Framework for Teaching*. Department for Education and Employment, London

DfEE (2001a) *Key Stage 3 National Strategy. Literacy Progress Unit. Phonics*. Department for Education and Employment, Annesley

DfEE (2001b) *Key Stage 3 National Strategy. Literacy Progress Unit. Spelling*. Department for Education and Employment, Annesley

DfEE (2002) *The National Literacy Strategy. Framework for Teaching. Glossary of Terms*. The Standards site. Literacy.http://www.standards.dfes.gov.uk/literacy/glossary

Ehri L.C. (1997) 'Learning to read and learning to spell are one and same, almost'. In Perfetti C.A., Rieben

L. and Fayol M. (eds) *Learning to Spell: Research, Theory and Practice Across Languages*. Lawrence Erlbaum Associates, Mahwah, NJ

Geddes and Grosset (1997) *Dictionary of Spelling*. Children's Leisure Products Limited, New Lanark

Hanna P.R., Hodges R.E. and Hanna J.S. (1971) *Spelling: Structure and Strategies*. Houghton Mifflin, Boston, MA

Hasenstab J.K., Flaherty G.M. and Brown B.E. (1994) 'Teaching through the learning channels instructor guide'. *Performance Learning Systems*, 62–64; 72–74. Nevada City, CA

Henderson E. (1985) *Teaching Spelling*. Houghton Mifflin, Boston, MA

Henry M. (1988) 'Beyond phonics. Integrated decoding and spelling instruction based on word origin and structure'. *Annals of Dyslexia*, 38: 258–275

McArthur T. (ed.) (1992) *The Oxford Companion to the English Language*. Oxford University Press, Oxford

Mather N. and Roberts R. (1995) *Informed Assessment and Instruction in Written Language: A Practitioner's Guide to Students with Learning Disabilities*. John Wiley & Sons Inc., New York

Ott P. (1997) *How to Detect and Manage Dyslexia: A Reference and Resource Manual*. Heinemann Educational Publishers, Oxford

Ott P. (2007) *Activities for Successful Spelling*, Routledge, London

Otterman L.M. (1955) 'The value of teaching prefixes and word-roots'. *Journal of Educational Research*, 48: 611–616

Phenix J. (1996) *The Spelling Teacher's Book of Lists*. Pembroke Publishers Limited, Ontario

QCA (2004) *Standards at Key Stage 2 English, Mathematics and Science*. Qualifications and Curricular Authority. QCA Publications, Sudbury

Stauffer R.G. (1969) *Reading Maturity as a Cognitive Process*. Harper and Row, NewYork

Steere A., Peck C.Z. and Kahn L. (1971) *Solving Language Difficulties: Remedial Routines*. Educators Publishing Service Inc., Cambridge, MA

TES (2002) 'Phonics at hub of literacy drive'. *Times Educational Supplement*. 5 December

The Times (1998) *Guide to English Style and Usage*. News International plc, London

The Times (2000) 'English spelling falls out of favor'. 25 November

Thorndike E.L. and Lorge I. (1994) *The Teacher's Word Book of 30,000 Words*. Teachers College, Columbia University, New York

Chapter 12

Bateman B. (1965) 'An overview – specific language disability'. *Bulletin of the Orton Society*, 15: 1–11

Balmuth M. (1982) *The Roots of Phonics*. Teachers College Press, New York

Brown G.D.A. and Watson F. (1991) 'Reading development in dyslexia: A connectionist approach'. In Snowling M. and Thomson M. (eds) *Dyslexia: Integrating Theory and Practice*. Whurr Publishers, London

Bryant P.E. and Bradley L. (1985) *Children's Reading Problems: Psychology and Education*. Basil Blackwell, Oxford

Bryant P.E., Bradley L., Maclean M. and Crossland J. (1988) 'Nursery rhymes, phonological skills and reading'. *Journal of Child Language*, 48: 224–245

Carroll J.B., Davies P. and Richman B. (1971) *The Word Frequency Book*. Houghton Mifflin, Boston, MA

Chambers (1999) *Chambers Twenty-first Century Dictionary* (Robinson M. ed.-in-chief). Chambers Harrap Publishers Ltd, Edinburgh

Cox A.R. (1980) *Structures and Techniques: Multi-sensory Teaching of Basic Language Skills*. Educators Publishing Service Inc., Cambridge, MA

Cox A.R. and Hutcheson L. (1988) 'Syllable division: A prerequisite to dyslexics' literacy'. *Annals of Dyslexia*, 38: 226–257

DfEE (1998) *The National Literacy Strategy. Framework for Teaching*. Department for Education and Employment, London

DfEE (2001) *Key Stage 3 National Strategy, Literacy Progress Unit, Phonics*. Department for Education and Employment, London

DfES (2001) *The National Literacy Strategy. Early Literacy Support Programme. Session Materials for Teaching Assistants*. Department for Educational Skills, London

Ferreiro E. and Teberosky A. (1982) *Literacy Before Schooling*. Heinemann, New York

Gillingham A. and Stillman B. (1956) *Remedial Training for Children with Specific Language Disability in Reading, Spelling and Penmanship* (fifth edition). Educators Publishing Service Inc., Cambridge, MA

Goswami U. (1986) 'Children's use of analogy in learning to read: A developmental study'. *Journal of Experimental Child Psychology*, 42: 73–83

Hanna P.R., Hanna J.S., Hodges R.E. and Rudorf E.H. (1966) *Phoneme–Grapheme Correspondences as Cues to Spelling Improvement*. US Department of Health, Education and Welfare, Washington, DC

Liberman I.Y., Shankweiler D., Fisher F.W. and Carter B. (1974) 'Explicit syllable and phoneme segmentation in the young child'. *Journal of Experimental Child Psychology*, 18: 201–212

Ott P. (1997) *How to Detect and Manage Dyslexia: A Reference and Resource Manual*. Heinemann Educational Publishers Oxford.

Ott P. (2007a) *Teaching Children with Dyslexia*. Routledge, London

Ott P. (2007b) *Activities for Successful Spelling*. Routledge, London

Rome P. and Smith Osman P. (1993) *Language Tool Kit*. Educators Publishing Service, Cambridge, MA

Schneider E. (1999) *Multisensory Structural Meta-cognitive Instruction: An Approach to Teaching a Foreign Language to At-Risk Students*. Peter Lang, Frankfurt am Main

Stanback M.L. (1992) 'Syllable and rime patterns for teaching reading; Analysis of a frequency-based vocabulary of 17,602 words'. *Annals of Dyslexia*, 42: 196–221

Steere A., Peck C.Z. and Kahn L. (1971) *Solving Language Difficulties: Remedial Routines*. Educators Publishing Service Inc., Cambridge, MA

Treiman R. (1985) 'Onsets and rimes as units of spoken syllables: Evidence from children'. *Journal of Experimental Child Psychology*, 39: 161–181

Treiman R. (1997) 'Spelling in normal children and dyslexics'. In Blachman B. (ed.) *Foundations of Reading Acquisition and Dyslexia: Implications for Early Intervention*. Lawrence Erlbaum Associates, Mahwah, NJ

Treiman R. and Zukowski A. (1991) 'Levels of phonological awareness'. In Brady S.A. and Shankweiler D.P. (eds) *Phonological Processes in Literacy*. Erlbaum Associates, Hillsdale, NJ

Wagner R.K. and Torgesen J.K. (1987) 'The nature of phonological processing and its causal role in the acquisition of reading skills'. *Phonological Bulletin*, 101: 192–212

Chapter 13

Adams M. and Huggins A. (1985) 'The growth of children's sight vocabulary: A quick test with educational and theoretical implications'. *Reading Research Quarterly*, 20: 262–281

Bridges R. (1999) *Homophones*. Tract II of the Society for Pure English

Brooks P. and Weeks S. (1998) *Individual Styles. Learning to Spell: Improving Spelling in Children with Literacy Difficulties and All Children in Mainstream Schools*. Research Report No. 754 DfEE, HMSO, Norwich

Burchfield R.W. (ed.) (1996) *The New Fowler's Modern English Usage* (third edition). Clarendon Press, Oxford

Carney E. (1994) *A Survey of English Spelling*. Routledge, London

Clark L. (2006) 'The A* pupils who only have a basic grasp of grammar'. *Daily Mail*. 18 July

Crystal D. (1995) *The Cambridge Encyclopaedia of the English Language*. Cambridge University Press, Cambridge

Crystal D. (1997) *English as a Global Language*. Cambridge University Press, Cambridge

Crystal D. (2002) *The English Language* (second edition). Penguin Books, London

DfEE (1998) *The National Literacy Strategy, Framework for Teaching*. Department for Education and Employment, London

DfEE (1999) *The National Literacy Strategy, Spelling Bank, Lists of Words and Activities for the KS2 Spelling Objectives*. Department for Education and Employment, London

DfEE (2001) *Key Stage 3 National Strategy. Framework for Teaching English. Years 7, 8 and 9*. Department for Education and Employment, London

DfES (2003) *Response to the March 2003 Phonics Seminar and Professor Greg Brooks' Report*. www.dfes.gov.uk

Ehri L.C. (1979) 'Do beginners learn words better in contexts or in isolation?' *Child Development*, 50: 675–685

Ehri L.C. (1996) 'Researching how children learn to read: controversies in science are not like controversies in practice'. In Brannigan G.G. (ed.) *The Enlightened Educator – Research Adventures in the Schools*. McGraw-Hill Inc., New York

Hanna P.R., Hanna J.S., Hodges R.E. and Rudorf E.H. (1996) *Phoneme–grapheme Correspondences as Cues to Spelling Improvement*. US Office of Education, Government Printing Office, Washington, DC

Levin J.R. (1996) 'Stalking the wild mnemos: research that's easy to remember'. In Brannigan G.G. (ed.) *Enlightened Educator: Research Adventures in the Schools*. McGraw-Hill Inc., New York

Moats L.C. (1995) *Spelling: Development, Disabilities and Instruction*. York Press, Baltimore, MD

Ott P. (2007) *Activities for Successful Spelling*. Routledge, London

Rohwer W.D. Jr, Lynch S., Levin J.R. and Suzuki N. (1967) 'Pictorial and verbal factors in the efficient learning of paired associates'. *Journal of Educational Psychology*, 58: 278–284

Schott B. (2002) *Schott's Original Miscellany*. Bloomsbury Publishing plc, London

The Times (1998) Austin T. (ed.) *The Times Guide to English Usage and Style*. News International, London

Truss L. (2003) *Eats, Shoots & Leaves: The Zero Tolerance Approach to Punctuation*. Profile Books, London

Chapter 14

Beard R. (2000) *Developing Writing 3–13*. Hodder & Stoughton, London

Becta (2000) *Dyslexia and ICT: Building on Success*. Becta, Coventry

Collison R.L. (1982) *A History of Foreign-Language Dictionaries*. Blackwell, Oxford

Crystal D. (1995) *The Cambridge Encyclopaedia of the English Language*. Cambridge University Press, Cambridge

Daily Mail (2001) 'Fingers do the talking in the month of 16th text messages'. 24 August

DfEE (1998) *The National Literacy Strategy Framework for Teaching*. Department for Education and Employment, London

Dorling Kindersley (1998) *Multi-Media: The Complete User Friendly Guide* (revised edition). Dorling Kindersley Ltd, London

Fischer Family Trust (2002) *High Impact ICT Resources.* www.fischertrust.org

Gookin D. (1996) *Word 97 for Windows for Dummies.* I.D.G. Books Worldwide, Inc., Foster City, CA

Gowers E. (1973) *The Complete Plain Words* (second edition) (revised by Fraser B.). Penguin Books Ltd, London

Hornsby B., Shear F. and Pool J. (1999) *Alpha to Omega* (fifth edition). Heinemann Educational Publishers, Oxford

Hutchins (2003) Personal communication

James A. and Draffan E.A. (2004) 'The accuracy of electronic spell checkers for learners'. www.dyslexia.com/database/articles

Keates A. (2000) *Dyslexia and Information and Communications Technology: A Guide for Teachers and Parents.* David Fulton Publishers, London

Kraynak J. (1995) *Your First Book of Personal Computing.* Alpha Books, Indianapolis

Martin J.R. (1989) *Factual Writing: Exploring and Challenging Social Reality* (second edition). Oxford University Press, Oxford

Moss H. (2000) 'Using literacy development programs'. In Townend J. and Turner M. (eds) *Dyslexia in Practice: A Guide for Teachers.* Kluwer Academic/Plenum Publishers, New York

Olson R.K., Wise B., Johnson M.C. and Ring J. (1997) 'The etiology and remediation of phonetically based word recognition and spelling disabilities: Are phonolological deficits the "hole" story?' In Blachman B.A. (ed.) *Foundations of Reading Acquisition and Dyslexia: Implications for Early Intervention.* Lawrence Erlbaum Associates, Mahwah, NJ

Ott P. (1997) *How to Detect and Manage Dyslexia.* Heinemann Educational Publishers, Oxford

Ott P. (2007) *Teaching Children with Dyslexia.* Routledge, London

Peacock M. (1992) 'Evaluating Word Processed Pupil Writing'. Unpublished PhD thesis, University of Leeds School of Education, Leeds

QCA (2005) 'QCA sets its sights on the curriculum of the future'. *Times Educational Supplement.* ICT in Education Online. January

Smythe I. (1996) 'Typographic Preferences in Dyslexic Students'. Unpublished paper

TechDis (2003) *Which Spellchecker is best?* TechDis Ezine. April

TES (2003) 'Disk's star turn for special needs'. *Times Educational Supplement.* January

Text Me (2000). Penguin Books, London

The Times Magazine (2000) 'A weekly posting from cyberspace'. 22 April

Which (2000) 'Help for left-handers'. March. Consumers Association, London

Glossary

Ayres J.A. (1972) *Sensory Integration and Learning Disorders.* Western Psychological Services, Los Angeles, CA

Backhouse G. and Morris (eds) (2005) *Dyslexia? Assessing and Reporting: The Patoss Guide.* Hodder Murray, London

Baron J. and Strawson C. (1976) 'Use of orthographic and word specific knowledge in reading words aloud'. *Journal of Experimental Psychology: Human Perception and Performance,* 2: 386–393

Bloomfield L. (1933) *Language.* Holt, Rinehart and Winston, New York

Borstrøm I. and Elbro C. (1997) 'Prevention of dyslexia in kindergarten: Effects of phoneme awareness training with children of dyslexic parents'. In Hulme C. and Snowling M. (eds) *Dyslexia: Biology, Cognition and Intervention.* Whurr Publishers, London

Bowey J. and Hansen J. (1994) 'The development of orthographic rimes as units of word recognition'. *Journal of Experimental Psychology,* 38: 504–514

Buzan T. (1993) *The Mind Map Book.* BBC Books, BBC Worldwide Ltd, London

Chambers (1999) *Chambers Twenty-first Century Dictionary.* Chambers Harrap Publishers, Edinburgh

Chambers (1999) *Chambers Twenty-first Century Dictionary* (Robinson M. and Davidson G. eds). Chambers Harrap Publishers, Edinburgh

Clymer T. (1963) 'The utility of phonic generalisations in the primary grade'. *The Reading Teacher,* 16: 252–258

Cripps C. (1984) *An Eye for Spelling.* Educational Software, Wisbech

Crumpler M. and McCarty C. (2004) *Nonword Reading Test.* Hodder Murray, London

Denckla M.B. and Rudel R.G. (1976) 'Rapid "automatized" naming (RAN): Dyslexia differentiated from other learning disabilities'. *Neuropsychologia,* 14: 471–479

Deponio P. (2004) 'The co-occurrence of specific learning difficulties: Implications for identification and assessment'. In Reid G. and Fawcett A. (eds) *Dyslexia in Context: Research Policy and Practice.* Whurr Publishers, London

DfEE (1988) (1995) National Curriculum. The Department for Education and Employment, HMSO, London

DfEE (1998) *The National Literacy Strategy: Framework for Teaching.* Department for Education and Employment, London

DfEE (1999a) *The National Strategy: Phonics, Progression in Phonics.* Department for Education and Employment, London

DfEE (1999b) *National Numeracy Strategy: Framework for Teaching Mathematics.* DfEE Publications, Sudbury

DfEE (1999c) *The National Literacy Strategy Training Modules 4 Phonics YR and Y1*. Department for Education and Employment, London

DfEE (2001) *Key Stage 3 National Strategy: Literacy Progress Unit, Phonics*. DfEE Publications, London

DfEE (2001) *Key Stage 3 National Strategy: Literacy Progress Unit, Phonics*. Department for Education and Employment, London

DfEE (2002) *The National Literacy Strategy. Framework for Teaching. Glossary of Terms*. The Standards site. Literacy.http://www.standards.dfes.gov.uk/literacy/glossary

DfES (2001a) *Special Educational Needs Code of Practice*. DfES Publications, London

DfES (2001b) *The National Numeracy Strategy: Guidance to Support Pupils with Dyslexia and Dyspraxia*. DfES, London

DfES (2006) *Primary Framework for Literacy and Mathematics: Primary National Strtegy*. http://www.dfes.gov.uk

Diack H. (1965) *In Spite of the Alphabet: A Study of the Teaching of Reading*. Chatto and Windus, London

Dolch E.W. and Bloomster M. (1937) 'Phonic readiness'. *Elementary School Journal*, 38: 201–205

Dolch E.W. and Buckingham B. (1936) *A Combined Word List*. Ginn and Company, Boston, MA

Dunn L.M., Dunn L.M., Whetton C. and Burley J (1997) *The British Picture Vocabulary Scale Testbook* (second edition). NFER-Nelson Publishing Company, Windsor

Dunn R. and Dunn K. (1978) *Teaching Students Through Their Individual Learning Styles: A Practical Approach*. Prentice Hall, Reston Publishing Company, Reston, VA

Ehri L.C. (1986) 'Sources of difficulty in learning to spell and read'. In Wolraich M.L. and Routh D. (eds) *Advances in Developmental and Behavioural Pediatrics*, 7. JAI Press, Greenwich, CT

Ehri L.C. (1997) 'Learning to read and learning to spell are one and the same, almost'. In Perfetti C.A., Rieben L. and Fayol M. (eds) *Learning to Spell: Research, Theory and Practice Across Languages*. Lawrence Erlbaum Associates, Mahwah, NJ

Evans B.J.W. (2001) *Dyslexia and Vision*. Whurr Publishers, London

Fawcett A.J. and Nicolson R.I. (2001) 'Dyslexia: The role of the cerebellum'. In Fawcett A. (ed.) *Dyslexia and Good Practice*. Whurr Publishers, London

Gardner H. (1983) *Frames of Mind: The Theory of Multiple Intelligences*. Basic Books, New York

Gathercole S. and Baddeley A. (1996) *The Children's Test of Nonword Repetition*. Harcourt Assessment, Oxford

Goodman K.S. (1986) *What's Whole in Whole Language: A Parent–Teacher Guide*. Heinemann, Portsmouth, NH

Goswami U. (2002) 'Phonology, reading development and dyslexia: A cross-linguistic perspective'. *Annals of Dyslexia*, 52: 141–163

Goulandris N.K. (1996) 'Assessing reading spelling skills'. In Snowling M. and Stackhouse J. (eds) *Dyslexia: Speech and Language. A Practitioner's Handbook*. Whurr Publishers, London

Gross R. (1996) *Psychology: The Science of Mind and Behaviour*. Hodder & Stoughton, London

Hanna P.R., Hanna J.S., Hodges R.E. and Rudorf E.H. (1966) *Phoneme–grapheme Correspondences as Cues to Spelling Improvement*. US Office of Education, Government Printing Office, Washington, DC

Hanna P.R., Hodges R.E. and Hanna J.S. (1971) *Spelling: Structure and Strategies*. Houghton Mifflin, Boston, MA

Henderson E. (1985) *Teaching Spelling*. Houghton Mifflin Company, Boston, MA

Kaplan B., Wilson B.N., Dewey D.M. and Crawford S.G. (1998) 'DCD may not be a discrete disorder'. *Human Movement Science*, 17: 471–490

Kreiner D. and Gough P. (1990) 'Two ideas about spelling: Rules and word specific memory'. *Journal of Memory and Language*, 29: 103–118

Lerner J. (2000) *Learning Disabilities: Theories, Diagnosis and Teaching Strategies*. Houghton Mifflin, Boston, MA

Liberman I.Y. and Shankweiler D. (1985) 'Phonology and problems of learning to read and write'. *Remedial and Special Education*, 6: 8–17

Lindamood P., Bell N. and Lindamood P. (1997) 'Achieving competence in language and literacy by training in phonemic awareness, concept imagery and comparator function'. In Hulme C. and Snowling M. (eds) *Dyslexia: Biology, Cognition and Intervention*. Whurr Publishers, London

Livingstone M.S., Rosen G.D., Drislane F.W. and Galaburda A.M. (1991) 'Physiological and anatomical evidence for a magnocellular defect in developmental dyslexia'. *Proceedings of the National Academy of Science*, 88: 7943–7947

Lloyd S.R. and Berthelot (1992) *Self Empowerment: How to Get What You Want From Life*. Kogan Page, London

McArthur T. (ed.) (1992) *The Oxford Companion to the English Language*. Oxford University Press, Oxford

Moats L.C. (1995) *Spelling: Development, Disability and Instruction*. York Press, Baltimore, MD

Mudd N. (1997) *The Power of Words: Guideline for Improving Spelling and Vocabulary*. United Kingdom Reading Association, Royston

National Institute of Child Health and Human Development (2000) *Report of the National Reading Panel of Teaching Children to Read: An Evidence-based Assessment of the Scientific Research Literature on Reading and its Implications for Reading Instructions: Reports of the Subgroups*. NIH Publications No. 00-4754. US Government Printing Office, Washington, DC

Nicolson R.I. and Fawcett A.J. (1990) 'Automaticity: A new framework for dyslexia research'. *Cognition*, 35: 159–182

Nicolson R.I. and Fawcett A.J. (2000) 'Long-term

learning in dyslexic children'. *European Journal of Cognitive Psychology*, 12: 357–393

O'Connor J. and Seymour J. (1990) *Introducing Neuro-Linguistic Programming*. Thorsons, London

O'Donnell M. and Munro R. (1949) *The Janet and John Series*. Nisbet, London

Orton J.L. (1966) 'The Orton–Gillingham approach'. In Money J. (ed.) *The Disabled Reader: Education of the Dyslexic Child*. The Johns Hopkins Press, Baltimore, MD

Ott P. (1997) *How to Detect and Manage Dyslexia: A Reference and Resource Manual*. Heinemann Educational Publishers, Oxford

Ott P. (2007) *Activities for Successful Spelling*. Routledge, London

Peer L. (2001) 'Dyslexia and its manifestation in the secondary school'. In Peer L. and Reid G. (eds) *Dyslexia: Successful Inclusion in the Secondary School*. David Fulton Publishers, London

Pumfrey P.D and Reason R. (1991) *Specific Learning Difficulties (Dyslexia): Challenges and Responses*. Routledge, London

QCA (1999) *The Revised National Curriculum*. Qualifications and Curriculum Authority, London

Rack J.P., Snowling M.J. and Olsen R.K. (1992) 'The nonword reading deficit in developmental dyslexia: A review'. *Reading Research Quarterly*, 27 (1): 29–53

Read C.(1971) 'Preschool children's knowledge of English phonology'. *Harvard Educational Review*, 41: 1–34

Rose J. (2006) *Independent Review of Early Reading*. www.standards.dfes.gov.uk/rosereview

Schonell F.J. and Serjeant I. (1939) *The Happy Venture Readers*. Oliver and Boyd, Edinburgh

Siegel L.S. and Himel N. (1998) 'Socioeconomic status, age and the classification of dyslexics and poor readers: The dangers of using IQ scores in the definition of reading disability'. *Dyslexia*, 4: 90–104

Snow C., Burns S. and Griffin P. (eds) (1998) *Preventing Reading Difficulties in Young Children*. National Academy Press, Washington, DC

Stanback M.L. (1992) 'Syllable and rime patterns for teaching reading: Analysis of a frequency-based vocabulary of 17,602 words'. *Annals of Dyslexia*, 42: 196–221

Stanovich K.E. and Siegel L.S. (1994) 'Phenotypic performance profile of children with reading disabilities: A regression-based test of the phonological-core variable-difference model'. *Journal of Educational Psychology*, 86: 24–53

Steere A., Peck C.Z. and Kahn L. (1971) *Solving Language Difficulties: Remedial Routines*. Educators Publishing Service Inc., Cambridge, MA

Stein J., Talcott J. and Witton C. (2001) 'The sensorimotor basis of developmental dyslexia'. In Fawcett A. (ed.) *Dyslexia Theory and Good Practice*. Whurr Publishers, London

Thomson M. (2001) *The Psychology of Dyslexia: A Handbook for Teachers*. Whurr Publishers, London

Thorndike E.L. and Lorge I. (1944) *The Teacher's Word Book of 30,000 Words*. Teachers College, Columbia University, New York

Torgerson C.J., Brooks G. and Hall J. (2006) *A Systematic Review of the Research Literature on the Use of Phonics in the Teaching of Reading and Spelling: A Report to the Department of Education and Skills*. DfES, London

Torgensen J.K., Wagner K. and Rashotte C. (1999) *Test of Word Reading Efficiency (TOWRE)*. Harcourt Assessment, Oxford

Treiman R. (1993) *Beginning to Spell: A Study of First-Grade Children*. Oxford University Press, New York

Vygotsky L. (1962) *Thought and Language*. MIT Press, Cambridge, MA

Vygotsky L. (1978) *Mind in Society: The Development of Higher Psychological Processes*. In Cole M., John-Steiner V., Scribner S. and Souberman E. (eds). Harvard University Press, Cambridge, MA

Waites L. (1968) 'Dyslexia International World Federation of Neurology: Report of research group on developmental dyslexia and world illiteracy'. *Bulletin of the Orton Society*, 18: 21–22

Wechsler D. (1992) *Wechsler Intelligence Scale for Children* (third edition) (*WISC-III*). Psychological Corporation, London

Wechsler D. (1993) *WORD: Wechsler Objective Reading Dimensions*. Psychological Corporation, London

Wolf M. and O'Brien B. (2001) 'On issues of time, fluency, and intervention'. In Fawcett A. (ed.) *Dyslexia Theory and Good Practice*. Whurr Publishers, London

Index

eBooks - at www.eBookstore.tandf.co.uk

A library at your fingertips!

eBooks are electronic versions of print books. You can store them onto your PC/laptop or browse them online.

They have advantages for anyone needing rapid access to a wide variety of published, copyright information.

eBooks can help your research by enabling you to bookmark chapters, annotate and use instant searches to find specific words or phrases. Several eBook files would fit on even a small laptop or PDA.

NEW: Save money by eSubscribing: cheap, online acess to any eBook for as long as you need it.

Annual subscription packages

We now offer special low cost bulk subscriptions to packages of eBooks in certain subject areas. These are available to libraries or to individuals.

For more information please contact webmaster.ebooks@tandf.co.uk

We're continually developing the eBook concept, so keep up to date by visiting the website.

www.eBookstore.tandf.co.uk